Natural Healing
for Dogs & Cats

Other Books by Diane Stein
Published by The Crossing Press

All Women Are Healers
A Comprehensive Guide to Natural Healing

The Natural Remedy Book for Women

Casting the Circle
A Women's Book of Ritual

Dreaming the Past, Dreaming the Future
A Herstory of the Earth

The Goddess Book of Days
A Perpetual 366-Day Engagement Calendar

The Goddess Celebrates
An Anthology of Women's Rituals

Lady Sun, Lady Moon
Poems

Natural Healing
for Dogs & Cats

by
Diane Stein

The Crossing Press, Freedom, CA 95019

For Cinde, Tiger, Dusty, Copper and Kali:
The Dogs Who Taught Me

The alternative healing methods of this book are not meant to take the place of expert veterinary care. When your pet is ill, consult a holistic veterinarian.

The author's opinions and descriptions of the Perelandra Flower Essences, publications or any process developed at Perelanda are her own, and may not reflect the intent or instructions published by Perelandra. The use of the Perelandra material in this book does not constitute an endorsement of this book by Machaelle Small Wright or Perelandra, Ltd.

Library of Congress Cataloging-in-Publication Data

Stein, Diane, 1948-
  Natural healing for dogs & cats / Diane Stein.
      p. cm.
  Includes bibliographical reference and index.
  1. Alternative veterinary medicine. 2. Dogs—Disease—
Alternative treatment. 3. Cats—Disease—Alternative treatment.
I. Title. II. Title: Natural healing for dogs and cats.
SF745.5.S74 1993
636.7'08958—dc20
                            92-42880
                            CIP

I would like to express special thanks to the following women, whose help added greatly to this book and made it possible. I owe a great debt to Laurel Steinhice and Marion Webb-Former for channeling and information on the chakras and auras of animals and for information on psychic healing and reincarnation. They put great amounts of time and care into the work. Thanks also to Mary Ann Simonds for book lists and networking, The Flower Essence Society for referrals and their newsletter, and Perelandra Flower Essences for their wonderful essences and information. Thanks also to Newton Laboratories, Inc. for extensive animal homeopathy information, and to Davida Johns for her photographs of myself, Kali and Copper. Without the help of Patti Callahan of Brigit Books, St. Petersburg, Florida this book could not have been researched.

Very very special thanks goes to Dr. Gloria Dodd, DVM for critiquing the manuscript for veterinary accuracy, for her encouragement and Foreword, and most especially for the additional material and personal research that she has so generously given to the book. I honor her and her work deeply and wish to see books of her own in print soon.

Thanks also and always to Elaine and John Gill of The Crossing Press, to Amy Sibiga for her drawings and to the wonderful people of the Press who publish my books with such dedication, competence and caring.

Contents

Foreword

Diane Stein has provided the reader with one of the most comprehensive encyclopedias of natural healing methods on the market today. She has gathered naturopathic techniques from the world's leading specialists in the field. She outlines acupressure, herbs, homeopathy, massage and many other disciplines that can be used to heal both people and animals. Stein's clear-cut explanations and illustrations make it easy for the reader to grasp these modalities and begin their use at home. In today's world of escalating medical and veterinary costs, this book provides a timely solution to utilizing ancient healing methods that have been historically proven effective, safe and gentle.

As a practicing veterinarian for thirty years (now retired), I was able to evaluate firsthand, the differences between orthodox veterinary practices of the use of drugs and surgery taught in this country with the naturopathic methods used in Europe and South America. After sixteen years of practice in traditional veterinary medicine, I began to realize some of these methods were repressive to the body's natural healing processes and did not address the *true* cause of dis-ease. I traveled to Germany, England and Colombia. There I studied with medical doctors who specialized in herbs, homeopathy, EAV (electro-acudiagnosis according to Voll), chiropractic, acupuncture, ozone therapies and natural diets made from uncontaminated food and spring waters. I returned home to California and adapted these modalities to my own veterinary practice. Soon I found I was able to do so much more in true healing of sick animals than I was capable of doing before. Utilizing the best of traditional medicine and my newly found knowledge of natural healing I saw dramatic recoveries in patients suffering from chronic degenerative dis-eases: arthritis, allergies, skin problems, pathologies of liver, kidney, heart and digestion, immune deficient syndromes, tumor formations and cancer. I had rediscovered the truths of healing known to the ancients! These were the women healers and nurturers of this planet, who long ago gently and lovingly kept the harmony and equilibrium between mankind and Nature (Mother Goddess of creation).

For one reason or another, we women gave up that power to men, who then became the dominant force in our destinies. Through their militant and brutal subjugation of Nature and Her life forms, the world today teeters on the brink of destruction, the magnitude of which has never been seen before. Dangers to the health of the planet, plants, animals and people are all around us: the depletion of the earth's ozone layer, the rapidly diminishing rain forests, the widespread pollution of our air, water and food by industry and agribusiness. Acid rain is releasing the earth's mineral aluminum, which now contaminates vast areas of subterranean water supplies and crops growing in the soil. There is a growing body of evidence that aluminum plays a major role in Alzheimer's Dis-ease, mental disorders, learning disabilities, premature aging and Senile Dementia as well as organic disease processes. Toxic food additives and preservatives have produced indisputable evidence of health hazards, yet our own governmental policies and the FDA turn a blind eye and even foster these practices by business.

Other countries, having banned some of the more toxic chemicals in foods and livestock feedstuffs, have pleaded with our government to do the same to no avail. Little known, but seriously affecting our health, are the noxious energy fields created by man's overelectrification of the planet. It is affecting the earth's own electromagnetic fields. Serious studies in Europe have revealed an increase in chronic degenerative dis-eases, malignancies and bizarre behavior in people and animals living in these fields.

This then is Diane Stein's most powerful message: the only hope of saving ourselves and future generations of all life forms is for *women to unite* and take back our God-given power of healers and nurturers. There are early warning signs that Mother Earth is convulsing. Through Her powerful forces She *will* wipe the slate clean of all life, and puny man will be helpless to prevent it. It's not too late, but we are running out of time.

Gloria Dodd, DVM

All Be-ings Great and Small

All life forms upon the earthplanet are connected to each other and to the planet itself.

All Be-ings hold within themselves a spark of Universal Life Force, a living self-linkage to All-That-Is.

All creatures great and small are spiritual. Into each species was breathed the Breath of Life, as it was in the Beginning.

All species have evolved spiritually, as well as physically, since the Beginning of timespace upon that entity which is called the Earth.

Life does not stand still upon itself. It *flows*.

In the age of transition in which the many veils are lifted, the many limitations are set aside in the process of co-creating new realities. New bondings are formed between one species and another. Old bondings are rediscovered, strengthened and renewed.

There is a sharing of new realities between humanity and other earthplanet life forms, and this sharing is an important part of the Reunion itself.

Each of us is unique. And we are all One.

Laurel Steinhice
(Under the Guidance of Earth Mother, Edgar Cayce and The Crystal Circle, 1992.)

In the very first times both people and animals lived on the earth, but there was no difference between them. A person could become an animal, and an animal could become a human being. There were wolves, bears and foxes but as soon as they turned into humans they were all the same. They may have had different habits, but all spoke the same tongue, lived in the same kind of house, and spoke and hunted in the same way.

Nalungiaq, An Inuit Woman

Close your eyes, remembering a place in Nature, that is special to you. Imagine an animal coming to you, an animal sent by the Goddess. Try moving as your animal would move, feeling how it lives in the world. What attributes of this animal can you adopt that will help you fulfill yourself?…Ask it what you can do to help our culture remember the sanctity of all forms of life….Lastly, how can you carry out the teachings of your animal in your daily life? When you are finished, thank the animal for coming to you and ask it to come back to you again in your dreams and meditations.

from Hallie Iglehart Austen,
The Heart of the Goddess

Introduction
Healing the Animals: Healing the Earth

Women are reclaiming their heritage as healers. They are regaining the life-respecting, noninvasive methods of older times as alternatives to dehumanized and frightening technological medicine that strips women of their self-respect and power. Women are returning the focus of health care to wellness instead of dis-ease, using time proven, gentle, ancient skills. Herbs and homeopathy, vitamins and minerals, psychic healing, flower essences, nutrition, massage and acupressure/acupuncture are some of the many methods being used to create a renaissance in women's healing and wellness. The resurgence of these methods has become a different medical system, an underground, growing grassroots movement in the last thirty years, and women are satisfied with its safety and effectiveness. They are fighting the patriarchal model that severely opposes and restricts this life-giving alternative, as it attempts to oppose and restrict others of women's rights.

Along with rediscovering the effectiveness and empowerment of healing themselves and their families, women are also reclaiming stewardship of the Earth, the need to take care of the planet. The time has come. There is urgent need to heal the environment and other Be-ings that we share the Earth with. The same methods of new/old alternative healing that work for women are effective for animals as well. Along with reclaiming women's healing methods for ourselves and our children, women are applying natural, noninvasive methods for farm animals, wild animals, and particularly for pets.

The concept is far from new, as women have always lived closely with animals, caring for them as for their children. The village/midwife/healer of Europe and other early farming cultures was often also the village veterinarian or animal healer. Later (nineteenth century) medicine shows remedies in the United States were the forerunners of today's over-the-counter drugs and often had directions reading "One for a man, and two for a horse." Animal and human healing were intertwined.

When the family cow was a source of nourishment for all the children, and the children grew up with her, had a name for her, and lived with her habits as a way of life, her care was as important as their own. When the cat who lived in the barn guarded the crops and was the family's best protection against rats and their dis-eases, her kittens and her times of illness were prominent concerns. When the family horse was the only source of mobility on the great plains and was also a hunting partner and puller of the plow, its health and wellness were paramount. When the family dog helped to hunt food, provide protection, herd the cows and sheep, and baby-sit the toddlers, that dog's well-being was as important as any other family member's. The February (Candlemas) birthing of lambs, calves and foals was the mystery and crisis time of the farming year, and all the women healers in the village were involved.

Women have become removed from this closeness with the Earth and are no longer part of the lives and life cycles of the planet unless they make conscious effort. Something vital and life-giving has been lost. Our industrialized culture raises farm animals in brutal factory conditions and even the friendly milk cows no longer have names, just numbers. Horses are obsolete as workers. Few women have ever helped a ewe to lamb, or a mare to birth her foal (or seen a human birth). Few women have spent the night in a barn watching over an animal in a healing crisis. Removed from the lives around us and numbed by centuries of "dominate and subdue" mentality, women's lives are far less intertwined with the smaller lives around them.

The animals as well have been removed. Today's farm animals live far away from the typical city family, and household pets have vastly different roles. Few of today's cats catch rats for a living, and today's dogs are seldom working animals or food-providing hunters. Most domestic pets are surgically neutered to prevent their fertility. Most are indoor companions frustrated by lack of exercise and freedom in small yards or city apartments. They are taken to the vet for routine injections, and during birth or illness, rather than being helped at home. They are fed poorly out of cans and bags, as poorly as humans feed themselves today. When their aging becomes a problem, they are quietly "put to sleep."

The intimacy between women and animals in their lives and life cycles has been seriously diminished, but pets remain important to women's well-being as a remnant of what's been lost—our closeness to the Earth.

Out of the sterility and barrenness of our patriarchal, underhumanized times, there is arising again a recognition of the oneness of all that lives. The Earth Herself is a Goddess and a living Be-ing, and women are learning to recognize and reclaim Her. Unless the planet's land, air and water are made clean again, and healed of the diseases (physical, emotional, mental and spiritual) of industrialization and masculine dominance and neglect, all life on Earth is in danger. Unless the forests are saved and the soil renourished, and threatened species of plants, insects, fish and animals are restored, the system that supports all our lives will perish. By returning the Earth to wellness—the realization that all life is one life, by returning to Her cycles and to the respect for all Her species, and to the healing of all the Earth's systems and Be-ings large and small—wellness and well-being for every creature is regained and assured. There is no separating people from animals, or people from trees, insects and ecosystems in this view. Such healing is now in women's hands—for the Earth, ourselves and the animals, both wild and domestic.

Machaelle Small Wright describes the concept of co-creative partnership between people and the natural world. Her several books, beginning with *Behaving as If the God in All Life Mattered* (Perelandra Ltd., 1987), describe what this means. The speaker here is the Overlighting Deva of Perelandra, a Nature Spirit:

We were always meant to work in partnership—we of nature and man. The very physical existence of man on Earth has depended upon all kingdoms of nature. In short, the very fact that man and nature co-exist on the planet has inherent in it partnership….From the moment man and nature came together on the planet, this link between us has not changed.[1]

As the patriarchal system has developed, with its denial of life and adulation of technology, the split between "man" and nature has widened. Women, with physiological cycles that tie their bodies irrevocably to the Earth's, have never fully accepted this split; but women along with the natural world have suffered from this split.

To deny the link between "man" and nature, however, is not to change the fact that all life is bound to the cycles of nature. Merely by being alive, all of us are part of these cycles. As the current mechanized system reaches its destructive limits and begins to deteriorate, a new order derived from partnership and co-creativity is being found.

That new order is actually an old one, pairing the creativity of nature with human intelligence. By working with, instead of against, the Earth for the good of all living things, the immense power of the natural world can be used for harmony and good. Substitute the words "Goddess" or "planet" for "nature" and the concept becomes familiar to women. The return to partnership with nature becomes the return to matriarchal, Goddess-centered values: caring and respect for all life; living and working within the cycles of nature/Earth/Goddess; and healing ourselves, the Earth and our animals of the negative split between people and the living Earth.

From Machaelle Small Wright again:

That which is nature is powerful beyond your imagination. And that which is human is also powerful beyond your imagination. Man and nature, come together as we have on this planet, hold the promise and potential of many times their individual power, if only they could work together to unlock that which nature holds and infuse the human ability to create expanded usefulness through the tool of applied intellectual knowledge.[2]

The results of utilizing this partnership fully are avenues that women explore when they do healing work, garden without chemicals, initiate conscious communication with their dogs, cats or other animals, midwife a human or animal birth or death, utilize with awareness crystals and gemstones, save or plant a tree, and live in ways that respect and preserve the environment. By learning about the Goddess Earth and living in partnership with Her and Her creatures, women return the balance that has been missing from modern life. By insisting on this partnership in the patriarchal world; by refusing the food irradiation and the factory foods, the chemotherapies and unnecessary surgeries for people and pets; by fighting against the oppression against animals, women and minorities; by fighting to preserve wild land and wetlands which are being turned into shopping centers; by fighting against the abuse of children, women and animals; women are insisting on returning health to human and nonhuman life by reaffirming the link with Goddess/nature.

Acknowledging, regaining and utilizing the link with Goddess/nature are essential.

If humans continue their reluctance to join us in the partnership we are suggesting, then surely out of human ignorance and arrogance, we will all continue to experience difficult challenges to our survival and, eventually, we will be faced with the full separation of spirit from matter.[3]

Healing this link with nature/Goddess is what is meant by healing the Earth, and means healing ourselves and our pets. The dogs and cats (and birds, small animals and horses) that women live with are the closest connection we have to the natural world. Their dis-ease and pain on all levels mirror our own, and their healing is intrinsic to our healing ourselves. By exploring natural/holistic healing methods for themselves as alternatives to patriarchal medicine, women reclaim a part of that link as well as self-empowerment and greater well-being. By extending these methods to our companion pets, they continue and affirm the link, co-creating greater wellness for other lives. Each return to a natural method is an affirmation of the link between women and nature, and women and Goddess. And each return offers an alternative to the life-destroying patriarchy. The choice, as written by Machaelle Wright's Overlighting Deva, is clear.

The Goddess as a connection with the natural world and specific animals is as ancient as the Earth herself, and that relationship reflects women's relationship with these animal representatives. Every aspect of life on Earth is embodied in the various aspects of the Goddess. She is known as the Lady of the Beasts, the Goddess/ Mother of both healing and animals, and Her link with them is universal. "They embody the deity Herself, defining Her personality and exemplifying Her power."[4] Animals are intrinsic to Her as Maiden, Mother and Crone, and act as mythic guides, dream bearers, soul carriers, totems and archetypes. Every culture equates animals with the Goddess, from the Arctic Circle to the southern tip of Africa.

Birds, spiders, lions and cats, dogs, jackals, coyotes and wolves, horses, cows, fish, bears, deer, serpents, insects, sheep and pigs are all Goddess-equated creatures. Dogs and cats, the central focus of this book, appear frequently, their images distributed widely across the Earth's cultures. Cats are sacred to the Egyptian Goddess Bast, who was portrayed as a domestic cat throughout the Nile Delta:

Bast's festivals,…were celebrated by hundreds of thousands of worshipers arriving in boats, playing flutes, singing, and feasting. Mistress of all kinds of pleasure and religious ecstasy, Bast, the Lady of Bubastis, carries the sistrum, symbol of joyous dancing and love-making.[5]

Cats were domesticated in Egypt and used to protect the granaries from mice. Along with Bast, they were also sacred to Isis. They were worshipped as a moon symbol, and described as an animal of Diana's, a Greek Goddess who originated in Egypt. Diana in Egypt was a daughter of Isis and a sister of Horus, and in earliest times was a Sun Goddess, so cats have been associated with both sun and moon. In Rome, statues of the Goddess of Liberty included a cat resting at the Goddess' feet. It is believed that cats were brought to Europe with the Roman conquest or sooner, and reached England by 200 C.E. or sooner.

Li shou was a Chinese cat deity who was worshiped by farmers, and in India a cat Goddess named Sasti was equivalent to Bast and a maternity Goddess. Cats in China had a mixed press. They were welcomed as rat catchers and were women's pets, but they were also suspect of bringing poverty to the family they lived with. Ceramic figures of seated cats gazing outward, some with hollow eyes used as candle-lanterns to frighten mice, were said to avert the bad luck. Cats are not included in the Buddhist list of protected animals or in the Chinese zodiac—it is said they fell asleep during Buddha's funeral. Or is it that, as representatives of Goddess and women, they were deposed from patriarchal favor during this era? Cats reached Europe and Asia by export from Egypt, though Egypt frowned on the trade. Some may have been abducted from Egypt by Phoenician sailors. Much later they were also an animal associated with the Scandinavian Goddess Freya.

Cat images have been found in Crete and off the coast of Florida, dating from 600 B.C.E. to 1500 C.E. Images of big cats—lions, lionesses, leopards and jaguars—are more widely prevalent than house cats, with lionesses and lions in Greece, Italy, China, France, Switzerland, Crete, Egypt, Iran, Turkey, and Mesopotamia. Jaguars and leopards are the "cats" in Anatolia, Turkey, and South and Central America. Several cultures equated lionesses with birth and portray them present with birthing women. The images of big cats, including Goddesses dressed in leopard skins or nursing leopard cubs, go back as far as 18,000 B.C.E. (a lioness engraved on the cave wall of Les Trois Freres, France).[6] Lion statues were used as guardians at building entrances in the United States into this century.

When the lion became extinct in China, the image was transferred to the Pekinese dog, a breed developed to resemble the lion. These Foo Dogs which were temple animals are seen widely in Chinese art as the guardians and protectors of crops and temple gates.[7] One of the two hundred images of the Goddess Kwan Yin shows her spilling the water of life from her sacred jar into a Foo Dog's mouth, and modern images of Foo Dogs are easy to find in import stores. The Celestial Dog of China is a storm deity.

Other images of Goddesses with dogs include Hecate and Diana/Artemis with their hounds, the Egyptian God Anubis and Goddess Bau, the Erinyes (Greek avenger Goddesses), the Nordic Underworld Goddess Hel, and the small Kalima dogs found throughout Central and South America and Mexico. In Neolithic Central Europe the dog was associated with the Mother Goddess and the Moon Tree, but was replaced by the lion (male) in the Bronze Age. Dogs are major Moon Goddess symbols throughout Europe and Eastern Europe, Egypt and Greece. They are associated with death and the underworld in Egypt, Babylonia, Scandinavia, India and Greece.

Isis is associated with Sirius or Sothic, the Dog Star, in Egypt, and the South American Aztec dog is associated with a star, as well. Hecate's dog (Greece and Egypt) that guarded the entrance to the Underworld was named Cerberus. Early Native American art frequently depicts dogs, wolves and coyotes. The ancient Irish name for dog is Madra (Mother). Dog images in ancient art are known from 5,000 B.C.E.[8] and, as the dog was domesticated far earlier than the cat, still earlier images could have existed. Dogs in early art are shown as dangerous, as well as gentle and playful. They are symbols of both death and life, and are always associated with the Goddess and the Night/Moon. Some cultures sacrificed dogs to the Goddess, and ancient cemeteries for both dogs and cats have been found. I discovered a red clay Mexican image of a Goddess nursing a puppy in an import shop a few years ago; the importer could not identify her.

Totem animals are a feature of many Native American cultures, with dogs and related animals prevalent. Jamie Sams and David Carson in their *Medicine Cards* book and tarot deck (Bear and Company, 1988) describe dog, wolf and coyote totems, as well as use the mountain lion to represent the cat family. Dogs in the southwest Plains tribes were used in hunting and as protectors; they were sources of warmth in the winter, and were seen as servant-soldiers, as well as child-minding guardians. Before the introduction of the horse to the Plains, dogs were used for hauling. They gave warning to the village in case of attack, and some tribes used them as a meat source. In the Pacific Northwest, a curly-coated dog breed was developed for its wool. As a totem animal, the dog represents service and loyalty.[9]

The coyote is the trickster (Raven in the Pacific Northwest), the sacred fool and wielder of the cosmic joke. A Native American friend has Coyote as his totem, and when Coyote visits, shiny and red objects disappear, to appear again later (if at all) in impossible places. Coyote moves from fiasco to fiasco, always surviving and coming out whole. It is one of the most sacred of totems and images.

The wolf is "the pathfinder, the forerunner of new ideas who returns to the clan to teach and share medicine."[10] Wolves are intuition and Moon (Goddess) energy, representing cooperation and living in accord. They take one mate for life (a trait that has been bred out of the domestic dog) and live in family-derived packs with a highly evolved social structure. It is tragic that today's image of the wolf is one of exaggerated danger; they are peace-loving creatures that rarely attack farm animals for food, preferring carrion and rodents. They offer no threat to people.

The Great Plains cat totem is the mountain lion, representing issues of leadership, independence, and the right use of power. It is considered a difficult totem, for the holder of this animal mentor may be blamed when things go wrong, and become a target for other people's insecurities.[11] The domestic cat is not mentioned in Plains Indian animal cosmology, but cats were well known as "familiars" and companions to witches in the Inquisition times in Europe. They were too often burned at the stake with their women, and some dogs also met this fate. The witches were remnants of the ancient Goddess religions, surviving underground. Baba Yaga, a grandmother folk figure/Goddess of Russia, is followed by a cat and identified as a witch, as is Cat Anna of the Celts.

With these things in mind, it is clear that cats and dogs (and other animals) have routinely been associated with Goddess, and Goddess women have been associated with cats and dogs. Women's link with animals is also a link with nature (who is Goddess/Earth), and this link has been the root of much of women's persecution under the patriarchal system. Animals under patriarchy are no more than objects, a part of what the male God decreed in Genesis that men were to "dominate and subdue." Women have been equated *as* animals, also, only men being viewed as fully human. These beliefs, not so old or ancient, only recently and gradually changing in some parts of the world, are the source of patriarchy's politics against women, animals and the Earth.

Susan Griffin, in her landmark 1978 book *Women and Nature: The Roaring Tide Inside Her* (Harper and Row Publishers), defines some of the beliefs gleaned from earlier historical writings. The connection between the oppression of women and the oppression of animals and the planet becomes very clear in the following series of quotes:

It is observed that women are closer to the earth. That women lead to man's corruption. Women are "the Devil's Gateway," it is said.[12]

And it is stated that the rational soul, which is immaterial, bears the image of its divine maker, has will, is endowed with intellect and is more noble and more valuable of being than "the whole corporeal world."

That Adam is soul and Eve is flesh.

It is argued now that animals do not think. That animals move automatically like machines. That passion in animals is more violent because it is not accompanied by thought. That our own bodies are distinguished from machines only by "a mind which thinks without reference to any passion."

But it becomes obvious that animals do not have immortal souls (and cannot think), since if one animal had an immortal soul, all might, and that "there are many of them too imperfect to make it possible to believe it of any of them...."

And it is said that the souls of women are small.[13]

All nature, it is said, has been designed to benefit man.[14]

And it is observed that woman is less evolved than man. Men and women differ as much, it is observed, as plants and animals do.[15]

Compare these quotes to those of Machaelle Small Wright's Overlighting Deva of Perelandra. Obviously there is much to heal, for women, the Earth, and the animals, not to mention the system that evolved into the extreme misogyny and life denial of above. That same negation of life, the Earth, women, animals and nature is the source of the pain, corruption, alienation and lack of values of our present order. Only by returning to matriarchal and New Age feminist values—respect for the oneness of all life, reaffirmation of the link between people and nature, the honoring of all Be-ings and of the Goddess-within in all living things—can the order be changed. By healing ourselves and healing the animals, women heal that link between people and the Earth and allow life to continue on this planet. There is clear and present danger to be addressed now, or as the Overlighting Deva of Perelandra warns, "we will be faced with the full separation of spirit from matter." The patience of the Earth, the Lady of the Beasts and Goddess of Women, is running out.

As a healer and woman, I consider the healing of animals and the Earth planet to be important and at this time of crisis in planetary herstory to be vital. The Susan Griffin quotes illustrate how we got to where we are, and the Machaelle Small Wright material points the direction for the future. We must evolve from Griffin to Wright on this beautiful Earth and do it now. For matriarchal Goddess women, the path is evident, but the return to a co-partnership with nature may not seem so obvious even to people who are aware of the danger. Having been raised in a world where the Susan Griffin material is only recently changing, the connection between healing women, healing the Earth and healing animals may be a new idea. It is hard to listen to nature over the roar of inner city traffic, or to make conscious contact with a pet or wild creature when we have been told that animals have no intelligence or souls. The change of attitude and change of heart, however, must come from women: few men have this awareness in any way at all, having been raised and trained in the patriarchal model and hold a vested self-interest in it.

This is not to say that men have no place in changing attitudes toward nature, for without their co-partnership the efforts can be only partially successful and ultimately will fail. The job for men is to become aware of how the patriarchal model harms *them* as well as the less dominant parts of the hierarchy. The realization that the patriarchal model has destroyed men's connection with the Earth as the Goddess' son-consort is a first step. When men realize how the mechanized view of the universe denies them their right to an emotional life, their freedom to be gentle and creative, and the knowledge of the oneness of all Be-ings, their change of heart begins. Once the contact is initially made with any aspect of nature/Goddess, the change has begun. There is no going back from growth and awakening.

Just as the mechanized view of the universe has created a health care system that is cold technology without regard for the quality of life, it has created a health care system for companion (and other) animals that is too often discompassionate and lifeless. As in the human medical system, many modern veterinarians view their patients as a collection of moving parts. If the animals do not respond to the textbook recommendation, they are written off or "put to sleep." There is almost no acknowledgment of an animal's feelings or wishes, nor is there any balancing of methods against results. It may be technically effective to remove a tumor and cancerous body part from the abdomen of a cat or dog, but is it humane to do so, when the animal's condition is terminal and the prognosis indicates more pain down the road? Is it valid to treat an animal as a dis-eased leg, liver or ear instead of as a Be-ing in its whole? Is it ethical to cause added suffering with side-effect drugs, or to reduce an animal's immune system with prolonged use of cortisone, when the cause of the illness could be removed by change of diet or the dis-ease treated by gentler (but nonpatentable, less profitable) means?

As veterinary medicine quickly moves into the over-technologized, over-use of drugs that are prevalent in today's medical system for people, the imbalances and lack of common compassion and sense become more pronounced. Women are becoming outraged at the unnecessary surgeries and dangerous side-effects of prescribed medications for themselves, and appalled at the costs. They begin to see these methods carried over for use on their companion pets, with the same negative and disquieting results.

Also as in women, the incidence of cancer, heart disease, arthritis, immune disorders, environmental allergies and stress-related illness is increasing by leaps and bounds in dogs and cats. The sickness of the Earth planet is reflected in the dis-eases of people and animals, and animals in their oneness with the Earth/Goddess are hurt sooner than humans and are more helpless. The lack of reasonable nutrition that undermines human health in the Typical American Diet (sugar, starch, animal fat, caffeine, preservatives, salt), also undermines animal health in shocking ways. The same polluted air and water, environmental radiation, ozone depletion, ELF and high frequency power lines, lack of exercise and high stress living that depletes women's health depletes that of our dogs and cats. The life expectancy rates for both animals and people in America is decreasing, despite the so highly lauded breakthroughs in medical drugs and technology. Cancer and heart dis-ease kill as high a percentage of companion animals as humans, and are showing up as tragically in animals of the wild.

Says Dr. Gloria Dodd, DVM:

Cancer and other chronic degenerative disease is not uncommonly found in the wildlife today, as man-made pollution becomes more serious. Fish and sea mammals such as whales and seals are showing an alarming frequency of tumors, virus and bacterial diseases unheard of in the past, and now the scientists are finding epidemics of pox viruses in seals and whales.

Migratory birds in selenium-polluted wetlands of California and elsewhere are showing grotesque birth defects in the dead and dying hatchlings; hence there are dwindling numbers of these birds now left to nest along the California shores.

Fish in the San Francisco Bay-Sacramento River Delta are so chemically polluted that they have tumors and large chemical burns all over their bodies. We are now being warned by Public Health not to eat these fish…because of the leakage of radioactive wastes from barrels dumped there by industry and the military. The veterinary professional authorities feel that increased chronic degenerative diseases of the heart, plus kidney failure, liver pathologies and skin diseases are due to this increased chemical and radioactive effect on the immune system of the organisms.

Of concern also are the increased frequencies of "beached" whales, dolphins and porpoises.…I (and others) feel that their sonar systems—which help guide these creatures' movements in migration and in catching their prey—are being seriously distorted by the increasing traffic of shipping on the waters and by sounds of communications systems linking in the ocean. Whales have an acute sense of hearing and were able to communicate with others of their species almost entirely across the oceans' expanse in the days before commercial shipping. But more important, I feel these creatures are suffering the effects of the electropollution gridding of the planet by man. This problem is reaching monstrous proportions with serious emotional, physical, mental and spiritual disease in all life forms: plants, animals and humans.[16]

Women are finding some answers in holistic methods of healing, beginning with optimal nutrition and continuing through such methods as herbs, vitamins and minerals, homeopathy, acupuncture and acupressure, stress reduction, massage, flower essences and psychic healing. There is an awareness that the physical body is only a part of the anatomy of any Be-ing, human, animal or plant, and therefore only a part of the healing concern. There is a growing awareness that return to Goddess/Earth-based values and to valuing and healing the planet are essential to the health and wellness of both pets and people. There is an understanding that all life is essential, no life form being less important than any other. And there is an understanding that healing for women/people can only come along with healing for the planet and for all that lives on it.

This book is a beginning survey of holistic healing methods for the Be-ings closest to people in women's daily lives. It is focused on cats and dogs, discussing and applying holistic healing principles and remedies to their needs. The urgency of finding alternatives to the current mechanized medical system is increasing, both for women and animals. Many women do not know that the alternative methods that make life more pleasant for people are also valid and effective for pets. How to use these methods is the purpose of this book.

I have not included other small animals, birds or horses in this work, though I am aware of their importance as pets and know that holistic healing is valid for them. I have little knowledge of other animals besides dogs and cats, and therefore leave other animals for those who are more experienced. In the field of horses, watch for books by Linda Tellington-Jones and Mary Ann Simonds. The methods in this book are all proven methods tried and used by either myself or the authors referenced. Some of the systems are fascinating and new, often with no rational explanation for the miracles they produce—Linda Tellington-Jones' work, psychic healing, and the effects

of flower essences are cases in point. Some of the methods are very ancient, known in the times of the matriarchies, as in the material on animal acupuncture. Some are well known to women as holistic methods for themselves—herbs, vitamins and minerals, homeopathy, and quality nutrition. Some of the remedies go beyond the physical, to have effect on the nonphysical bodies. All the subjects are written for the laywoman, with the exception of acupuncture, but acupuncture done without needles (acupressure) requires no specialized training.

The remedies of this book are geared toward increasing wellness and well-being in companion pets. They are suggestions for preventing minor dis-eases from becoming serious and are not meant to take the place of veterinary assistance. Holistic methods work best in early stages, and they are also used along with veterinary care. The primary focus, particularly in the areas of nutrition and vitamins and minerals, is prevention of dis-ease by total health. In every case, the methods described give a foundation for each discipline, enough to give the lay person a beginning working knowledge. Each of the methods merits (and usually has) full texts, to which the reader can go to learn more.

The animals in our care deserve the best that we can give them and the current medical model for both pets and women is failing us. Organized medicine in the west operates to take away women's power over their bodies, wellness and lives, and does the same when modern medical methods and attitudes are applied to cats and dogs.

The rising costs of health care for people are also reflected in the rising costs of veterinary medicine. The routine yearly immunization visit for a dog has grown from $15 to $75 in the past five years. Routine spaying or neutering has doubled in price in that time, with fewer low-cost spay/neuter clinics available as veterinarians protect their high fees. (This is especially an issue in Florida.) The cost has risen but the quality of care has grown more toxic, with greater risk of iatrogenic (doctor-caused) dis-ease.

Women reclaiming their own bodies now have an option for reclaiming some of the quality of life for their pets. Holistic methods are gentle, effective, and low cost. They are based on promoting wellness instead of offering heroic interventions. The methods reduce the need for drugs and surgeries and in general increase the animals' length and quality of life. They offer alternatives also for many illnesses that have no allopathic answers beyond "putting them down." Many supposedly hopeless cases—cats with feline leukemia and feline AIDS, dogs with hip dysplasia and severe skin ailments—have been healed by alternative methods when technology has failed. At very least, women need to know that these options exist.

My own experience with alternative animal care has been through twenty years of co-partnership with Siberian Husky dogs. I have also been a professional, practicing dog groomer. As my research over the past thirty years with holistic health care for women has grown, I have gingerly moved into using the same methods for my pets. The braver I have become at this, the more exciting the results. I remember too clearly the times when such healing would have made life-saving differences in the past. One of my dogs' lives was saved by a $3.50 homeopathic remedy, when half a dozen vets and astronomical expenses over six months did nothing for him. One of my dogs' lives was lost because I did not have the necessary information for her when we needed it. Three of my animals died too young of cancer over a twenty-year period because I had no knowledge of the politics of animal nutrition, a mistake I will not make again. In my years of experimentation, I have never seen an alternative healing method cause harm, add to an animal's (or human's) pain, or reduce its life span.

You will find much of the information in this book to be an "ah-ha" experience; "I didn't know animals needed that." Most holistic remedies for people carry over to pets, with adjustment for their smaller body sizes. The information on dog and cat chakras and auras, thanks to the help of psychics Laurel Steinhice and Marion Webb-Former, has never been available in print before. My discussion of the death experience at the end of this book incorporates Goddess and New Age awareness to discuss life's most mysterious event.

I offer these methods and this book as a step in Machaelle Small Wright's co-creative partnership with the animals and the planet. Our dogs and cats deserve no less.

Full Moon in Sagittarius
May 16, 1992

[1] Machaelle Small Wright, *Behaving As if the God in All Life Mattered: A New Age Ecology*, (Jeffersonton, VA, Perelandra, Ltd., 1987), p. xiv.

[2] *Ibid.*, p. xv.

[3] *Ibid.*

[4] Buffie Johnson, *Lady of the Beasts: Ancient Images of the Goddess and Her Sacred Animals*, (San Francisco, CA, Harper and Row Publishers, 1988), p. 3.

[5] *Ibid.*, p. 106.

[6] *Ibid.*, p. 100–111.

[7] *Ibid.*, p. 111.

[8] *Ibid.*, p. 114–119.

[9] Jamie Sams and David Carson, *Medicine Cards: The Discovery of Power Through the Ways of Animals*, (Santa Fe, NM, Bear and Co., 1988), p. 93.

[10] *Ibid.*, p. 97.

[11] *Ibid.*, p. 105.

[12] Susan Griffin, *Women and Nature: The Roaring Inside Her*, (San Francisco, Harper and Row Publishers, 1978), p. 7–8.

[13] *Ibid.*, p. 17–18.

[14] *Ibid.*, p. 22.

[15] *Ibid.*, p. 26.

[16] Dr. Gloria Dodd, DVM, Personal Communication, August 27, 1992. All reference to her is from this source unless otherwise noted.

Physical & Nonphysical Anatomy

Dogs and cats, as mammals, have physical anatomics quite similar to that of people. Their bodies contain the same systems and organs as the human body, and with respect to their four-footed structures, the organs are essentially in the same places. Dogs and cats have similar skeletons, as well, with a familiar organization of bones, vertebrae, joints, muscles, tendons and ligaments, again with regard to their different body needs. Animals walk on four legs, people on two, so their structures are organized differently. (Many women with bad backs are aware of the stresses of the human upright pose.) Cats, dogs and horses possess the same body systems as humans: lymphatics, glands, nerves, organs, skin, brain and spine, eliminative systems, digestive, circulatory and respiratory systems, and a similar but enhanced sensory system. Their muscular structures reflect the different uses of the animals' bodies: cats are built for pouncing, climbing and jumping, dogs for chasing, running and the pulling down of prey.

The cat body has 244 bones, forty more than the human adult. It has a short jaw and thirty teeth (people have thirty-two), designed for cutting meat, rather than for tearing or chewing grass—cats are unable to chew at all. There are 500 skeletal muscles in the cat body, compared to 650 in the adult human. Cats have narrow chests and thin, reduced or missing collar bones, allowing greater flexibility of movement than people or dogs have. They walk on their toes (as dogs do, also) for speed, longer stride and precise control of their movements.[1]

Cats are closer to being true carnivores than dogs or humans, requiring a diet of primarily meat to live and

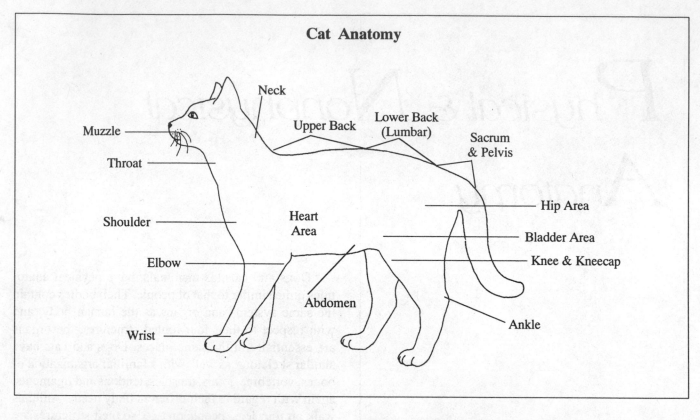

Cat Anatomy

thrive. A cat cannot survive on an all-vegetarian diet, though people can and do. Dogs require less meat than cats. Cats' digestive and eliminative systems are arranged to utilize raw meat. The cat's urinary system is more closely linked to its reproductive tract than to the intestinal/excretory system. The kidneys are the primary waste-disposal organs, and they regulate the body's water balance. Cats are desert animals in origin, and when water is scarce the body's fluids become more concentrated as a way of conserving water; this is a factor in domestic cats' tendency to urinary tract infections.[2]

The cat circulatory system contains a half-pint of blood which circulates the body in eleven seconds, and the heart rate is 110–180 beats per minute. Cats breathe thirty to fifty breaths per minute, four times faster than humans. The size of domestic cats ranges from about five-and-a-half to ten pounds for females and males that are castrated when young, and eight to fifteen pounds for intact adult males. The size range is uniform compared to dogs. The cat body contains more than four million cells, and normal body temperature averages 101.5°F (the same as in dogs).[3] Cat gestation time is sixty days, plus or minus five (sixty-three to sixty-five days is the average gestation in dogs).

Cats' sensory system, compared to humans, is highly evolved. The sense of touch, considered the least of cat senses, is most developed on the hairless nose, tongue and paw pads, and the paws' sensitivity to vibration helps the cat's hearing. Cats' dislike of having their feet handled results from this extreme sensitivity. The guard hairs of the coat contain several types of touch receptors that operate at close range, and the vibrissae or whiskers on face and elbows sense close objects and air currents, and are also essential for a cat's balance. The hair roots and skin between hair follicles are highly sensitive, as well.[4]

Hearing in cats is vastly expanded from human limits. The human high sound range ends at twenty kilohertz (Khz) or 20,000 cycles per second, while cats' range reaches sixty-five kilohertz or 65,000 cycles. Cats' lower range hearing goes down to thirty hertz, thirty cycles per second. The ear structure is internally the same in cats, dogs and people. Cat vision is best from about seven to twenty feet. They lack the ability to focus well close up. There is a mirror-like surface that lines the back of the retina, the tapetum lucidum, that enhances the eyes'

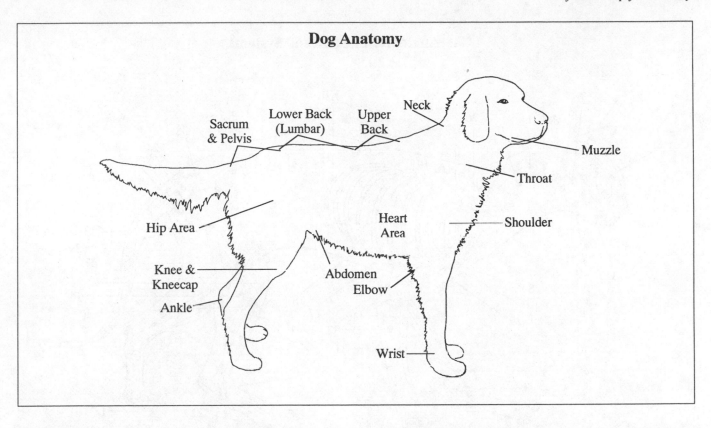

Dog Anatomy

sensitivity to low light and causes the glow-in-the-dark of dogs' and cats' eyes caught by a light at night.

Cats see better in low light than humans do but cannot see in total darkness. Their resolution of details is less clear than in humans; things appear fuzzy at night, and even in bright light have less detailed focus than humans. The third eyelid, called the nictitating membrane, closes under the external eyelids when the cat sleeps; its appearance or partial appearance over the open eye can be a sign of illness. Cats do see colors: they can distinguish red, blue and white, though green, yellow and white probably look the same, and red appears to cats as grey. The two eyes take in separate images, which the cat learns to compensate for. Kittens achieve full adult eyesight only at about three months old. Vision, of all the cat's senses, is the most developed and depended upon.[5]

Smell and taste are vital to cats. Like dogs, a cat gets to know people and objects by smelling them. Food is sniffed first and eaten only if it smells right. Sexuality and aggressiveness also use the senses of smell and taste. An organ lost to humans, the Jacobson's vomeronasal organ in the roof of the mouth, increases a cat's taste/smell sensitivity. Cats make faces using it, called the flehemen reaction. Their tongues are rough, with backward-facing hooks to help clean the bones of fed-upon prey. They are sensitive to salt, bitter and acid tastes. When salt is added to foods, the sense of sweet is invoked (cat food companies make use of this). Cats that cannot smell will not eat.[6]

Dogs have 319 bones, the same in all breeds and all sizes, though the bones themselves may differ in size and shape. (People have 204 bones, cats 244). There are forty-two teeth in the adult dog and twenty-eight in puppies. The jaw size in dogs varies with the breed; short-faced, short-jawed breeds may have fewer teeth, and some breeds carry a mutation gene for missing ones. Despite the great variation in size and body shapes, the general dog anatomy remains the same for all breeds, large or small. Their bodies are designed for endurance running with speeds up to forty miles per hour in the racing hounds (wolves run at thirty miles per hour). Like cats, dogs run and stand on their toes.[7]

A dog's front limbs move only a few degrees away from the chest and body, unlike the flexible cat. The forelegs are held by skin against the chest wall, limiting shoulder movement to a backward-forward motion only.

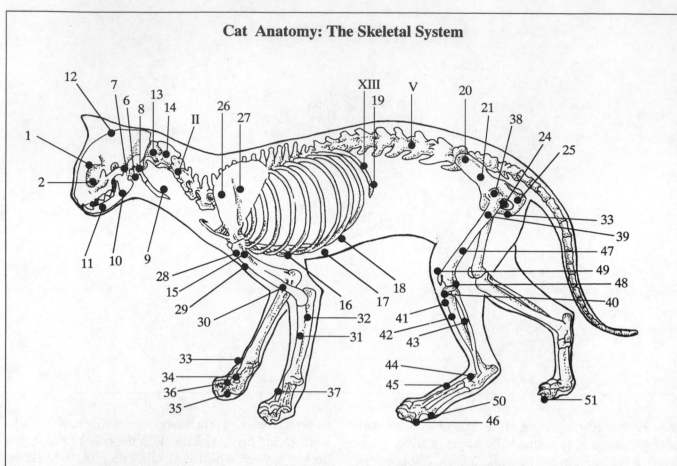

Cat Anatomy: The Skeletal System

1. Zygomatic process
2. orbit
3. zygomatic arch
4. maxilla
5. external acoustic meatus
6. tympanic bulla
7. temporomandibular articulation
8. angular process
9. hyoid bone
10. mandible
11. mental foramen
12. external sagittal crest
13. atlas
14. axis
15. manubrium
16. sternum
17. xiphoid process
18. costal arch
19. costal cartilage

20. crest of ilium
21. ilium
22. sacrum
23. pubis
24. obturator foramen
25. ischium
26. scapula
27. spine
28. clavicle
29. humerus
30. supracondylar foramen
31. radius
32. ulna
33. carpus
34. metacarpus
35. phalanges
36. third digit
37. first digit
38. head of femur

39. greater trochanter
40. tibial tuberosity
41. cranial margin of tibia
42. tibia
43. fibula
44. tarsus
45. metatarsus
46. fifth digit
47. femur
48. popliteal sesamoid bone
49. patella
50. plantar sesamoid
51. second digit
III. third cervical vertebra
V. fifth lumbar vertebra
VI. sixth thoracic vertebra
X. tenth caudal vertebra
XIII. thirteenth rib
(From Sis. 1965.)

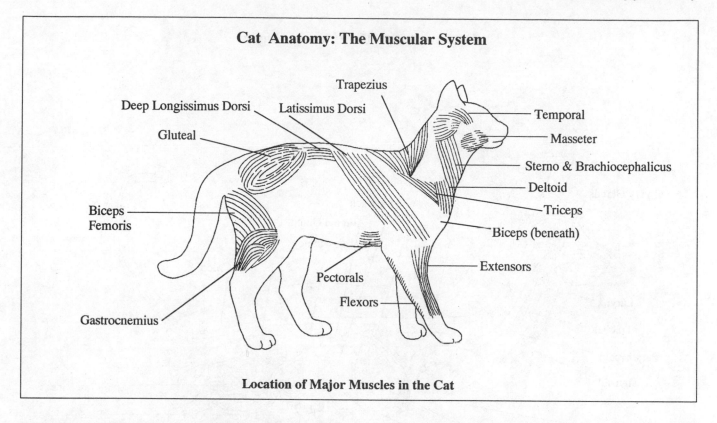

Cat Anatomy: The Muscular System

Trapezius

Deep Longissimus Dorsi

Latissimus Dorsi

Gluteal

Temporal

Masseter

Sterno & Brachiocephalicus

Deltoid

Triceps

Biceps
Femoris

Biceps (beneath)

Extensors

Pectorals

Flexors

Gastrocnemius

Location of Major Muscles in the Cat

People and cats have far greater arm/foreleg mobility, but horses have even less than dogs. This arrangement enhances the dog's long distance running specialty but results in the loss of other kinds of movement.[8] Dogs carry 75% of their weight on the shoulder joints and front end of the body, where humans carry all their weight on the hips. The hock in the dog is the human heel bone.[9] Unlike cats, dogs have fixed, nonretractable claws that are mainly used for traction in running. They do not have the cat's ability to manipulate objects with their paws, or to use their claws for fighting, grasping, climbing or hunting. Dogs use their jaws instead.[10]

Dogs are more carnivorous than humans but less meat dependent than cats. They require a diet of about 40% fat plus protein, where cats require 65%. (Dr. Gloria Dodd prefers 60–63% fat plus protein and 23% carbohydrate for both cats and dogs.) As hunters of plant-eating prey, dogs and wolves go to the contents of their kill's stomach first. This means that they are seeking partially digested grass and seed matter, vegetables. Dogs can survive on an all-vegetarian diet (if the diet is well-planned), but they are not happy or healthy on it; cats on such a diet will die within a year. Dogs and cats both have the shorter intestinal length of carnivores for rapid digestion of raw meat. Because dogs lack the cat's ability to concentrate body fluids in times of water shortage, they seldom have a problem with urinary tract infections. Both animals need fresh water available at all times, of course.

The heart rate in dogs averages 70–130 beats per minute, as opposed to 110–180 in cats. Respiration/breathing rate at rest is 10–30 breaths per minute and rapid breathing at rest is considered a sign of dis-ease. While dogs' ancestor the wolf has a relatively uniform size, today's domestic dogs may range from as small as three pounds for the teacup toy breeds, to as large as over two hundred pounds for a Saint Bernard or Newfoundland. Normal body temperature ranges from 100 to 102.5°F, and averages 101.3°F. Gestation time is from fifty-nine to sixty-six days with sixty-three to sixty-five days as average.[11]

Like cats, dogs' sensory system is far advanced of humans. The sense of touch, as in cats, is the least developed sense and is probably less acute than in cats. Dogs' foot pads are hard and their hair thick, compared to cats' tender paws and thinner coats. The foot pads and

Cat Anatomy: The Internal Organs

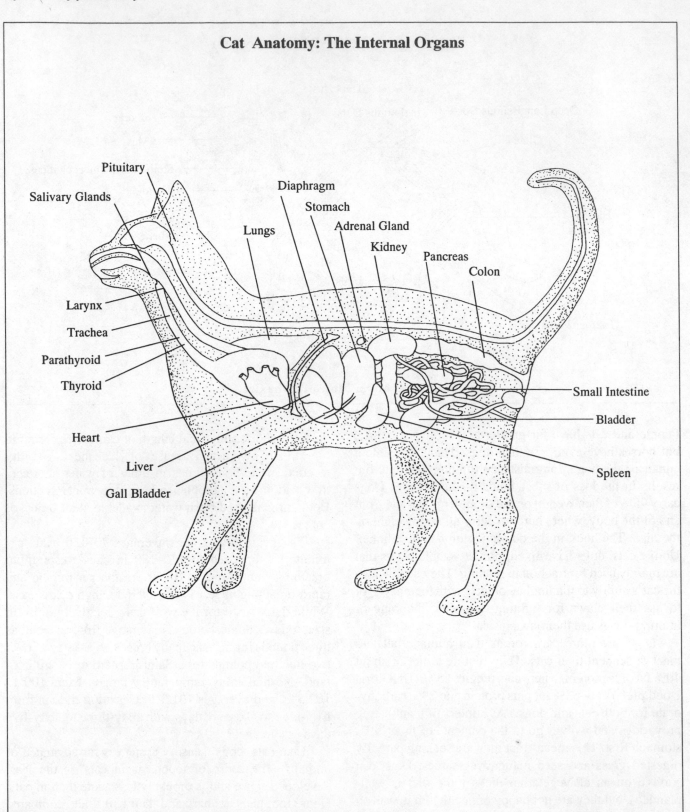

Pituitary

Salivary Glands

Diaphragm

Stomach

Lungs

Adrenal Gland

Kidney

Pancreas

Colon

Larynx

Trachea

Parathyroid

Thyroid

Small Intestine

Heart

Bladder

Liver

Gall Bladder

Spleen

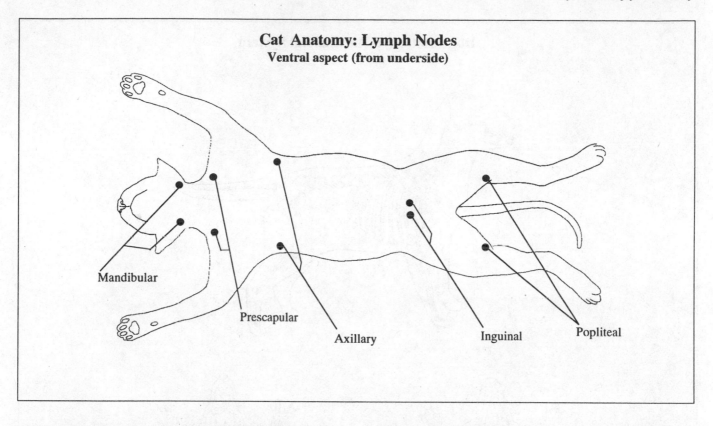

Cat Anatomy: Lymph Nodes
Ventral aspect (from underside)

Mandibular

Prescapular

Axillary

Inguinal

Popliteal

nose contain the only sweat glands of the dogs' body. Dogs have the same vibrissae/whiskers that cats do, but seem to rely on them less. Newly born puppies use the sense of touch (other sources say smell) as their means of locating the mother's nipple before other senses have opened. Dogs *do* sense vibrations through their feet and skin. They are more sensitive to some stimuli, such as electric shocks, than people are.[12]

Dogs' sense of hearing is extremely acute, far beyond that of either humans or cats. They can hear into the ultrasonic frequencies, with a high range of 70,000 to 100,000 cycles per second, by some reports. Sounds inaudible to people are easily heard by dogs, and what a human can hear at a hundred yards a dog can hear over a quarter of a mile away. The mobile outside earflaps accurately locate where a sound is coming from.[13]

Experts state that dogs have no color vision, but they seem able to distinguish between shades of colors. They are near-sighted and do not see things in sharp focus. Objects are recognized by form and the dog is highly sensitive to the slightest movement. They have superior night vision and ability to see well in dim light, and their eyes contain the tapetum lucidum that also aids light

reflection in cats. Dogs have a wider visual field and larger eye pupil than humans do. Because their eyes are in the front of their heads, rather than on the sides, dogs are unable to see behind them without turning. Their binocular vision is half that of humans, but their field of vision is about seventy degrees greater. The third eyelid, the nictitating membrane, exists in dogs as well as in cats and aids in cleaning and lubricating the eyes; it is more visible in some breeds than in others. Dogs have eyelashes on their upper eyelids, none on the lower ones.[14]

Sense of smell in the dog is forty times stronger than in people, and is dogs' most developed and depended upon sense. There are 200 million olfactory cells, compared to five million in humans. A dog can detect a teaspoonful of salt (odorless to humans) in thirteen gallons of water, and the sense of smell increases threefold when the dog is hungry. Dogs rely on their noses for most of their perceptions of people or situations, and the sense of smell is important in dogs' social rituals (territory marking, greeting, mate finding, etc.). Their sense of smell is used by people for detecting gas leaks, finding drugs, contraband and explosives, rescue work and hunting. No technology has ever replaced it. In a healthy dog,

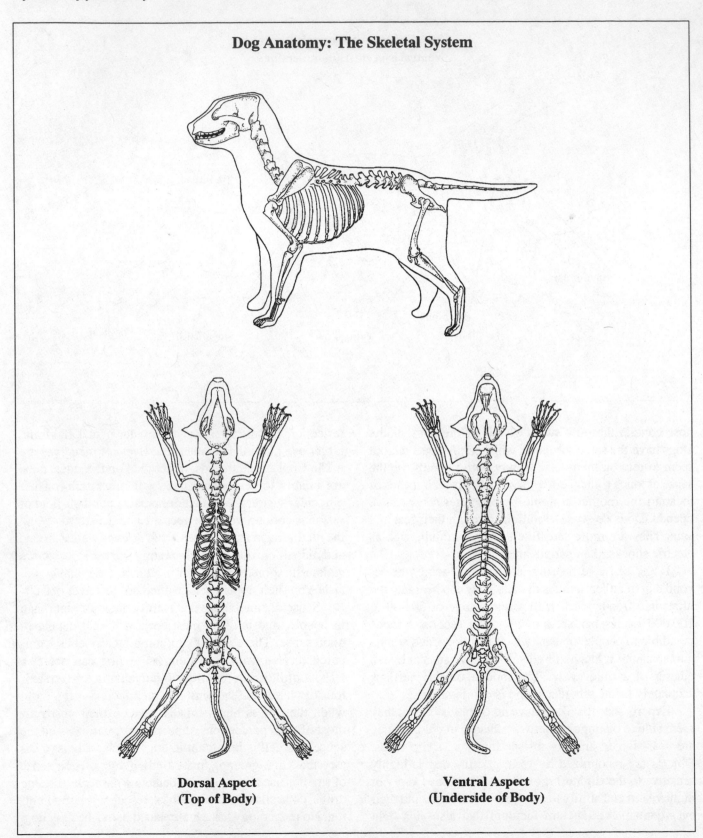

Dog Anatomy: The Skeletal System

Dorsal Aspect
(Top of Body)

Ventral Aspect
(Underside of Body)

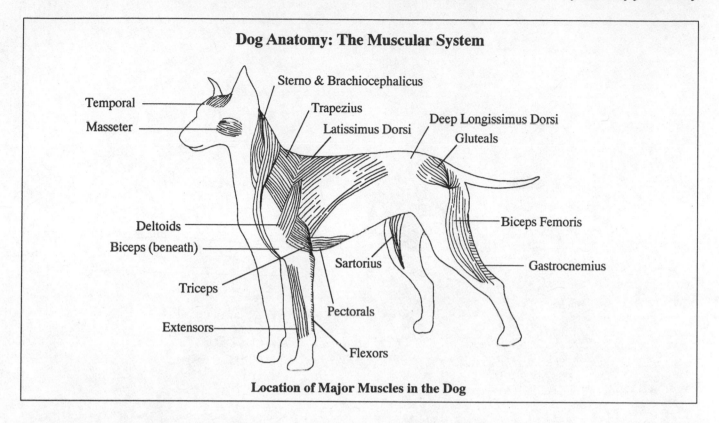

Dog Anatomy: The Muscular System

Temporal — Masseter — Sterno & Brachiocephalicus — Trapezius — Latissimus Dorsi — Deep Longissimus Dorsi — Gluteals — Deltoids — Biceps (beneath) — Triceps — Extensors — Flexors — Sartorius — Pectorals — Biceps Femoris — Gastrocnemius

Location of Major Muscles in the Dog

the nose is usually cool and wet, but there are individual variations. Mucus glands create the moisture and there are sweat glands in the dog's nose.[15]

Less is known about dogs' sense of taste; they gulp food down without tasting it, depending more on the sense of smell before eating. There are taste buds in the tongue, however, and the sense may be more refined than is known.[16] Most dogs will eat anything and are too easily at risk for poisoning and for ingesting unsafe objects. In my own experience, dogs have clear taste preferences, with food aversions and favorites.

This is only the briefest overview of dog and cat anatomy and, like people, dogs and cats (and all living things) have a nonphysical or beyond-the-physical anatomy as well. Dogs, cats and horses have a highly developed and distinctive chakra and aura energy system. (The animal meridian system will be discussed under acupuncture.) Where the standard medical and veterinary awareness treats only what it can see and touch, holistic healing goes beyond the physical to the energy bodies from which all life is comprised. Along with treating the physical body, holistic methods incorporate the emotional, mental and spiritual bodies. Without healing that reaches

the nonphysical levels, complete resolution of dis-ease cannot take place. These energy levels are receiving increasing study and attention in people; the concept carries over to dogs and cats. Where physical anatomy is derived from scientific research, nonphysical anatomy comes from psychic observation that may not be scientifically provable at this time. (See Appendix I: *Scientific Methods of Detecting the Nonphysical Anatomy* by Dr. Gloria Dodd, DVM.)

Different holistic methods work on different energy levels. Herbs, vitamins and minerals, nutrition and massage affect the physical body specifically and have their significant responses on that level. Homeopathic remedies, which may be diluted to the point where no molecule of the actual remedy substance remains, work on the nearest nonphysical level—the etheric double—as well as on the emotional and mental bodies. Flower essences reach even further, extending from the etheric to the spiritual range. Acupuncture, with its focus on the energy channels of the body, works on the unseen levels as well as on the physical. Healing that takes place on the energy levels filters down to the physical body. A "cure" is not complete until all of the levels are cleared of dis-ease,

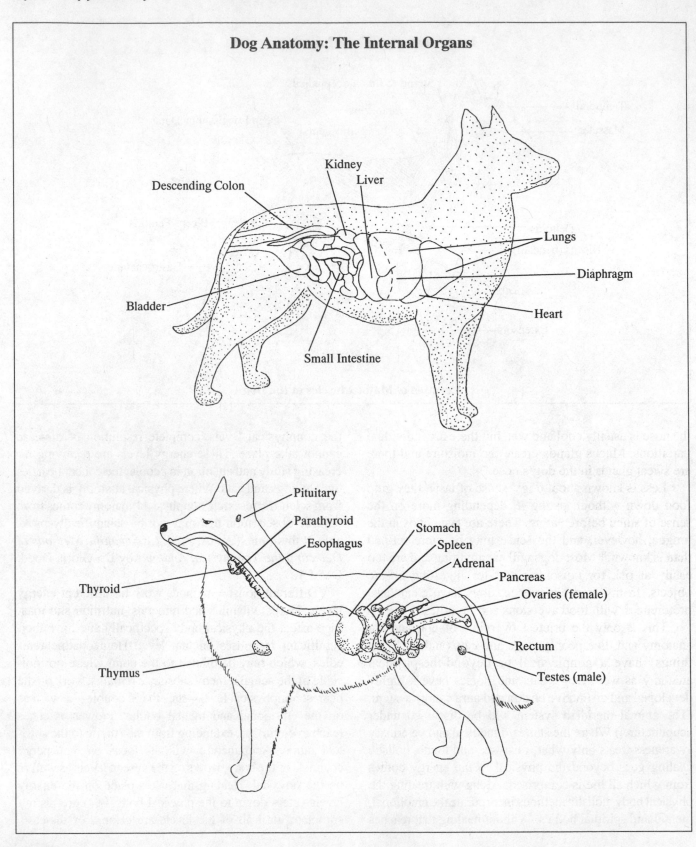

Dog Anatomy: The Internal Organs

Descending Colon

Kidney

Liver

Lungs

Diaphragm

Bladder

Heart

Small Intestine

Pituitary

Parathyroid

Esophagus

Stomach

Spleen

Adrenal

Pancreas

Ovaries (female)

Thyroid

Rectum

Thymus

Testes (male)

Anatomy Comparisons

	Cat	Dog	Human
Bones in the Body	244	319	204
Teeth in Adults	30	42	32
Heart Rate—Beats Per Minute	110–180	70–130	70
Respiration Rate—Breaths Per Minute (Average)	30–50	10–30	18
Body Size—Pounds (Average)	5 1/2–15	3–200	100–200
Body Temperature—Average	101.5°F	101.3°F	98.6°F
Gestation Time—In Days	60±5	59–66	266
Hearing—High Range in Cycles Per Second	65,000	70,000–100,000	20,000
Tapetum Lucidum	yes	yes	see note
Nictitating Membrane	yes	yes	no
Jacobson's Vomeronasal Organ	yes	no	no

Note: The Tapetum Lucidum exists in humans in only one people, the aboriginal people of Australia. My thanks to Dr. Gloria Dodd for this information.

Michael Wright and Sally Walters, Eds., *The Book of the Cat* (New York, Summit Books, 1980), p. 102-113; Delbert G. Carlson, DVM and James M. Griffin, MD, *Dog Owner's Home Veterinary Handbook* (New York, Howell Book House, 1986), pp. 161, 225-226, 355-356, and Dr. Ian Dunbar, *Dog Behaviour: Why Dogs Do What They Do?* (Neptune, NJ, TFH Publications, Inc., 1979), p. 36-49.

whatever the problem from hip dysplasia to depression. The medical/veterinary technological model, working only on the physical body, does only a small part of the job.

A brief description of the four bodies, the aura layers and the chakras of dogs and cats follows. For more detailed information based on people, see Diane Stein, *All Women Are Healers* (The Crossing Press, 1990) and Diane Stein, *The Women's Book of Healing* (Llewellyn Publications, 1987). The basic energy structures are the same, but there are variations between human and animal nonphysical anatomies.

The physical level—the physical body that can be touched and seen—has an energy twin called the etheric double. This is the first of the energy bodies or aura layers. Whatever the health state is of that double, the animal's physical body reflects it. If dis-ease begins in the physical body, it moves through the etheric double to the energy bodies. If it begins on any of the other levels—emotional, mental or spiritual—the dis-ease filters through the energy layers to the etheric double and then to the physical body. Energy moves from the physical/ etheric double to the emotional to the mental to the spiritual body. It also moves in the opposite direction in

the same order: from the spiritual to the mental to the emotional to the etheric double and finally into the physical animal's body. A dis-ease that is only on the physical level is far easier to clear than one that has emotional or mental consequences. Women who see auras can assess the state of a person or a pet's health. They often see dis-ease developing in the etheric or emotional body levels before it becomes apparent in the tissues and organs.

The next energy/aura body is the emotional body. Women who see auras see it as a rainbow of colors. Most holistic and many progressive medical healers believe that every dis-ease has an emotional coordinate that must be released for full healing to take place. This in humans has been the major work of Louise Hay (*You Can Heal Your Life*, Hay House, 1984). Emotional pain leads to physical dis-ease in both people and animals. The dog that has been abused will show more than physical effects—it may be afraid and shy even in a safe home (emotional effects), show aberrant behaviors (mental effects), or even give up, languish and actually die (spiritual effects). These things continue long after the dog is in a caring environment. When that dog develops a physical dis-ease, more than physical healing is required.

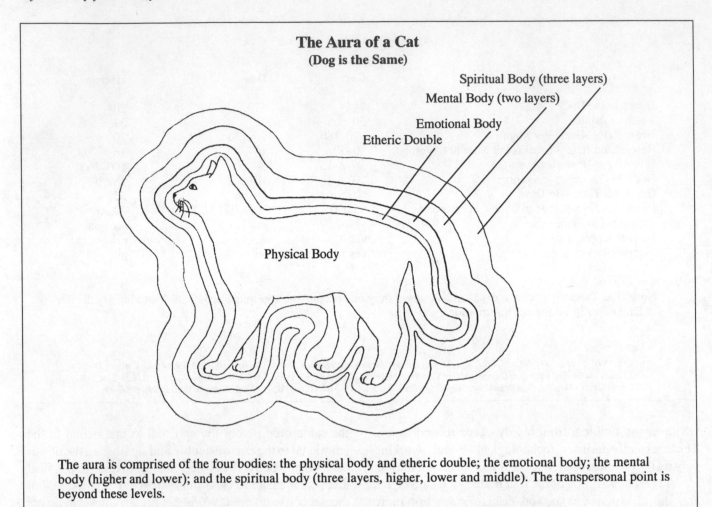

The Aura of a Cat
(Dog is the Same)

Spiritual Body (three layers)

Mental Body (two layers)

Emotional Body

Etheric Double

Physical Body

The aura is comprised of the four bodies: the physical body and etheric double; the emotional body; the mental body (higher and lower); and the spiritual body (three layers, higher, lower and middle). The transpersonal point is beyond these levels.

Likewise, a cat I knew that had been raped by other cats in her family became enormously obese. She was attempting to protect herself from further attacks, on an emotional and mental level, by being "bigger." Putting this cat on a reducing diet would not heal her. The emotional body is the subconscious mind and is highly active in pets. The energies of both healing and dis-ease always pass through the emotional body. When dis-ease originates there, the emotions must be healed before the physical body will respond to treatment.

The mental body is the next level. Fewer aura-seeing women can view this body, and those who do perceive it as shooting projectiles of light and color. Animals certainly think, and their perception of the world differs greatly from people's. An idea made in time of crisis or decided upon without full understanding can be a source of dis-ease later. In the base of the abused dog, such an idea might be that "this person hurt me, so all people will hurt me. I'll hide from them." In the case of the obese cat, it might be "I'll make myself bigger than they are, then they'll be afraid of me and leave me alone." To heal both cat and dog these thought-forms must be changed—the dog must be shown that not all people will hurt her, and the cat shown that there are other ways to protect herself. Many aberrant animal behaviors (and human ones) come from misguided thought processes like these. By healing the thought-form, positive effects reach all the levels and affect the animal's physical well-being.

Pets are as spiritual as people, if not more so, and the spiritual body is also a factor in healing animals. Dogs and cats have a oneness with the Earth and nature that few humans experience. Just as the Earth is wounded now, so are Her animals and people. Spiritual healing is not only a human concept. Had the abused dog in the examples above not found a safe home, or if that home came too late, she might decide that she has no place on the planet to belong and choose to die. To put that plan into effect, she might stop eating, run deliberately in front of a car, or contract and not fight a dis-ease. Dogs and cats can and do commit suicide. Spiritual level healing means connection with Goddess and with one's purpose on the planet. Animals as much as people need to know why they are here, what their job is in this life, and where and with whom they belong. Much of the suffering is spiritual, and healing on the spiritual level is profound healing indeed. It is where a great deal of today's healing work for both people and pets is being accomplished. A cat, dog or human whose illness has reached the spiritual level will not have a healthy body. Despite these implications, spiritual healing happens every day, and can begin on any of the four levels with any of the healing methods of this book.

The four body levels also comprise the eight levels or layers of the aura in humans or animals. Some levels are visible to some women. The etheric double is the closest layer to the physical, a single aura layer, and the next layer beyond it is the emotional body. The mental body follows with two aura layers, called the higher and lower mental bodies. The emotional body level is the subconscious mind; the lower mental body is the conscious mind, and the higher mental layer is the creative or inspirational mind. The spiritual body follows as three aura layers, the lower, middle and higher spiritual areas (the Maiden, Mother and Crone). This is the super-ego or higher self, and animals have it as well as people. Above the body completely is a further layer, the transpersonal point. The aura layers surround the physical body like an egg surrounds the unborn chick or the mother's womb surrounds a developing mammal fetus.

Marion Webb-Former describes the aura layers of cats and dogs:

As with all life forms, earthly animals do indeed possess auras. Auras are as much a part of the whole being as are the bones, the flesh and the tissue. They may not be as visible as is the flesh, but auras are equally as viable.

The layers of auras of dogs, cats and other animals are different from those of humans in their extent. In animals, the etheric body, because it extends directly from the higher soul...is minimal....The second layer of the aura, which is known as the astral or emotional level, extends far wider than that of humans.

It stretches beyond the boundaries of any total human aura because animals participate as much at the astral level as they do at the physical....Cats in particular prefer the astral level of existence. The lower and higher mental layers of the auras of animals are quite narrow, for...they do not utilize their mental abilities to any great extent. Lastly, the spiritual layer of animal auras is similar in size to that of the astral and for both these levels this is a consequence of the abundance of Source consciousness within the animal.[17]

Animals also can see auras and use the information much more fully than humans can:

Whereas the ability to see auras is latent in many humans, it is a natural sense, if you will, within the animal kingdom for the crown and third eye chakras are one. Thus the ability to "see" and function at the astral level is greatly enhanced. Dogs and cats recognize one another and their human companions primarily by "seeing" the aura of another and not from physical sensory input. That is why recognition can take place sometimes even at great distances, for the animals' aura extends so widely that contact can be made with another's aura long before physical contact takes place. This auric contact is much more than seeing, smelling, hearing, touching and speaking. It resonates throughout all the inner senses of the animal. It is a melding of one aura with another.[17]

Each of the bodies and layers has a direct connection to the physical body through a series of energy centers located on the etheric double. These energy centers are called chakras, a Sanskrit word that means "wheel." Each energy layer of the aura corresponds to a chakra, and each chakra to a portion of the physical body. The chakras are much the same in animals as they are in people. Humans generally have eight major opened chakras, depending on the individual's level of development, and as many as forty-nine altogether, including a variety of smaller and minor energy areas. Dogs and cats essentially have the same chakras, with individual variations as to which ones will be developed and operating. Most pets have at least five active primary chakras and up to twenty-one minor ones. Unlike people's chakras, animal chakras are not placed in a straight line down the body's center.

Different parts of the body are accessed by different chakras, and a healing for a particular part of the body involves working with and healing that energy area. In humans, as well as cats and dogs, the eight primary areas are as follows. Each chakra is accompanied by a color. The root center, located at the vagina in women, works with issues of survival and living in the world. Its color is

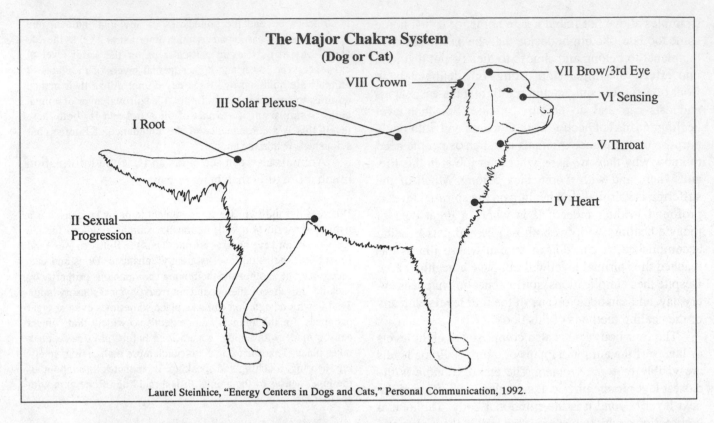

The Major Chakra System
(Dog or Cat)

VIII Crown
VII Brow/3rd Eye
III Solar Plexus
VI Sensing
I Root
V Throat
IV Heart
II Sexual Progression

Laurel Steinhice, "Energy Centers in Dogs and Cats," Personal Communication, 1992.

red; it corresponds to the uterus and the etheric double energy level. The belly chakra is orange, located at the ovaries or spleen. It corresponds to issues of taste/preference, sexuality and reproduction, and the emotional body. Pictures of past events as well as first impressions are stored here, and this is a major center for animals. The solar plexus (yellow) is the energy assimilation center of the body. It is the lower mental level, the conscious mind, as well as the organs of digestion. Energy is brought into the body at this center and distributed to the other chakras and energy layers.

The heart center is described as green or rose in people, and is often an undeveloped (because not needed) energy area in pets (more on this below). This is the higher mental body, the imaginative mind and the place of compassion for others. Development of these qualities in animals is so far advanced that the heart center is no longer required for them. They do not need a heart center; they are all heart. The throat center in people is likewise less developed in animals, they communicate from the solar plexus telepathically. The color is blue; people speaking to dogs or cats with conscious intent use

their throats and third eyes. The throat center is the lower spiritual body level.

Two more levels of the spiritual body are the third eye/brow chakra, the place of psychic gifts (indigo) and the crown chakra at the top of the head (violet). The crown is the place of women's connection with Goddess. In animals the crown and brow (middle and higher spiritual layers) are combined, as are the root and belly chakras (etheric and emotional layers). Pets operate fully on psychic levels and are totally connected with Goddess/the Earth and Universe. One further center, located beyond the physical body, is the transpersonal point. Described as clear in color and comprised of all the colors of light combined, this layer is the full aura, and all the chakras are incorporated within it. As with humans, animals have all of these centers, but their use and development are differently arranged. Animals as well as people have a number of additional smaller chakras, including those on the hands and feet (paws). The centers in the paws are highly important for pets.

Two psychics, Marion Webb-Former and Laurel Steinhice, describe the chakra system of dogs and cats.

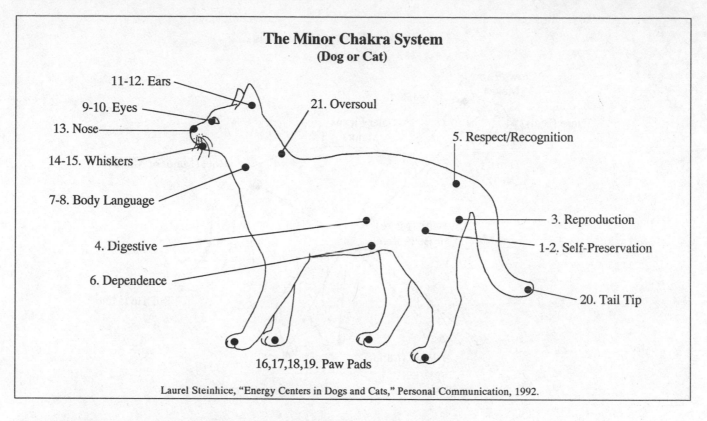

The Minor Chakra System
(Dog or Cat)

11-12. Ears

9-10. Eyes

13. Nose

14-15. Whiskers

7-8. Body Language

4. Digestive

6. Dependence

21. Oversoul

5. Respect/Recognition

3. Reproduction

1-2. Self-Preservation

20. Tail Tip

16,17,18,19. Paw Pads

Laurel Steinhice, "Energy Centers in Dogs and Cats," Personal Communication, 1992.

Their descriptions complement each other, with Marion describing what is most active in animals, and Laurel going into fuller detail about all of the centers, developed or not. Marion focuses on the energy channels, the movement of life force energy among the chakras, and these channels come into play most clearly in the sections on acupuncture and psychic healing. The chakra centers and channels are central information for doing psychic energy work and balancing on pets. Both women were featured in *Dreaming the Past, Dreaming the Future* (Diane Stein, The Crossing Press, 1991). Both women are accomplished animal healers, Laurel with cats in particular, and Marion with her dogs. I thank them deeply for their participation in this book.

Marion Webb-Former describes three or four major chakras. There are two additional minor centers and three bud chakras. Major chakras are essential and fully developed energy centers in all pets: these are the crown/brow, solar plexus and belly/root chakras. Minor chakras are smaller and less major energy points but still essential and universal. In cats and dogs, these are at the bottoms of all four paws and at the tip of the tail. Bud chakras are small energy centers that may be more or less developed, with variations among individual animals; they are subject to growth and change. The chakra at the base of the tail may be considered either minor or major; it is equivalent to another root center. In Marion's chakra analysis, the belly and root chakras are combined into one major center, located in the underbelly of the dog or cat. I have listed the center at the base of the tail as the root chakra, and describe it as a major center, since Laurel Steinhice also notes it this way. The combined chakra in the underbelly is designated as the belly chakra.

That no heart center is listed as a major chakra for animals is surprising. (Laurel Steinhice describes the heart as present but awakened only in some pets.) Marion Webb-Former explains it as follows:

You will note that in animals there is no equivalent to the heart chakra and this is because there is no need of that chakra within animals. Due to their abundance of Source consciousness they have not lost the concept of love, of agape, whereas man (sic) has and he needs that chakra to reaffirm and realign himself with the love which is all existence.[17]

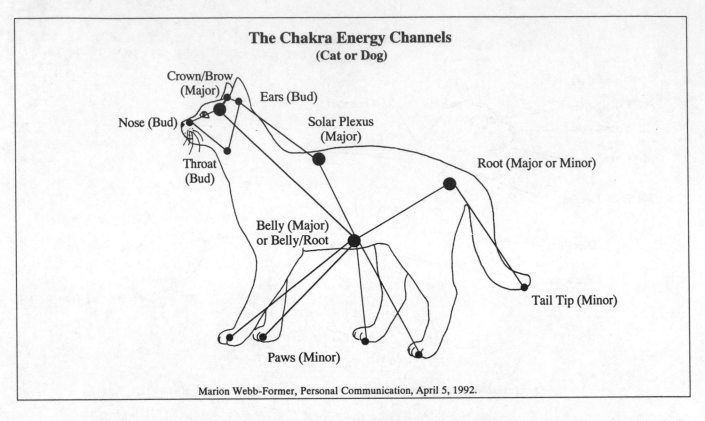

The Chakra Energy Channels
(Cat or Dog)

Crown/Brow (Major)

Ears (Bud)

Nose (Bud)

Solar Plexus (Major)

Throat (Bud)

Root (Major or Minor)

Belly (Major) or Belly/Root

Tail Tip (Minor)

Paws (Minor)

Marion Webb-Former, Personal Communication, April 5, 1992.

In psychic explorations with my dogs and a friend's cat, I had felt highly active heart energy. I questioned Marion about this:

What is being sensed or 'seen'…is the direct channel which allows the linkage between the head and belly chakras. It is of equal if not more importance than the major chakras for without it animals would have to always utilize the channel from the head chakra, to the solar plexus chakra, and down to the belly chakra in order to connect with the Earth Mother. Think of this alternative channel as the pathway of pure love along which…the Source can travel freely in either direction, for it is the substance of the Source. The variation of colors which Diane has perceived within the chests of her dogs denotes the directional flow of Source consciousness; reds and pinks would indicate an upward thrust; greens, blues and violets would signify a downward movement.[17]

These energy channels that connect the chakras are of apparently more significance than the chakras themselves. The three major chakras—crown/brow, solar plexus and belly/root—comprise the central two-way energy channel in the form of a triangle. (Energy in the human chakras moves in a vertical, double straight line, along the spinal column.) Energy from the Earth and Universe (feet and head) is brought into and out of the dog or cat's body in both directions through this energy triangle. The energy flow runs as follows:

Think more in the geometrical form of a triangle with animals, starting at the belly chakra for grounding, going up to the small of the back for utilizing that energy into the physical form and traveling on up to the head to take that energy and transfer it back into Source energy, Source consciousness. In order to complete the figure of a triangle there is also a a direct connection between the head and belly chakra which bypasses the second chakra (solar plexus). This linkage is possible because once again I say that animals have not forgotten their heritage, the Source from which they came. Both their head and belly chakras assimilate the consciousness of the Source and, as you have been taught, "as above, so below." Animals do not use this particular linkage constantly, but it is theirs to command whenever they so choose. With it they manifest what they require when their physical aspect is in need of food and shelter. It is also the channel…through which they communicate with one another and with man (sic).

Man also possesses this linkage between his crown and root chakras, but it has fallen into decay because his preoccupation with the physical plane has led to separation from much of his Source energy….For those individuals who promote and utilize

The Chakra System
(Cat or Dog)

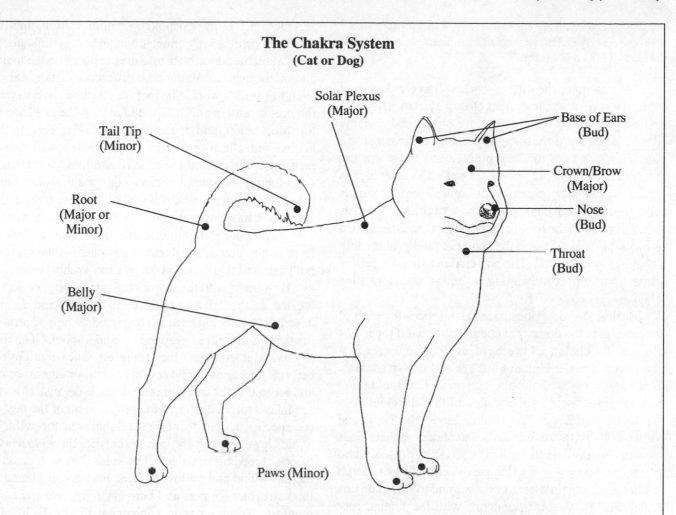

Major Chakras		
Crown/Brow	Head	Green, Blue, Purple
Solar Plexus	Back	Orange or Golden
Belly	Root	Bright Red
Root	Base of Tail	Dark Red

Minor Chakras	
Paws	Ruby
Tail Tip	Dark Red

Bud Chakras	
Nose Tip	
Throat	
Base of Ears	Pale Yellow, become Aqua
	or Blue when developed

Marion Webb-Former, Personal Communications, March 18, and April 5, 1992.

this energy channel there are wondrous rewards for there is the ability to perceive all dimensions of consciousness and communication within all life forms.[17]

As in people, the energy chakras have colors, and these are similar to the human chakra system. Different animals may vary these colors for shade and density. Marion describes the crown/brow center as ranging from pale green or blue to deep purple, and these are the spiritual body colors in people, as well. The solar plexus chakra is orange or golden yellow, and the belly center is bright red. The root chakra at the base of the tail, listed as either a minor chakra or a smaller major one, is described as black or dark red, as is the center at the tip of the tail. The paws are ruby red. The bud chakras are pale yellow while undeveloped, changing to aquas and light blue when awakened.

Marion also describes specific purposes for each of the chakras in the dog or cat energy system. Of the major centers, the chakra in the head of dogs and cats is a combination of the human third eye and crown chakras. This energy center links the personality of the animal with its higher self or oversoul, and that oversoul with the Goddess/Source. The chakra along the backbone corresponds with the human solar plexus. It manifests physical energy and the animal's physical presence and attributes. Marion notes that many animals like to rub this body area against trees or the ground to stimulate this center. Animals' correspondence with the human root and belly chakras is the major center located in the underbelly. Its purpose is for grounding and for alignment with the Earth Mother.

The underbelly chakra works in conjunction with the minor chakras in the bottoms of the paws. The centers in the paws lead the dog or cat to harmonious energy spots; when found, the animal will lie down there, and the belly chakra opens to draw in the energy. Both dogs and cats are very particular as to where they lie down, and the chakras in the feet are uniquely sensitive to Earth energy. The minor/major chakras in the tail also help to guide the animal to energy sources, but they are less primary than the paw chakras.

A smaller energy triangle runs from the bud chakras in the ears to the nose and throat centers. The throat in most pets is a closed bud, as dogs and cats use their solar plexus centers to communicate psychically with instead. The ears and nose are more highly developed centers,

and more active in nonspoken communication, and the three bud centers are connected in an energy linkage.[17]

Laurel Steinhice goes into deeper detail on the major and minor chakras, with some differences from Marion Webb-Former's work. She includes the bud chakras with the minor centers and lists the chakra at the tail base as the root center and a major chakra. Her description begins with the root for the major centers and moves forward to the crown. (See the illustration for comparison.) Laurel's system describes eight major chakras and twenty-one minor ones. Several of these remain undeveloped in most animals, and development of these centers is often an individual matter with wide variations from dog to dog or cat to cat. The system is the same in both cats and dogs, as it is for Marion Webb-Former.

Beginning with the major chakras, the root chakra is located at the tail base. Its color is red, and Laurel describes it as being oval in shape and "wrapped around the spine as thread is wrapped around a spool." The root is survival instinct and for grounding. She describes the belly as the sexual progression chakra, orange in color, and located at the internal reproductive organs. This is a sexual overdrive designed for propagation of the best of the species, an aid to natural selection in the wild. In domestic pets, it helps to counterbalance the weaknesses of poor breeding practices. The solar plexus, located at the mid-spine and yellow gold is, for pets and humans, the key center for pets and humans to interact and communicate. When active in a dog or cat, this center links to the solar plexus of the participating person and both are energized by the linkage. When the relationship between human and animal has become fully co-creative and cooperative, the linkage is no longer needed and deactivates.

Only a few individual animals have developed heart chakras, and the loving energy is shared between animal and human. The color is green, and Laurel Steinhice notes that the trend is moving toward a wider use of the heart center in animals. Very few animals have developed their throat chakras, though the potential is there. Pets' instinctive communications (bark, howls, cries, purr, etc.) come from the root center, where throat chakra energy is used for conscious communication with intent. Another center with wide variations in individual animals is the sensing chakra located at the bridge of the nose between the eyes (not the third eye). It is pale silver blue and governs sensory intake and the transmission of sensory input to the brain. The center is more developed in highly sensitive animals, and is overdeveloped in some while underdeveloped in other individuals.

The third eye/brow crown chakras are often combined in cats and dogs. The third eye is located on the forehead, above and between the eyes. It is usually indigo, but is sometimes seen as silver with or without crystalline flecks. As in humans, this is the center of psychic sight, and many pets are psychically developed far beyond their humans' abilities. The crown is usually violet in color and is located just behind the top of the head. It is the life force connection, the connection with Goddess in both people and pets. Alternate colors for this center are golden or white, and the center can appear as a funnel shape, pear shape, camera lens shape, or the traditional lotus. The combined crown/brow is highly active.

The twenty-one minor chakras work directly with the major ones. The self-preservation centers, one on each hip (1–2), are shaped like starfish with one longer arm that runs down the hind legs. The centers boost the energy of the root center in fight or flight situations (adrenal), and are less developed in pets than in wild creatures. Take note of the high current incidence of hip dysplasia in dogs with this chakra information in mind; the dis-ease is a reflection of the adrenal burnout and depletion of living on a wounded planet. The reproduction chakra (3) is placed at the external reproductive organs under the tail; its color is red-orange, and the center governs basic reproduction. It works in conjunction with the root chakra. Also subordinate to the root center is the digestive self-preservation chakra (4), located at the tip of the liver and rust-red in color. This usually underdeveloped center helps animal instinct to avoid poisons and other inedibles that could cause harm if ingested. In most pets, this center is completely atrophied (cats have more sense with this than dogs do).

The friend/foe/respect/recognition center (5) operates in conjunction with the sexual progression/belly chakra. It is located at the spine, slightly above the internal sexual organs, and is golden in color. The center regulates territory and social customs beyond the individual animal's pack or household. It is also activated by each species' oversoul intelligence to sense gene-pool impact in territorial issues—the animal whose reproduc-

tion is best able to enhance the species is deferred to.

Coordinate with the solar plexus major center, the underbelly dependence chakra (6) is the place of independence, trust and obedience with people, as well as dominance-submission behavior between animals. The color of this minor center is citron yellow. No minor chakras are connected with the heart chakra, but a pair of minor chakras are linked to the throat. They are listed as body language centers (7–8). These are located on either side of the chest slightly toward the body center from the shoulder joints. The colors are blue, and thin pathways run from them to either side of the body, along the spine and down into all four legs and paws. Body language behavior in intentional communication is regulated by these chakras. These communications include tail wagging, purring, pawing, body position, imitating humans, etc.

The sensing chakra in the bridge of the nose is the seat of the other sensing minor centers. Do not confuse it with the brow/third eye. These minor chakras include the small ones in the eyes (9–10), the pair at the base of the ears (11–12), the nose tip (13), the whiskers on each side of the face (14–15), all four paw pads (16, 17, 18, 19) and the tail tip (20). No colors are given for these small centers. The species oversoul linkage (21) is connected with the combined crown/brow major chakra. This is a small, dense energy area located at the base of the skull. Many women believe there is a similar center now activating in people, and Katrina Raphaell calls it the causal body.[18] (She also refers to the transpersonal point as the soul star.) The color for this center cannot be clearly seen and has no earthplane name. Laurel Steinhice describes it as white/silver/living-grey.

Laurel describes an "accelerated activation and opening of chakras previously little used or long unused" in individual animals as they interact closely with people. She describes also several new energy flow formats developing and several new chakras. These are experiments that may or may not be adopted for permanent incorporation and use. Animals' rate of development, along with people's, is increasing and rising at this time. Co-creation between animals and people is a key to this rising evolution.[19] More on this in the next chapter, Communication and Psychic Healing.

From this brief overview, it is apparent that animal anatomy both physical and nonphysical is a complex and detailed subject. I have given enough information to show women where to start. The information on psychic anatomy of dogs and cats has never been published before, and I thank Laurel and Marion for their very expert help. Women can assess the energies of their own pets to determine which chakras are active and how the energy flows operate in their individual animals.

Anatomy and nonphysical anatomy are the beginning of healing work in people and no less so for healing with animals. Knowledge of both forms of anatomy provide an understanding and basis necessary for all healing methods. The next chapter deals with a necessary healing skill—conscious communication between women and their pets—and an introduction to energy work and psychic healing with animals.

[1] Michael Wright and Sally Walters, Eds., *The Book of the Cat*, (New York, Summit Books, 1980), p. 102–105, and 118.

[2] *Ibid.*, p. 102–105.

[3] *Ibid.*

[4] *Ibid.*, p. 108.

[5] *Ibid.*, p. 109–111.

[6] *Ibid.*, p. 112–113.

[7] Dr. Ian Dunbar, *Dog Behaviour: Why Dogs Do What They Do* (Neptune, NJ, TFH Publications, Inc., 1979), p. 36–43.

[8] *Ibid.*, p. 40.

[9] Delbert G. Carlson, DVM and James M. Griffin, MD, *Dog Owner's Home Veterinary Handbook* (New York, Howell Book House, 1986), p. 225–226.

[10] Ian Dunbar, *Dog Behavior*, p. 49.

[11] Delbert Carlson and James Griffin, *Dog Owner's Home Veterinary Handbook*, p. 99–101.

[12] Ian Dunbar, *Dog Behaviour*, p. 49.

[13] *Ibid.*, p. 45–46.

[14] *Ibid.*, p. 43–44, and Delbert Carlson and James Griffin, *Dog Owner's Veterinary Handbook*, p. 99–101.

[15] Ian Dunbar, *Dog Behavior*, p. 46–48.

[16] *Ibid.*, p. 48–49.

[17] Marion Webb-Former, Personal Communication, May 16, 1992.

[18] Katrina Raphaell, *The Crystalline Transmission: A Synthesis of Light* (Santa Fe, NM, Aurora Press, 1990), p. 33 ff.

[19] Laurel Steinhice, "Energy Centers (Chakras) in Dogs and Cats," Personal Communication, 1992.

Communication & Psychic Healing

Two quotes, one from Laurel Steinhice and the other from Penelope Smith, are the keynotes of this chapter. From Laurel Steinhice:

Dogs and cats are bridges between humanity and *all* other life forms, because of their highly developed and time-honored interspecies relationship to humanity, and because there are so many of them living as an accepted part of human society. They are beloved and familiar; they occupy a position of trust in the human family. Their service is multifaceted and widely acknowledged.[1]

And from Penelope Smith, author of *Animal Talk: Interspecies Telepathic Communication* (Pegasus Publications, 1989):

The proof of the spiritual nature of human and nonhuman alike is that when you address them accordingly, with respect and helpfulness, you can improve the condition of the whole being. In my work, a key element is recognizing the individual animal as a spiritual being inhabiting or enlivening a particular form. In communicating and counselling them this way, upsets and behavior problems are resolved, illnesses and injuries are more readily healed, and the individual becomes more alive, aware, and happy.[2]

Before women can begin communication with their pets or other animals, they must recognize animals' spiritual nature which is their bond with the Earth Mother. In the eyes of the Goddess/Earth all life is one life, and any force that harms any of Her creatures harms them all. Likewise, any energy that helps any animal or person helps and heals the Earth as well. Because so much harm has been done to the creatures of the planet—including human creatures—we are in a time of clear and present danger to the planet as a whole. Healing the animals heals the Earth, and heals women as well.

This recognition that all life is spiritual (a part of Goddess) is what is meant in the concept of the oneness of all life, and a part of what women attempt to heal by alternative healing. This is what a co-creative partnership with the Earth means; by working with (instead of ignoring or working against) animals and the rest of nature, people create with nature a planet that is conscious of everyone's needs (not only humans'), a place of safety, abundance and love for all. Animals, as spiritual Be-ings, deserve no less. Dogs and cats, as the animals that directly share humans' everyday lives, are the beginning and, perhaps because they share our lives so closely, they are the first in need.

Women helping to heal animals and the planet cannot do it alone. It is a clear offense and violation of free will to interfere with another Be-ing without permission and without knowing what is needed and wanted. This is as much true in healing animals as it is with people. Before women can help, they must find out what is needed and find it out directly. Before women can help, they must get to know the spiritual Be-ings they are working with. In short, the first step in healing with animals is to learn to communicate with them. When there is clear, conscious two-way talk, the animals tell us themselves what they want and need from us, as healers and as partners on the Earth.

Because dogs and cats do not speak does not mean that they are "dumb" or unable to communicate. Their body language in itself is eloquent and gets many messages across, and is a primary way in which animals speak to each other. A cat or dog's ears and tails alone speak volumes. Their body positions show mood, emotion and intent. A dog with her head lowered to her chest and her teeth bared is a dog that will bite. A cat with her back arched and fur standing on end is ready to attack. Anyone who lives with a dog or cat learns at least some of this language; they are aware of their pet's moods, even if they cannot define what gives them the information. The illustrations from the work of Jean Craighead George show a sampling of cat and dog facial and tail positions and what they mean.

The communication of this chapter, however, goes beyond animal behavior and body language to direct interspecies communication. It is quite possible, and even easy, to talk directly with your pet, once you show her you are serious about it. The key to doing so is the meditative state, and the attitude of co-creating partnership. If you come to your pet with the patriarchal model of "I'm the boss and you're the cat," don't expect any response. If you come to your pet with the attitude of "I love you and want to learn about you," a whole new world begins to open. The first phase illustrates what's wrong between humans, animals and the Earth, and the second is a start in healing it.

For a first step, try a meditation. Get into a quiet place and quiet space, maybe at night with a candle burning, and clear your mind of outside distractions. Take the phone off the hook, and make sure you will be undisturbed. Next imagine a lioness or she-wolf running free; run with her a while, and with her pride or pack. Feel the wind on her fur, which becomes your fur. Go home with her to her/your den and experience her life, which is without human interaction….Next imagine a dog or cat on the street, struggling for survival. Feel her hunger and her fear, and the world from her point of view. Far from nature, humans have abandoned her. Become her for a while, and send her healing, comfort and love.…Then imagine your own dog or cat, and enter her life for a time. Experience her Be-ing through her own senses, and experience her view of humans, including yourself. Be the dog or cat taking care of her person, and realize how your pet takes care of you…Be yourself again, sending your animal (and all the animals) love. Come back to now.[3]

The change of viewpoints is enlightening. The world from the eyes of a wild cat or dog is far different from that of one hungry and lost on dangerous city streets. The world of the dog or cat that you live with appears very different through her senses than it does through your own. By slipping in and out of your pet's reality, your recognition of her Be-ing and your respect for it grows. With that respect, compassion and love in mind, you are ready to begin speaking to your animal.

The procedure here is from Penelope Smith's *Animal Talk: Interspecies Telepathic Communication*.[4] It is the clearest and simplest of the communication methods I've seen, and is based on two abilities well known to Goddess spirituality and New Age women—meditation and visualization. If you need help in learning these skills, see Diane Stein, *the Women's Book of Healing*.

Animal Communication
The dog's major facial expressions

Calm

Worried — ears back

Suspicious — wrinkled brow, lowered ears

Defensive — threat stare, lips pulled back

Ready to Bite — fangs exposed

Remorseful

adapted from Jean Craighead George, *How to Talk to Your Dog* (New York, Warner Books, 1985), p.68.

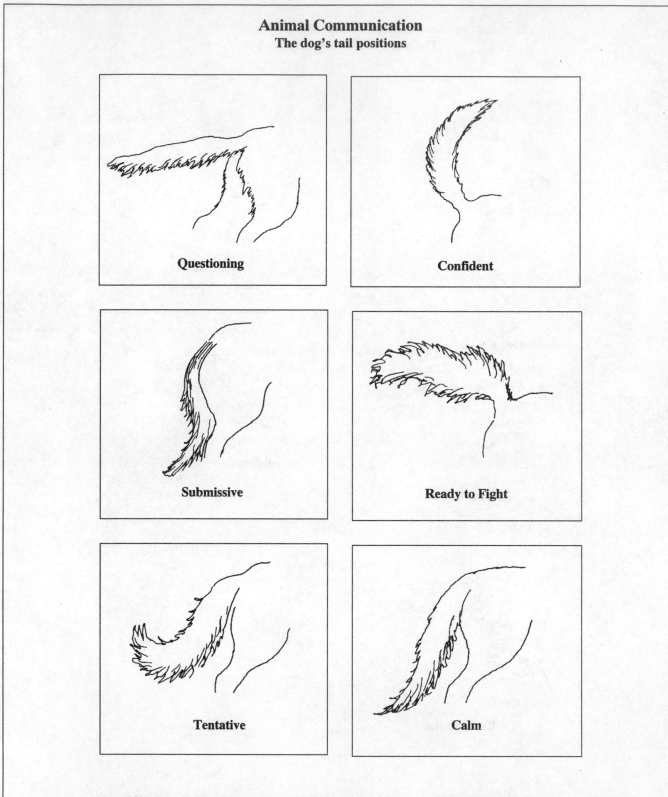

Animal Communication
The dog's tail positions

Questioning

Confident

Submissive

Ready to Fight

Tentative

Calm

adapted from Jean Craighead George, *How to Talk to Your Dog* (New York, Warner Books, 1985), p. 81.

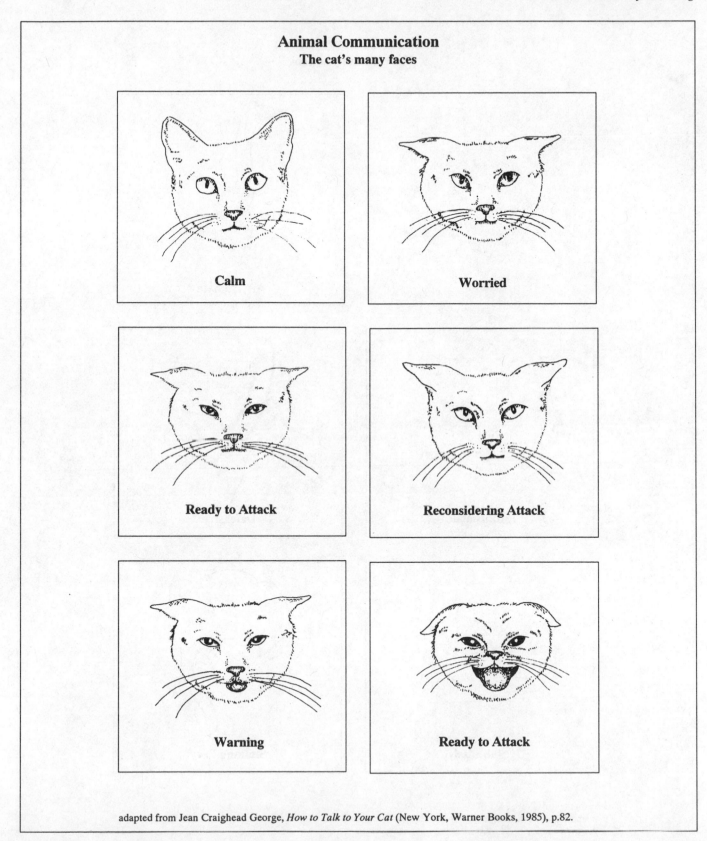

Animal Communication
The cat's many faces

Calm

Worried

Ready to Attack

Reconsidering Attack

Warning

Ready to Attack

adapted from Jean Craighead George, *How to Talk to Your Cat* (New York, Warner Books, 1985), p.82.

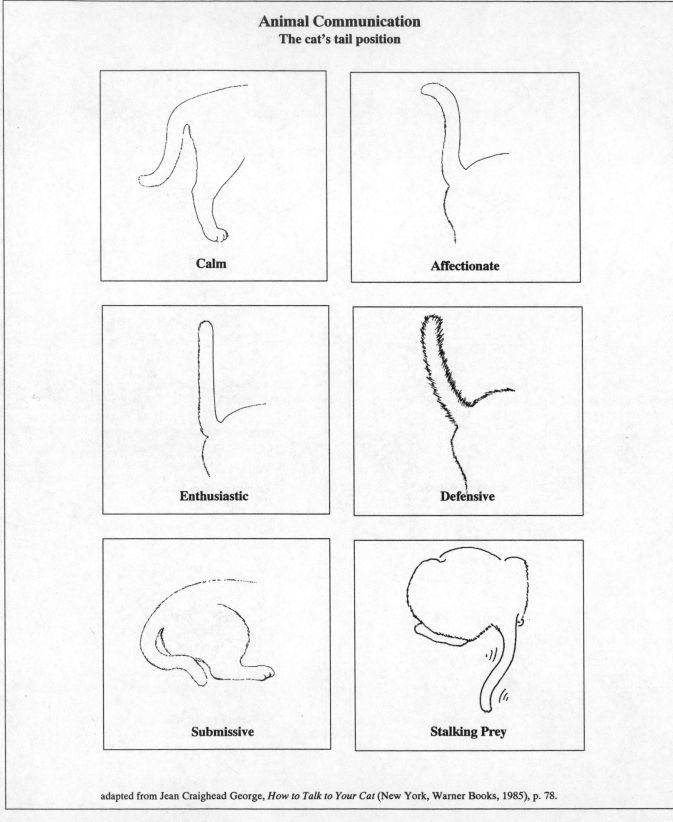

Animal Communication
The cat's tail position

Calm

Affectionate

Enthusiastic

Defensive

Submissive

Stalking Prey

adapted from Jean Craighead George, *How to Talk to Your Cat* (New York, Warner Books, 1985), p. 78.

Begin by observing your pet quietly—in the meditative state. Sit with her in a room at a distance comfortable to you both, without trying to get the animal's attention. Be open to whatever comes. Look at your pet, focus gently upon her, and let other distractions slip away. Increased awareness and clearer perceptions begin with this. The skill may not come immediately if you are not experienced at meditating. Try working with it for fifteen or twenty minutes each night before bed. This is the first basic step in animal communication, setting up a safe space in which both you and your pet can be receptive.

Try the next step, getting your animal's attention. Do this in the meditative state above, by softly speaking the resting dog or cat's name, or touching, rubbing or patting her gently. Do not expect the pet to look directly at you while you speak to her, but if the animal is distracted or doing something else, she will not be paying attention to you or hearing you. Speak to your pet aloud or in your mind (telepathically), and with your words use pictures that illustrate what you mean. Use a soft tone. Most animals respond more clearly to pictures than to words, and the combination of both makes for clearer communication. Keep it simple, with the words and pictures (visualizations) sending the same message. Gentle touching while you talk adds to the sensitivity of both of you. First, say "hello."

Once you are comfortable with sending messages, practice receiving them. In the quiet meditative state, observe your animal calmly and simply listen. Keep other thoughts and distractions out of your mind and be open to "hearing" and receiving. The animal's words and pictures appear in your mind, just as yours were spoken in your mind when you sent them to her. Do not anticipate what your pet might say; it's never what you expect. Let her make her own words. When you first say "hello," imagine her "hello" coming back to you. Then get your pet's attention and ask a question, "How are you doing?" or "What's happening?" and wait for the response. Listen without tensing up, and accept what you hear without adding your own thoughts. Acknowledge what comes through.

Says Penelope Smith:

People are better at picking up thoughts of animals and people they are close to than they give themselves credit for. A major barrier to receiving communication is invalidating what you perceive or doubting your own ability to do it. Take my word for it. You have the ability. Practice, and build your own confidence.[5]

Pets are usually eager to communicate but may not believe it at first, feeling you have not wanted to hear them before. They may ask you if you really want to know, or tell you, as a horse that a friend worked with said, "You aren't ready to know." Most of my own animals have simply joined in the game, as if we had always done it that way. Dusty's response was, "I hear you but I'm not talking: you're my mom." My first contact with Kali, a young puppy, was all giggles. Copper wanted to know what I was so excited about. Emerson, a friend's cat, felt I was "not to be trusted since I smelled of dogs." Keep trying, though you may have to prove your sincerity and intent. It's worth the effort.

Tanith has lived with Onyx, a large black Newfoundland dog for fourteen years. I asked about how they communicate:

It is hard to really write anything on how we communicate, we just do. We both seem to just know. She has a rather large vocabulary and listens to me talk, but the real communication is non-verbal. We work together in counseling sometimes. I have been taking her to the office on occasion, especially when I have a client in crisis coming in. Clients always seem to end up on the floor petting Onyx and finally able to voice their issues and fears. She comforts people and gives them a sense of peace and safety. I have had many people tell me that they can see her aura, which is a deep clear blue. In fact when teaching people to read auras I often have them start with Onyx, as hers is so easy to see.[6]

Marion Webb-Former writes about the beginning of her fifteen years with Earl, a German Shepherd:

I first saw Earl when he was four days old. I picked him out immediately, he was one of eight puppies. For a few moments I held him in my hands, he was then so tiny, and during that time I had my first realization that what I had always considered to be my thoughts about an animal was actually it communicating with me. I experienced his total sense of fear at not only being held by me, but more importantly being separated from MOTHER. I am writing that word in capitals to try to convey how intensely he communicated to me his feelings at that early stage of his life of what she meant to him. She was everything, she was existence. I wanted to hold onto him because he was so tiny and so adorable, but I quickly put him back with his mother. I believe at that moment we bonded forever because he knew I had understood him and respected his overwhelming need for maternal warmth, comfort and love.

Techniques for Sharing Awareness with Other Animals

The following O.F.F.E.R. (Open-Friendly-Focused-Empathetic-Respectful) techniques are presented to assist people in sharing awareness with other animals. These techniques are based on the author's experience of over 20 years of observing and recording data relating to animal-animal and animal-human interactions, as well as interviews with other wildlife biologists and behaviorists. Since every animal being is as unique as every person, these techniques work best with animals and people that are open and aware.

1. *Be Open*—Often our belief systems, attitudes and judgements prevent us from being open and learning new knowledge. Paying attention as an observor to your thoughts and where they come from, will help your mind to be open.

2. *Be Friendly*—Maintain a joyous and friendly attitude with the animal.

3. *Be Focused*—The average person can only focus on one subject for approximately 4 seconds. (People that meditate can hold much longer.) Practice holding your attention on a leaf, or a blade of grass examining every little detail. Don't be upset if other thoughts creep into your mind, just allow them to go through. Watch them like clouds passing by. Focus your attention.

4. *Be Empathetic*—Empathy implies compassionate feeling "with," not "at," another animal. The more you can project your own consciousness into the animal's, the more understanding of the animal you will gain. Having a good understanding of the animal's behavior, ecology, physiology, perception, and needs in life is helpful, but not necessary.

5. *Be Respectful*—This is something that is difficult even for many animal lovers. We have been programmed from childhood to believe in the paradigm that we are responsible for caring for animals and, thus, although we may feel very close to them, they are "below" humans intellectually. Respect implies absolute honest feelings of dignity, worth, and esteem for another. When a person understands the value of the presence of another "being," whether for beauty or for the function that it performs, it becomes easier to truly respect another animal.

"There must be the . . . generating force of love behind every effort destined to be successful."

Mary Ann C. Simonds, *Techniques for Sharing Awareness with Other Animals* (handout).

Throughout the fifteen years we were together he always communicated his needs to me…At times, he would look at me and his "words" would be crystal clear in my head.

Penelope Smith felt she could not ask Peaches, her cat, to stop hunting birds, it was her nature, but that she could ask her to keep her prey outside:

When my cat, Peaches, and I first moved to the country, she used to present mice or birds at the foot of my bed in the morning. I did not scream and go "yuck," although this was a shock to my bare feet. I thanked her wholeheartedly for the gift, really validating her ability as a huntress. When I was sure she really felt acknowledged, I asked her to take the body out of the house, or I'd take it out, explaining that I'd prefer if she kept her prey outside. She understood, and after a few times ceased to bring back dead or half-dead animals.[7]

For a period of eleven years I talked constantly with my black and white Siberian Husky, Tiger. She had an opinion on everything and made sure I heard it. I could call her telepathically from anywhere in my apartment or house, and she always wanted to know what I wanted before she would come. (She always came if I told her it was chocolate ice cream or that I wanted to rub her ears.) Her daughter Dusky would talk to anyone else who tried but refused to speak to me except on special occasions. She told others to tell me that she loved me. Once before a snowstorm I told her we were going to be snowed in. Her infrequent response came loud and clear—"Do we have pizza and puppy food? Then I guess it's okay." When she had lung cancer and was dying at thirteen years old, she asked me to put her to death.

My newest Siberian Husky is Kali, a red and white nine-month-old puppy who was a pound rescue. She came to me limping and would bite when I touched her back or hind legs, and finally she told me her story. She had fallen out of a moving car and been injured and bruised, though nothing was broken. She was furious her people hadn't come back for her (they apparently couldn't find her). She followed someone else's dog home and was taken to the shelter where a man abused her. She also told me she had been Dusty in her last life (Dusty had died two years before and this puppy has an uncanny resemblance to her.) She knew she was supposed to be with me and promises to talk to me this time around.

Copper also came from a shelter, and came to me with parvovirus. It's a dis-ease that many well cared for dogs do not survive, and Copper had not been well cared for. I asked him if he would live and come home with me, and it took some convincing, as he'd been both neglected and abused. He lived and is happy and healthy today, and he named himself. Copper only talks when he really wants something. When I ask him to do (or not do) something, he usually says, "Fat chance!"

When you hear your pet's response, even if you think you imagined it, acknowledge it. If you didn't understand, ask her to clarify or to tell you again. If your pet wants something done or something changed, do so. Listen to and acknowledge whatever your dog or cat wants to tell you, even if it is off the subject. Ask, "Is there anything you want to tell me?" Acknowledge the answers, and if the pet refuses a particular question, don't push it, at least not at first, but ask again at another time.

Practice this with other animals, not only your own, and not only with pets. Wild animals will talk to you also. Once you have opened the communication channels with your dog or cat, make it an everyday part of life. Remember to send love, appreciation, caring and respect to your pets and to other animals you make contact with. Though telepathic communication feels strange at first, especially if it's new to you, time and experience prove how real it is. Using it adds a whole new perspective and dimension to your life and to your cat's or dog's, and is a first step in making a co-creative partnership with your animal.

Anitra Frazier uses telepathy and visualization with her cats:

Communicating clearly with your cats is mostly a matter of simplifying your own thinking and looking at the situation from the cat's point of view....Cats perceive our thoughts in terms of mental pictures, sense memories (see, hear, taste, feel, and smell) and accompanying emotions. This last is the most important. Cats are very emotionally oriented.

My simple "Goodbye, I'll be back tonight" communication is transmitted with accompanying thoughts that go something like this: "We'll see-touch each other with gladness when it's black dark night outside the window." I picture and feel myself seeing and touching Purr. Then I add the emotion of gladness and picture the dark window in the background to give a time reference.[8]

When she needs to leave her cats for a period of time with a house sitter, she uses the same procedure but sends the visualization of night/day/night/day for the number of days until she returns, and then picture of the sitter coming to take care of them. Her animals know when to expect her home, and that she will definitely be back.

Machaelle Small Wright, in *Behaving as if the God in All Things Mattered*, also comments on emotion as part of dogs' and cats' role:

The animal kingdom functions as a full partner within nature by serving both the planet and mankind as one of the buffers....
Animals absorb, and to a limiting degree transmute, human projections and imbalances on an emotional level. Our lives would be much harsher, more difficult physically, were it not for the animal kingdom functioning as a sheath around us and working with us on unconscious levels. The wild animals take in the imbalanced energy of massive group actions such as war, famine, poverty and mass death. The animals who are more in touch with individual humans take care of the emotionally imbalanced environment around that human.[9]

With emotions so intrinsic between animals and their people, it is important to make the visualized emotions positive, as well as to protect pets from people's emotional traumas.

This is both a visualizing and a healing issue, as Dr. Gloria Dodd observes (personal communication):

We must protect the animals from the trauma of people's negative emotions. I saw an awful lot of physically ill pets with emotionally disturbed owners. Depression in pet owners produces depression in the pets—if it is strong enough and long enough it breaks down the immune system (remember the Chinese acupuncture flow relationships of negative emotions— liver— immune system). This impaired immune system affects every organ in the body. It in time will manifest in many pathologies: skin diseases, digestion problems, deficiencies in the body's endocrine system (hypothyroidism, adrenal exhaustion due to prolonged stress), heart, liver and kidney dysfunctions. The emotions of anger and resentment are the most destructive.

Anitra Frazier's technique of aura stroking her cats is both a method of communication and a beginning of psychic healing. She calls it the "almost" touch, stroking just above the cat's physical body: "Just pet the aura and you may be very surprised at the response."[10] By stroking the aura nonphysically in this way, the change in energy sensations over the animal's body tells you where there is a "stuck" or "ruffled" spot in the cat's or dog's auric field. Where there is, the area feels different than the energy over the rest of the pet's body. Such spots need to be "unstuck" or "unruffled" by the following technique. Hold both hands palms down over the area, not touching the animal's body. The sensations in your palms increase and may feel hot, cold, vibrating, an electrical feeling, or other sensations. Hold your hands still or "comb" them through the aura and, when the sensations smooth out lift your hands. You may want to shake the energy off them. Check the aura energy flow again by stroking above the animal's body—the "stuck" places are usually gone. If the area is a pain spot, the pain is lessened or gone, also by this technique.

Both dogs and cats are highly receptive to energy work and aura healing. Any form of psychic healing, laying on of hands, Reiki, distance healing, crystals and gemstones, energy balancing or color work that is positive for people is also positive for pets. The rapport and communication between human and animal is enhanced by doing this work, and energy work is highly useful along with other forms of healing (medical/veterinary, herbs, homeopathy, flower essences, etc.) It does not interfere with the effects of other healing or therapeutic methods and, in fact, enhances them. It offers love and well-being on a level pets fully understand.

All animals are sensitive to energy. In doing Reiki or laying on of hands healing with pets, the session takes a fraction of the time that it does on a person. Place your two palms flat and resting gently (touching) over a pain area or anywhere on the animal's physical body. Hold them there for several minutes—you will know when to stop—sending healing and love through your hands. When the energy is not needed, cats may resent it (they invented this energy, after all, and aren't sure they want to share it), and dogs get silly about it ("I love you,

Mommy," as they bounce away). When they are hurting, however, they accept the healing. Pets take this energy from your hands usually for a very short time, then indicate they've had enough. They often return for it repeatedly when they need it and accept it when you offer it later. This is a form of laying on of hands healing that can never do harm and often does great good. It is highly soothing for an animal upset or in pain. The difference here from aura stroking is that this method uses gentle physical touch.

Laurel Steinhice suggests a simple way of doing aura/chakra healing on dogs and cats. Place your right (sending) hand on the spine at the back of the animal's head, and your left hand on the spine at the base or tip of the tail. If you are Reiki trained so that both hands send energy equally, either hand can be in either position. You will feel the energy running along the spine between your palms, sending spent or negative energy (pain) out of the pet's body through the tail tip and less so out through the paws. Some of the releasing energy may collect in the healer's left hand; shake it off, rinse your hands after finishing, or otherwise disperse it. A small crystal taped to your own left wrist can help.[11]

Another suggestion is to cup your palms on each side of the dog or cat's face and, with or without physically touching, look the animal in the eye. "Let the love-energy flow from your eyes and the Breath-of-Life energy flow from your breath, as you give Light through your hands."[12] Speak lovingly while doing this and listen for your pet's response. Follow up by giving energy to the spine, using the back of head and base of tail positions above.

While doing this healing, or other forms of psychic energy work, Laurel suggests focusing on the *value* of your pet as an individual and on the *value* of all pets of her species. Focus on what these species mean to humanity and the Earth, and extend the love and healing to all cats and dogs. This strengthens the bond immensely between the individual pet and person.[13]

Marion Webb-Former suggests a similar method of healing, which also enhances human-animal communication and rapport:

During this form of healing, the projective hand should be placed over the head chakra and the receptive hand over the belly chakra. Visualizations and projections of love, peace, harmony and the oneness of all things should fill the healer's mind and heart and be given to the animal. Depending on the severity of the soul sickness of the dog or cat, several sessions may be required....Either the animal or the healer will initiate an end to each session.

She suggests that the person to do this healing be someone who has a deep rapport with the cat or dog, as the pet may react unpredictably to it with someone she does not know well. Hands placed on these chakra positions will also initiate or deepen telepathic communication between human and animal. When using these methods, it becomes clear that love, communication and understanding do more to prolong animal lives than all the medical care in the world.

Whatever type of healing method, always make sure that the animal really wants it. Use the communication techniques of this chapter to tell the pet what you want to do, and ask permission. This is as important when working with animals as it is with people. The dog or cat may not want help, and the healer is honor-bound to respect this. Both Dusty and Tiger in their final days refused all help, until it was time to die and they each in turn asked to be released. Touch healing will not hold back an animal that is passing over; it aids and comforts her, but if she refuses healing the healer must respect her wishes. Also remember to ask the pet what she needs; it may be something you haven't thought of. If an area of the animal's body is injured and touch would cause more pain, do the healing by holding your hands just above the body and stroking the aura over the injury.

Reiki is a method of laying on of hands that I recommend to any woman interested in human or animal healing. The system uses a series of positions over the chakras to balance energy all through the body, clear the energy centers, repair tissues, calm and ease pain. The method is positive for use on animals (and plants, people, babies, elders, even cars). Without the special attunements that boost and tune the healer's energy, use the Reiki positions as therapeutic touch or laying on of hands.

The standard Reiki positions used on people are less feasible for use on animals, though the chakra maps of the last chapter also map the hand placements. Most animals do not have the patience to sit or lie still through a number of placements, especially considering that it takes about five minutes for the energy to rise and fall to complete the position. Place your hands instead on a major chakra (crown/brow, solar plexus or belly), resting them gently. You can also place your hands anywhere else on the animal's body, over an energy center or not. Hold your hands in place and notice the sensations that develop in them—this energy rise and fall varies in sensation. Your hands may vibrate or even feel some temporary pain. When the sensations reduce to body warmth again, move to another chakra or position—unless the animal has indicated enough. This method is a combination of the aura stroking and touch healing described above. The Reiki practitioner has received energy attunements that bring the healing energy into and through her hands.

Do energy healing as soon after injury as possible, and as often as it is accepted during injury or illness. Use Reiki/laying on of hands in conjunction with other methods—first aid, homeopathy, herbs, veterinary care. The more serious the dis-ease the more frequent the healing sessions. Let the animal tell you what she needs.[15] Start at a position closest to or on the head and move downward on the body, in the head to tail direction.

I have used these healing methods on all of my dogs, and on a lot of other people's dogs and cats, and recommend them highly. It calms an excited or frightened animal, relieves pain, and I have seen some miraculous cures with it in pets and people alike. The meditative state it initiates in the healer helps with animal communication, as well. It is excellent for revitalizing an animal that is exhausted or ill, and wonderful for reassuring one that has been abused in the past and is afraid to trust people when hurting.

Another method to use along with laying on of hands or aura work is color. This is another visualization: the healer chooses the color she feels best for the situation and "imagines" it flowing through her healing hands into the dog or cat's body. An animal that is in pain is soothed by blue or green, the universal healing colors. A depleted animal welcomes life-force red to warm and vitalize. An animal in need of love and calming trust responds to pink, rose, red-violet or violet. Metallic gold is good for infectious dis-eases and intensive healing, and metallic silver for healing broken or injured bones. A good rule in using color is to visualize and send it only as "light," allowing it to become whatever color is best for the pet's needs. Send the energy out, in meditation for a distance healing, or through your hands in a direct one, and let the Goddess/Earth and the animal choose how to use it and what color to use it as. Gemstones in the pet's chosen color are also helpful in direct healing; place the stones around the cat or dog while doing Reiki, laying on of hands, aura stroking or chakra balancing.

If your pet refuses to be touched, is unable to be touched, or is somewhere other than physically with you, try the full healing from a distance. This again depends on the meditative state and visualization, and the full healing can be completed in moments by doing it this way. I used it with Copper when I first brought him from the animal shelter—he spent five days on IV's at my veterinarian's. I was able to make clear contact with him there from my bedroom, to talk telepathically with him, do numerous healing sessions, and watch him respond to the energy.

To do distance healing, first get into the meditative state, probably a little deeper into meditation than direct healing work requires. In that state, imagine/visualize the dog or cat standing in front of you; it will not be a photographic image, but either a silhouette or a fuzzy representation. When you have the image, ask in your mind (telepathically) what the pet needs, even if you already know. Then ask for permission to do healing to help her. If she agrees to accept energy from you, there are a few ways to do it. One is to send light and color as described above, letting the pet's higher self choose what color the light turns into. Another way is to imagine that you are physically there with your animal, doing the healing with your hands. You can vary this by growing extra pairs of arms to heal in several areas at once. You can imagine/visualize that the dog or cat is resting on your lap, and use your seated knee and leg to represent the animal's body. The cat or dog's "head" is your knee. Then do laying on of hands healing on your knee, focusing the energy to reach your pet. Another method is to imagine your pet shrunk small enough to hold between your hands, and send love and healing through your hands to the animal's whole body.

A further method of distance healing, which I call Tinker Woman healing, is to telepathically "fix" what needs fixing. If the cat has a broken leg, repair it in the distance healing meditation with Goddess Tape. If the dog has a cut or injury, sew it up with a Goddess needle and thread. If there is a fever, visualize a thermometer with the high reading, pile imaginary ice around the thermometer and the pet, and watch the reading drop to normal. To make sure there are no errors in this method, before leaving the meditation visualize the cat or dog as completely well and healed.

A distance healing meditation of this nature takes a matter of seconds to do, less time than it takes to read the description of it. Like any healing skill, the more practice you do, the more proficient you become. A distance healing can be done as often as needed until the pet no longer needs the energy. It can take only once for a minor problem, or require several healings a day for some time in a major dis-ease. The dog or cat will tell you when the healing is completed. Using distance healing becomes a very individualized thing, and no two experienced healers will work at it in exactly the same way. At first, doing it feels contrived or made up, but like communication with your pet, it's very real. It is a good idea to visualize the animal totally healed at the end of each distance healing session. Once you have left the meditation and returned to daily life, let the energy go—do not dwell on the healing or the pet's dis-ease. Such holding on prevents the healing from happening.

One further healing method for cats, dogs and other animals is guided healing. Many women at this time are working with spirit guides and helpers, and "the other side" is eager to participate in any healing activity for people, pets or the Earth. If you are currently in contact with such guidance, simply invite their presence whenever you do healing with your pet, whether the healing is distance or hands-on direct. If you have not made contact with your guides—everyone has them—and wish to, read Laeh Maggie Garfield's *Companions in Spirit*, (Celestial Arts Press, 1984) or the Meeting Spirit Guides ritual in *Casting the Circle*, under Other Rituals (Diane Stein, The Crossing Press, 1990). If you have not worked with spirit guides until now, I highly recommend it. Doing so is a great joy and brings wonderful results in healing work.

Machaelle Small Wright has developed a guided healing system that invokes the help of nature and is very profound and powerful.

To use this healing system, you will need an hour of uninterrupted time in a quiet room alone with your cat or dog. Quiet yourself and allow your pet to get quiet, and enter the meditative state. The following charts are from Machaelle Small Wright, *Nature Healing Conings for Animals*.

This all sounds too simple to be real, but I can assure you it is profound, awesome and *very* real. From the first coning session, the healer clearly feels the other presences, and the most skittish of animals cooperates and

Nature Healing Conings for Animals
For companion animals or pets

Use this nature healing coning when you know the animal and choose to participate in the healing process. This can involve taking the animal to the vet, if necessary, giving medicine or special food and opening additional nature healing conings, if needed.

1. Open a nature healing coning. Do this by asking to be connected to:

   a) the Deva of Animal Healing
   b) Pan and/or the nature spirits working with this animal
   c) the higher self of the animal
   d) your higher self

Allow about 15 seconds for the coning to fully activate and settle in.

2. Explain what you observe and know about the animal's condition. Do this as fully as you can. Then let the coning work with the animal for 30 minutes. (Your explanation lets those in the coning know what you understand about the animal's condition. This is important since you will be participating in the animal's healing process.

During this time, you may feel/sense/hear you are to test the animal for flower essences. Ask the coning if your intuition is correct. (Test using kinesiology. See *Flower Essences*) If so, then give the animal a flower essences basic test and administer the essences that are needed. (Don't do a dosage test here.)

3. At the end of the 30 minutes, ask the coning any questions that come to mind having to do with what the animal needs and how you may assist. Should the animal go to the vet? If so, should another nature healing session be held after the vet's visit? Should the animal's diet be changed, and how? Is this change temporary? If so, how long should it go on? Should there be additional healing sessions even if the animal doesn't go to the vet? If so, how many and when? Continue asking any questions like this until you feel you have all the information you need. (You can receive your information by formatting every question in the simple yes/no format and testing using kinesiology.)

4. Test the animal for flower essences once more. Include a dosage test. (In the next nature healing session, when you get to this step, do a new flower essence and dosage test. Then, if you are still giving the previous essences ask if that solution is to be continued for the remaining days of its dosage along with this new solution. For a few days, you may be giving the animal two different solutions.)

5. The session is now finished. It is important to disconnect or dismantle the nature healing coning. Do this by asking each participant to disconnect, one by one (the Deva of Animal Healing, Pan and/or the nature spirits working with this animal, the animals higher self and your higher self), from the coning. Allow about 5 seconds for each disconnection to occur. The session is over. Test yourself for flower essences to make sure you're clear.

Machaelle Small Wright, *Nature Healing Conings for Animals: Perelandra Papers #8* (Jeffersonton, VA, Perelandra Ltd., 1993), pp. 2-4.

Nature Healing Conings for Animals
For wild animals

This coning is for those who wish to assist injured or sick wild animals or other animals in need to whom you are a stranger. In both cases, the only thing you have to offer is a healing coning. In most cases, it is not appropriate to follow up with any assistance on your part—such as giving medicine or taking the animal to the vet. Consequently, you (your higher self) do not have to be part of the coning. (If you are going to assist a wild animal through a healing process, use the nature healing coning as set up for pets/companion animals.) For wild animals, you just set up the coning. Here's what you do:

1. Connect with the animal's higher self. (Do this exactly as you would when connecting to your own higher self—ask to be connected. Verify the connection using kinesiology, if you know how to test.)

2. Ask if it is appropriate to assist this animal by opening a nature healing coning.

If you get "no," go no further. The animal doesn't wish to be disturbed, doesn't want your assistance, and for you to do so anyway would be an interference.

If you get "yes," go on to step 3.

3. Ask to open a nature healing coning. Then ask the following participants to activate in the coning:

> a) Deva of Animal Healing
> b) Pan and/or the nature spirits working with this animal
> c) Animal's higher self

Allow about 15 seconds for the coning to fully activate and settle in.

4. The healing coning will know what to do for this animal. All you have to do is sit quietly for 30 minutes.

5. At the end of the 30 minutes, you may test the animal for needed flower essences, if you wish. For these animals, do not try to administer the essences in the mouth. Simply put the drops anywhere on the body. With some wild animals it may be foolhardy or impossible to test and administer flower essences. If this is the case, skip this option.

6. Close the cloning. Do this by asking that each participant, one by one (the Deva of Animal Healing, Pan and/or the nature spirits working with this animal, and the animals higher self), disconnect from the coning. Allow about 5 seconds for each disconnection to occur. The session is over and you can leave.

(7. Option. Check yourself for essences to make sure you are clear.)

Machaelle Small Wright, *Nature Healing Conings for Animals: Perelandra Papers #8* (Jeffersonton, VA, Perelandra Ltd., 1993), pp. 2-4.

relaxes for the healing. The effects of this method are incredible—and I recommend it strongly.

When my Siberian Husky puppy Kali came to me, she was obviously in pain (she bit me when I touched her hindquarters) and showed signs of having been abused (extreme shyness, fear biting, biting when I tried to lead her by a collar or touch her feet). She was unsteady on her hind legs and cried when getting up from a prone position. Within three coning. sessions she was running and playing, no longer swaying on her hind legs, had stopped most of the biting and all of her crying out in pain. She lost a major portion of her shyness and started coming to me with wet puppy kisses. For a few days, she released a lot of anger; her first family hadn't come to take her home. Kali turned from a sad abused creature to a normal puppy getting stronger every day, all in just a few weeks time. I've asked the Team now for help with house training! Machaelle Wright's coning system is impressive, to say the least.

The nature healing coning system is used in conjunction with the Perelandra Flower Essences, discussed later in this book, but can be used without them. I recommend Machaelle's books and essences highly and thank her for the major breakthroughs in human and animal healing that her work has brought. For more information, write for the Perelandra catalog at POB 3603, Warrenton, VA 22186 or call (703) 937-2153. Her work is useful for the beginning and advanced healer alike.

One last note on the subject of psychic healing and animals: On some occasions, a pet may be subject to a spirit attachment, an animal spirit that has died but not found its way to the spirit world. These, as in humans, are usually lost entities rather than negative ones, but they may cause inexplicable illnesses and behavioral changes in domestic dogs and cats (wild animals are seldom affected by them). This is not something to be frightened of, only be aware this exists.

Says Laurel Steinhice, whose expertise is in working with such attachments:

Most animal spirit attachments are to other animals, and are casual and opportunistic rather than directed and intentional. They can change the animal's personality, however, and should be promptly cleared as soon as they are discovered. Animal spirits also sometimes attach to sympathetic humans.

In rare instances, animals may also suffer from intentional attachment by negative entities or energies of various sorts (whether animal, human, primitive earth-energies, extraterrestrial, etc.). This doesn't happen often. When it does, a ritual blessing of the animal may be helpful. Otherwise, clearing is best achieved through the services of an experienced professional.[16]

When a loving pet suddenly becomes angry and belligerent or exhibits sudden negative habit changes for no apparent reason, look for a spirit attachment. Also suspect it when an animal's aura colors or energy flows change suddenly, and change into unattractive muddy colors (both symptoms can also indicate physical disease). Do a cleansing ritual: smudge the dog or cat with sage smoke (not so close as to choke her), and state clearly and firmly, "Whoever is there that does not belong, now leave." If the entity resists, insist more firmly. "No one will harm you. It is safe to return to the Goddess." Invite your pet's spirit guides in to protect her, and the entity's spirit guides in to take it where it properly needs to go. Be firm but gentle and make sure you have cast a circle of protection around yourself and your pet before beginning. Insist that the entity return to the Goddess for healing. Once that attaching spirit leaves, and you know your pet is cleared of it completely, put protection around her (place her in a bubble of blue light). Be sure that the entity has completely left your house and premises before opening the circle; if it does not leave, insist upon it doing so until it has obeyed. Be in control, and there is nothing to fear in doing this type of healing.

To help animal spirits that have died to pass over completely, Laurel suggests that, particularly when passing dead animals on the road, make a small blessing to assist them on their way. Say something simple like, "Go in peace, little one. Go to the Goddess." This prevents lost animal spirits from following you home by helping them to find where they need to go.

No book on alternative animal healing could ignore the psychic aspects of dealing with animal dis-ease or the ideas of interspecies communication and the oneness of all life. While most of the methods that follow are alternative holistic systems, the information of the past two chapters is vital for any understanding and healing of dogs and cats. The human and animal body consists of much more than can be seen and touched physically, and the lack of healing on the nonphysical levels is the reason why technological medicine is only partly effective. By adding the nonphysical to the physical healing methods, animals (and people) heal more quickly, fully and satisfactorily. The next chapter begins healing from the physical body level, starting with animal nutrition and earthplane pet food politics.

[1]Laurel Steinhice, "Energy Centers (Chakras) in Dogs and Cats," Personal Communication, 1992.

[2]Penelope Smith, *Animal Talk: Interspecies Telepathic Communication* (Point Reyes Station, CA, Pegasus Publications, 1989), p. 11.

[3]Diane Stein, *Casting the Circle: A Women's Book of Ritual* (Freedom, CA, The Crossing Press, 1990), p. 128. The Lammas ritual is a Blessing of the Animals.

[4]Penelope Smith, *Animal Talk*, p. 25–35. This is her method.

[5]*Ibid.*, p. 32.

[6]Tanith and Marion Webb-Former, Personal Communication, 1991.

[7]Penelope Smith, *Animal Talk*, p. 49–50.

[8]Anitra Frazier with Norma Eckroate, *The New Natural Cat: A Complete Guide for Finicky Owners* (New York, Plume Books, 1990), p. 25.

[9]Machaelle Small Wright, *Behaving As If the God in All Life Mattered* (Jeffersonton, VA, Perelandra Ltd., 1987), p. 163–164.

[10] Anitra Frazier, *The New Natural Cat*, p. 8.

[11]Laurel Steinhice, "All Beings Great and Small," Personal Communication, 1992.

[12]*Ibid.*

[13]*Ibid.*

[14]Marion Webb-Former, Personal Communication, April 12, 1992.

[15]Larry Arnold and Sandy Nevius, *The Reiki Handbook* (Harrisburg, PA, PSI Press, 1982), p. 89–97.

[16]Laurel Steinhice, "All Beings Great and Small," Personal Communication, 1992.

Optimal Nutrition

People in America, the richest nation in the world, are suffering from malnutrition, actually starving amid plenty. I am not referring to the many women and children (primarily) able to eat only what food stamps will buy or the many elders and working poor ineligible for food stamps and without enough to eat. I am referring to the "Typical American Diet" sold to us by the food industry, television, and the FDA (Federal Food and Drug Administration). Americans live on nutritionless white sugar (average consumption over three pounds per week per person), white flour (starch, empty of food value), red meat (fed heavily on antibiotics and hormones), and preservatives, dyes, additives and chemicals (many known to be carcinogens and many more totally untested).

With a rating of only fifteenth in life expectancy among the developed nations, a third of Americans die of heart dis-ease, a third of cancer, and a third of other causes. Ill health in old age and dependence on the medical system are expected. With a polluted environment, eroded and overcropped soil, and massive overuse of chemical fertilizers, pesticides, and growth enhancers, even the supposedly healthy vegetables and fruits are no guarantee of adequate nutrition. The motive of profit-above-all-else and uncontrolled self-interest keeps the government a co-conspirator, and the food industry free to profiteer upon the human population. Then the FDA insists that vitamins and supplements are unnecessary when eating a "balanced diet."

If it's that bad for human food and health—and it is worse—what about pet food? The same poor quality of life and early death is affecting dogs and cats, and the same dis-eases are killing them in increasing numbers. Cancer, heart dis-ease, arthritis and immune deficiency dis-eases are the same top killers of domestic pets as they are of people. Virulent skin dis-eases and allergies are running rampant among dogs and cats, along with liver failure in older pets, chronic kidney dis-ease, epilepsy, lethargy and hyperactivity. Mental and emotional disturbances are frequent today that were unheard of twenty years ago, and none of these dis-eases exist among animals in the wild. Poor animal nutrition, and poor human nutrition, are direct causes of much suffering for people, cats and dogs.

Says Dr. Richard Pitcairn, holistic veterinarian and author of *Dr. Pitcairn's Complete Guide to Natural Health for Dogs and Cats* (Rodale Press, 1982):

Since I graduated from veterinary school in 1965, I've noticed a general deterioration in pet health. I believe that the chemical additives in pet food play a major part in that decline.[1]

Veterinarian Alfred Plechner, researcher into pet allergies and nutrition, reports that "more than thirty percent of the ailments I treat in my practice are directly related to food."[2] And from *Consumers' Digest* as long ago as 1979:

There is mounting evidence that a lifetime of eating commercial pet foods can shorten your pet's life, make him fatter than he (sic) ought to be and contribute to the development of such increasingly common disorders as cystitis and stones (in cats), glaucoma and heart disease (in dogs), diabetes, lead poisoning, rickets and serious vitamin-mineral deficiencies (in both cats and dogs).[3]

How can this be, when every television commercial assures that its product is the best and most tasty, giving pets everything they need for long, healthy lives? But pet food doesn't, just as the "Typical American Diet" doesn't, and the result is the same as it is for humans. People are dying, and pets are dying, in the name of commercial greed. The same patriarchal self-interest and disregard for life that is destroying and using up the Earth is destroying and using up humans' and animals' natural rights to good health.

The pet food industry is mega big business. According to the U.S. Department of Commerce, there were 52.4 million dogs and 54.6 million cats in the United States in 1987 (most recent available figures). This was a decrease in dogs of three million from 1983 (55.6) and an increase in about two and a half million cats from 1983 (52.2). That's a lot of pet food sold, and television expenditure for network advertising of pet products was $134 million dollars in 1989 (latest figure, down from some other recent years).[4] Pet food, with sales amounting to five billion dollars a year, is the most profitable aisle in the supermarket. Americans spend twice as much on pet food as they do on cereal, macaroni and flour products (starch in the "Typical American Diet"), and four times as much on pet food as on baby food.[5]

Dr. Plechner says:

There is one major reason that considerable tonnage of pet food is nutritionally inadequate, and that is competition....On one end of the battle line is price, causing the use of cheap ingredients, and on the other is the quest to enhance appeal through the use of chemicals.

Feeding cheaply can cost more in the long run—in veterinary bills.[6]

The cheap grade generic pet foods are highly suspect but are not the only offenders. Even the high quality veterinary line foods can be responsible for the ill health and deaths of pets, and there have been recalls of some of these in the last few years, as well. There is no requirement of government or FDA inspection for dog or cat foods and no supervised quality control. Most of the ad information is designed to sell products, is not nutritionally sound, and advertising claims are misleading at best. There is no way to know if a bag or can contains the dietary or vitamin and mineral content claimed, how much of the nutrient content is biologically available (usable to the animal), or how much has been lost to processing and shelf deterioration.

A food that claims to be a "complete and balanced diet" may not be so for every cat or dog. There are individual needs, as well as different requirements at different life stages and different states of health. The actual nutritional needs of pets, particularly of cats, has never been scientifically determined. (The information on human nutritional needs is far from adequate, also.) Nutrition is the stepchild of the American food and medical industries. Little or no research is funded, and any attempt to upgrade official government standards is met with fierce opposition from the industries involved.

What is contained in dog and cat food, labeled a "complete and balanced diet," can make you sick just to know the ingredients, or the between-the-lines truth. That our animals have to live on this stuff, usually everyday for as long as they live, is appalling.

To begin with, let us look at what commercial pet foods are composed of in general. The Pet Food Institute says: "Forty percent of all pet food is meat by-products and offal (wastes)." One would think that the other sixty percent would have to be better than that, but the Pet Food Institute goes on to say that the other sixty percent is grain and soy meal not used for human consumption because of foreign odors, debris, germs, etc.[7]

The term "meat by-products" sounds good, but what does it really consist of? Beef by-products are made of cow hooves, horns, bones, skin and hair, esophagus, leftover organs, and glands. Chicken by-products include feathers, beaks, feet, claws, waste material, and leftover parts after processing. More by-products include: gristle, lungs, pig feet, pig snouts, tails, cheeks, udders, and condemned hog livers. Slaughterhouse wastes and organs condemned for human use go into dog and cat food: disease-ridden or dying animals and animal parts, pus, tumors, and animals found dead on the feed lots. These by-products can also include: moldy, rancid or spoiled processed meats, as well as tissues too severely riddled with cancer to be eaten by people. Much of what is not directly harmful is indigestible. "Vegetable fiber" is the term used for ground up corn husks and peanut shells.[8]

Then there are the additives and chemical contaminants. First of all, meat and poultry animals are fed an unsavory stew of pesticide laden fodder, antibiotics and hormones, and this is an issue for people who eat meat as well as for pets. What an animal or human eats of these chemicals becomes part of its tissues. Many of these toxins are not eliminated from the cow or chicken's body by the time of slaughter. The animals that die of agricultural chemicals—and there are many of them—go into pet food, as well. These hormones and drugs have been implicated in the high cancer rates of this country in women.

The U.S. Government's General Accounting Office issued a report in 1979 indicating that all commercially sold meat is contaminated to some degree with chemicals. Something like "fourteen percent of the dressed raw meat and poultry sold in supermarkets might contain illegal residues of chemicals suspected of causing cancer, birth defects or other toxic effects..."[9]

If this is the case in human foods (another agricultural chemical seems to make the news almost daily), how much more is it the case in pet foods that are not inspected and that legally contain the lists of horrors given above. No one knows how much of these chemical residues survive the processing; pet food meat and poultry are steamed to kill bacteria, but most of these chemicals are not destroyed by heat. That pet foods use internal organs and tissues primarily is a further concern for these residues, which accumulate in bones, fat and the eliminative organs. Cancer in women is directly related to the hormone levels stored in meat animal fat; how much of the rising cancer rate in pets is from the same cause? Perhaps a separate issue, many dogs are allergic to beef, as well.

That's the base ingredient, the meat and poultry by-products, and what about the additional additives deliberately put into the finished pet food products? Many of these are known to be toxic, yet are legally included in both human and animal foods. Here are some of the worst offenders, present in virtually every supermarket dog and cat food, and in too many processed foods for people:[10]

Sodium Nitrite and Red Dye No. 40: These are artificial colorings used to give pet foods a fresh meat appearance. They are especially used in canned foods. Both have been linked to cancer, epilepsy and birth defects in laboratory animals. Both are widely used in this country, but have been banned in several European countries. People have died of nitrite poisoning. The FDA listed these as toxic as long ago as 1972, but they are still being used. Another of the many dyes used in pet foods, Blue No. 2, increases dogs' sensitivity to fatal viruses.[11] The nice color is for people-appeal, not for the cats and dogs; it has no nutritional value.

BHA, BHT and MSG: Butylated hydroxysanisole (BHA) and butylated hydroxytoluene (BHT) are used as preservatives to prevent the fat in pet foods from going rancid. They have been implicated in liver and kidney problems, birth defects, slow growth rates, behavior problems, metabolic stress, increased cholesterol levels, allergic reactions, baldness and brain defects in laboratory animals. They may also be carcinogens. These are prevalent in most pet foods, wet or dry. They have been banned in several countries other than the United States. And they are not necessary: vitamins C and E are safe preservatives. Monosodium glutamate (MSG) is also a preservative and flavor enhancer; used in Chinese restaurants, it gives some humans migraines.

Sodium Metabisulfite is another preservative used in pet foods. In humans, this chemical has been known to cause brain damage, difficulty in swallowing, weakness, loss of consciousness, and more.

Lead: This is a serious health hazard for children in particular, along with too many other forms of heavy-metal poisoning from the damaged environment. Lead is in the air in cities, in chemical pesticides used on plants fed to meat animals, and it accumulates in meat animals' bones and organs. From there it is passed on to pets and people.

Many canned pet foods contain so much lead that an animal eating only six ounces a day of these foods might be taking into his body *four times* the level of lead potentially toxic to children.[12]

Lead damages the nervous system, red blood cells, the enzyme and immune systems, and also causes mental impairment, hyperactivity, anemia and cancer. Cat food is the worst offender here, and lead may be a factor in cat's feline leukemia and immune disorders, and epilepsy in dogs.[13]

Artificial Flavorings: These are added to pet foods to tempt hungry animals into eating what they otherwise would never touch and probably would not recognize as food. These are the additives that have been proved to cause hyperactivity and autism in children; in pets they cause nervousness, anxiety, hostility, allergic reactions, and a variety of behavior problems.

Salt: Heart dis-ease and high blood pressure kill a third of the people of this country, and the overuse of salt is a major cause. Salt is used in pet foods as a preservative in amounts as high as a thousand times what would be there naturally. As much as six percent of a pet food can be salt; it can irritate the stomach and intestines causing abnormal thirst and drinking that in turn leads to vomiting. A cycle of this drains the pet's body of minerals and eventually can lead to death. High blood pressure and heart dis-ease were unknown in pets forty years ago, but are all too common now.

Sugar and Propylene Glycol: Semi-moist dog foods are as much as twenty-five percent sugar (sucrose, caramel or corn syrup), again used as a preservative and to keep the foods moist. In cat foods this is replaced by about ten percent propylene glycol, since cats are not as attracted as dogs to sweets. Dogs become addicted to sugar and, since the advent of these foods, are developing diabetes in record numbers. Sugar is also implicated in hypoglycemia, overweight, nervousness, cataracts, tooth decay, arthritis, and allergies, and it drains vitamins and minerals from the body. Propylene glycol causes unexplained "irregularities" in cats' red blood cells; in dogs it causes severe skin problems, hair loss, dull coats, diarrhea, overweight and death. It is a chemical used in antifreeze, oil and waxes. Why must we feed it to our pets?

Cats are fussy eaters known to be addicted to certain foods; pet food companies foster these addictions with chemicals like propylene glycol. Formalin is also used as a preservative in moist foods, a chemical used for embalming. The semi-moist foods are the worst offenders for dangerous chemicals and lack of real nutrition; they should be avoided at all costs. Many pet treats also contain high amounts of sugar.

Ethoxyquin: This is the newest controversial chemical on the pet food market, used as a fat preservative in many or most of the dry foods, including the high quality veterinary lines. The FDA says ethoxyquin is safe and so do a number of the pet food companies that use it—several of them have defensive literature on the subject. Grassroots outcry has said otherwise:

This preservative has been blamed for most of the chronic maladies that have been affecting purebred dogs with increasing frequency.

The nearly tenfold increase in the frequency and recognition of immune-related diseases in companion animals has coincided with the premium brands of pet foods.[14]

Other implications in dogs and cats have been for itchy skin, lethargy, hair loss, thyroid problems, kidney problems, reproductive disorders, birth defects, and cancer. The chemical was developed by Monsanto Corporation as a rubber hardener and all of the research to date has been done only by Monsanto. It has also been used as an herbicide and insecticide (anti-scale agent) for apples and pears. At this time, there is no real evidence that ethoxyquin is safe. It is used in both dog and cat foods with great frequency. See Appendix II for more information.

Fungi, Bacteria and Germs: Canned pet foods are heat sterilized, but up to one percent of dry dog foods (cat foods were not tested) has been shown to carry salmonella bacteria. This contamination can make the animal sick with vomiting and diarrhea within thirty-six hours, the classic symptoms of food poisoning. This and other bacterial infections can be the cause of unexplained sporadic dis-ease in pets and, in some cases, can be transmitted to people in the same household. How widespread this may be is unknown.[15]

The point of all this is not to make you sick, but to impress upon women who live with pets the need for making some real changes. This need has become evident in human food, and pet food is only a carbon copy of the foods humans are expected to eat. Carvel Tiekert, DVM, head of the American Holistic Veterinary Association, lists the choices in pet feeding on a desirability scale of one to ten—ten being the most desirable from the viewpoint of wholesome, clean nutrition for cats and dogs:

1. A home-made diet made incorrectly. This is usually an all meat diet, which…is going to leave the animal deficient, particularly in essential minerals.
2. Soft-moist diets. These diets are extremely high in sugars, chemicals and dyes.
3–4. Generic dry foods. We all know the problems with these.
5. Standard commercial diets.
6–8. "Topshelf" lines—Iams, ANF, Science Diets, etc.
9. Natural Life Pet Foods. No artificial preservatives or chemicals. Preserved with vitamin C and vitamin E.
10. Home-made diets done correctly. A good starting place to work from are the diets in Dr. Pitcairn's book.[16]

There are a number of preservative-free pet food lines now available (Natural Life was the first and is highly respected). These are usually relatively small companies that do little advertising and mostly sell their products through health food stores, veterinarians, and pet and feed stores. They are far less available than the supermarket or veterinary line brands (Iams, Science Diet primarily), but virtually all of the companies will refer you to the closest outlet in your area and/or ship the foods direct to you. Even in Florida I have had no difficulty locating these pet foods. I find them only marginally more expensive than the veterinary lines. With a quality food, the cat or dog gets more nutrition per pound and therefore eats less. She also uses more of what she eats and eliminates less waste. Addresses for several pet food companies are listed in the resource section at the end of this book.

My own experience with dog foods has led me from the generics to the preservative free (with additions). I used a popular and widely advertised dry supermarket brand for many years and then switched to a cheaper feedstore brand during hard times, having no idea there would be a difference. When I switched back to the supermarket brand from the generic, I saw some improvement in my dogs' coats; they seemed to eat less and make less waste, but there was no significant change. When I switched form the popular supermarket brand to a veterinary line dry brand (Iams Eukanuba), I couldn't believe the difference. There was less stools, better coat, less susceptibility to fleas, higher vitality and overall health, and a change for the better in Copper's hyperactivity.

At that point I began supplementing. I started with a Pet Tab multiple vitamin daily and began adding about 1/8 pound of raw meat (usually heart) and some raw veggies to Copper's food. He calmed down even more, his coat became extremely soft and with less overall shedding, and a four-year chronic ear infection disappeared in about three weeks with no medication. (He had been at the vet's for this about three times a year, but it never seemed to go away completely.) When I switched to a preservative free brand (Nature's Recipe), the changes were even more pronounced and people on the street started asking if I show him. At about six years old, he looks and acts like a puppy. The hyperactivity and behavior problems are totally gone. I use raw carrots and asparagus ends for dog biscuits and they are eagerly accepted. I use less than twenty pounds of the dry dog food a month, at $17 a bag, for a sixty-five pound Siberian Husky male. Needless to say, I would not go back to the supermarket brand or generic. Beef heart in the supermarket (less chemical residues than the eliminative organs, the liver or kidneys) costs about a dollar a pound.

If you are now using supermarket brands, semi-moist or generic pet foods, try switching to a preservative free brand. Look for one that uses vitamins C or E for preservatives, and without ethoxyquin or by-products. Your dog or cat may balk at something new—the pet food companies foster food addictions in both cats and dogs—but they will accept it if you mix it with the old food and increase the amount gradually. At the same time begin adding in the extras—small pieces of raw meat, chopped up raw veggies (any whole foods people eat), occasional cottage cheese, slightly cooked eggs, or cooked whole grains. These may be refused at first by some pets; cut them small, mix them in and keep trying. I recommend a pet multiple vitamin and mineral supplement.

After a few days on the new diet, your pet may go through a cleansing reaction as the chemicals and toxins start to leave her body. There may be some diarrhea, lethargy, thirst, frequent urination, even vomiting. This lasts less than a week and is no cause for alarm. In a few weeks, the animal may shed her old coat out of season and do so more thoroughly than usual. The new coat that grows in shows the difference—shinier, fuller, thicker and richer in color—better in every way, with clearer skin to match. She will be healthier and her increase in vitality will surprise you.

Too much raw meat can cause an increase in aggressiveness, so it should not be a large part of the diet. Avoid using pork because it contains the highest amounts of chemical additives and its fat raises pets' cholesterol levels. Avoid tuna for cats and limit the amount of fish in the diet, as cats become "tuna junkies" and refuse to eat anything else. The oil in tuna depletes vitamin E in the body, risking a serious deficiency dis-ease called steatitis.[17] Make sure that the pet food you choose is truly preservative free—not all the health food brands are. Read the labels and watch for the additives noted in this chapter, especially BHA and ethoxyquin. Preservative-free pet foods, dry or canned, are the central factor of your improved diet, unless you choose to cook for your pet. Look for one that does not use by-products.

Cats and dogs are both carnivores, cats more so, but neither can live well on an all-meat diet (or a meatless one). Dogs are not happy or healthy on a meatless diet but can survive if it is well-balanced nutritionally. Cats require the amino acid taurine, found only in animal protein. Without it, they develop enlarged hearts, congestive heart failure and blindness. Dogs require ten essential amino acids, cats eleven, and few plant proteins or protein combinations can provide these. Cats require higher amounts of protein and fats than dogs, about thirty-five percent protein and thirty percent fat. Dogs require about twenty percent protein and twenty percent fat. Protein means meat, poultry, fish, eggs, cheese, and plant protein, while fat is meat or poultry gravies or vegetable oils. Dogs need about sixty percent carbohydrates in their diets, cats thirty-five percent. Carbohydrates are starches from plants, grains, potatoes, corn, rice or cereals.[18] The major components in the pet diet are protein, fats and carbohydrates, as well as vitamins and minerals.

Veterinarian Gloria Dodd disagrees with the above standard analysis, stating that many holistic veterinarians recommend sixty to sixty-three percent protein and fat and about twenty-three percent carbohydrates for both dogs and cats. In her personal communication to me dated August 27, 1992, she states:

We feel a much higher percentage of protein and lower percentage of carbohydrates make an ideal carnivore diet. One way to tell if your dog or cat is getting enough protein is to feel the muscles—is there a firm tone to them or do they feel mushy? Also, shave a small half-inch area on the body and see how long it takes the hair to grow back. You should start to see hair growth within a few days, with one to two weeks full growth in long-haired animals if protein in the diet is sufficient—not months for hair to grow like I've seen on twenty percent protein diets.

Yet, the very high protein in commercial pet foods—poor quality protein and too many chemicals and toxicities—is implicated as a cause of kidney dis-ease in older dogs and cats. A high quality diet will not cause this. My own animals, on a preservative-free dry dog food (Nature's Recipe Puppy and High Performance Formula) with twenty-five percent protein and fifteen percent fat, exhibit the above sufficient protein indicators. The dogs are solidly muscled and grow hair rapidly; they are pictures of vital good health. Raw meat added to the prepared meal also raises the quality protein level of their diets.

The easiest way to provide optimal nutrition for a cat or dog is to use the preservative-free pet food as a base and supplement it (with raw meat, veggies, vitamins). It is not terribly hard to create this high quality diet by cooking at home. The pet food companies discourage supplementing their foods or giving table scraps, but if the supplements and scraps are healthy whole foods (no sugar, white flour, salt or additives), the pet benefits tremendously. (If the supplements and scraps are the "Typical American Diet," forget it.) In buying a pet food, using Pitcairn's standard analysis, look for foods listing for cats an average of forty percent protein, thirty-two percent fat, twenty-two percent carbohydrate, and six percent ash. For dogs, the average is twenty-two percent protein, seventeen percent fat, fifty-three percent carbohydrate, and eight percent ash.[19] Don't make the mistake of assuming that the higher the protein the better the food; too much protein in the diet is a clear cause of kidney failure in animals' old age.

Also be aware, that like people, dogs and cats can be (and too often are) subject to food sensitivities and allergies. These can cause anything from chronic stomach upsets and skin ailments to pancreas, liver and kidney dis-ease, urinary tract infections, weight gain, chronic fatigue and excess mucus. The allergens are usually items from the animal's daily diet. Pet allergy expert Alfred Plechner offers his Allergic Hit List of the most frequent things pets are intolerant to:

Dogs
1. Beef and beef by-products
2. Milk
3. Yeast, yeast-containing foods, brewer's yeast
4. Corn and corn oil
5. Pork
6. Turkey
7. Eggs
8. Fish and fish oils
9. Wheat and wheat by-products (when in combination with 1–8)

Cats
1. Beef and beef by-products
2. Tuna
3. Milk
4. Yeast and yeast products
5. Pork
6. Turkey[20]

A dog or cat with chronic diarrhea and gas or skin problems, or a cat with frequent urinary tract infections, may be suffering from a food allergy. Beef is the worst offender, the most frequent allergen in both cats and dogs; Plechner takes his sick animals off beef first and many recover just by that. Most of the preservative-free pet foods are lamb and rice or chicken-based, rather than the beef so prevalent in supermarket brands. Over eighty percent of cats and dogs cannot tolerate cow's milk—it causes gas, vomiting and diarrhea. Yeast in some pets, despite its benefits as a vitamin supplement, can cause skin allergies in sensitive animals. Wheat and corn allergies induce vomiting and itchy skin.

Tuna has been mentioned previously; it can also cause skin problems in cats, as well as intestinal upsets and pancreas, liver and kidney problems. It contributes to urinary tract infections and urinary blockage (FUS). Pork and turkey may cause diarrhea and vomiting, and ham may cause pancreas damage. Eggs can be allergenic to some pets. For all animals they should be cooked

before feeding, as an enzyme in egg whites robs the body of biotin, an important B-complex vitamin. Cooking deactivates this enzyme. Eggs and chicken parts in Florida recently have been discovered to carry salmonella bacteria (food poisoning)—I learned this only after my own dogs got sick on raw egg yolks, very sick for almost a week. Cooking also kills this bacteria.

Other allergens may include: peas, beans, nuts, shellfish, chocolate, fruit, grapes, pineapple, tomatoes, cabbage, chard, broccoli, cauliflower, mushrooms and spices.[21] This does not mean that all pets are allergic to all of these things, but means that any animal (or human) can be. If your cat or dog suffers from any chronic disease, food allergies are a likely cause, and change of diet to a different brand of food that excludes the likeliest allergens may be all that is needed. Pets should never be fed chocolate or alcohol—they can be fatal. Remember also, that food additives, dyes, preservatives and other chemicals are highly suspect for causing health problems in both dogs and cats. The change from the supermarket brand to a preservative-free one can be the key.

For optimal health, supplement the dog's or the cat's basic diet as described below. Several recipes by several experts are given as choices. These supplements are absolutely essential if you are feeding a supermarket pet food, but can also make a good diet into an optimal one when using the better quality and preservative-free foods. When cooking for your pet, rather than using already prepared pet foods, the following supplements prevent any chance of something being missing from the diet and should be considered essential. The ingredients are easily available from health food stores. It may seem expensive to buy them all at once, but on a week to week basis they are very inexpensive. The mixtures are made up in quantity and used by the teaspoonful each day, added to their daily food. When using vitamin tablets, crush them with a mortar and pestle (or a hammer) and sprinkle them on the meal. Be careful of some health food store bone meal and kelp products that may be high in lead and heavy metals. Dr. Dodd suggests that K.A.L. brand bone meal tests "fairly clean," and kelp harvested in Scotland. American-harvested kelp is too high in toxicities for safe use.

The first and most highly recommended supplement recipes are from Dr. Richard Pitcairn.[22] For cats, feed a teaspoon of the Cat Powder Mix and a teaspoon of the Cat Oil, along with thirty to fifty IU's of vitamin E daily.

Cat Powder Mix
1/2 cup nutritional yeast
1/4 cup bone meal
1/4 cup kelp powder (can use part alfalfa powder)

Cat Oil Mix
3/4 cup vegetable oil
1/4 cup cod liver oil
20–40 IU vitamin E (to prevent spoilage)

Below are the recipes for making Dog Powder Mix and Dog Oil Mix in quantity. Since dogs vary so greatly in size, a chart showing the amounts to feed them is also given.

Dog Powder Mix
2 cups nutritional yeast
1-1/2 cups bone meal
1/2 cup kelp powder (can use part alfalfa powder)

Dog Oil Mix
1-3/4 cups vegetable oil (safflower oil is best)
1/4 cup cod liver oil
50–100 IU vitamin E (to prevent spoilage)

Daily Quantities for Dogs

Weight	Powder	Oil	Vitamin E
5–15 pounds	2 tsp.	1 tsp.	50 IU
15–30	4 tsp.	2 tsp.	100 IU
30–50	2 T.	1 T.	150 IU
50–80	3 T.	1-1/2 T.	200 IU
80–110	1/4 cup	2 T.	300 IU
110+	1/3+ cup	2-1/2 +T.	400 IU

Mix or shake the ingredients together well and store in sealed jars (one for powder, one for oil). The oil is best kept in the refrigerator, the powder on a dark shelf. Brown bottles for storage are preferred, especially for the oil. Do not make large amounts of these mixes in advance. If you are still using supermarket pet foods and wish to add these mixes, reduce the bone meal for large animals and omit it for small ones. Also use a little less of the cod liver oil. These things will already be present in the supermarket brands.[23]

Cat expert Anitra Frazier buys her preservative-free cat foods in cans by the case. She adds the following Vita-Mineral Mix to each cat's meal, one teaspoonful of mix twice (two meals) per day. Again, the recipe makes up a substantial quantity.[24]

Vita-Mineral Mix
1-1/2 cups yeast powder (any food yeast: brewer's, tarula or nutritional)
1/4 cup kelp powder (*or* 1/4 cup mixed trace mineral powder)
1 cup lecithin granules
2 cups wheat bran
2 cups bone meal, calcium lactate or calcium gluconate

In addition, for the oils, she gives each cat once a week:

400 IU vitamin E (alpha-tocopherol, not mixed tocopherols)
10,000 IU vitamin A and 400 IU vitamin D (one capsule)

If the cat will not accept the capsules punctured and squirted onto food, pierce them with a pin and squirt them directly into the cat's cheek pouch or diagonally across the tongue. Be careful not to squirt these liquids (or any liquids) down the cat's throat, as she may choke on them that way. There are health food store oil supplements for pets that contain these vitamins, as well. Anitra Frazier notes the following changes from using the Vita-Mineral Mix and oils, along with a change from supermarket cat foods.

After implementing this regime for one month, approximately 85 percent of my clients noticed the following changes: dandruff gone, oiliness diminishing and disappearing; matting diminishing and disappearing; shine appearing; texture becoming thick, rich and plushy. Of the other 15 percent, most noticed the changes after two, three or six months because the cats were older and had slower metabolisms, or because the owners were slower to make a complete change in diet.[25]

Along with this program, she notes that it is absolutely essential with cats not to leave food available between mealtimes. Feed twice a day, and anything left after half-an-hour must be removed.

Dr. Wendell Belfield, pioneer in the use of vitamins and minerals for pets, begins with a balanced pet multiple vitamin and mineral tablet[26] (a human *low potency* multiple can also be used). Make sure that the minerals are included in the tablet. Also at the health food store, purchase a bottle of vitamin C powder (or tablets to crush), and a bottle of vitamin E capsules (100 IU for small dogs and cats, 200 IU or 400 IU for large dogs).

While Anitra Frazier says that alpha-tocopherol E is the only acceptable form for cats, Belfield says that for dogs the cheaper mixed tocopherols are okay.

Here is Dr. Wendell Belfield's daily protocol for supplementing cats:[27]

1. Weaned and adult cats receive a multivitamin and mineral. Follow the dosage instructions on the label of the product. These cats also receive extra vitamin C (500–750 mg).

2. Pregnant and lactating cats and aged cats receive a multivitamin and mineral plus extra C and E. (Pregnant and lactating cats: 1000 mg vitamin C and 100 IU's vitamin E). Aged cats: 500-750 mg vitamin C and 50 IU's vitamin E.

3. Preweaned kittens receive vitamin C pediatric drops. (1–5 days use 20 mg; 5–10 days, 35 mg; and to weaning 65 mg. For weaned kittens, the vitamin C starts at about 250 mg and increases by six months to 500 mg.)

To administer, most cats will take the multi-tablet from your hand as a treat, or they can be crushed and sprinkled on food. Do not give small kittens whole tablets, crush them. The vitamin C can also be sprinkled on the food or mixed into it, but if refused the C tablets can be dipped in corn oil or butter and cats will usually accept them. For vitamin E, puncture the capsule and squirt it onto food—50 IU is half a capsule, the rest will keep till the next day in the bottle. Avoid trying to force pills down the cat's throat—it's an unpleasant experience for all. To avoid diarrhea with vitamin C, start with a very low amount and increase it gradually, dividing it into two daily doses, with each meal. If the cat develops diarrhea, cut the dose very slightly and stay at the lower level. This is called going to bowel tolerance. A sick animal will take much more vitamin C than a well one.[28]

Below is the daily protocol for dogs. It is somewhat more complicated as dogs vary in size, but the information is basically the same as for cats.[29]

1. Preweaned puppies: Vitamin C pediatric drops (from a pharmacy). Use the following amounts.

Small breeds: 1–5 days old 20 mg; 5–10 days old 35 mg; to weaning 65 mg. *Medium breeds:* 1-5 days old 35 mg; 5-10 days 65 mg; and to weaning 100 mg. *Large or giant breeds:* 1–5 days old 65 mg; 5–10 days old 100 mg; to weaning 135 mg.

2. Weaned puppies: Multiple vitamin and mineral tablet, follow directions on the bottle. Begin vitamin E at six months old. For vitamin C use the following.
First six months: *small breeds* 250 mg; *medium breeds* 500 mg. Six months to a year, gradually increasing to adult levels: *small breeds* 250–500 mg; *medium breeds* 500–1500 mg.

First four months: *larger breeds:* gradually increase from 500 to 1000 mg; *giant breeds:* 750 to 2000 mg.
From four to eighteen months gradually increasing to adult levels: *large breeds* 1000 to 3000 mg; *giant breeds* 2000 to 6000 mg. (1000 mg = 1 gram).

3. Adult dogs: Multiple vitamin and mineral tablet, follow directions on the bottle. Vitamin C and E:

	Small	Medium	Large	Giant
Vitamin C	500–1500 mg	1500–3000	3000–6000	6000–7500
Vitamin E	100 IU	200 IU	200 IU	400 IU

4. Pregnant and lactating dogs and dogs under high stress: Multiple vitamin and mineral supplement, follow directions on the bottle, and vitamin C and E:

	Small	Medium	Large	Giant
Vitamin C	1500 mg	3000	6000	7500 mg
Vitamin E	100 IU	200 IU	400 IU	600 IU

5. Aged dogs: Multiple vitamin and mineral supplement, and vitamins C and E:

	Small	Medium	Large	Giant
Vitamin C	250–750 mg	750–1500	1500–3000	3000–4000
Vitamin E	200 IU	400 IU	400 IU	800 IU

Use these in the same ways as for cats, sprinkling them on the food if the dog won't accept them from your hand. I find dogs tend to wrinkle their noses at the sour taste of C, but within a few days are taking it easily in food. Pet multiple vitamin and mineral tablets are tasty and make good treats. Puncture the E capsules and put the oil onto food. Always give vitamins and minerals with meals. Much more information on vitamins and pets is given in the next chapter—there are miracles here.

An alternative to any sort of prepared pet foods is cooking for your animals at home. If you eat a quality diet yourself, it becomes very easy to do this. When switching over to such a diet, do it gradually by mixing half of the old food in with half of the new diet, then gradually increase the amount of the new food. Cats are finicky about the changes, but dogs think table scraps and usually wolf it down. Make sure that when using a home diet you also use the vitamin supplements to prevent anything being missing nutritionally. All of the supplement choices above are good with the home made feeding programs.

Anitra Frazier offers "The Superfinicky Owner's I'll-Do-Anything-For-My-Cat Diet." The diet contains:[30]

60 percent protein: Use raw ground chuck, raw organic chicken, raw organic egg yolk; cooked egg white; tofu (only in small amounts); cooked chicken, turkey, lamb or beef (no cooked poultry bones).

20 percent vegetable: Use finely grated raw zucchini or carrot; finely chopped alfalfa sprouts; lightly steamed broccoli, carrot, or corn; baked winter squash, Chinese broccoli in garlic sauce; a little yam or sweet potato.

20 percent grain: Use soaked oat bran, cooked barley, millet, oat flakes, brown rice, teff, quinoa, amaranth, sweet corn, or mashed potato.

Into each portion add: 1 teaspoon Vita-Mineral Mix; 1/4 teaspoon feline enzymes (for the first month only; then they're optional). Once a week give each cat: 1 capsule 400 units vitamin E...and 1 capsule vitamin A and D (10,000 units A and 400 units D).

Frazier notes that yeast should not be used for cats with active feline urological syndrome (FUS, urinary tract infections), and that the vitamin E should be alpha-tocopherol form only.

Pat Lazarus, in *Keep Your Pet Healthy the Natural Way*, offers "The Optimal Preventive Diet" for dogs and cats. She follows the Wendell Belfield method of supplementing the meals with a multiple vitamin and mineral tablet, plus vitamins C and E. Here is her recipe for dogs:[31]

Meat: One-third to one-half the daily ration should be meat, preferably raw. Approximately one-sixth of the weekly meat ration should be organ meats—heart, kidney, gizzard, spleen, tripe. Provide fish perhaps twice a week and chicken and turkey often.

Vegetables, Fruits and Grains: The rest of the daily ration should be grated raw carrot or other grated raw fruits and vegetables; cooked brown rice or whole grain breads or cereals, or chopped nuts.

Milk Products: Yogurt or raw (unpasteurized) milk should be given several times a week.

Fats: Polyunsaturated fat daily (in the form of soybean oil, sesame oil, etc.).

Eggs: One or two raw egg yolks (no whites), or soft-cooked whole eggs a week.

Dry Dog Food (optional): Supplement your dog's ration with one of the purer dry foods from a health food store.

Pure Water

Lazarus suggests that before going to home cooking, you switch your pet to a noncommercial, preservative-free pet food for a few weeks at first. This breaks food addictions and gives the dog's (or cat's) body a chance to detoxify before making the radical change to whole foods. From the recipes above, it is clear that different experts have different opinions on what foods to use and how to use them. I have presented several choices for this reason.

Here is her "Optimal Diet" for cats:[32]

Meat: About seventy-five percent of the daily food ration should be meat, raw preferably. Approximately one-sixth of the weekly meat ration should be organ meats—heart, kidney, gizzard, spleen, tripe. Provide fish perhaps twice a week and chicken and turkey often. Do not give any type of bones.

Vegetables, Fruits, Grains: Most of the rest of the daily ration should be cooked brown rice or cereal, cut-up raw fruits and vegetables, and occasionally chopped nuts.

Milk Products: Yogurt or raw (unpasteurized) milk should be given several times weekly.

Fats: Polyunsaturated fat daily (in the form of safflower oil, sesame oil, etc.).

Eggs: One or two eggs a week.

The Pat Lazarus cat diet also includes optional dry cat food, pure water (always), and the vitamins and minerals suggested by Wendell Belfield for cats. One caution here for home cooking advocates: while meat for human use is far cleaner than that put into commercial pet foods, it is still filled with more hormones and chemical feed residues than are healthy for anyone. These residues concentrate in the organ meats, especially the eliminative organs (liver, kidneys, gizzards). If you are using large amounts of these meats in pet or human foods, buying organics would be the best way to do it.

Chicken has the highest level of hormone residues. Notice too, that in any of these diets the foods are whole, unprocessed foods. There are no sugars, white flour starches, or packaged dinners with preservatives or dyes.

Different animal experts have different systems for feeding cats and dogs whole food diets without commercial pet foods. There are a number of books on cooking for pets, and a variety of individual recipes. Remember the Carvel Tiekert dietary scale that lists a correctly done home-made diet as the best that can be offered (but an incorrectly done home-made diet as the worst of the possibilities). For the woman who wishes to feed her cat or dog correctly in this way, I recommend the following sources: Richard Pitcairn, DVM, *Dr. Pitcairn's Complete Guide to Natural Health for Dogs and Cats* (Rodale Press, 1982); Anitra Frazier's *The New Natural Cat* (Plume Books, 1990); Joan Harper's *The Healthy Cat and Dog Cookbook* (Pet Press, 1988); and Juliette de Bairacli Levy, *The Complete Herbal Handbook for the Dog and Cat* (Faber and Faber, Sixth Edition, 1991).

The next chapter discusses vitamins and minerals as a way of healing dis-ease in dogs and cats.

[1] Dr. Richard H. Pitcairn, DVM, PhD, and Susan Hubble Pitcairn, *Dr. Pitcairn's Complete Guide to Natural Health for Dogs and Cats* (Emmaus, PA, Rodale Press, 1982), p. 14.

[2] Alfred J. Plechner, DVM and Martin Zucker, *Pet Allergies: Remedies for an Epidemic* (Inglewood, CA, Very Healthy Enterprises, 1986), p. 11.

[3] Quoted in Wendell O. Belfield, DVM and Martin Zucker, *How to Have a Healthier Dog* (New York, New American Library, 1981), p. 18.

[4] US Department of Commerce, Bureau of the Census, *Statistical Abstracts of the United States 1991* (Washington, DC, US Government Printing Office, 1991), p. 234 and 564.

[5] Alfred Plechner, DVM, *Pet Allergies: Remedies for an Epidemic*, p. 11.

[6] *Ibid.*

[7] Pat Lazarus, *Keep Your Pet Healthy the Natural Way* (New Canaan, CT, Keats Publishing, Inc., 1983), p. 3.

[8] Alfred Plechner, DVM, *Pet Allergies: Remedies for an Epidemic*, p. 12–13.

[9] *Ibid.*, p. 16.

[10] *Ibid.*, p. 15–16, and Pat Lazarus, *Keep Your Pet Healthy the Natural Way*, p. 3–5.

[11] Richard Pitcairn, DVM, *Dr. Pitcairn's Complete Guide to Natural Health for Dogs and Cats*, p. 14.

[12] Pat Lazarus, *Keep Your Pet Healthy the Natural Way*, p. 4.

[13] Wendell Belfield, DVM, *How to Have a Healthier Dog*, p. 34–37. Also, Wendell Belfield, DVM and Martin Zucker, *The Very Healthy Cat Book* (New York, McGraw-Hill Book Co., 1983), p. 28–31.

[14] W. Jean Dodds, DVM, "Nutritional Approach Can Help Immune Competence," in *DVM: The Newsmagazine of Veterinary Medicine*, Vol. 22, no. 4, April, 1991. Reprint.

[15] Wendell Belfield, DVM, *How to Have a Healthier Dog*, p. 37–40.

[16] Carvel G. Tiekert, DVM, "An Overview of Holistic Medicine," handout of the American Holistic Veterinary Association, p. 1.

[17] Anitra Frazier with Norma Eckroate, *The New Natural Cat: A Complete Guide for Finicky Owners* (New York, Plume Books, 1990), p 51–53.

[18] Joan Harper, *The Healthy Cat and Dog Cookbook* (Richland Center, WI, Pet Press, 1988), p. 13–15.

[19] Richard Pitcairn, DVM, *Dr. Pitcairn's Complete Guide to Natural Health for Dogs and Cats*, p. 17–18.

[20] Alfred Plechner, DVM, *Pet Allergies: Remedies for an Epidemic*, p. 20.

[21] *Ibid.*, p. 21–23.

[22] Richard Pitcairn, DVM, *Dr. Pitcairn's Complete Guide to Natural Health for Dogs and Cats*, p. 23–26.

[23] *Ibid.*, p. 25–26.

[24] Anitra Frazier, *The New Natural Cat*, p. 55.

[25] *Ibid.*, p. 56.

[26] Wendell Belfield, DVM, *How to Have a Healthier Dog*, p. 150–163, and *The Very Healthy Cat Book*, p. 147–158.

[27] Wendell Belfield, *The Very Healthy Cat Book*, p. 152–155. Information is combined.

[28] *Ibid.*, p. 155–157.

[29] Wendell Belfield, DVM, *How to Have a Healthier Dog*, p. 156–160.

[30] Anitra Frazier, *The New Natural Cat*, p. 61–62.

[31] Pat Lazarus, *Keep Your Pet Healthy the Natural Way*, p. 18–19.

[32] *Ibid.*, p. 34.

Vitamins & Minerals

By feeding the optimal diets and supplements of the last chapter on a daily basis, dogs and cats regain and keep full wellness. A quality diet extends the life-span of pets, increases their quality of life, and offers a more comfortable, less veterinary-dependent old age. Animals fed quality nutrition without chemical additives are less likely to have fleas, skin ailments, infectious dis-eases, ear infections, cancer, immune dis-eases (feline leukemia, feline AIDS, arthritis), epilepsy, heart or kidney failures, diabetes or behavioral problems. The better diet saves money in the long run. Over twenty years' time, I lost three beloved dogs in a row to cancer, and wish I had had the nutritional information from the beginning.

Alfred Plechner, in his work with chronic allergy and immune dis-ease in dogs and cats, begins with changing their diets and for many animals this is all that is needed. If that fails or the healing is incomplete, there are three more factors to look for. One is to add a mineral supplement to the pet's food; the second is to test for digestive enzyme system deficiency; and the third is to test for cortisol (a vital adrenal hormone). In Plechner's discoveries, it became clear that nutritional and vitamin deficiencies—direct results of poor feeding—were the cause of most animals' health problems. The lack of minerals and/or of digestive enzymes are remedied easily once the change of diet has occurred.[1]

The last of the factors, adrenal cortisol deficiency, is less apparent and a last resort. Plechner blames this factor on bad breeding, the way that breeders of purebred cats and dogs have incorporated genetic defects in exchange for what is deemed beautiful (or fashionable) bodies. To achieve the long thin heads of collies, for example, detached retinas and blindness were also bred into a once hardy, working dog. To achieve the dog-like faces of Siamese cats, the unwelcome results include poor vision (squinting), kinks in the tails, and "dingbats." Such breeding practices are another aspect of American greed, and are unnecessary and unfortunate. One of the results of this overbreeding and unintelligent breeding is adrenal cortex deficiencies in both dogs and cats, leading to immune dis-eases, allergies, reproductive hormone problems, skin dis-eases, feline urologic syndrome (FUS), feline leukemia and AIDS, epilepsy, lick granulomas, tendency to viral and bacterial infections, and behavior aberrations.[2]

In treating a pet with chronic or multiple health complaints, Plechner changes the diet and adds immediately the minerals and digestive enzymes (trypsin). If this does not make the changes—and the changes are often dramatic ones—it takes veterinary testing to define a cortisol deficiency and to treat it. Plechner found that in animals with healthy adrenal systems, prolonged use of cortisone is highly detrimental, as it damages the immune system and creates more problems than it cures. In animals with genetically defective adrenal systems, treating with cortisone—sometimes for life—is the only way to remedy what the body is not naturally producing.[3]

Adrenal therapy/cortisol replacement is a last step on a long road, the first three steps of which are simple for the laywoman. If your cat or dog suffers from any of the above complaints, first change her diet to a preservative-free one or even a hypoallergenic diet if the preservative-free one fails after several weeks' trial. (The Natural Life Co., founded by Alfred Plechner, specializes in hypoallergenic formulas.) Next, try the vitamin and mineral daily formulas suggested in the last chapter, making sure that the supplements include minerals (Dr. Pitcairn's Dog and Cat Powder and Anitra Frazier's Vita-Mineral Mix do). Digestive enzymes for dogs and cats are available from Natural Life and other pet products companies (see Resources section), or from veterinarians, and can be ordered through health food stores or pet supply shops.

The information from Plechner's work is to illustrate a point: pets (or people) that are deficient in any of the complex nutrients and factors required for optimal health experience dis-ease. By replacing what is missing from the diet or what the animal's body is not producing naturally, the dis-ease state can be changed to well-being. Replacing what is missing, the vitamins, minerals,

enzymes, glandulars, amino acids or other nutrients, is the work of clinical nutrition. In humans this science, named by Dr. Linus Pauling, the founder of vitamin C, is called orthomolecular medicine. Holistic healers call it vitamin therapy or using megavitamins.

Vitamins, minerals and other supplements are never a substitute for food or for an optimal diet. They work *with* an optimal diet and are geared to the individual animal's (or person's) healing needs. Vitamin C and calcium are important for dogs with hip dysplasia, for example, while kittens with skin ulcers may need zinc and vitamin E. The intent is to feed a full-nutrient diet, a good basic diet supplemented with balanced vitamins and minerals, and then to see if the animal or human needs something else. Every animal (or human) is an individual, and what may be enough vitamin C or zinc for one may be too much or too little for another. Animals under stress also need higher levels of vitamins, minerals, and nutrients than the adult norm, as do growing puppies and kittens, and pregnant or nursing mothers. Aged animals may also have different needs. Where optimal nutrition still leaves something left to heal, targeting it with the proper vitamin, mineral or supplement can effect a major cure.

Pets hampered by the effects of bad breeding practices can be helped significantly with vitamins and minerals. Some of the effects are tendencies to produce too little of a catalyzing enzyme or to have intestinal organizations that absorb too little of one or more nutrients. If a dog has the inability to absorb enough zinc from the intestines, for example—Siberian Huskies and other northern breeds are known for this—she may need supplements to prevent zinc deficiency dis-eases even though her diet contains adequate amounts. (Generic dog foods are notoriously deficient in zinc.)[4]

A dog or cat with zinc deficiencies will usually show it first in skin problems, demodectic mange, poor coat, allergic reactions, and eventually in more significant reduced immune response. Zinc in the body is necessary for healing tissues and wounds, and for healing burns. It is an antibacterial and a regulator of the enzyme and immune systems. Cat deficiency symptoms include emaciation, vomiting, conjunctivitis, retarded growth and general debility. Immune system dis-eases are far too prevalent in people and animals now; our bodies and immune systems are overloaded with stress and environmental pollutants, and weakened by chemicalized, denutritionalized food. Zinc deficiencies are more common now for this reason, as well as other deficiencies, and more is needed in some pets.

Other mineral deficiencies are implicated in a wide number of pet disorders. Minerals enter the human or animal body through diet (eating the meat animals that live on plants, or by eating the plants themselves). Plants take in minerals from the soil, and these are passed upward along the food chain. The weak link in the chain in the past fifty to seventy-five years has been in poor agribusiness practices that cause depletion of minerals from the soil. Erosion, single-crop farming and overcropping have resulted in mineral-depleted land worldwide and the specific mineral deficiencies—and toxicities—vary geographically (see Appendix III, *Aluminum Toxicity*):[5]

Over the years veterinarians have traced deficiency diseases to a wide number of minerals. They include nitrogen, phosphorus, calcium, potassium, magnesium, sodium, iron, chlorine, copper, manganese, zinc, molybdenum, cobalt, iodine and selenium.

There are other minerals with a variety of exotic names and often little known functions. It is probably the case also, that all the minerals and vitamins needed to sustain mammal life have not been defined yet. Most of these are needed by the pet or human body in only minute amounts, and they are called trace minerals. (Calcium, magnesium and phosphorus are needed in more significant quantities and are called bulk minerals.) Alfred Plechner has found that supplementing pets' diets with a trace mineral combination can show the following improvements over six months:

1. Darker, thicker hair coat with increased lustre.
2. Reduced scratching.
3. Reduced flakiness of skin.
4. Better maintenance of body weight with reduced caloric intake.
5. In geriatric cats and dogs, increased activity, weight gain, and improved condition of hair coat.
6. Animals with heavy flea and fly infestations appear to be less attractive to insects after three weeks of supplementation.
7. Improvement in general health.[6]

Supplementation has also been helpful in controlling food allergies, flea allergy dermatitis, pancreatic deficiencies, endocrine-immune imbalances, chronic active hepatitis and airborne allergies in dogs. In cats, mineral supplementation has proved helpful in miliary dermatitis, leukemia and infectious peritonitis.[7] The minerals are given in full mineral complexes, rather than as individual items, with some exceptions like zinc or calcium/magnesium supplements. They can obviously make a significant difference in pet health and well-being.

Of the vitamins, vitamin C is probably the best known in human or animal healing. The human body produces no vitamin C and the bodies of dogs and cats produce too little for the stresses of modern life. (Dogs and cats produce 40 mg per Kg of body weight per day of vitamin C. A kilogram is 2.2 pounds.)[8] A deficiency in vitamin C is a deficiency in the healing, glandular, circulatory, immune and regenerative abilities of the body. It is a major factor in the formation and maintenance of bones and tissues, prevents cancer, and may prevent atherosclerosis. The classic vitamin C deficiency disease is scurvy, with gum dis-ease, loss of teeth, weakened bones, bleeding, bad breath and general debility. Signs of clinical scurvy have been apparent in dogs under stress.

In cats the effects of vitamin C deficiency are weak and dying kittens, fatal viral dis-eases, urinary tract infections and blockages, and poor coats with general ill health.[9] Supplementing with C can change a feline leukemia/feline AIDS blood status from positive to negative by going to bowel tolerance with the vitamin over a period of a few months. In dogs, it can totally resolve the problems of dysplastic hips in younger dogs and arthritis in older ones, as well as help or cure spinal myelopathy, ruptured discs, allergies, viral infections (including distemper), and skin problems.[10] After the "cures," the pet needs to stay on C, but in lesser amounts.

The attitude of veterinary medicine on the subject of vitamin C is that cats and dogs produce what they need in their own bodies, and no supplementation is needed. Most pet multiple vitamin and mineral tablets contain a very low amount of vitamin C, if any at all (this is also true of human supplements). The vitamin is an antioxidant, a pollution fighter that cleans toxins from the blood and tissues. In an environment that is heavily polluted, the small amount of C produced in an animal's body is not enough for the increased requirement. Stress also is a vitamin C depleter (as well as other nutrients). Vitamin C additionally helps to protect the body against lead toxicity and nitrites, as well as other heavy metals. It protects against the side-effects of some veterinary drugs (including steroids/cortisone), and it is a major pain reliever. It keeps the teeth strong in aging pets and retards the aging process.[11] Supplementing with vitamin C is a major disease preventive, therefore it's emphasized in the daily feeding plans. Supplementing with vitamin C can mean the difference between life and death in the case of a sick cat or dog. Contrary to myth and rumor, vitamin C will not cause kidney stones, it dissolves them.

Here is a run-down of other major vitamin needs in cats and dogs. The information is primarily from Wendell Belfield, whose work is the only vitamin information currently available for use on pets. (Alfred Plechner has mineral information, as does Belfield.) The material is from his books, *The Very Healthy Cat Book* (McGraw-Hill, 1983), and *How to Have a Healthier Dog* (New American Library, 1981). Much more research and work in this field is needed. The information below is condensed and also is referenced to James Balch, M.D. and Phyllis Balch, C.N.C., *Prescription for Nutritional Healing* (Avery Publishing Group, 1990).

Vitamin A deficiencies cause most skin and infection problems in both dogs and cats. Short-term use of 10,000 IU of vitamin A daily in cats and small dogs (25,000 IU in large dogs) can be enough to clear up many skin dis-eases, followed by a daily multiple vitamin and mineral supplement that contains vitamin A in less amounts. Like vitamins C and E, vitamin A is an antioxidant that helps prevent cancer, retard aging, and protects the body from damage by pollutants and chemicals. It is also important in eyesight and eye dis-eases, infectious dis-eases, and the formation of bones and teeth. In cats other signs of vitamin A deficiency include: cataracts and retinal degeneration, pneumonia, convulsions, watery diarrhea, emaciation, weakness in the hind legs, and increased susceptibility to infections and infectious dis-eases. In dogs, vitamin A deficiency leads to nerve degeneration, birth defects, reproductive failures, night blindness, muscular incoordination, seizures, lack of weight gain, and deafness, as well as skin disorders and increased susceptibility to infections.[12] Cats cannot derive vitamin A from beta-carotene, as dogs and people can; they therefore cannot get their vitamin A from vegetables, and A supplements cannot be beta-carotene.

The B-Complex vitamins are a range of vitamins necessary for a healthy nervous system. Cats need almost twice as much of these vitamins as dogs do for proper absorption of nutrients throughout the body (fats, proteins and carbohydrates). These vitamins require each other to work, and so are taken in the B-complex unit, with occasional additions of other single B-vitamins. Mouth, eyes, skin, gastrointestinal tract, and reproductive organs are B-deficiency dis-ease sites, as well as behavior, intelligence, and brain and nerve function. Stress depletes the B-vitamins, as it does vitamin C, and so does extremely cold weather. The individual B-vitamins known to be primary for pets are listed briefly.

B-1 (Thiamine) is a major issue in cats, as supermarket cat foods may not provide enough of it. The results of this deficiency are brain damage, seizures, loss of movement control, and can lead to death. Treatment with the vitamin by injection effects full recovery within twenty-four hours.[13] Most cat breeders supplement with B-vitamins, and B-1 also helps hyperactivity, internal muscle weakness, flea resistance, appetite, learning ability and intelligence. Cats that eat fish and cats or dogs on supermarket pet foods are more likely to be thiamine deficient.

In dogs, B-1 deficiency signs are lack of appetite, vomiting, unsteadiness, and spasticity of the hind legs. Dogs also respond to B-1 as a flea repellent. A tablespoonful of brewer's yeast contains 1.25 mg of B-1, but some pets are allergic to yeast, and it should not be used on cats during urologic (FUS) attacks. A B-complex-50 from the health food store contains 50 mg, and can be bought yeast free cheaply.[14]

B-2 (Riboflavin) deficiency may lead to cataracts in both dogs and cats. Bloodshot eyes and conjunctivitis are often deficiency symptoms.[15] This vitamin is necessary for red blood cell formation, antibody production, food metabolism and growth. Riboflavin prevents birth defects and dandruff.

B-3 (Niacin) deficiency may cause blacktongue in dogs which is the equivalent to human pellagra. Niacin is an immense help in controlling seizures and reducing behavior problems; it reduces cholesterol levels, improves blood circulation, and aids central nervous system function. In cats, niacin deficiency signs are: mouth ulcers; thick, foul smelling saliva that drools; weight loss, lack of appetite, weakness and apathy, finally leading to death from respiratory dis-ease.[16] Raw meat and brewer's yeast are good niacin sources. Cooking destroys many B-complex vitamins; because of the hot flush effect, niacin is usually given only as part of the full B-complex or as niacinamide. Cats need more of it than dogs do.

B-5 (Pantothenic Acid) adds to animals' (and humans') longevity. It is important for good immune system and adrenal function, vitamin and food utilization, and essential in fighting allergies, inflammations, asthma and infections. Vitamin C and B-5 together are highly important for skin dis-eases and allergies in both cats and dogs. The presence of allergies or infections is considered a B-5 deficiency symptom. It also helps animals to combat stress, reduce depression and ease anxiety. Exact requirements are not known in pets, but supplementing is important.[17]

B-6 (Pyridoxine) deficiency symptoms include failure to grow and thrive, epilepsy, anemia, water retention, and kidney stones or kidney damage in dogs and cats. Its deficiency is also implicated in artery dis-ease, cancer, arthritis, asthma and allergies in pets and people. B-6 is essential for the metabolism of protein (and more protein is needed by cats than by dogs). It is required in the utilization of some minerals, for a healthy nervous system, red blood cell production, good brain function, and a strong immune system.[18]

B-9 (Folic Acid) deficiency results in reproductive problems, birth defects when the mother is deficient, weight loss and anemia, erratic appetite, low energy, seizures, eye discharge, depression and anxiety, as well as decreased immune function in both cats and dogs. Red blood cell formation, DNA synthesis and protein metabolism are dependent upon this vitamin.[19]

B-12 (Cobalamin) deficiency in humans results in anemia that if left untreated leads to death. Dogs also can suffer from B-12 deficiency anemia, but how much they actually require (or that cats require) is still unknown. Supplementing pregnant animals with vitamin B-12 results in stronger, larger and healthier young, with better dis-ease resistance.[20] This vitamin prevents nerve damage, aids fertility and promotes normal growth and development. It is necessary for normal digestion and proper food absorption. Raw liver is the best animal food source.

Biotin deficiency results in hair loss and in hair and skin disorders in cats and dogs, but the exact requirements for it are unknown in both. This B-vitamin is essential for thyroid and adrenal health, strong nervous systems and nerve tissue, healthy reproduction, normal sweat glands and bone marrow, and healthy skin. It is necessary for utilization of fat, proteins and carbohydrates in the body. Biotin is a cure for dogs that eat their feces; they may be looking for this vitamin, which is produced to some extent in the intestines. Raw egg whites contain an enzyme that depletes biotin, and for this reason eggs fed to pets should be cooked to deactivate the enzyme.[21]

Vitamin D deficiency leads to rickets, a bone deformity dis-ease that dogs may be more prone to than cats. This vitamin prevents osteoporosis and hypocalcemia, and is essential for normal teeth, bones and growth, and absorption of calcium and phosphorus. Vitamin D in nature is formed on the animal or human skin by sunlight—indoor cats have no way to synthesize it for themselves and the vitamin is not included in most pet foods. Cod liver oil is a prime source. Little is known about animal requirements, but tropical zoo animals deprived of sunlight in northern winters need supplements to prevent crooked bones.[22]

Vitamin E is one of the wonder vitamins, and both dogs and cats need supplements. It is essential for healing dis-eases of the circulatory system (and preventing them), including heart tachycardia and arteriosclerosis. It promotes fertility, slows aging, prevents cataracts, boosts the immune system, protects the body against pollutants and cancer, prevents or heals scarring, and heals the skin. Vitamin E prevents steatitis in cats and boosts muscle power and endurance in working dogs. It helps in dissolving tumors, especially in breasts, and in relieving posterior paralysis and disc problems in dogs (also see a chiropractor for this). The vitamin oxygenates the blood and improves the function of all internal organs; its antioxidant abilities protect the lungs. In humans, vitamin E deficiency disorders include heart dis-ease, muscular dystrophy, brain and neurological problems, and reproductive failures.

Doses range from 100 IU per day for cats, to 400 IU or more for larger dogs (in healing dis-ease). I have used up to 800 IU per day on a forty-five pound puppy for a period of three months with good results and no side effects; higher doses in this individual animal resulted in vomiting. Wendell Belfield used amounts of 1200 IU per day to cure cats of steatitis, a vitamin E deficiency dis-ease.[23] This is one of the vitamins to supplement daily as part of the routine diet. It is a must for cats that eat fish, and for dogs with skin ailments.

Supplementing with mineral combinations and the mineral zinc have been discussed earlier, but a few of the other major ones deserve mentioning.

Calcium and Phosphorus need to be in balance in

the animal and human body (along with magnesium). Few pets or people are phosphorus deficient, but calcium is another story. Calcium deficiencies can cause eclampsia in breeding and nursing female cats or dogs. This mineral is essential for bone, tooth and muscle growth, blood clotting, normal heart rate, and transmission of nerve impulses. It helps the body to eliminate lead and other heavy metal poisoning. Calcium deficiencies (sometimes brought on by high meat diets, as meat contains an unbalanced amount of phosphorus) can result in nervousness, lameness, muscle spasms, heart palpitations, eczema, decrease in bone density, osteoporosis, gum erosion, increased cholesterol levels, seizures, hemorrhages, high blood pressure, arthritis, breeding difficulties, and bone fractures.

Cats that are calcium deficient hide in dark corners and fight being handled. For cats, supplement calcium in the amount of 500 mg to every 100 grams of meat fed, and many breeders supplement calcium during pregnancy and nursing. For dogs, supplement high amounts of calcium only in the first year of life, or during pregnancy and nursing, as too much can cause kidney stones. (Use vitamin C along with calcium to prevent this totally). Many people believe that calcium deficiency causes hip dysplasia in dogs, but the lack of vitamin C is really the cause. The Dog Powder Mix and Vita-Mineral Mix of the last chapter contain all an animal needs of this mineral. Vitamin D is required to activate calcium.[24]

Iron can be deficient in both dogs and cats, causing anemia, fatigue, diarrhea, pale gums, and hair loss particularly in animals fed on low meat diets. Dogs with low iron levels are especially susceptible to hookworm infestations. Iron is important in cats, as it combats the lead poisoning that too easily comes with commercial cat foods.[25] Iron is needed in the creation of hemoglobin (red blood cells), enzyme function, immunity and energy, and may be important in protecting against feline leukemia. Cats need about 5 mg per day, which is usually included in a pet multiple vitamin and mineral tablet.

Magnesium helps to detoxify the body of lead and other heavy metals, and is important for the nervous system, enzyme function, heart rate, bones and muscles. Deficiency symptoms include heart arrhythmia, high blood pressure, seizures, bone pain, nervousness and irritability, twitching, depression, muscle spasms and retarded weight gain. For dogs with arthritis, a calcium/magnesium tablet is a great pain reliever. Dogs should

seldom be fed aspirin, cats never (it can be fatal for cats); calcium/magnesium tablets are a substitute. They are calmative, as well, and for arthritis work best with vitamin C. Dogs that chew plaster are probably looking for minerals missing from their diets, primarily magnesium and calcium.

Manganese is necessary for enzyme utilization, lactation, normal reproduction, bone, cartilage and collagen growth, fat and protein assimilation, blood sugar regulation, healthy nerves and immune systems, and normal function of the pituitary gland (that regulates all the other glands). It is needed for utilization of thiamine and vitamin E. Animal requirements have not been determined,[26] but humans need 2 mg per day of this trace mineral.

Potassium and Sodium must be kept in balance in the body, and the current overuse of salt (sodium) in the American diet and American pet food diet has become a hazard to pet and human health. It is very rare, other than in cases of heat exhaustion, that sodium needs to be supplemented in pets. Heat exhaustion with loss of equilibrium, decreased water intake, dry skin, hair loss, retarded growth, and an inability to maintain body water balance are signs of sodium deficiency. Potassium deficiency symptoms include restlessness, heart arrhythmia, poor growth, muscular paralysis, tendency to dehydration, and heart or kidney lesions. Potassium helps prevent strokes. Some diuretic and heart medications deplete potassium in the body.[27] An excellent and easy source of potassium replacement is apple cider vinegar. Place one teaspoon to each pint of water in the cat's or dog's waterbowl daily. (Never use aluminum or galvanized bowls.)

Selenium deficiency dis-eases include heart dis-ease, cancer, tumors, and immune deficiencies. Lameness, muscular weakness, skin problems, low fertility, and retarded growth rates are also selenium deficiency symptoms. This trace mineral is required in very minute amounts as an antioxidant that helps to slow aging and regulate the pancreas (blood sugar). It works very well with vitamin E; although recognized as essential in small amounts in dogs, it has not been investigated in cats.[28]

These are not all of the known vitamins and minerals, but are a few of the major ones whose role in pet health have been determined. Too little research has been done on vitamins, minerals and supplements for animals or people. For extensive information on these in humans, that can carry over to pets, see Balch and Balch's

Prescription for Nutritional Healing as a recommended source. Also see Diane Stein, *All Women Are Healers,* and *The Natural Remedy Book for Women* (The Crossing Press, 1990 and 1992).

The same vitamins, minerals and supplements that are used to heal human dis-eases are also effective on pets, in doses that reflect their smaller sizes and body weights. Where the adult human dose for zinc is 50-100 mg (stay under 100 mg), use 5–10 mg zinc gluconate lozenges on a cat or small dog. Where vitamin C to bowel tolerance in people might be three to ten grams (3000–10,000 mg), a large dog might reach that point with 2000 mg, or a cat with feline leukemia as high as 5000 mg daily. The sicker the animal the higher amount of C without diarrhea. When using C to heal dis-ease go to bowel tolerance, then decrease the amount gradually after the animal is healed.

Animals and people get virtually all their vitamins and minerals from their food. The water soluble vitamins are substances that must be taken into a dog's or cat's diet daily, as the excess is not stored but is excreted in the urine. These vitamins include all except A, D, E and K, which are oil soluble and are stored in the body—the excess is not excreted but held. Oil soluble vitamins, because they are stored, should not be overdosed. They are given in small amounts or not everyday. Too much of any of these will cause vomiting or digestive upsets as warning long before any overdose harm is done. Reports of vitamin toxicities are often highly exaggerated, in a medical system attempt to frighten people away from self-care. Minerals are used in very small amounts and a balanced trace mineral formula, or multiple vitamin with minerals, is usually the place to start. Avoid using mineral oil as a laxative or lubricant for dogs, cats or people— it depletes the vitamins and minerals from the body. If oils are needed, as for cats' hairballs, use cod liver oil or vegetable oils instead.

Some orthomolecular remedies for cat and dog diseases follow. In general, the information women have learned over the years about vitamins, minerals and supplements for themselves is valid for pets. Carry it over for use on cats and dogs, in smaller doses, and the results are as miraculous for animals as they are for people (and sometimes even more so). Vitamins and minerals are used along with diet and other healing methods including herbs, homeopathy, flower essences, massage, psychic healing and acupuncture, as well as veterinary care and medical drugs. The information that follows assumes that you have changed your pet's diet to a preservative free or whole foods one, and are supplementing with at least a daily pet multiple vitamin and mineral tablet. Adding the additionals of the last chapter—Dog or Cat Powder Mix and Oil Mix, Vita-Mineral Mix, or additional vitamin C and E are recommended. These keep your pet healthy. The remedies below are for some common pet dis-eases.

One further note: most holistic animal experts recommend that a dog or cat in acute illness (sudden, self-limiting sickness) be fasted for a few days until the disease abates. This does not mean a pet with long-term chronic hip dysplasia, but does refer to an animal with an upset stomach, fever or infectious dis-ease. Start the fast by easing the animal into a simpler diet for a day, then into all liquids (pure water, vegetable juices or clear soups) until healing is underway. When breaking the fast, ease into a normal diet slowly again. If a pet refuses food completely, do not force it; let her fast while she needs to, keeping pure water and nutritious liquids available at all times. Fasting usually lasts from one to four or five days, no more.[29] Do not fast a pet that is diabetic. When an animal is fasting, give her vitamins by crushing them into the liquids.

The dis-ease suggestions below can in no way be considered complete, but are a sampling of what vitamin therapy can offer. Major sources are: Wendell Belfield, DVM, *How to Have a Healthier Dog* and *The Very Healthy Cat Book;* Anitra Frazier, *The New Natural Cat;* Pat Lazarus, *Keep Your Pet Healthy the Natural Way;* and Richard Pitcairn, DVM, *Dr. Pitcairn's Complete Guide to Natural Health for Dogs and Cats.*

Allergies: First begin with a change of diet and the daily vitamin-mineral supplement program. Read Alfred Plechner's *Pet Allergies: Remedies for an Epidemic.* Recommended vitamins are: vitamin C to bowel tolerance, B-complex and pantothenic acid (B-5), and vitamin E. Pet digestive enzymes (dog or cat) are also recommended and helpful. To reference amounts by body size, for a cat use twice a day (two meals): 500 mg vitamin C, 1/2 low potency B-complex tablet (yeast free); 1/4 tsp. feline enzymes or 1/2 digestive enzyme pill. Once a week add: 400 IU vitamin E and a capsule containing 10,000 IU vitamin A and 400 IU vitamin D.[30]

Arthritis and Hip Dysplasia: For arthritis, vitamin C 500–3000 mg per day, 10–20 mg B-complex (when using Dr. Pitcairn's Dog or Cat Powder, substitute B-complex for the yeast), and vitamins E, A and D.[31] Anitra Frazier additionally suggests digestive enzymes (1/4 tsp. feline enzymes per meal), 1-1/4 tsp. Vita-Mineral Mix per meal, and 250 mg of vitamin C per meal. Once a day add 2 mg zinc, 100 IU vitamin E, and 5000 units vitamin A (for one month, then go to the recommended weekly A, D and E amounts).[32] In dogs, Wendell Belfield suggests vitamin C to bowel tolerance for arthritis or dysplasia. Avoid steroids and aspirin. This alone can result in full cures for hip dysplasia in younger dogs and major relief for older ones. Belfield equates hip dysplasia with subclinical scurvy, a vitamin C deficiency dis-ease.[33] Put a teaspoonful of apple cider vinegar in each pint of the pet's drinking water.

Cancer and Tumors: Use vitamin C to bowel tolerance, B-complex, selenium and zinc; deficiencies in any of these have been known to stimulate cancer and tumor growth in laboratory animals. Also vitamins A and E.[34] Use high amounts tailored to body weight. Dr. Pitcairn suggests 2000–6000 mg (2–6 grams) of vitamin C daily, four times the usual level of vitamin E (400 IU daily), and double the amount of cod liver oil/vitamin A. The natural diet is a must here.

Pat Lazarus lists the following supplements for both cats and dogs, using amounts that are high for the animal's body weight. She suggests vitamin A, B-complex, large amounts of vitamin C, large amounts of vitamin E, and pancreatic enzymes or bromelain.[35] Suggested amounts: C to bowel tolerance, vitamin A 5000 IU per day with 400 IU of D, B-complex 20 mg, 400 IU vitamin E, pancreatic enzymes by body weight (check the label). Use 50 mcg selenium, and 5–10 mg zinc for a medium sized dog of about forty-five pounds. Lazarus also reports significant success with vitamin B-17 (laetrile), and recommends raw thymus glandular extract, and evening primrose oil.

Cataracts: Pat Lazarus states that B-15 eye drops used twice daily "will dissolve most early cataracts" and about thirty percent of advanced ones. She recommends vitamin E and selenium in addition, and stresses the need for a preservative free diet.[36] Wendell Belfield recommends high amounts of vitamin C, plus E (300 IU for a large dog), selenium (50 mcg) and vitamin A (20,000 IU a day). Optimal treatment is begun intramuscularly (by injection) and continued at home by mouth.[37] Anitra Frazier uses 250 mg of vitamin C per meal for cats, with

100 IU vitamin E a day for two weeks (then reduce to 400 IU of E per week). She also stresses a high quality diet with the daily supplements.[38]

Constipation and Diarrhea: For chronic constipation, again change the diet to a preservative free high quality one, and add one teaspoonful of bran per pound of food. For cats, use 750 mg vitamin C per day and 100 IU vitamin E.[39] (Increase these amounts for larger pets.) Richard Pitcairn suggests that chronic constipation in dogs or cats can be a result of heavy metal (aluminum) toxicity. Avoid using aluminum cooking pots or bowls, processed cheeses, table salt, white flour or tap water which may all be high in this metal. Detoxify with high levels of vitamin C, 500–3000 mg per day, plus zinc (5 mg for a cat or small dog, 10 mg for a medium sized dog, and 20 mg for a large dog).[40] Also note that vitamin C in doses approaching bowel tolerance becomes laxative. Avoid using mineral oil as a lubricant or laxative (use olive oil instead), as it drains the body of vitamins. For diarrhea, when chronic suspect food allergies and change the diet to a preservative free one with supplements. For acute diarrhea, see future chapters.

Diabetes: Feed a low fat, sugar free, preservative free diet with supplements, divided into several small meals per day. Reduce the Dog Oil Mix to 1/4 cup each of vegetable and cod liver oil, and feed only 1/2 tsp. of the Mix daily. Increase the amount of vitamin E. Add a trace mineral combination that contains chromium, manganese and zinc; vitamin C 500–3000 mg divided into two daily doses; and 1/2-1 tsp. of liquid lecithin per day.[41] Pat Lazarus suggests vitamin E (up to 300 IU per day), digestive enzymes or bromelain, and a natural foods diet. For pancreatitis, use the diabetic diet with vitamin C and digestive enzymes. Add a small amount of sesame oil to the food.[42]

Anitra Frazier's recipe for cat diabetes is:[43]

Add to each meal:
1 tsp. Vita-Mineral Mix
1 tsp. chopped alfalfa sprouts
250 mg. vitamin C powder
1/16 tsp. potassium chloride (salt substitute)
1 drop stevia extract

Daily: 100 IU vitamin E, after two weeks reduce to 400 IU of E weekly.
Weekly: 10,000 IU vitamin A and 400 IU vitamin D.

If your pet is on insulin, make very sure to monitor blood sugar levels, as these can change with the supplements. When using supplements for diabetes, it is extremely important to be consistent. The minerals chromium and manganese, and raw pancreas glandulars, have been proven important for people with hypoglycemia or diabetes; they lower blood sugar levels. Try them with pets, in amounts based on body weight.

Feline Leukemia: The big news is that this major killer of cats can be cured totally, asymptomatic animals with positive testing reverting to negative status in about ten to twelve weeks. Sick animals take longer. The recipe: vitamin C to bowel tolerance, 3000–5000 mg per day divided into two mealtime doses. Start small and increase the amounts gradually. Use the improved diet and a pet multiple vitamin and mineral supplement; once testing negative, the cat still needs to remain on the supplements. Do not allow medication with steroids/cortisone.[44]

Anitra Frazier adds other vitamins to 1000 mg of vitamin C per day: with each meal use 1 tsp. Vita-Mineral Mix, 1 tablet bioplasma (homeopathic), 1 capsule of liquid calcium (400 mg), 1/4 tsp. feline enzymes, 10 mg Co-enzyme Q10, 1/8 tsp. olive oil, 10,000 IU vitamin A or 1/2 tsp. cod liver oil, 2–3 mg zinc and 1 tsp. chopped alfalfa sprouts. She uses 400 IU vitamin E once a week.[45] The experts suspect lead poisoning may be a primary factor in the cause of this dis-ease. Vitamin C helps to detoxify the body, and the changed diet removes lead from daily ingestion. Use the recipes above for feline AIDS, as well.

Gloria Dodd, DVM comments on feline leukemia:

On August 15, 1992 a lady by the name of Minke Prince called me from Arizona. They've been curing a large number of their feline leukemia cats in the "no kill" shelter where she works, with a blue green algae called "Cell Tech." Minke said she had cancer herself and cured it by removing the silver amalgam fillings (oh yes, Voll found out twenty years ago that silver amalgam fillings leach out mercury that poisons the whole body) and the use of the Cell Tech. I have asked her to send me a sample of the Cell Tech for EAV analysis in the body, and all the facts and statistics about the feline leukemic cats.

Cell Tech, and other blue-green algaes, are available in health food stores.

Heart Dis-ease and Hypertension: These were both unheard of in pets forty years ago, and unheard of in people before the manufacture of white flour and white sugar. Change of diet is essential. Vitamin E is primary in all forms of heart dis-ease and hypertension; use 100 IU daily for cats and small dogs; 200 IU for medium dogs and large ones, and 400 IU for the giant breeds. Double the dose for aging pets. Use a pet multiple vitamin and mineral tablet and vitamin C, as well.[46]

Pat Lazarus suggests vitamin A, C and E in high doses, adding the vitamin E only after the weak heart has been stabilized. She recommends weight reduction, no-salt diets, a natural diet, and moderate exercise. When using A or E in high amounts, try the water soluble (dry) forms that cannot be overdosed, and use vitamin C in the ascorbic acid (salt free) form. For high blood pressure (hypertension), she recommends the minerals magnesium and potassium.[47] For potassium, put a teaspoonful of apple cider vinegar in each pint of drinking water. Dr. Richard Pitcairn prescribes the following: a complete B-complex (20–50 mg), dolomite powder instead of bone meal in the Dog and Cat Powders, trace minerals containing selenium and chromium, and zinc 5–20 mg daily.[48]

Injuries, Cuts and Burns: After standard first aid and/or veterinary care, the improved diet with multiple vitamin and mineral supplements are important. Vitamins to aid the healing of cuts, internal and external injuries, wounds and burns are: vitamins C, E, A and zinc.[49] All speed healing. Vitamin C reduces bruising and bleeding, prevents infection, and reduces inflammation. Vitamin E induces healing of skin and internal tissues and prevents scarring—it is particularly important both internally and externally for burns. Zinc is necessary for wound and burn healing, and boosts the immune system to speed healing and prevent infections. Where there has been shock or trauma, the B-complex is also important. Use these vitamins after surgery for rapid recovery. Increase the daily dietary amounts when higher levels for healing are needed. These supplements are routinely used for people, as well.

Skin and Coat Ailments: When a dog or cat has chronic skin problems, hair falling out, bald patches, rashes, dandruff or poor coat, the causes are virtually always dietary. Change to a preservative free diet and supplement with the daily pet multiple vitamin and mineral tablet, and vitamins C and E. This usually does the job. Many skin problems are specific deficiencies, including vitamins A, E, C or zinc. Animals on vegetable oil or cod liver oil tend to need more vitamin E. Chronic skin ailments, demodectic mange or seborrhea usually respond to vitamin C; rashes, eczema and hair loss are often vitamin E deficiencies; abscesses and sores respond to zinc; and bacterial skin eruptions, scratching or sebaceous cysts require vitamin A.[50] Use 200 IU daily of vitamin E, 10,000–20,000 IU vitamin A, 5–20 mg of zinc, and vitamin C 500–3000 mg per day.

Pat Lazarus suggests the following vitamin amounts for a fifty pound dog with skin problems. These are added to the daily vitamin-mineral supplement. Vitamin C 1000–2000 mg, vitamin E 400 IU per day, B-complex-50 with B-12, and two tablespoons of cold pressed vegetable oil (sunflower or sesame) per meal. Additionally, she uses 2 tsp. kelp powder, zinc 30 mg, selenium 50 mcg, one tablespoon per day of bone meal, and two wheat germ oil capsules per meal. She advises a change of diet to natural, preservative free foods beginning with a veterinary-supervised fast on distilled water for a few days. Do not fast a diabetic pet unless advised by a veterinarian.[51] Anitra Frazier suggests that the fast be on her High Calcium Chicken Broth; the recipe is in her book (p. 243).

Spinal Problems: Too many dogs in particular have died (been euthanized) for spinal myelopathy, spinal degeneration, posterior paralysis, or disc troubles. Modern chiropractic and veterinary acupuncture can help tremendously here. Vitamin supplements also can work wonders, particularly vitamin C to bowel tolerance (as much as 6000 mg per day) with a multiple vitamin and mineral supplement. Response time varies with the individual and the severity of the problem. Intravenous injections of vitamin C work faster than oral dosage.[52] Pat Lazarus adds vitamin E (400 IU), trace minerals, and manganese to the above.[53]

Urinary Tract Infections, Kidney and Bladder Disease: Feline Urologic Syndrome (FUS) is a leading cause of dis-ease and often death in cats. It can almost always be prevented by feeding a preservative free natural diet and vitamin-mineral supplement, along with vitamin C. Anitra Frazier suggests at the first sign of urinary infection to withhold solid food and give 500 mg vitamin C in a teaspoon of chicken broth, plus 100 IU vitamin E. During an attack, along with veterinary care, use a B-complex 10 mg twice a day, 100 IU vitamin E daily for a month (then decrease to 400 IU once a week), and 1/4 tsp. cod liver oil or 10,000 IU vitamin A with 400 IU vitamin D. After attacks, continue vitamin C (500 mg

per day divided into two meals), and vitamins E, A and D weekly.[54] Her information on diet, supplements, care and medication is highly recommended.

Richard Pitcairn offers the same protocol for cats and adds the following recommendations for bladder infections and kidney stones in dogs: vitamin A as cod liver oil or 5000 IU vitamin A capsules daily for cats and small dogs; 5000–10,000 IU for medium dogs, and 10,000–20,000 IU for large dogs. Use vitamin C twice daily: 500 mg per day for cats and small dogs, 1000 mg daily for medium sized dogs, 500 mg three times a day for large dogs. Use a 10 mg B-complex for cats and small dogs and 20 mg for larger ones. Where there are kidney stones in dogs, add 50–300 mg of magnesium depending on the pet's size.[55]

Wendell Belfield uses vitamin C to bowel tolerance to dissolve kidney stones in cats and dogs, 500–800 mg per day. For interstitial nephritis and kidney degeneration, use high amounts of vitamins C, A and E. For cats with FUS, he uses a catheter douche of 25 percent vitamin C solution (sodium ascorbate), followed by a change in diet with a multiple vitamin-mineral supplement and 1000–1250 mg of vitamin C per day divided into two meals. Serious cases of FUS take as long as six months to heal completely and stop returning.[56] The supplements can prevent recurrences, veterinary drugs, catheterizations, surgeries, and even death.

Viral Dis-eases: These are the infectious dis-eases that require yearly vaccinations, but sometimes the vaccinations don't work. An animal that is on a natural diet and supplements has a better chance of resisting these diseases, or surviving them if she gets sick. Wendell Belfield treats these dis-eases by megadoses of vitamin C administered intravenously, in amounts of half a gram (500 mg) of the vitamin per pound of animal body weight twice a day. Vitamin E and selenium are added, as well as zinc, the B-complex, pantothenic acid (B-5), and B-6. The treatment must be done twice daily without missing a single treatment for a period of about five days in cases of canine and feline distemper, influenza, kennel cough and parvovirus in dogs, and upper respiratory dis-eases in cats. He has achieved remission of FIP (Feline Infectious Peritonitis—usually considered fatal) if treatment is started early enough. Raw thymus extract along with the vitamin C may help to boost the immune system. Fluids are also given intravenously to prevent dehydration.[57]

If IV injection of vitamins is out of reach, along with veterinary treatment try the following. Give no solid food while fever and vomiting are present. In cats, use a liquid fast and high amounts of powdered vitamin C dissolved in water. Use 100 mg per hour of vitamin C in this way for kittens and 250 mg per hour for adult cats. For larger dogs, increase the amounts.[58] Vitamin E 50–100 IU three times per day, and cod liver oil (vitamin A) 1/4–1 tsp. three times per day can be added. When using high doses of vitamins, decrease them gradually after the animal no longer needs them. For recovery from viral dis-eases, continue with smaller amounts of vitamins C and A, calcium/magnesium, selenium, vitamin E and B-complex. These can also alleviate central nervous system damage residues. Acupuncture is recommended in cases of nervous system damage from distemper.[59]

These suggestions are a beginning of what vitamin therapy can do in healing dogs and cats of dis-ease. The best method is to feed well and supplement daily to prevent these dis-eases, as an animal (or human) in top health will be resistant to most illness. In many cases, vitamins can have spectacular results, and in the least cases they add measurably to an animal's full recovery. Vitamin therapy is a mainstay of holistic healing. Herbs, the subject of the next chapter, is one of the oldest of holistic healing methods for people and pets.

[1] Alfred Plechner, DVM, *Pet Allergies: Remedies for an Epidemic* (Inglewood, CA: Very Healthy Enterprises, 1986), p. 95.

[2] *Ibid.*, p. 67.

[3] *Ibid.*, p. 65.

[4] *Ibid.*, p. 45, and Wendell Belfield, DVM, and Martin Zucker, *The Very Healthy Cat Book* (New York: McGraw-Hill Book Co., 1983), p. 82.

[5] Alfred Plechner, DVM, *Pet Allergies: Remedies for an Epidemic*, p. 43.

[6] *Ibid.*, p. 44.

[7] *Ibid.*

[8] Wendell Belfield, DVM, and Martin Zucker, *How to Have a Healthier Dog* (New York: New American Library, 1981), p. 51.

[9] Wendell Belfield, DVM, *The Very Healthy Cat Book* (New York: McGraw-Hill Book Co., 1983), p. 38.

[10] Wendell Belfield, DVM, *How to Have a Healthier Dog*, p. 49.

[11] *Ibid.*, pp. 56–60, and *The Very Healthy Cat Book*, pp. 49–53.

[12] Wendell Belfield, *How to Have a Healthier Dog*, pp. 67–69, and *The Very Healthy Cat Book*, pp. 58–61.

[13] Wendell Belfield, *The Very Healthy Cat Book*, p. 63.

[14] Wendell Belfield, *How to Have a Healthier Dog*, pp. 70–72.

[15] *Ibid.*, p. 72, and *The Very Healthy Cat Book*, p. 65.

[16] *Ibid.*, p. 72–47, and *The Very Healthy Cat Book*, pp. 65–66.

[17] *Ibid.*, p. 74–76, and *The Very Healthy Cat Book*, p. 66–68.

[18] *Ibid.*, p. 76–77, and *The Very Healthy Cat Book*, p. 68-69.

[19] *Ibid.*, p. 77–78, and *The Very Healthy Cat Book*, p. 68–69.

[20] *Ibid.*, p. 78–79, and *The Very Healthy Cat Book*, p. 69–70.

[21] *Ibid.*, p. 79–80, and *The Very Healthy Cat Book*, p. 70–71.

[22] *Ibid.*, p. 80–81, and *The Very Healthy Cat Book*, p. 71.

[23] *Ibid.*, p. 81–88, and *The Very Healthy Cat Book*, p. 72–76.

[24] *Ibid.*, p. 88–90, and *The Very Healthy Cat Book*, p. 77–78.

[25] *Ibid.*, p. 91, and *The Very Healthy Cat Book*, p. 79.

[26] *Ibid.*, p. 91, and *The Very Healthy Cat Book*, p. 79.

[27] *Ibid.*, p. 92, and *The Very Healthy Cat Book*, p. 79–80.

[28] *Ibid.*, p. 92, and *The Very Healthy Cat Book*, p. 80–81.

[29] Richard Pitcairn, DVM, PhD and Susan Hubble Pitcairn, *Dr. Pitcairn's Complete Guide to Natural Health for Dogs and Cats* (Emmaus, PA: Rodale Press, 1982), pp. 159–160.

[30] Anitra Frazier with Norma Eckroate, *The New Natural Cat: A Complete Guide for Finicky Owners* (New York: Plume Books, 1990), pp. 276-277.

[31] Richard Pitcairn, DVM, *Dr. Pitcairn's Complete Guide to Natural Health for Dogs and Cats*, p. 182.

[32] Anitra Frazier, *The New Natural Cat*, pp. 278-282.

[33] Wendell Belfield, *How to Have a Healthier Dog*, pp. 175–176, 190–198.

[34] *Ibid.*, pp. 230–235.

[35] Pat Lazarus, *Keep Your Pet Healthy the Natural Way* (New Canaan, CT: Keats Publishing Co., 1983), pp. 159–166.

[36] Ibid., pp. 84–85.

[37] Wendell Belfield, *How to Have a Healthier Dog*, pp. 181–182.

[38] Anitra Frazier, *The New Natural Cat*, pp. 317–318.

[39] Wendell Belfield, *The Very Healthy Cat Book*, pp. 190–191.

[40] Richard Pitcairn, DVM, *Dr. Pitcairn's Complete Guide to Natural Health for Dogs and Cats*, pp. 194–196.

[41] *Ibid.*, pp. 199–200.

[42] Pat Lazarus, *Keep Your Pet Healthy the Natural Way*, pp. 125–131.

[43] Anitra Frazier, *The New Natural Cat*, pp. 301–305.

[44] Wendell Belfield, *The Very Healthy Cat Book*, pp. 163–176.

[45] Anitra Frazier, *The New Natural Cat*, pp. 326–330.

[46] Wendell Belfield, *How to Have a Healthier Dog*, pp. 185–189.

[47] Pat Lazarus, *Keep Your Pet Healthy the Natural Way*, pp. 145–155.

[48] Richard Pitcairn, DVM, *Dr. Pitcairn's Complete Guide to Natural Health for Dogs and Cats*, pp. 215–216.

[49] Wendell Belfield, *How to Have a Healthier Dog*, pp. 226–227.

[50] Wendell Belfield, *The Very Healthy Cat Book*, pp. 199–211.

[51] Pat Lazarus, *Keep Your Pet Healthy the Natural Way*, pp. 95–97.

[52] Wendell Belfield, *How to Have a Healthier Dog*, pp. 218–221.

[53] Pat Lazarus, *Keep Your Pet Healthy the Natural Way*, p. 72.

[54] Anitra Frazier, *The New Natural Cat*, pp. 331–336.

[55] Richard Pitcairn, DVM, *Dr. Pitcairn's Complete Guide to Natural Health for Dogs and Cats*, pp. 186–190.

[56] Wendell Belfield, *How to Have a Healthier Dog*, pp. 119–203, and *The Very Healthy Cat Book*, pp. 1

[57] *Ibid.*, pp. 226–254.

[58] Richard Pitcairn, DVM, *Dr. Pitcairn's Complete Guide to Natural Health for Dogs and Cats*, p. 206.

[59] Pat Lazarus, *Keep Your Pet Healthy the Natural Way*, pp. 112.

Herbal Healing

Domestic and wild animals go to plants naturally when they need medication or internal cleansing. Every dog owner has seen her pet eat grass and selected weeds, and vomit within the hour. The animal is not the least upset, and if more is needed, she goes and looks for more. Cat owners are also aware of their pets' eagerness for grass and houseplants (some houseplants are poisonous and should be out of reach). Animals need greens for nutrition and proper digestion, and when needing a plant medicinally they intentionally seek it. Wild animals know what plants to use when they need healing, also and wild animals with their natural diet and free access to natural herbs do not suffer the dis-eases of civilization (heart disease, diabetes, kidney failure, cancer, arthritis) that plague people, dogs and cats. (This is only true today for wild animals in a clean, unpolluted environment however.)

Perhaps by watching animals medicate themselves, women first discovered herbal healing. Using plants as medicine is the oldest of the healing arts, going back many ages before written records, by oral tradition. In early foraging cultures, plants were the mainstay of the food supply, and in the search for new foods the effect on the body of various plants was noted and used. Each tribe or culture developed an herbal pharmacy, knowing what plant to use for what dis-ease, and the information was passed on from mother to daughter. Most tribes had one primary healer, trained from generation to generation by her foremothers, who was an expert in plant use and healing. As animals became domesticated, the healers treated them along with the people.

The oldest books and written treatises known, from China, India, Egypt and the ancient Middle East, contain information on using herbs to heal dis-ease in people and animals. By the time this information became written down, it had been used and refined over centuries of direct use. Egypt, seat of the western world's learning for thousands of years, housed noted schools of healing run by the healer queens. These women—among them Queen Mentuhetop (2300 BCE)—trained the herbalists who then spread the learning throughout the ancient world. They in effect started the first medical schools.[1] Their students came from Egypt, Greece, Italy, Africa and the Middle East, and they took their knowledge back to these countries. Most cultures were animal-dependent by this time—for protection, transportation, hauling, farming, wool, leather and meat. Keeping the animals well was almost as important as keeping people well.

The highly respected system of Chinese healing goes back to at least 3000–5000 BCE, when Asian herbal medicine was developed in western China. Fu Hsi is credited with the development of animal domestication and agriculture (around 4000 BCE), and Sheng Nung (around 3000 BCE) is credited with the founding of Chinese medicine. The Yellow Emperor, author of the earliest book of Chinese medicine still known, lived around 2700 BCE. The oldest remaining edition of his book is from 400 BCE, called the *Huang Ti Nei Ching* or *Nei Ching* (*Yellow Emperor's Classic of Internal Medicine*). It is still studied. It contains detailed information on herbs for healing a variety of dis-eases, as well as the basic information on acupuncture and acupressure that is still used today.[2] This book reflects the first written volume on a tradition whose exact age is unknown. Five hundred herbs and their uses are recorded in the *Nei Ching,* used in combinations of five to fifteen items. The high reputation of Chinese medicine is based primarily on its herbals.

Herbal healing was taught in classical Greece and Rome, and every world culture, tribe and geographical location had its own plants and knowledge. By the time of the resettlement of Europe in the wake of the Roman victories, the information of matriarchal peoples and their conquerors merged into a unified system of healing in the west. The early Christian convents were centers of women's learning later and were the first hospitals. The convents' method of healing was based on herbs. Hildegard of Bingen (1098–1179) wrote an herbal (*Liber Simplicis Medicinae*) that contained information on 213 plants and 55 trees. This book is considered the foremother

of the current drug industry. After her time, women's freedom and scholarship were curtailed, and so was the information on medicine that was mainly women's work. As women's status fell, so did the status and treatment of animals.

The Inquisition in Europe from the thirteenth to seventeenth centuries killed nine million people, most of them women. The target of the Church courts was certainly, if not primarily, women healers, who were the advanced medical people in each village. They were the only access to expert midwifery and health care for the lower classes, as well as for the farm and working animals of each locale. The emerging male medical system taught men only and had very little medical knowledge. Many women in Europe and some in the United States died because of their herbal healing skills, prosecuted by the Church courts for their success and hung or burned at the stake. Women who practiced the ancient Goddess/ Earth religion were also targets for the Inquisition courts and many of these were the village healers. There became no room in a "dominate and subdue" order for lifepaths or skills that were close to nature/Goddess. Animals regarded as "the witches' familiars"—usually cats, but often dogs and other small pets—frequently died at the stake, along with the witches. The mass execution of cats led later to rat-carried plagues that decimated the European population by a third.

The Inquisition destroyed the chain of thousands of years of oral tradition in Europe, and much of the knowledge of herbal medicine died with the healers and witches. With so many dead, there were few healers left to teach the traditions to their daughters and granddaughters, and those who survived were probably afraid to continue using the old traditions. The highly developed art of herbal medicine was mostly lost, and the remaining bits of knowledge (along with the Goddess/Earth religion) went underground. Much of what remained survived only in non-Church cultures, in Africa, South America, Asia, Native America, and the Near and Middle East. After the witch burnings ended, the remaining herbal traditions were ridiculed and discredited in the west by the new male medical system.[3]

The witch/midwife/healers were far from ignorant, even by today's technological standards. They knew midwifery procedures that are now lost but that are sorely needed, and unlike modern harsh drugs and invasive methods, their healing did much good and no harm. They had ergot to ease labor and shepherd's purse to stop bleeding. They used foxglove (the plant from which digitalis was synthesized) for heart dis-ease, belladonna (atropine) for an anesthetic, and white willow bark (herbal forerunner of aspirin) for pain, arthritis, inflammation and headaches. They used valerian root (natural valium) for more serious pain relief, and comfrey to heal broken bones after setting. (Remains going back to neolithic times show a knowledge of bone-setting, and of heart and even brain surgery.)

Plants were used as antiseptics, tonics, anti-spasmodics, painkillers, anti-inflammatories, contraceptives, and abortifacients; herbs were also used to promote fertility and birth. There were remedies to ease menopause symptoms, for wound and infection healing, for indigestion, for the reduction of tumors and fevers. The healers were also aware of the need for at least basic sanitation, something discovered by male medicine only much later. Nuns in the Middle Ages, long before the advent of penicillin, knew about the bread-mold that healed seemingly hopeless infections.

Since the 1960s herbal healing has been rediscovered in the United States and is celebrating a revival throughout the west. Much of the lost knowledge is being relearned and reclaimed, and women are satisfied with the effectiveness and safety of herbs. Because herbs are considered foods, the FDA so far has had little control over them, though increasingly repressive laws are being introduced in Congress. The multi-billion dollar a year drug industry looks upon herbals with a jaundiced eye—they take money from the corporations by reducing their sales—but so far has had no success in curtailing their use.

Various herbs like lobelia (for chest and lung congestion, coughs and pneumonia) have been claimed to be "toxic" and removed from the market, to return by popular demand sometime later. The latest claims of toxicity are for comfrey and sassafras—comfrey for bone and internal healing, and sassafras for menopause and tonics—but the claims are totally unfounded, usually based on one case of misuse with no other validation. These herbs have been used by women for healing people and animals for thousands of years and are thoroughly researched by time and tradition. The big business interests are threatened by herbal medicine because it works.

Herbs compare favorably to medical drugs in a number of important ways. The drug industry isolates and synthesizes a plant's "active ingredient" so it can patent it and call it a drug. Herbs, as foods, are not patentable and therefore not subject to monopolies and high profits. Because herbs contain the complete and natural plant, however, herbals hold all instead of only one of the plant's full properties. This use of the whole plant compound is a primary reason why herbs for healing have none of the negative side effects that occur with synthesized drugs. Herbs contain lower concentrations of the active ingredient than medical drugs, and they contain them in natural (rather than synthesized/artificial) form. An herb may take somewhat longer for healing, but it heals without harm or discomfort and just as effectively. A well-made herb tincture is powerful, yet offers no negative effects; it does not make people or pets sicker than they already are, as so many medical drugs do. Herbalists feel that safe healing can come only from the full herb. By isolating the known active property from the full plant, necessary ingredients with benefits that may not be known are lost.

Another advantage to herbs is that they have a long herstory. When a women uses valerian or echinacea, for example, she knows exactly what it will do since many generations of healers have learned its properties. This information is increasingly available in books and other sources. Most medical drugs are put on the market with dubious amounts of testing and without the test of time. Many medical drugs have severe side effects, with damage that may not be apparent until years later. The medical/veterinary system refuses to acknowledge the negative effects of drugs, though high percentages of users may experience them in varying degrees of seriousness. None of this is an issue with herbs. Herbalists consider anything a drug or herb does to be its properties; negative properties are not side effects, they are the drug's real effects. Any herb with negative properties has been dropped from the pharmacopia long ago. There are no negative side effects with healing herbs.

Cost and availability are other factors that make herbs desirable. If a healing plant cannot be picked fresh in one's backyard, it can be found almost as easily in a health food store and at very low cost. Herbs are inexpensive—under a dollar an ounce for raw dried plant matter, under two dollars for a box of herbal tea bags, about six dollars for most bottled herb tinctures, or under ten dollars for a hundred prepared capsules. Medical drugs are much more expensive, the average prescription today costing as much as seventy-five dollars, and veterinary prescriptions have gone up considerably as well.

Using herbs gives people back some of the power to take care of themselves and their pets and to be free from a domineering, seemingly uncaring, medical system. Too much money and greed goes with today's medical/veterinary technology. The drug companies push their newest products at the highest price the traffic will bear; doctors and veterinarians are coerced into using these items. They are told they are depriving their patients if they don't use them. The result is higher and higher prices for both medical and veterinary care, with more and more people dissatisfied with the results for themselves and their pets. The high pressured abuse by greed, and the over-use of ineffective drugs and technology, keeps more people and animals medically and veterinary dependent, but not getting well. People feel more and more helpless, faced with their own suffering and their pets'. Moreover, the life expectancy of people and animals is decreasing. By working with herbs, which are totally safe, inexpensive and have no negative side effects, women take back their empowerment—and heal themselves and their dogs and cats.

There are several reasons then, why herbal healing is desirable. It is far cheaper than veterinary drugs and far safer. The products are easily available and require no prescription. Using them removes people and pets from the greed of the drug companies and their coercion of the medical/veterinary system. When the means for healing is easily available and known to be safe and effective, women are also more likely to begin treatment earlier. Instead of waiting until the illness becomes a crisis, healing is started at the beginning when any dis-ease is the most easily cured. Herbs become a first line of defense. If the condition doesn't improve or worsens, the trip to the veterinarian is next. Herbs can take the place of many veterinary or human medical drugs and can often be used along with them.

Herbs for animal healing come in several different forms. Loose dried plant matter is generally made into a tea or infusion (decoction is the term for roots or barks). They can be used dry by sprinkling them onto pet food, as well. Make sure the herbs you buy are fresh and buy only as much as needed. They should smell good with a strong green smell and have good color, with no apparent mustiness or mold. Dried herbs last, if kept in a dark cool place, for about a year but gradually lose their potency

over time. Some more common herbs come in supermarket or health food store tea bags, like chamomile, peppermint leaf or raspberry leaf. They are already premeasured for herbal teas, but are on the weak side. Again, smell them for freshness and keep on the shelf no longer than a year. Teas made of herbs are used by the spoonful, placed into the cat's or dog's mouth or lapped up in water or food.

Healing herbs also come prepared in gelatin capsules, but these are less recommended for pets, and freshness is an issue here, also. Dogs and cats are both carnivores with better ability to digest and assimilate meat than plant matter. Herbs administered in capsules must be digested before they can reach the animal's bloodstream and begin having healing effects. And first you have to get the capsules into the pet to begin with, often involving an unpleasant wrestling match.

Herb tinctures are a further way to use herbs, in my experience the easiest and most potent. They are preserved in alcohol and are highly concentrated. Kept in brown bottles in a cool place they never lose potency, so freshness isn't an issue. Administered with an eyedropper into the cat's or dog's cheek pouch or put into food, are the easiest methods to get herbs into an animal. The pet may not like the taste, but it goes down fast. Instead of going through the digestive system, the liquid goes right into the bloodstream and begins working immediately. Only a couple of drops of an herb tincture are used in pet healing, so the tinctures last a long time and are highly economical.

To prepare an herb tea or stronger infusion using plant leaves, flowers or stems, put a teaspoon to a tablespoonful of dried herb matter into a tea basket and mug. If you are using fresh green plants, use three times the amount. Add a cup of boiling water made in a stainless steel, ceramic, enameled or glass container (no copper, aluminum or teflon) to the herbs and let steep. A good tea or infusion is made in five to thirty minutes' steeping, though the herbs become bitter if left longer than fifteen minutes. A tea uses the lesser amount of herbs and steeping time, an infusion greater amounts of herbs and more time. Strain out the plant matter and cool. Give a half-teaspoonful for a kitten, one or two teaspoonsful for a grown cat or small dog, and increase the amount accordingly for larger dogs. Give the remedy three or four times a day. In short-term healing, the tea may be needed only for a few days to a week; for longer chronic conditions use the tea twice a day for as long as several weeks, decreasing gradually. Leftover tea, once strained, can be kept in the refrigerator overnight; make sure it doesn't sour.

When the tea is made from harder plant parts, bark or woody stems, put an ounce of plant matter into a pot with a pint of water and bring to a boil. The flame can be shut off when the water reaches the boiling point and steeped or boiled for two minutes. Cooled and then strained, it is used the same way as a tea. To make a decoction, a very strong tea, boil the herbs for as long as thirty minutes, until half the water is gone.[4] A decoction is *strong,* use the same amounts for a much stronger dose, and use it two to four times a day.

Juliette de Bairacli Levy, dog breeder and herbalist, makes her tea infusions somewhat differently. For a standard infusion, she uses two heaping tablespoonsful of the dried herb to a pint of cold water. Simmer to near boiling, but do not boil. Then take the pot off the heat to steep for four hours. Do not strain, but pour into a clean covered jar, where it will keep for two to three days without souring. Her average dose for a medium sized (cocker spaniel) dog is two tablespoonsful morning and night. She gives the liquid by placing it in a plastic squeeze bottle, putting the nozzle in the animal's cheek pouch, and slowly squeezing the dose in.

To make a strong infusion, she uses two heaping tablespoonsful of herbs to each cup (half pint) of water. Heat to the boiling point, boil for no longer than three minutes, then take the pot off the heat. Steep overnight or for at least seven hours, keeping the mixture tightly covered. After steeping, pour into a jar, do not strain.[5]

If using store-bought tea bags, it takes two to make a reasonably strong tea/infusion, steeped as for loose herbs. Loose dried herbs can also be made into small balls with honey and pushed all the way down a dog's throat—I don't recommend this with cats—or sprinkled on the animal's food. Like capsules, however, the herb must go through the digestive system when given as a solid, where liquids move much faster. This takes longer to have effect, and as dogs and cats assimilate plant matter less easily, some of the healing properties of the herb may be lost. Some herbs, like raw garlic for an antibacterial/antiviral, may be easier fed to a cat in capsules, though most dogs like a garlic taste. Other herbs, like goldenseal, taste too bad for any pet to accept by mouth, and here's where herb tinctures are so useful.

Herb tinctures are easily bought in health food stores but also can be made at home. They are used in very small amounts, five drops of a tincture is the equivalent to a teaspoon of loose dried herb matter. They are highly concentrated and the dosage for a cat is only about two drops used three or four times per day. The drops can be put into the cheek pouch of the animal's mouth, or placed in food or a teaspoon of water or broth. (Placed in a teaspoonful of *hot* water or broth, the alcohol content evaporates off.) Herb tinctures are always fresh; they keep permanently and never spoil because they are prepared in alcohol which is a preservative. Tinctures may also be prepared in apple cider vinegar, but these keep a maximum of two years.

To make a tincture at home, place six to eight ounces of dried plant matter into a quart jar, and fill the rest of the jar up with sixty proof or higher drinking alcohol (brandy or vodka). Let stand for two to six weeks, shaking the bottle night and morning. Then strain out the herbs, squeezing them to keep as much of the plant matter in the liquid as possible, and discard the used herbs. Store the tincture in brown glass eyedropper bottles with glass eyedroppers. Women who use these must make them in advance and many keep a medicine cabinet of prepared tinctures. They are the most potent way to use herbals, and the easiest to administer because of the amount used.[6]

These are internal ways to use herbs; they also may be used in poultices or compresses externally for wounds or skin dis-eases. A compress is made by wetting a washcloth in an herbal tea, usually hot but not uncomfortably so, and placing it on the animal. When the cloth cools, replace it with another one also soaked in the tea. A poultice is made by using the tea dregs, with the plant matter usually strained out, in a gauze packet bound to the skin by bandages. Use as hot as can be comfortably tolerated, but be careful not to burn sensitive pet skin. Dried herbs can be made into a paste with a few drops of boiling water, then cooled and also used as a poultice.[7] Herb tinctures can be used as compresses externally. Remember, however, that they are made with alcohol, and if the alcohol might burn the skin dilute it with water. Herbs are also used externally as salves, mixed with softened beeswax or calendula cream and placed on the skin. They are safe if licked off and very soothing.

One further way to use herbs is based upon homeopathy (see the next chapter), and is preferred by holistic veterinarian Dr. Richard Pitcairn. The method is described by Anitra Frazier in *The New Natural Cat* (Plume Books, 1990):[8]

1. Into a new one-ounce glass dropper bottle put 2/3 bottle full of distilled or spring water and 3 drops of herbal tincture.
2. Cover and shake vigorously 108 times, hitting bottle against a thick rug or padded arm of a chair each time.
3. Shake 12 times before each use.
4. Dosage is 1/4 dropperful 20 minutes before meals.
5. Keeps in refrigerator 7 days.

More on how and why this homeopathic remedy works in the next chapter. She suggests that where herbs are used as nutrients, use the tincture; when they are used to heal a dis-ease or condition, use the elixir.

As was noted in the last chapter, infectious dis-eases and fevers are more easily healed when treatment is used with a liquid fast. Juliette de Bairacli Levy insists on the importance of this with herbal healing, and also supports it with a daily laxative (she uses senna pods, an herb) or warm water enemas. Her reasons for this are given below.

Treatment must begin with a fast of at least two days on water or honey-water only. Two to three days is usually sufficient to cure a straightforward fever case. During fasting all the body powers released from food digestion are concentrated on elimination of internal toxins, and therefore chances of curing the ailments are made more favorable. Urgency of toxin elimination supplies the important reason for use of a daily laxative when fasting or on the fluid diet of milk and honey. During long fasts if there is no natural bowel action, a warm-water enema is given. Until the temperature is normal and steady at normal, fasting *must* be continued. To feed solid foods during a fever means complication of the ailment and often also fatal results.[9]

One further caution: while the same herbs used for healing humans are also used safely for both dogs and cats, there are a couple of notable exceptions. Cats are highly sensitive and some herbs may affect them differently than they would a dog or a person. Marigold, marijuana, and cocoa are poisonous to cats, and catnip is an aphrodisiac (where in humans and dogs it is a sedative and digestive calmative).[10] When in doubt, check with a holistic veterinarian or herbalist. The leaves, sprouts and tubers of the common food potato plant, and the rhubarb plant, are also poisonous to both dogs and cats. A chart is given of some common houseplants—*not* medicinal herbals—that are also poisonous to cats. Many of them are

poisonous to dogs as well. Other than marigold and catnip, which are safe for dogs and humans, you will not see any of these recommended for herbal healing here or elsewhere. Since they are in the daily environment, however, women need to be aware of them, and a chapter on plants seems the place to make them known. Again, these are not healing herbs.

With these things in mind, some recommendations follow for treating cat and dog dis-eases with herbal healing. I have used the same list of dis-eases in the last chapter. Herbs are used along with vitamins and optimal nutrition for pets, and the optimal nutrition is essential. Major sources for the remedies that follow are: Juliette de Bairacli Levy, *The Complete Herbal Handbook for the Dog and Cat* (Faber and Faber, 1955 and 1991), Dr. Richard Pitcairn's *Complete Guide to Natural Health for Dogs and Cats* (Rodale Press, 1982), and Anitra Frazier, *The New Natural Cat* (Plume Books, 1990). My years of healing with herbs is added.

Says Dr. Richard Pitcairn, respected holistic veterinarian, about herbal veterinary medicine:

As compared to their pharmaceutical counterparts, herbs exhibit a slower and deeper action. They assist the healing process by helping the body to eliminate and detoxify, thus taking care of the problem the symptoms are expressing. For instance, they may stimulate physiological processes like the emptying of the bowels or urination. In addition they can serve as tonics and builders that resonate with and strengthen tissues in specific parts of the body (or the whole body, depending on the herb in question). Finally, they can be highly nutritious, containing large amounts of various vitamins and minerals.[11]

Allergies: Avoid cortisone and steroids. Herbal healing for this begins with a few days' fast to eliminate toxins, followed by a whole foods or preservative-free diet. Support the detoxifying process with warm-water enemas and such herbs as yarrow, yellow dock, dandelion or red clover. Remember the vitamins of the last chapter. Anitra Frazier makes the following recommendations as part of her extensive allergy protocol for cats, and the same herbs in larger doses are fine for dogs, as well.

For a stuffy nose, give three drops in each nostril of warm saline nose drops. If you add two drops of goldenseal extract to 1/4 cup of the solution it will kill germs and viruses and shrink swollen tissue. For red itchy eyes you can use the same solution for eye drops.

Some Common Poisonous Plants
The plants in the following chart are poisonous to humans as well as cats.

Plants	Poisonous Parts	Symptoms
Bittersweet *Celastrus* spp.	Bark, leaves and seeds	Vomiting, diarrhea, convulsions, coma
Dumb cane *Dieffenbachia*	All parts	Swelling in throat, vomiting, diarrhea; death can result.
Poison hemlock *Conium maculatum*	All parts	Dizziness, all loss of muscular control, disordered vision (within 15-45 minutes)
Ivy, English and Baltic *Hedera helix*	Berries and leaves	Labored breathing, diarrhea, coma
Jimson weed, thorn apple *Datura* spp.	All parts (extremely poisonous)	Intense thirst, rapid pulse, convulsions, coma, death
Marigold, marsh marigold *Caltha palustris*	All parts	Mouth irritation, salivation, diarrhea, nervousness
Marijuana, hemp *Cannabis sativa*	Resinous substance	Blurred vision, coma, drowsiness, and loss of coordination
Mistletoe *Phoradendron serotinum*	White berries	Vomiting, diarrhea, convulsions, coma
Oleander *Nerium oleander*	All parts (extremely poisonous)	Vomiting, abnormal heartbeat, coma, death may occur.
Philodendron *Philodendron* spp.	All parts	Swelling of mouth and throat, vomiting and diarrhea; death may result from blockage of windpipe
Poinsettia *Euphorbia pulcherrima*	All parts	Rash or blistering of skin, mouth and throat irritation, vomiting and diarrhea
Poison Ivy *Rhus radicans*	All parts	Itching, redness of skin, small blisters; local swelling of flesh may occur
Potato *Solanum tubersum*	Unripe tubers, sprouts from tubers	Vomiting, diarrhea, coma, stupification
Rhubarb *Rheum rhaponticum*	Leaf blades	Vomiting, muscular weakness, slow pulse, coma and death, even from small amounts

Judy Fireman, Ed., *Cat Catalog: The Ultimate Cat Book* (New York: Workman Publishing Co., 1976), p. 198. (The text of this chart is adapted from *Arnoldia,* a publication of the Arnold Arboretum of Harvard University.)

For itchy skin, massage in Lemon Rinse (an herb tea made by pouring a pint of boiling water over a thinly sliced skin-and-all lemon; let stand twenty-four hours.

For diarrhea and/or vomiting, give one teaspoon slippery elm syrup before each meal.

For asthma, put three drops of oil of eucalyptus in a cup of boiling water and let the patient breathe the fumes.[12]

Willow bark is also an herbal antihistamine. You should not use it on cats. Another is Kyolic, odorless garlic, which comes in liquid or capsules. It is also a detoxifier.

Many pets suffer allergic reactions from the bites of fleas and are miserable all summer with the resulting skin rashes. Feeding a combination of brewer's yeast and garlic (raw or powder) makes the dogs or cats less attractive to fleas, as does putting a teaspoon of apple cider vinegar in each pint of drinking water. These must be continued every day. Instead of chemical flea collars, which contain nerve gases, and which many cats and dogs are allergic to, try an herbal collar scented with oil of pennyroyal, citronella, cedar or eucalyptus. Pat Lazarus says: "A necklace made of eucalyptus nuts seems to be more effective for getting rid of fleas than all the highly touted chemical flea powders. . . ."[13] Use brewer's yeast as a flea powder, also.

Susan R. Griffin, pet groomer and developer of Critter Oil, a natural flea shampoo, suggests making your own citrus rinse as follows:

Take oranges, lemons, grapefruit, etc., and boil them down in a large pot—skins and all—then strain out the residue; or eat the fruit first and use the rest to boil. Depending upon the strength of the mixture, dilute this further before using it on your pet. You can also add this to your basic pet shampoo and make it into a flea shampoo.[14]

She has developed a safe herbal product for use in her grooming shop. It is mixed with shampoo, plain water, or placed straight on pet collars, in pet bedding and in home carpets. Critter Oil is made of herbal essential oils of lemon, cedarwood, grapefruit, pennyroyal, eucalyptus, sage and other herbs. It smells great and it works, even in Florida. Note however that fragrant oils used on or around a pet can antidote homeopathic remedies, if homeopathy is being used for healing. For more information on Critter Oil, write to the SuDi Company, P.O. Box 12767, St. Petersburg, FL 33733.

Arthritis and Hip Dysplasia: Begin here also with a fast, followed by a change of diet. Vitamin C is highly important. The classic herb tea for arthritis is equal parts of alfalfa, white willow bark and burdock. For cats, leave out the willow, as cats are aspirin intolerant. This is a detoxifier (alfalfa, burdock), anti-inflammatory and pain reliever (willow), and nutrient high in all the vitamins and minerals (alfalfa). It tastes good, and as a nutrient is better made in a tea/infusion than used in tinctures or elixirs. Mix with food or give by placing the liquid in the dog's or cat's cheek pouch, if they will not accept it unforced.

A variation of this is to feed two to six alfalfa tablets per day, especially for thin, nervous dogs or cats with a tendency to digestive problems along with the joint pain. For overweight animals with hip pain, especially those that eat high meat diets, add a third to three cloves of grated garlic to each meal.[15] Garlic may also be used in odorless form, Kyolic, which comes in liquid, tablets or capsules. Alternatives to alfalfa include kelp tablets, or yucca. These are nutrient herbs that may be used long term.

Anitra Frazier suggests Kombu broth, which is similar to kelp, in the amount of up to a quarter cup per meal for cats (more for dogs). Other choices are celery seed infusion (one teaspoon per meal) or dandelion root decoction (a quarter teaspoon per meal). For pain, try infusions or tinctures of chickweed, valerian root or feverfew.[16] Feverfew is highly recommended, and scullcap is a less sedative pain reliever than valerian. She also suggests a poultice or compress of rosemary leaves, used externally over affected joints. Her dosage for alfalfa tablets is half a tablet added crushed to food once a day for cats.

Herbalist Juliette de Bairacli Levy uses rosemary internally, and feeds chopped raw parsley and comfrey leaves with the pet's food. Nettles is also a detoxifier. Use an external massage lotion made of four tablespoons olive oil, one tablespoon linseed or sunflower oil, and a half teaspoon eucalyptus oil.[17] Castor oil packs used externally over the affected area can also help tremendously.[18] Place the oil on a washcloth or on the inside of a disposable diaper and bind into place. Leave for about an hour; the same pack is reusable. Discourage the animal from licking this—it is laxative. Wash off with baking soda in water.

All of these choices are familiar to women who use herbs, and they are also effective on people. All of these are easy to locate in health food stores, and many of them grow easily in wild places or garden herb patches.

Cancer and Tumors: A strong infusion of red clover and blue violet leaf taken twice daily over a period of time has been known to reduce and dissolve tumors in humans and pets. It is particularly helpful in breast tumors. Juliette de Bairacli Levy also suggests garlic, turnip, aloe vera juice or organic grape juice used internally (and externally) as choices.[19] In the case of breast tumors, check thyroid function, and use raw thyroid extract glandular or Edgar Cayce's Atomidine if the thyroid checks low. Castor oil packs can also help greatly.

In her critique of this manuscript, Gloria Dodd, DVM also suggests:

Breast tumors can be related to disturbed energies in the teeth. Voll found interrelationships of organs to teeth. A specific tooth is related to a specific organ and vice versa. For example, the lower molars and upper premolars are related to the breasts. The third lateral incisor (canine) tooth is related to the liver, hip joint and the visual part of the eye (hence "eye tooth").

Check the teeth for abscesses or other pathologies; healing these may cause the tumor to dissolve with no other treatment.

Richard Pitcairn uses goldenseal tincture made into an elixir, using one drop twice a day for cats and small dogs, two drops twice a day for medium sized dogs, and three drops twice a day for large or giant breeds.[20] If the symptoms worsen, stop; and repeat the dosage when the condition stabilizes again. Most animals show consistent improvement. See the chapter on homeopathy for more on this, as an elixir is a homeopathic remedy.

Another herbal recipe for cancer, leukemia and other immune system dis-eases is called Essiac. This is a human recipe that may also be used for pets. The formula requires:

6-1/2 cups burdock root
16 ounces sheep sorrel (the active ingredient, make sure it is sorrel and not a substitute)
1 ounce turkey rhubarb root
4 ounces slippery elm bark

In a stainless steel pot, bring five gallons of sodium-free distilled water to a boil. Stir in one cup of the Essiac formula and boil for ten minutes. Turn off stove, scraping the herbs from the pot sides, cover, and steep for twelve hours. Then turn on the stove to full heat for twenty minutes. Strain the liquid twice, pour it hot into dark bottles, and refrigerate. To use for a medium sized dog, heat a tablespoon of distilled water in a stainless steel pot and add a tablespoon of Essiac (four tablespoons each for humans). Take once daily on an empty stomach. For more information and the source of this recipe, contact Dr. Gary Glum, Silent Walker Publishing Company, P.O. Box 92856, Los Angeles, CA 90009.

Other anti-cancer herbs include pau d'arco, chaparral, Jason Winters' Tea, echinacea, black radish, Oregon grape root, dandelion, yellow dock, burdock or periwinkle (vinca). Herbalist May Bethel in *The Healing Power of Herbs* offers the following recipe:[21]

1 ounce red clover
1 ounce burdock seed
2 ounces Oregon grape root
1/2 ounce bloodroot

Steep these in a pint of water and a pint of apple cider vinegar for two hours, strain, and take four times a day for growth and tumors anywhere in the body. For humans use a glassful; for pets use a teaspoon to a tablespoon, depending on the size of the animal. These herbs are also available in tinctures.

Cataracts: A natural diet is essential, beginning with a few days' detoxifying fast. The chemicals in supermarket foods are much to blame for the development of cataracts in animals and people. A natural remedy that has proved successful for Dr. Richard Pitcairn is eucalyptus honey: apply a small dab inside the lower eyelid once a day with the blunt end of a toothpick, or put one drop in each eye with an eyedropper. The process takes several weeks. Order the honey from Natural Sales Co., P.O. Box 25, Pittsburgh, PA 15230.[22] Cineraria eyedrops can also do the job, or eyebright tea (not tincture) used internally and as eyedrops. Another herbal favorite for cataracts is greater celandine tea used twice daily as an eyewash.

Constipation and Diarrhea: To alleviate constipation in dogs or cats, mix a teaspoonful for cats or more for dogs of grated raw carrot, grated raw garlic or raw fruit into the food. This can be used a couple of times a week as a preventive, or add half a teaspoon to a tablespoon of bran to meals as needed. A little milk, olive oil, or melted butter are also laxative for pets. Juliette de Bairacli Levy uses dried fruits—figs, dates, coconut, raisins, and especially prunes.[23] Avoid chemical laxatives and mineral oil. For pets with chronic constipation, take a close look at the animal's diet.

For constipation in cats, Anitra Frazier uses a half teaspoon of powdered bran mixed with a half teaspoon of butter; cats accept this as a treat. She uses a stool softener treat as follows:[24]

1 Tbsp. babyfood vegetables and meat
1/2 tsp. melted butter
1/8 tsp. *ground* psyllium husks
1/8 tsp. powdered bran
2 Tbsp. or more of water

Also use the ground psyllium husks and water by themselves as a laxative.

For diarrhea, withhold solid food and give slippery elm syrup, or carob powder mixed with water and honey (half to two teaspoonsful three times a day for three days).[25] For dogs catnip tea helps. Add a quarter teaspoon of cinnamon to these, it is binding. Blackberry tea, easily found in supermarkets as tea bags, also stops diarrhea. Anitra Frazier uses Kombu seaweed in chicken broth (liquid diet) for cats, and one-eighth teaspoon of liquid chlorophyll three times a day in the broth. A teaspoon of liquid acidophilus helps to restore intestinal bacterial balance. For serious cases, put five drops of goldenseal tincture into half a cup of water; give one or two teaspoonsful twice a day between meals.[26]

Kaopectate is also an alternative, as are activated charcoal tablets. Use a teaspoon of Kaopectate for cats and small dogs and up to four tablespoonsful for large dogs every four hours. Charcoal is good for absorbing toxins and poisons (food poisoning, garbage can raiding) but it interferes with normal digestion. Use half to one teaspoon of the powder or one to three tablets, every two or three hours for twenty-four hours only.[27] Honey with lemon juice, apple juice, or garlic capsules are also recommended.

Diabetes: Along with a sugar free, preservative free natural diet, some food herbs are helpful in reducing blood sugar levels. These include grated carrots, Jerusalem artichokes, garlic, alfalfa (sprouts or dried herb), dandelion greens, and onions. Herbs for diabetes include

dandelion, buchu, mullein, alfalfa, parsley, and periwinkle. Yarrow tea contains some of the active ingredients of insulin, and goldenseal can reduce blood sugar levels significantly. Stevia, an herbal sweetener, also balances blood sugar.[28] Anitra Frazier suggests giving cats a teaspoon to a tablespoonful of dill seed or horsetail grass made into a tea with each meal, as well as one drop of stevia and a teaspoon of chopped alfalfa sprouts.[29] Amounts are higher for larger dogs.

In using these suggestions with pets, it is essential to monitor blood sugar levels carefully, as these can change the animal's insulin needs. It is also essential to use whatever herb or method you choose consistently; once begun, it must be used every day, or the insulin levels change. If it is at all possible to control your pet's blood sugar without insulin, with diet and holistic remedies, the animal will be much better off.

Feline Leukemia: Vitamin C is the key to feline leukemia, which many pet experts believe is caused by chronic lead poisoning. Pat Lazarus recommends laetrile, the vitamin B-17 made from fruit pit kernels (apricot, apple, peach), 50 mg orally two to three times per day, for reducing high fevers in feline leukemia (also cancer). This substance has been banned by the FDA because of its potentially toxic cyanide content. Lazarus says that once the fruit pits have been ground up, they should be refrigerated and should not be put in water, as water will release the cyanide (ingestion will not). She states that in recommended doses, laetrile is not toxic, though it can be toxic when overdosed. She believes in it as a cure.[30] For those wishing to try laetrile, seek the advice of an expert.

Two drops of goldenseal tincture (or one drop made into an elixir) are more frequently used, along with the vitamin C. If the cat's symptoms worsen, stop; repeat the dosage when the condition stabilizes. Most cats respond by consistent improvement. (See the homeopathy chapter for information on using the elixir, which is a homeopathic remedy.) Anitra Frazier also suggests an infusion/tea made with Korean white ginseng and caraway seeds in equal parts. This stimulates appetite and adds minerals. Put a teaspoon of this tea into each meal.[31]

Heart Dis-ease and Hypertension: Hawthorne berry is the traditional herb for strengthening the heart and reducing blood pressure. It may be used as a tea, tincture or elixir daily long term. The major heart drug, digitalis, was synthesized from the foxglove plant and has been used by herbalists for centuries. It should be used only under expert supervision. A safer herbal with digitalis-like properties is lily of the valley flowers, used as a heart tonic. However, use this herbal only with knowledgeable help.

Juliette de Bairacli Levy recommends rosemary tea with honey as her central herbal for heart dis-ease and heart weakness in dogs or cats. She adds one level teaspoonful of pure honey to every tablespoon of rosemary infusion administered. Use in addition, dandelion and/or watercress in one meal daily, as a diuretic and for their mineral contents (iron, potassium, copper). Heartsease (wild pansy) is another heart tonic herb.[32]

Parsley or dill seed tea (like dandelion and watercress) make excellent herbal diuretics. These can take the place of medical drugs. Bearberry (uva ursi), juniper or buchu are also herbal diuretics. Alfalfa is important to regulate blood pressure and reduce cholesterol, and it increases the action of other herbs taken with it. Scullcap is a safe calmative, as is peppermint tea, and a combination of scullcap, cayenne and goldenseal is a heart strengthener. (This tastes bad, so use it in capsules.)[33]

Injuries, Cuts and Burns: These are for injuries and burns not serious enough to require veterinary care. For cuts, stop the bleeding by sprinkling goldenseal powder directly into the wound. Goldenseal is an antiseptic, often working when bleeding is hard to stop. (Cayenne pepper will do the same thing, but it smarts.) Goldenseal tincture, five drops added to a cup or less of pure water, can be used to clean out cuts and wounds, as well as to irrigate abscesses. On the final rinse, add five drops of calendula tincture for rapid healing. A saline solution or hydrogen peroxide are also used to wash out cuts and wounds, even in sensitive cats.[34]

Hypericum tincture (St. John/Joan's wort) taken internally eases pain and speeds healing where tissues have been torn or nerves damaged. Where cuts are severe, use echinacea or garlic internally to prevent infection. For infected cats, echinacea or goldenseal in a compress (also taken internally) are antibiotics. Keep the animal on either for a few days longer once the infection seems healed. A number of "green salves" are available, containing such ingredients as goldenseal, comfrey and chickweed, or comfrey and plantain, or calendula and hypericum, or goldenseal and hypericum. These are wonderful for healing cuts, rashes and abrasions, and are highly soothing.

Burns (first or second degree, scalds) are first treated by immersing the area in cold water for at least ten to fifteen minutes. Then bathe the injured area in apple cider vinegar, and afterwards spread honey thickly over the burn. On long haired animals, clip the hair away from the burn or scald before applying the honey. Grated raw potato pulp also makes a good poultice for burns,[35] as does honey with calendula, or honey with comfrey. Aloe vera is the classic herbal for burns; break off a leaf of the plant and use the gel, which can also be mixed with vitamin E. Increase the animal's vitamin C intake during the time of healing to prevent infections.

Skin and Coat Ailments: Begin with a detoxifying fast, then change the pet's diet to a preservative free or hypoallergenic diet with the vitamin supplements discussed earlier. Additions of kelp for iodine, and a teaspoon of apple cider vinegar to each pint of drinking water for potassium, can make a significant difference in cases of hair loss and skin problems.[36] A classic skin remedy is to wash the areas with a cooled infusion of blue violet leaf and red clover—this has been known effective even for skin cancers, and can also be taken internally. Use goldenseal tea or infusion as a wash or compress for open sores, especially where there is pus.

Dr. Richard Pitcairn uses a poultice or wash of very strong green or black tea, or a strong infusion of goldenseal root made with two teaspoons of the herb to a pint of water. Aloe vera is also helpful. For long term itchy, greasy skin, use internally three capsules of garlic or Kyolic daily, or a quarter to one clove of grated garlic placed daily in the pet's food. Bathe the animal weekly if the skin is greasy, and use Lemon Rinse at the end of the bath.

To make Lemon Rinse, cut a whole lemon into thin slices (including the skin). Pour a pint of boiling water over it, and let steep for twenty-four hours. When used as a skin rinse, it need not be washed off.[37] For dry skin, add a teaspoonful of olive oil to food once a day until the skin condition is relieved, then use the oil daily or twice a week. Dog Oil or Cat Oil will take the place of this. For blood cleansing, important in most skin conditions, use burdock with red clover, yarrow, sassafras, Oregon grape root, alfalfa or parsley internally.[38] These can be used during the liquid fast.

Spinal Problems: Scullcap or hypericum (St. John/Joan's wort) are herbs that help to repair the nervous system and ease pain. Valerian, scullcap or feverfew are pain relievers and relaxants, and white willow is an anti-inflammatory (not for use with cats). Alfalfa is an important nutrient. All of the above are used internally.

The best hope in treating spinal problems in dogs and cats is not in herbs but in acupuncture and chiropractic. The above herbs can help with pain and inflammation and are calmative. They support the bodywork, but do not replace it.

Urinary Tract Infections, Kidney and Bladder Disease: At first sign of bladder infection, replace a third of the pet's drinking water with unsweetened (health food store) cranberry juice. This can stop many urologic infections quickly and completely; like vitamin C it acidifies the environment and makes the bladder and urinary tract inhospitable to the infection bacteria. Herbs for bladder infections/feline urologic syndrome (FUS) include juniper, buchu, couchgrass, cornsilk, parsley, marshmallow (mallow) root, nettles, dandelion, watercress, uva ursi (bearberry) or yarrow. Bearberry, sage and horsetail grass used together are a good combination, and parsley or nettles are highly recommended. Antibiotic herbs include echinacea, goldenseal or pau d'arco.[39]

Dr. Richard Pitcairn recommends horsetail grass for cats with chronic FUS (feline urologic syndrome). Steep two teaspoons of the herb in half a cup of hot water, and give a quarter of a teaspoon of the infusion three times a day for a week or more. Urtica urens (stinging nettles) is another recommended herb for cats. For cats or dogs with bladder or kidney stones, use barberry root. Briefly boil a teaspoon of the root in a cup of water, let it steep five minutes and strain. Give three times a day in the following dose amounts: one teaspoon for a cat or small dog; two teaspoons for a medium-small dog; a tablespoon for a medium sized dog; two tablespoons for a large dog; and three tablespoons for the giant breeds.

He suggests sarsaparilla root where there are small stones and gravel in the urine. Use a teaspoon of the root to a cup of water, steep until cool and strain. Give it three times a day in these amounts: two teaspoons to a cat or small dog, four teaspoons to a medium-small dog; two tablespoons for a medium sized dog; four tablespoons to a large dog; and six tablespoons for a giant dog.[40]

Viral Dis-eases: For feline or canine distemper or other infectious dis-eases, use the vitamin C therapy described in the vitamin chapter. According to Juliette de Bairacli Levy, the high incidence of death in these diseases has been because of the practice of forced feeding. Animals with infectious dis-eases should be on a liquid fast for as long as the fever continues, and not started on solid foods until the normal temperature remains steady

(about 101.5°F for dogs and cats). Liquids used in the fast include honey-water, health food store pure grape juice or apple juice, with an average dose for a cocker spaniel sized dog two tablespoonsful three times a day. Fresh water should be available at all times, and there can be honey in the water.

Also give several tablespoonsful of water with very diluted lemon juice (a teaspoon of the juice to two tablespoons of water). Clean the eyes and nose with cotton balls dipped in infusions of rosemary, elder flowers, or chickweed. After the fever, break the fast with slippery elm powder added to water or milk, with a half teaspoon of cinnamon to each cup of slippery elm if there is still diarrhea. Use antibiotic or herbs during the full treatment: goldenseal, echinacea or garlic. Levy says that when the fasting is observed, there is seldom or never the nervous system damage that occurs when an animal with distemper is force-fed.[41]

Dr. Pitcairn uses the above protocol and adds the following herb combinations for canine and feline distemper. For dogs, use either the goldenseal elixir, or the following herb combination:

7 parts powdered goldenseal root
2 parts powdered licorice root
1 part powdered ginger root

Stir the powder into a little water, or put the dry powder into capsules. Use the following amounts: an eighth teaspoon for puppies and very small dogs given twice a day; an eighth teaspoon for small dogs given three times a day; a quarter teaspoon twice a day for medium sized dogs, and a quarter teaspoon three times a day for large dogs.

For cats, mix a teaspoon of tincture each of echinacea and boneset; give two drops every half hour until there is improvement, then give two drops every two hours until the cat recovers. If the cat is comatose or nearly so, place a drop of camphor-based ointment (Tiger Balm or Sunbreeze) in front of the cat's nose for a few breaths, and repeat every fifteen minutes until there is response.[42]

For dogs with kennel cough, use an herbal cough syrup adjusted to the animal's weight, and peppermint tea/infusion. Make the infusion strong; steep three tablespoons of the dried leaves in two cups of boiling water for fifteen minutes. Strain and add a teaspoon or two of honey. Give a half teaspoonful to a tablespoonful every three hours. Another herb alternative is mullein, using a heaping teaspoonful per cup of water, steeped twenty minutes; strain and add honey.[43]

Pat Lazarus recommends fruit pit derived laetrile for feline distemper. For parvovirus in dogs she uses Kyolic/garlic as an antibacterial, and nutrient herbs to build the liver. These include: dandelion, red beet powder and parsley. For respiratory dis-eases in cats and dogs, she recommends an herbal combination of fenugreek and comfrey.[44] Use these along with the vitamin C protocol. An herb to relieve congestion and phlegm in the lungs is lobelia. Use this sparingly and along with other herbs; it heightens their effects. The animal may vomit from too much, but will bring up the fluid that needs to be removed. Antibiotics for infectious dis-eases include goldenseal, echinacea and garlic. Make sure to use enough of these and to continue using them for at least several days after all symptoms are gone. I use goldenseal for infections that have digestive symptoms, and echinacea for upper and lower respiratory dis-eases. Garlic is an antibacterial, antiviral, immune builder and detoxifier.

Herbs were the earliest beginnings of what became modern medicine and the pharmaceutical industry. They are still powerful and effective as healers today, and are important in healing pets holistically. They are probably the first basis for all holistic healing of dis-ease. With the many books on herbalism available, the information on using herbs medicinally is within anyone's reach. The advantages of using these whole natural plants over synthesized and chemical drugs are many. When used well, their ability to heal gently and thoroughly is apparent. The next chapter discusses homeopathy, a method of using very minute amounts of an herb or other substance as a powerful and safe healer. In healing dogs and cats, homeopathy is also a primary method.

[1]Judy Chicago, *The Dinner Party: A Symbol of Our Heritage* (New York: Doubleday Books, 1979), pp. 116–119.

[2]Sheldon Altman, DVM, *Introduction to Acupuncture for Animals: A Teaching Manual* (Monterey Park, CA: Chan's Corporation, 1981), p. 13.

[3]Diane Stein, *All Women Are Healers* (Freedom, CA: The Crossing Press, 1990), pp. 184–186.

[4]Anitra Frazier with Norma Eckroate, *The New Natural Cat: A Complete Guide for Finicky Owners* (New York: Plume Books, 1990), pp. 259–260.

[5]Juliette de Bairacli Levy, *The Complete Herbal Handbook for the Dog and Cat* (London and Boston: Faber and Faber, Ltd., 1955 and 1991), pp. 136–137.

[6]Anitra Frazier, *The New Natural Cat*, p. 260, and Diane Stein, *All Women Are Healers,* p. 189.

[7]Anitra Frazier, *The New Natural Cat*, pp. 234 & 261, and Diane Stein, *All Women Are Healers*, p. 190.

[8]Anitra Frazier, *The New Natural Cat,* p. 260.

[9]Juliette de Bairacli Levy, *The Complete Herbal Handbook for the Dog and Cat,* pp. 139–140.

[10]Anitra Frazier, *The New Natural Cat,* p. 252.

[11]Richard Pitcairn, DVM, PhD and Susan Hubble Pitcairn, *Dr. Pitcairn's Complete Guide to Natural Health for Dogs and Cats* (Emmaus, PA: Rodale Press, 1982), p. 145.

[12]Anitra Frazier, *The New Natural Cat,* p. 277.

[13]Pat Lazarus, *Keep Your Pet Healthy the Natural Way* (New Canaan, CT: Keats Publishing Co., 1983), p. 99.

[14]Susan R. Griffin, *Winning the Flea War Naturally . . . Without Toxins* (St. Petersburg, FL: The SuDi Co., 1990), p. 6. Pamphlet.

[15]Richard Pitcairn, DVM, *Dr. Pitcairn's Complete Guide to Natural Health for Dogs and Cats,* pp. 182–183.

[16]Anitra Frazier, *The New Natural Cat,* pp. 280–281.

[17]Juliette de Bairacli Levy, *The Complete Herbal Handbook for the Dog and Cat,* p. 152.

[18]Pat Lazarus, *Keep Your Pet Healthy the Natural Way,* p. 65.

[19]Juliette de Bairacli Levy, *The Complete Herbal Handbook for the Dog and Cat,* pp. 161–162.

[20]Richard Pitcairn, DVM, *Dr. Pitcairn's Complete Guide to Natural Health for Dogs and Cats,* p. 193.

[21]May Bethel, *The Healing Power of Herbs* (North Hollywood, CA: Wilshire Book Co., 1968), p. 136.

[22]Richard Pitcairn, DVM, *Dr. Pitcairn's Complete Guide to Natural Health for Dogs and Cats,* p. 213.

[23]Juliette de Bairacli Levy, *The Complete Herbal Handbook for the Dog and Cat,* pp. 166–167.

[24]Anitra Frazier, *The New Natural Cat,* p. 295.

[25]Richard Pitcairn, DVM, *Dr. Pitcairn's Complete Guide to Natural Health for Dogs and Cats,* pp. 201–202.

[26]Anitra Frazier, *The New Natural Cat,* pp. 306-307.

[27]Richard Pitcairn, DVM, *Dr. Pitcairn's Complete Guide to Natural Health for Dogs and Cats,* p. 201.

[28]Diane Stein, *The Natural Remedy Book for Women* (Freedom, CA: The Crossing Press, 1992), p. 177.

[29]Anitra Frazier, *The New Natural Cat,* pp. 303–304.

[30]Pat Lazarus, *Keep Your Pet Healthy the Natural Way,* pp. 166 & 170.

[31]Anitra Frazier, *The New Natural Cat,* p. 330.

[32]Juliette de Bairacli Levy, *The Complete Herbal Handbook for the Dog and Cat,* p. 199.

[33]Diane Stein, *The Natural Remedy Book for Women,* p. 197.

[34]Anitra Frazier, *The New Natural Cat,* pp. 358–359.

[35]Juliette de Bairacli Levy, *The Complete Herbal Handbook for the Dog and Cat,* p. 246.

[36]Pat Lazarus, *Keep Your Pet Healthy the Natural Way,* pp. 95–104.

[37]Richard Pitcairn, DVM, *Dr. Pitcairn's Complete Guide to Natural Health for Dogs and Cats,* pp. 238–239.

[38]Anitra Frazier, *The New Natural Cat,* pp. 317–318.

[39]*Ibid.,* p. 169.

[40]Richard Pitcairn, DVM, *Dr. Pitcairn's Complete Guide to Natural Health for Dogs and Cats,* pp. 186–190.

[41]Juliette de Bairacli Levy, *The Complete Herbal Handbook for the Dog and Cat,* pp. 173–175.

[42]Richard Pitcairn, DVM, *Dr. Pitcairn's Complete Guide to Natural Health for Dogs and Cats,* pp. 203–207.

[43]*Ibid.,* pp. 247–248.

[44]Pat Lazarus, *Keep Your Pet Healthy the Natural Way,* pp. 114–118.

Homeopathy & Pets

Homeopathy bridges the healing gap between the physical and nonphysical bodies. A homeopathic remedy, made by a process of successive dilutions and potentizations, may contain little or no molecular content of the original herb, mineral or animal substance it is made from; yet, with each successive dilution it becomes more active and more potent for healing physical, mental and emotional dis-ease. The remedies are chosen on the basis of symptom pictures—what are the total symptoms that need healing in the animal or person?—rather than by dis-ease names or labels. Each homeopathic remedy incorporates a dis-ease picture, with symptoms on physical, mental and emotional levels. When the remedy is chosen that closest matches the animal's dis-ease description, and the remedy is administered, the results can be a healing so rapid that it can only be described as miraculous. The skill in homeopathy is in locating the right remedy, the one that matches what the dog or cat (or human) needs.

Homeopathy is used alongside of or as part of the standard medical and veterinary systems in most countries. Over half of the physicians in England are homeopaths, and this is also the case in France, Brazil and India. In India there are over 100,000 homeopathic doctors and 120 homeopathic medical schools. The method is practiced in Mexico, Greece, Belgium, Italy, Spain, Australia, Nigeria, South Africa, and the Soviet Commonwealth countries, to name only a few.[1] Before 1900, over a fourth of American medical doctors were also homeopaths, but increasing repression by the American Medical Association closed the homeopathic medical schools and refused homeopaths the right to practice. The AMA was founded in 1846 for the purpose of ridding itself of its major competition—homeopathy—just as the Inquisition that ended only a hundred years before got rid of women healers. Most homeopaths in the United States today are laywomen.

While the focus in homeopathic medicine has been in its use on people, it has always been used on animals, as well. The procedure is the same for infants, puppies, kittens, adult humans and grown dogs and cats. The dosage is the same for everyone—the potency of the remedy is the question, not how many pellets or drops are taken of that potency. Unlike medical drugs, the testings (provings) of homeopathic remedies are done on people (often students of the method) rather than on laboratory animals. The dilutions make the remedies safe, no matter what the base substance may be.

Humans and animals have many similarities in their make-up and in the illnesses and diseases from which they suffer. The remedies therefore can apply equally well, according to symptoms presented, to all the members of the household whether human or animal. The same remedy may be safely given, usually in the same dose, whatever the pet may be—a horse, pony, donkey, dog, cat, guinea pig, hamster, gerbil, white mouse or even a tortoise. Homeopathic remedies may also be used to treat pet birds of any kind and, of course, fish—where the remedy can readily be put into the water.[2]

The method is also used for farm animals, wild animals and zoo animals.

When I first began studying homeopathy, in the research for *All Women Are Healers,* the system seemed too academic and complicated to be real or useful. Then I saw it in action. In February, 1989 I found Copper, one of my current Siberian Huskies, at the Humane Society in Pittsburgh. He had parvovirus, a dis-ease that few dogs in his run-down condition survive, and the Society was going to put him down. The dog weighed thirty-five pounds and was just over a year old; he was a rack of bones. He had a coat like yellow straw, and on later examination was determined to have infected ears and four kinds of intestinal worms—after he survived the parvo. When I presented him to my veterinarian, he strongly suggested that I have him euthanized. I refused. The dog had a strong aura and a hopeful, outgoing personality; he had been badly abused but was still young. I knew he would live.

He spent five days on intravenous fluids at the veterinary hospital and refused all food. I visited him daily, did distant and direct healing work with him, then brought him home. He continued an after-residue of intestinal and digestive problems that were damage left from the virus. There was chronic diarrhea, also recurrent periods of vomiting and bleeding, as well as periods of extreme irritability and depression in an otherwise bouncy animal. Despite six cups a day of dry dog food (still supermarket, unfortunately), he only gained three pounds in a period of several months. I took him to every vet in the area, each of whom gave me drugs to stop his digestive processes ("and let them rest") for a few days, after which the symptoms returned. They all said nothing more could be done. Several suggested euthanizing him, and all of them charged me a lot with no results. I had become quite attached to Copper by this time.

Then, while I was writing the homeopathy chapter for *All Women,* I happened to ask Sidney Spinster, who is an experienced homeopath and was checking my accuracy, "What can I do for this dog?" She suggested a homeopathic remedy of *Phosphorus,* made up into the 12C potency in a twenty percent dilution liquid; she said to give one dose only and expect to see some improvement within a week. I ordered the remedy, it cost $9 in the liquid ($3.50 in pellet form), and put a few drops on the dog's tongue. Within fifteen minutes Copper, who was very hyperactive, curled up and went to sleep in the kitchen and slept for most of that day. The diarrhea stopped right then, as did the vomiting. His digestion and elimination stabilized within twenty-four hours, and within two weeks he gained fifteen pounds!

In about ten days the symptoms began to recur, though less severely, and I gave a second dose of the homeopathic *Phosphorus.* Improvement was again immediate, and when the symptoms recurred once more (much less severely) three weeks later, I gave a third dose. No more was ever needed, and no more veterinary visits. Copper gained weight consistently, and has become a very stable, gentle, outgoing animal. He now weights sixty-five pounds, has no further damage from the dis-ease, and is in full good health. I still have most of the bottle of his remedy.

The Boericke *Materia Medica,* a guide listing and describing the homeopathic remedy characteristics, describes the person or animal that responds to *Phosphorus.* In its non-homeopathic form, phosphorus is a toxin, and the description is of the sickness caused by it. That same sickness is what the homeopathic form treats, whether caused by phosphorus itself or not.

Phosphorus irritates, inflames and degenerates mucus membranes, irritates and inflames serous membranes . . .; disorganizes the blood, causing fatty degeneration of blood vessels and every tissue and organ of the body and thus gives rise to hemorrhages, and hematogenous jaundice.

Produces a picture of destructive metabolism. Causes yellow atrophy of the liver and sub-acute hepatitis. Tall, slender persons, narrow chested, with thin, transparent skin, weakened by loss of animal fluids, with great nervous debility, emaciation, amative tendencies . . . .[3]

The language is archaic, and for women politically unaware, but the remedy pictures work. Descriptions under *Mind* included Copper's mental state: "excitable, outgoing, periods of depression, irritability, and restlessness." Descriptions under *Stomach* and *Stool* fit his digestive symptoms. Even the physical descriptions matched. The remedy picture for *Phosphorus* fits the dog's symptoms and personality, and therefore was a cure—a spectacular one. The correct homeopathic remedy healed what half a dozen experienced veterinarians with as many chemical drugs could not. Homeopathic veterinarians would have healed him a lot sooner.

There is more than magick operating here. Homeopathy is an exact science, based upon scientific testing, with recorded and proven results. It was developed in 1796 by a German physician, Samuel Hahnemann (1755–1843), who based his work on a theory of healing that goes back to the Delphic Oracle: "That which makes sick shall heal."[4] This philosophy of healing was highly prevalent in the ancient world, but was one of the ideas that fell into disregard in the west with the loss of the traditional healers. The theory, expressed as "like cures like" (*similia similibus curentur*) is the basis and first law of homeopathy. It means that a substance which causes in a healthy person or animal a particular set of symptoms, will also cure a sick person or animal with those same symptoms. For example, a dog that expresses the symptoms of phosphorus poisoning as Copper did, will be cured by a homeopathic preparation of *Phosphorus*.

This sounds good, and Hahnemann found that it works, but some of the symptom-causing substances are also toxic. The second law of homeopathy came from the discovery that diluting those toxic substances (and all homeopathic remedy substances) increases their healing power, while simultaneously making them safe to use. This is called the Law of the Minimal Dose and is the second basis of homeopathic medicine. It is precisely the opposite of the theories of the standard medical system and synthetic drug industry.

The process of creating a homeopathic remedy is a process of diluting the substances to such minute amounts that it seems impossible that anything at all could happen. Yet, by the process of dilution used with potentization (of striking/succussing the remedy a specific number of times for each dilution), the *energy* properties of the original substance are released and activated. A homeopathic remedy beyond a 24X or 12C potency no longer contains any physical molecules of the original substance, but the greater the dilution the more powerful the healing.

The remedies are created in the X (tenth) or C (hundredth) dilutions. A 1X potency means that one drop of a Mother Tincture (usually herb tincture) is added to ten drops of alcohol, and potentized by striking the bottle vigorously a number of times. A 1C potency is made by putting one drop of the Mother Tincture into a bottle with ninety-nine drops of alcohol, and potentized by striking the bottle vigorously a number of times. Obviously a 1X has more of the Mother Tincture in it than a 1C, but the effect is the opposite—the 1C has a much stronger healing potency than the 1X. The Mother Tinctures are made from herbs, minerals, organic or inorganic substances. They can also be made from dis-ease bacteria (called nosodes), which are rendered harmless by the potentizing process. The preparation process removes any possibility of side effects or toxicity, while activating and releasing the nonphysical level energy patterns of the substances.

When a single drop of the 1X potency is placed in a second bottle with nine more drops of alcohol and potentized again, the result is a 2X remedy. A 3X remedy is made by again taking one drop of the 2X liquid, adding it to nine more drops of the alcohol, and again potentizing. A 2C remedy is made by taking one drop of the 1C remedy, adding it to ninety-nine drops of alcohol, and potentizing.[5] This is how the remedies are made, though today they are usually made by machine rather than by hand. Anitra Frazier's herb elixir of the last chapter (from Richard Pitcairn) is a homeopathic remedy, made by placing three drops of an herb tincture (Mother Tincture) into a one-ounce eyedropper bottle filled two-thirds full of water. She potentizes the remedy by shaking the bottle vigorously 108 times and striking it against a thick rug or padded armchair surface each time.[6] The result is probably a 1C remedy (one drop of tincture to each ninety-nine drops of water).

Homeopathic remedies come in the X (tenth) dilutions and the C (hundredth) dilutions for home use; professionals sometimes use higher potencies. The X remedies are considered smaller/less active, and they are slower acting and less long-lasting or far reaching than C remedies. Lower numbers are less potent; for example a 6X is less stronger than a 12X, or a 6C remedy less than a 12C potency.

What size remedy to use is a matter of opinion. Some homeopaths prefer the smaller doses for home use (Standard Homeopathic Co. makes their line in 6X; Newton Laboratories mostly in 10X and 15X potencies). Others prefer the consistently higher doses: 9C, 12C or 30C. These are higher but still relatively small; professionals often use 200C remedies or constitutional remedies diluted into the thousandths and more. I myself prefer a general 12C or 30C with people and pets, believing that the 30C dose has to be repeated less often and has better chance of clearing the dis-ease quickly without its returning. The dose that cured Copper was a 12C. Since the remedies are so thoroughly diluted, there is no risk that any dosage of any substance will be unsafe, but with higher doses there is the possibility of what homeopaths call an aggravation.

An aggravation is a worsening of symptoms for a short period of time, before the dis-ease symptoms suddenly clear or start getting better (ameliorate). In a 30C remedy, the aggravation usually lasts less than half an hour, with a temporary intensification of symptoms that is not frightening or extreme and that leaves quickly. If the symptom being treated is diarrhea, for example, there may be more of it but only for a few minutes. When that few minutes ends, there is a significant improvement quickly in the person or animal's well-being. The onset and clearing of the aggravation are the beginning of the healing and are sometimes called a healing crisis. A larger potency remedy may have a stronger aggravation, and a very low potency may have none at all. The potency with the aggravation, however, is the potency that will more fully cure the dis-ease. Aggravations are considered positive indications that the remedy is a correct match. They don't always happen, but come and go quickly when they do.

After choosing the remedy that seems to match, using a *Materia Medica and Repertory* or other homeopathy guide, give a dose of the potency decided upon (guidebooks often specify a dose, or use what's available, or use the 12C or 30C). When using the remedies in liquid form, put two to six drops on the animal's tongue (or better under it); when using the more often available pellets, crush two of them between two teaspoons and sprinkle the powder into the animal's mouth. The remedies should not be touched with your hands or allowed to drop on the floor. If some spills, don't worry about it, as long as some of it gets in. The actual amount of the remedy doesn't matter—with two pellets or ten it is still a dose of the same potency. After administering the remedy, sit back and observe. It is best to withhold food for at least half an hour after giving remedies, and water for fifteen minutes.

As one possible guideline, for low potency remedies (6X, 12X), veterinary homeopath Francis Hunter suggests giving remedies with the following frequency for cats and dogs. In the case of acute, urgent attacks, give one dose every fifteen minutes up to four doses, then every two hours up to another four doses. For less urgent conditions, give the remedy three or four times a day for a few days. For chronic long-term dis-eases, give the remedy three times a day for four to seven days, then wait and repeat if needed.[7]

OR—and again there are differing opinions—give one dose of whatever potency, wait for reactions and changes, and do not repeat until the changes stop. Wait at least an hour to see, except in urgent acute situations. Several things may happen here. The animal may suddenly improve, as Copper did. She may seem to get worse, indicating an aggravation. Or nothing at all will happen, in which case it may have been the wrong remedy, or the remedy may have antidoted (more on this in a moment). Watch carefully for these changes, they may be subtle. I prefer this method of dosage.

If the animal improves, no more doses of the remedy are needed until that improvement stops. When it seems that the improvement is no longer continuing, or worsening begins again, repeat the dose (unless the dog or cat is healed and no more is needed). If the animal seems to worsen, an aggravation is indicated; give no more remedy until the aggravation ends and the subsequent amelioration (improvement) that follows it ends. Then repeat the dose if the dis-ease is still present. Sometimes one or two doses is enough.

If nothing happens at all, try a second dose under Francis Hunter's guidelines. If nothing happens within a few hours of the second dose, discontinue using the remedy as it is probably the wrong symptom match. Go back to the guidebook or *Materia Medica* and re-evaluate the choice; try a different remedy that more clearly fits the animal's symptoms and emotional state. A variety of factors can also antidote (cancel) homeopathic remedies, as they are extremely fragile. Never touch them with your hands while administering the remedies; for pellets tip a few into the container cap, pour them into a teaspoon, crush them to powder with a second teaspoon, and tip them onto the pet's tongue. For liquids, drip them from the eyedropper onto the tongue. If the animal's mouth touches the dropper, rinse it before returning it to the bottle.

Strong fragrances can cancel homeopathic remedies, including camphor, menthol, and peppermint. Peppermint in any form, including peppermint tea, will antidote a remedy, as will fennel. A number of antidoting factors that affect the remedies are not used by animals—coffee and peppermint toothpaste—and make homeopathy easier to use on pets than on people. The remedies can be antidoted by being stored in sunlight, exposed to heat, or stored beside things that could affect them (don't keep them in the drawer with moth flakes). Keep the containers closed. Extreme emotional trauma in the pet taking the remedy can also sometimes cancel it. When a remedy seems to be working and then suddenly stops, suspect an antidote. If a remedy is antidoted, remove the cancel factor, and repeat the dose.

Dr. Richard Pitcairn, describing the use of his goldenseal herb elixir for cancer and feline leukemia, gives the following instructions. Goldenseal in its homeopathic remedy name is the plant's Latin name, *Hydrastis canadensis.*

As soon as *any* reaction seems evident (the animal gets weaker, symptoms worsen or the appetite is lost), temporarily discontinue the treatment. Usually the animal will improve, only to have some of its previous symptoms return. At that point begin the goldenseal treatment again, but as soon as an aggravation of symptoms is seen (even after one dose), discontinue again. On the other hand, if the animal shows only improvement after the initial dosages (as is more common), continue the treatment as long as improvement goes on. When a plateau is reached, in which things get neither better nor worse, then make a 1:100 dilution *of the first dilution . . .* and continue from there.[8]

The instructions are based on twice a day dosage, one to three drops per dose. The herb elixir/homeopathic remedy is a very low potency, probably about a 1C; the second dilution described would increase the dose to a 2C. When using remedies in the 12C or 30C potencies or higher, give the first dose then wait and watch for reactions. The remedy may not require repeating everyday, but might be every other day, or as in Copper's case only after a week or more.

Healing occurs in homeopathy by Hering's Law of Cure. This describes the pattern the healing process takes, and is more often seen in healing deeper, more serious dis-ease issues than in superficial or immediate/acute ones. The first pattern is that healing in homeopathy occurs in a movement from internal to external levels. An external dis-ease, like a skin rash, is easier to heal than, say, a heart or liver dis-ease. In a deeper dis-ease, the healing will occur first at the internal level, the liver, and a movement of symptoms outward may appear. The cat with liver dis-ease symptoms, for example, may show great improvement in liver symptoms but develop a skin rash. A skin rash is considered less serious; an improvement from dis-ease in the internal organ; the remedy is working. The rash is temporary and clears as the rest of the dis-ease clears. Likewise, if psychological symptoms improve but the physical symptoms seem worse, the change is considered a beginning of healing. Again the remedy is working. An example of this might be a cat treated for allergies that refuses to be touched; her temperament improves but her runny eyes seem a little worse. More healing will follow this first change.

The second part of Hering's Law of Cure states that healing proceeds from upper to lower parts of the body. If a dog treated for skin rashes has an improvement in the rashes on her face, but none on the rashes near her tail, the healing has begun. The rash on the lower part of her body will take longer to clear, and that on her feet may clear last.

I am treating my new puppy Kali for the abused and traumatized state in which she arrived from the dog pound. She has an infected ear, she seems to have an injured lower back or hips, and she came to me an angry biter. On 30C doses of *Pulsatilla* (which matches her physical and emotional description—she is light colored with blue eyes, of changeable temperament and usually very loving and affection-craving), the biting stopped first. Now her ear is almost healed, and I watch for improvement in her lower body. Her tendency to house-training accidents has also stopped; whether that was physical or emotional is undetermined. So far two doses, ten days apart, have done the job.

The third part of Hering's Law is that symptoms disappear in order of their appearance. What occurred most recently disappears first. There may be a temporary return of old symptoms (homeopaths call them "old sores"), especially if medical drugs were used in the healing of them. This process and the temporary return of symptoms thought gone is positive. Again, they are indications that the remedy is working. Sometimes with dogs and cats, the whole process happens so rapidly that the changes are barely noticed. Aggravations should never be suppressed with any chemical or drug (and definitely *never* with cortisone).[9] Let them run their course. The healing moves through the layers of the dis-ease, like peeling an onion, until full wellness is reached.

Homeopaths feel that chemical drugs, particularly steroids and cortisone, suppress a dis-ease and drive it deeper. Their classic example is asthma, which they feel always begins with a skin rash that has been suppressed. When a dis-ease goes deeper into the body it becomes more serious, and chemically suppressing a symptom causes worsening and greater harm. The deepening may not appear right away. Often homeopathy releases multiple layers of a dis-ease: asthma, when released from the lungs, may reappear for a time on the skin, as the original rash is released instead of suppressed. If the skin rash had been treated homeopathically instead of with steroids, it never would have gone inward and become asthma to begin with. Homeopathy is particularly successful in treating both asthma and skin rash dis-eases.

Vaccination of pets is another issue. First of all, the vaccines are not a hundred percent effective. The woman who says, "My cat can't possibly have feline distemper, she was vaccinated for it," can be wrong. Homeopaths feel that routine vaccinations, particularly when a number of vaccines are given at once as they usually are, can do more harm than good and will cause dis-ease reactions and a breakdown of the immune system sooner or later. This is becoming a serious controversy in other areas of holistic healing, as well. Few veterinarians who are not

homeopaths will make the connection between a dog or cat's chronic long-term illness and vaccination reaction (vaccinosis).

Animals can have immediate adverse reactions to the yearly "shots," some of them serious. They may even develop the dis-ease they were vaccinated for. One of my dogs, Tiger, was vaccinated very early for rabies. She had been weaned early and started on the other vaccinations early, as her mother could only breast feed for three weeks, and the puppies were then hand raised. After the rabies shot at four months, Tiger developed a high fever and was lethargic for several days during the time she was shedding her puppy teeth. Her adult teeth came in brown, without the white enamel outer layer, and remained that way all the dog's life. She had earlier tooth decay, many more cavities and broken teeth, and very bad breath as compared to other dogs. My veterinarian denied that it could have been the vaccination, but I knew otherwise.

Anitra Frazier credits multiple vaccinations as the source of many long-term auto-immune dis-eases in animals (and people). These include asthma, arthritis, allergic dermatitis, warts, tumors, gum dis-ease and irritable bowel syndrome.[10] She feels that the combination of antigens confuses the animal immune system, sometimes enough to turn it against itself. Richard Pitcairn, a veterinarian very interested in homeopathy, states that often in homeopathic healings the symptoms of vaccinosis appear and are released, and the animal makes rapid healing gains afterwards. Watch for the cat or dog that becomes sicker after vaccination with whatever dis-ease she has, or that gets sick directly from the injections. The effects can be antidoted with homeopathic *Thuja*.

Since vaccinations are required by law in most states, and since they do protect at least from some deadly dis-eases, what are the alternatives? Dr. Richard Pitcairn makes these suggestions: (1) only vaccinate for dis-eases that are prevalent in your area; (2) vaccines are not to be repeated frequently; and (3) killed or modified-live virus vaccines should be used instead of live-virus ones. He gives specific instructions for dogs and cats.

For dogs, rabies vaccination is required by law and should be done every two years, the first vaccine not given before four months of age. Distemper and hepatitis shots are given at eight weeks and twelve weeks, with a booster in a year. After, give a distemper vaccination every three years; no further hepatitis shots are needed.

Leptospirosis vaccination is not very effective, only lasting a few months. Parvovirus vaccine should be given under special circumstances, when the dog will be exposed to other animals that could be ill with it, as in a boarding kennel. Give two injections about two weeks apart, before expected exposure. He does not recommend repeated and continuous immunization; protection lasts only a few months and the long-term effects can be harmful.

For cats, Pitcairn recommends distemper (feline panleukopenia) injections at eight and twelve weeks of age, repeated every five years. No other vaccinations are recommended for cats.[11]

Another alternative to injection vaccinations is to use homeopathic oral vaccinations, made from nosodes of the dis-eases. These require dosing over a period of time, not as easy as taking the animal to the veterinarian once a year for a shot. Like other homeopathic methods, there are conflicting protocols, but here is a representative one. Give a dose of the nosode night and morning for three days, then once a week for four weeks, and then monthly for six months. Gloria Dodd uses this protocol with one exception: after weekly doses for a month she waits for a month, then doses monthly for six months. She uses a half dropperful of the nosode, 30C in liquid form.

Says holistic veterinarian Dr. Dodd:

My vaccination philosophy . . . is this: If you have an indoor dwelling dog or cat I do not recommend Rabies vaccination due to its destructive effect on the brain and nervous system rendering the animal open to developing chronic degenerative diseases. Many holistic veterinarians have become aware that Rabies vaccination is the basis of every skin case we see—including rapidly aging processes of the body's organ systems. German Shepherds are particularly sensitive to its paralytic consequences.

However, if one is forced to give a Rabies vaccine—either the dog is exposed to an endemic rabies wildlife population, county licensing pressures to have the vaccine, or if you must show or kennel your dog and they require certification of the vaccine— then I recommend the KILLED Rabies vaccine, *not* the modified live vaccine which is the most destructive form. Immediately following the killed Rabies vaccination I dispense a homeopathic nosode of the killed Rabies and the lymph drainers for the nervous system and brain. Through my Dermatron/EAV studies I find a complete neutralization of the vaccines' noxious effects, yet the antibody titer protection is still intact.

For protection against the rest of the infectious diseases, I use the homeopathic oral nosodes, which I find not only protect for those diseases specifically, but build the immune system to protect for other diseases. For example: I had a lady who breeds Boston Terriers call me from Connecticut about a very resistant Parvo outbreak in her kennel despite traditional vaccination for Parvo. I sent her the oral nosode for Parvo, instructed her to give 2 drops to each newborn puppy on a daily basis for 2 weeks, then go to my vaccination schedule (above). For the adult dogs, put them on the routine oral vaccination schedule. After that she never had another case of Parvo infection in her dogs. She also found that her dogs became resistant to Kennel Cough when they were exposed to an outbreak at a Boston dogshow she attended, yet all the other dogs belonging to the other people who were showing their dogs, did. Kennel Cough is EXTREMELY contagious and is spread in the air as infective droplets through the dogs' coughing.

Says homeopathic veterinarian George Macleod:

Oral vaccination . . . gives a more solid immunity in as much as it incorporates the entire defense system, which is mobilized as soon as the vaccine is taken into the mouth and builds up protection with each further dose . . . .

Another advantage in protection by homeopathic means is that vaccination can be started very early in the kitten's (or puppy's) life *e.g.* within the first week if necessary. This does not interfere with the presence of any maternal antibodies.[12]

If a homeopathic veterinarian works in your area, this is a method to seriously consider. With the damaged environment reflected by depressed immune systems in people and animals, I cannot recommend *not* vaccinating dogs and cats. Use one method or the other, the medical injections or the homeopathic oral vaccines. For home use, nosodes are becoming difficult to order by lay people from the homeopathic pharmacies; prescriptions are needed. The FDA is harassing homeopaths again, as well as the herb and vitamin industries. Oral vaccines are effective, but the protocol of doses must be followed conscientiously. The controversy on pet vaccinations extends to vaccinating children and adults; see your homeopathic physician.

While classical homeopathy considers it extremely important to give only one remedy at a time, many modern homeopaths mix remedies. If a patient has a skin dis-ease, for example, the homeopath may select several possible remedy matches and include the most likely ones in a liquid remedy. One advantage of this is that if any of the remedies in the bottle is the right one, the combination initiates an immediate cure without trying each possibility one at a time until the correct match is found. The disadvantage is that by using a combination, it is impossible to know which remedy actually worked. When one component of a combination is the right one, that is the only remedy to have effect; the others do neither harm nor good on short term use.

Another advantage is that combination remedies, while not teaching the student how to use homeopathy, take the guesswork out of the method. By using one combination for diarrhea, for example, the remedy is highly likely to work—and without trial and error. Where the experienced homeopath can usually pick the correct single remedy on the first or second try, this is a complex science that takes time to learn. Your cat's diarrhea cannot wait for you to study homeopathy over a period of maybe years to become expert at it. (But the studying is well worth the effort.)

Two homeopathic companies market a series of dog and cat combination remedies. Dr. Goodpet's Natural Remedies, made by Alfred Plechner (*Pet Allergies: Remedies for an Epidemic*), include homeopathic combinations with the following titles: Flea Relief, Scratch Free, Calm Stress, Diar-Relief, Good Breath, and Ear Relief. The liquid remedies are $8.95 each from Dr. Goodpet Laboratories/Very Healthy Enterprises, P.O. Box 4728, Inglewood, CA 90309. The individual ingredients/remedies in the combinations are not given in the company's literature.

Newton Laboratories, Inc. also offers a homeopathic remedy combination series for dogs and cats (as well as the single homeopathic remedies). The Pets-A-Care combinations include: Skin, Nervousness, Kidney Help, Back Ache, Cough, Worms, Diarrhea, Ear Relief, Doggy Breath, and Leukemia. They also produce a wound ointment, bruise ointment, and sore muscle liniment. The remedies are liquids in eyedropper bottles, and sell for $8 each. Several of them recommend use with a homeopathic Drainer (detoxifier) that is also $8. The ointments are $5.95, and the company also has a series for horses. I have tried the Drainer with the Ear Relief combination and found it highly effective.

The Back Ache remedy contains the following: *Rhus tox* 10X, *Ruta* 10X, *Guaiacum* 10X, *Strychninum* 10X, and *Colchicum* 10X, in twenty percent alcohol dilution. The remedy for Ear Relief contains: *Graphites* 10X, *Mezereum* 10X, *Viola tricolor* 10X, *Capsicum* 10X and *Rhus tox* 10X. The Nervousness combination contains: *Gelsemium* 10X, *Coffea* 10X, *Hypericum* 10X, *Iodum* 10X, and *Argentum nitricum* 10X, again in the twenty percent alcohol dilution. These are an easy and effective way to begin use of homeopathy with animals, and they are recommended. The address for the company is: Newton Laboratories, Inc., P.O. Box 936, Lithonia, GA 30558 (1-800-448-7256).

Cell Salts are often included with homeopathic remedy prescriptions, though they are slightly different from standard homeopathic remedies. They come usually in 6X potency and are more nutritional than therapeutic in effect. Developed by homeopathic physician Wilhelm Schuessler in the nineteenth century, they are based on the theory that the individual cells require a balance of water, organic substances, and inorganic substances. If that balance is disturbed, dis-ease results; if it is regained, health is regained.[13] Some of these remedies are included among the homeopathic suggestions for diseases that follow. Cell or tissue salts are usually more easily available in health food stores than the homeopathic remedies—perhaps because there are only twelve of them. In personal experience, I find them less effective by a great deal than the correct homeopathic remedy in the 12C or 30C potency. As nutrients, however, cell salts can be taken daily over long periods of time.

The following homeopathic suggestions for dog and cat dis-eases use the same dis-ease list as the vitamin and herb chapters. Doing this provides a comparison of methods, besides a number of alternatives for the woman whose pet is in need. The material in this section references to a number of sources, including *Dr. Pitcairn's Complete Guide to Natural Health for Dogs and Cats* (Rodale Press, 1982), and Francis Hunter, *Homeopathic First-Aid Treatment for Pets* (Thorsen's, 1984). Also several books from British homeopathic veterinarian George Macleod: *Cats: Homeopathic Remedies* and *Dogs: Homeopathic Remedies* (C.W. Daniel Co., Ltd., 1990 and 1983); *A Veterinary Materia Medica and Clinical Repertory* (C.W. Daniel Co., Ltd., 1981). A further source is K. Sheppard, *The Treatment of Dogs by Homeopathy* (C.W. Daniel Co., Ltd., 1972). All of these are highly recommended, particularly the Pitcairn and Sheppard books, and George Macleod's *Cats:* and *Dogs: Homeopathic Remedies*. All but Dr. Pitcairn's book were published in England, and were written by English veterinary homeopaths.

The same remedies in the same doses and amounts apply to dogs, cats and people of all ages. For further homeopathic guidance, therefore, see books that apply to human use. The remedies are chosen by symptoms, and if these are the same as for a human dis-ease, the same remedy applies. See Stephen Cummings, FNP and Dana Ullman, MPH, *Everybody's Guide to Homeopathic Medicines* (Jeremy Tarcher, Inc., 1984); Diane Stein, *The Natural Remedy Book for Women* (The Crossing Press, 1992); and Diane Stein, *All Women Are Healers* (The Crossing Press, 1990), as well as other of the many homeopathic guides. Homeopathic remedies may be used at the same time as herbals and vitamins and should be used with optimal nutrition. They are a first choice over chemical drugs. For simplicity's sake, I have not footnoted every entry; they are from the sources above with much duplication of information.

Allergies: If the animal's symptoms are skin problems, see the section under Skin in this and other guides. If they are digestive, also see the categories that fit. Homeopathic remedies are prescribed by symptom descriptions, rather than dis-ease labels. A rash from whatever source is treated the same way. Here are some basic suggestions:

For runny, reddened eyes and runny nose with no other symptoms, use homeopathic *Euphrasia* (eyebright), a dose every hour or two up to six doses in low potency. Euphrasia eyedrops are also available. Allergic swellings or sudden blotchy rashes on head or body are treated with *Urtica urens* (stinging nettles). *Rhus tox* is for the early stage of contact dermatitis; use it for itching, burning rashes and particularly for poison ivy exposure. There may be fluid filled blisters on the skin. *Rhus tox* is homeopathically prepared poison ivy.

Sulfur may be helpful in any type of skin rash, particularly when it has not responded to other remedies. Rashes of fine, dry bumps, especially on the face, with the animal irritable and wanting to be left alone, respond to *Bryonia* (wild hops). Bee stings, or allergic reactions that look like bee stings, respond to *Apis mellifica* (honeybee venom). The skin is hot and dry with angry red lesions, and the animal is depressed and may be irritable.

Anaphylaxis is a severe allergic reaction, dramatic and sometimes life threatening. First aid measures include homeopathic *Aconite* (monkshood) at first onset. This is also used for shock and may stop the attack entirely if used immediately. Dr. Dodd recommends *Apis* 6X and Rescue Remedy rubbed into the gums; in acute cases dose every ten minutes for an hour, then hourly as needed. Homeopathic *Camphora* (camphor) is for collapse, with diarrhea and extreme coldness. Use *Carbo veg* (vegetable charcoal) when breathing is impaired. These are first aid measures; the animal may need cardio-pulmonary resuscitation if unconscious and veterinary care quickly if the remedies fail.

Arthritis and Hip Dysplasia: In addition to the remedies listed below, Dr. Dodd suggests *Kali carbonica* (potassium carbonate) as a joint fluid and lymph drainer. When the animal is sore and stiff on getting up, but moves more easily once started, try *Rhus tox* (poison ivy); in the opposite, where pain seems worse for movement and the animal is lame, the remedy is *Bryonia* (wild hops). This may be a younger animal—she doesn't want to move. *Arnica* (leopard's bane) is for swelling, bruising or pain; try one pellet three times a day for a few days. When there is swelling in the joints, with pain, sudden onset, and reddened skin, the dis-ease may respond to *Apis* (honeybee venom).

Caulophyllum (blue cohosh) is used where smaller joints are affected, particularly in the feet and neck. This is targeted for female animals with a herstory of genital and reproductive problems. The less powerful cell salts, *Natrum phorphoricum* (*Nat. phos.* or sodium phosphate) and *Natrum sulphuricaum* (*Nat. sulph.,* sodium sulfate) may help mild arthritic conditions; give them daily together for several weeks.

Actea racemosa (black snakeroot, also listed as *Cimicfuga racemosa*) is for arthritis and rheumatism that seems to affect the whole body, joints as well as surrounding muscles. The animal's movement is slow and heavy. Lower vertebrae and hips are affected, and this is a remedy for hip dysplasia in dogs. Another remedy for dysplasia is *Conium maculatum* (hemlock); the animal's hind legs tend to sway, there is difficulty of movement in the hindquarters, loss of body control, and painful stiffness. This remedy is for seriously advanced dysplasia. Remember *Arnica* for pain, or *Hypericum* (St. John/Joan's wort) where there has been nerve damage. For general stiffness, or when other remedies fail, try *Sulfur*.

Remember the natural, preservative free diet and vitamin C, and avoid raw meat and sugar.

Cancer and Tumors: I once treated an eleven-year-old tomcat with tumors all over his body. He responded to *Thuja occidentalis* (tree of life, arbor vitae) 30C and the tumors were gone within two weeks. This is a remedy for warty tumors, malignant or benign, and for vaccination reactions—is one caused by the other? For breast tumors in dogs or cats, try *Phytolacca decandra* (pokeroot); Richard Pitcairn uses this in an herb elixir 1C potency. It will reduce the size and hardness of breast growths. In older animals where the tumors are accompanied by lymphatic swelling and muscular weakness, especially of the hindquarters, try *Conium maculatum* (hemlock). There may be chronic ulcers with discharge. *Iodum* (iodine) is indicated in too thin animals with great appetite and small hard lymph glands. The animal seems shriveled looking, and the tumors may be superficial. Try *Bellis perennis* (daisy) when the growth was caused by an injury. Gloria Dodd suggests success in reducing hard stone-like tumors with *Baryta carb* (carbonate of baryta) in 30C potency, followed by nosodes of the specific tumor/cancer and lymph drainers.

Richard Pitcairn suggests the following tissue salts: *Kali muriaticum* (*Kali mur.*, potassium chloride) where the tumors feel soft and are sensitive to pressure; *Kali phorphoricum* (*Kali phos.*, potassium phosphate) where the tumors discharge a smelly secretion, and the animal is high-strung or exhausted; or *Silicea* (silica) where there is pustular discharge and hard swelling. Use these three times a day over a period of time.

For cancer in general, he uses *Hydrastis canadensis* (goldenseal). Cancer nosodes include *Schirrhinum* or *Carcinosinum* in 30C or 200C potency, and these are also recommended. Cancer is considered a constitutional dis-ease, with treatment by an experienced homeopath advisable.

Cataracts: This is best treated in the earliest stages and diet change is essential. Remember the eucalyptus honey of the herb chapter. *Conium maculatum* (hemlock) may help, especially in older weakened animals; vision is dim and worse in artificial light. There may be excessive tearing and sensitivity to sunlight. *Phosphorus* is a possibility for cataracts, glaucoma and retinal degeneration. *Euphrasia* (eyebright) helps where there is tearing, but will not remove the cataract, and *Silicea* can delay the progress—Dr. Dodd recommends it as primary for mature cataracts in dogs. Use these up to two or three times daily for low potencies. *Cineraria* (Dusty Miller) eyedrops, the Mother Tincture, are used in a dilution of one to ten with pure water, and placed in the eyes (two to three drops) daily for about two months.

Three of the cell salts, especially when used in higher homeopathic potency (30C for example, instead of the usual 6X), are indicated for healing cataracts by several sources. Use *Calcarea fluorica* (*Calc. fluor.*, calcium fluoride) in 30C potency daily for about two weeks to prevent further degeneration in early stages of the dis-ease. *Natrum muriaticum* (*Nat. mur.*, sodium chloride) is used when the cataracts also accompany kidney dis-ease. The dog or cat is noticeably thirsty and is also in run-down condition. Use one dose daily for three weeks in 30C potency. *Silicea* (silica) can resorb scar tissue and is recommended in 200C potency, giving one dose weekly for eight weeks. Richard Pitcairn suggests these in 6X cell salt strengths for use four times a day over several weeks. My personal recommendation is for the higher doses.

Constipation and Diarrhea: These respond very well to homeopathic remedies, but change of diet in chronic cases is essential. *Nux vomica* (poison nut) is usually the remedy of choice for simple constipation or diarrhea. This is for general digestive disturbances, often related to overindulgence (eating too much, stealing the pizza, too many bones, garbage can raiding), or emotional upset. There may be vomiting, gas and abdominal (liver area) tenderness. The animal may be irritable and avoid being touched; she may strain to eliminate but produce little. After her binge, she is off her feed. Give small doses after each attempt to eliminate (6X), larger ones three times a day (6C) or watch for reaction.

Alumina (aluminum) is for the animal suspected of aluminum heavy metal poisoning; there is chronic constipation with sticky or messy stools. There may be frequent vomiting and lymphatic involvement. When *Bryonia* (wild hops) is the remedy, the dog or cat prefers not to move. Stools are hard and look burnt, and the mucus membranes are dry. Try *Lycopodium* (club moss) when liver involvement is suspected; symptoms are worse in the afternoon and the pet may have respiratory problems. If the constipation goes with skin trouble, try *Sulfur*, and if there is gas with simple constipation, try *Carbo veg* (vegetable charcoal).

Gloria Dodd has worked extensively with aluminum poisoning, see Appendix III. To treat it homeopathically, she uses *Alumina* along with lymphatic drainers *Zinc cyanatum* and *Agaricus musc* (poison mushroom) for brain and nervous system clearing. Use 30C potency or higher. She comments that aluminum toxicity has been present "in *every animal I have ever tested* with hair analysis and EAV."

Returning to constipation and diarrhea—*Natrum muriaticum* (*Nat. mur.*, sodium chloride) can be used in cell salt strengths (6X) or in higher homeopathic concentrations. This is an especially useful remedy for cats. There may be excessive thirst, sores in the mouth and general weakness. Stool seems dry and hard to expel but there are other watery discharges (watery eyes, watery vomiting, heavy salivation or urination). If the animal can't seem to expel the bowel movement, try *Silicea* (silica), again in either cell salt 6X potency or higher homeopathic strength. If constipation alternates with diarrhea, the remedy is *Graphites* (black lead); the anus is sore and the animal is timid. Also try *Nux vomica*. Use *Sepia* (cuttlefish ink) for constipation during pregnancy.

For diarrhea in cats or dogs try the following, matching the remedy closest to the animal's symptoms. *Arsenicum* (arsenic) is used when diarrhea is accompanied by vomiting. The vomiting can be frequent and the animal is extremely restless and feels cold to the touch. She is thirsty, but vomits back water almost immediately. When there is frequent diarrhea with straining but no vomiting, try *Mercurius corrosivus* (corrosive sublimate). These are for acute situations, with dysentery or food poisoning suspected, but chronic diarrhea may respond to the same remedies. For dysentery with vomiting, try *Ipecac* (ipecacuanha, ipecac root).

Phosphorus is the remedy for copious, chronic debilitating diarrhea; *China* (quinine) when there has been great loss of body fluids and debility after a long attack of diarrhea; and *Colocynthis* (bitter cucumber) when diarrhea comes with colic and pain. The animal is extremely irritable and angry.

Newton Homeopathic's combination remedy for diarrhea includes in 10X potency: *Baptisia* (wild indigo), *China* (quinine, Peruvian bark), *Elaterium* (squirting cucumber), *Iris versicolor* (blue flag), and *Lycopodium* (club moss).

Diabetes: This is best controlled by diet and holistic means, if possible. George Macleod says it affects primarily neutered male cats, and female dogs over five years, as well as elder animals of both sexes. Every source that talks about diabetes in pets comments on its increasing incidence. *Syzygium* (jambol seeds) seems to be the remedy of primary choice. Says the Boericke *Materia Medica* of the remedy:

A most useful remedy in diabetes mellitus. No other remedy causes in so marked degree the diminution and disappearance of sugar in the urine. Prickly heat in upper part of the body small red pimples itch violently. Great thirst, weakness, emaciation. Very large amounts of urine, specific gravity high. Old ulcers of skin. Diabetic ulceration.[14]

Gloria Dodd uses *Syzygium* in combination with *Diabetogenic factor* (a nosode), and *Cactus grandiflora* (night-blooming cereus) as a lymph drainer. If the patient is at very low energy and has body discharges, she adds *Carbo animalis* (animal charcoal), or *Carbo veg* (vegetable charcoal) if the pet is fat and lazy. *Senna* is used if the skin is very dry, along with the *Syzygium* combination. For diabetes with skin involvement, a homeopathic preparation of *Insulin* may also be indicated. Boericke suggests this in a 3X to 30X dose.

Uranium nitricum (nitrate of uranium) is used for diabetes with emaciation and dropsy; there is frequent urination, abdominal bloating that is prominent, and dry mucus membranes. Dropsy (kidney and liver involvement) calls for this remedy. George Macleod suggests a 30C potency for either cats or dogs, used three times a week for six weeks. *Iris versicolor* (blue flag) is a good general pancreatic remedy; the animal has loose yellowish looking stools. *Iodum* (iodine) is the remedy where diabetes is accompanied by yellowish green urine with a milky appearance, and stool is light colored and loose, sometimes frothy.

When there is great debility *Phosphoricum acidum* (phosphoric acid) may help. When there are cataracts with diabetes, try *Calcarea fluorica* (calcium fluoride) or *Silicea* in 30C potency. Also see the section on cataracts. These remedies do not replace insulin therapy, but in early and mild cases may be enough with change of diet to prevent the need for insulin. Again, as in all holistic remedies for this dis-ease (or for insulin use), the remedies must be used carefully and consistently. Stopping and starting can result in the animal's death. Monitor insulin levels frequently.

Feline Leukemia: Richard Pitcairn uses homeopathic goldenseal for this, *Hydrastis canadensis,* in the 1C potency, one drop twice a day. Follow his protocol given earlier in this chapter. I would also try higher potencies, particularly once the animal's improvement plateaus on lower ones. He also suggests two of the cell salts (6X), *Natrum muriaticum* (*nat. mur.*, sodium chloride) one tablet three times a day for a weak cat with severe anemia and dehydration, and *Calcarea phosphorica* (*Calc. phos.*, calcium phosphate) one tablet twice a day. The *Calc. phos.* is the secondary remedy, use them together but do not give the two remedies at the same time.

George Macleod calls any treatment for feline leukemia, even by homeopathy, speculative at this time. A nosode of FeLv infected blood is available, and another is made from homeopathically prepared lymphosarcoma tumor tissue. Some cases respond to these remedies, others do not. One cat with a lymphosarcoma tumor responded to a combination of the nosode and homeopathic *Phosphorus*. He also suggests *Calcarea Fluorica* or *Silicea* for swollen lymph glands. The nosodes are being used as an oral vaccine, as well.[15]

Newton Laboratories markets a combination remedy for feline leukemia made of the following homeopathics in 10X potency: *Baptisia* (wild indigo), *Lachesis* (bushmaster snake venom), *China* (quinine), *Phosphorus* (itself), and *Pulsatilla* (wind flower). The remedy is designated for leukemia and for weight loss due to ill health. Remember also the vitamin C treatment. Use it with the homeopathic goldenseal or other homeopathic remedies.

Gloria Dodd, DVM comments on her work with feline leukemia:

Feline Leukemia—extremely difficult to treat and almost impossible if the cat has had treatment with corticosteroids. Corticosteroids depress the already depressed immune system by the virus further until there is irreversible damage. A feline leuk. cat with nonresponsive anemia is almost impossible to treat also. The problem with a holistic veterinary practice is that we almost never see the animals early in the disease but after all the orthodox doctors have loaded the cat's system with so many drugs that we find little we can do. However there have been some recoveries and cats have reverted to Feline Leukemia Negative.

You have to be careful how you evaluate a FeLv negative status. The FeLv virus is capable of going dormant in the bone marrow, the cat is asymptomatic, all blood tests are negative but the cat is still carrying the virus. Dr. Pederson at the University of California Veterinary School research FeLv colony has found that these cats will break with the clinical disease again if stressed with X-rays, steroids, or vaccinations. The EAV method (See Appendix I) is the only way you confidently know if the cat truly has kicked the virus or not.

DO NOT, I repeat, DO NOT expose a seemingly recovered FeLv cat to any of these immune stressing factors, nor let your cat outdoors (both as a precautionary measure that the virus may be shed by your cat, nor the pressures and stresses of cars, other cats, and dogs). Absolutely DO NOT vaccinate a "recovered" FeLv cat with the FeLv vaccine. In fact, we saw so many cats break clinically with FeLv after the shot we don't recommend it—we prefer the oral homeopathic vaccination for FeLv.

My treatment for corticosteroid depressed FeLv cats was detoxification, stimulation of the immune system and supportive therapy for the involved organs. Detoxification of the steroids by the homeopathic steroid, weekly administration of potentized homeopathic FeLv with weekly increased potencies (I may start at 30C and go up to 10M before completely ridding the cat of the virus). I also used the EAV to detox with nosodes for Rabies Vaccination, FDVRTC combination vaccines, any pesticides and drugs found. A home-made clean diet detoxed by Parcell's method of clorox soaks, ozone injections, and I had a pulsating electromagnetic machine that I used at the setting of 50 guass–2 cycles per second frequency at 30 minutes.

I taught my clients to stimulate the acupuncture points for the immune system (the chart is included in the chapter on acupuncture) on a two times daily basis and the use of the color to augment treatment. Usually the cat is in adrenal gland exhaustion and anemic—red color light therapy (and Rescue Remedy) is very useful to "lift" the life force and stimulate new RBC (red blood cell) formation. My "Energyzing" Halter (See Appendix I) was worn night and day, and quartz crystals were placed in water dishes to charge the water molecules the cat drank. I had the owner do visualization techniques and play a lot of Mozart (charges all 7 chakras). Of course mega-vitamin therapy (basic 3 legged support under the cat were vitamins A, E and C plus a good multivitamin/mineral tablet).

All noxious energy fields were removed from the environment and a hair analysis was done to analyze the imbalances in the electrolytes and minerals. All heavy metals were also detoxed with nosodes. In my practice these were very sick cats, some almost comatose and it took many months to bring a good majority back. Some didn't make it, but the ones that did live became completely FeLv free—and even bred and had FeLv negative (and viral-free) kittens.

Heart Dis-ease and Hypertension: *Crataegus oxycantha* (hawthorn berries) is the traditional heart remedy for an animal with extreme breathlessness on exertion. She has an irregular, weak or intermittent pulse, symptoms that worsen for warmth, and high blood pressure. The dog or cat is nervous and irritable. *Crataegus* strengthens the heart and heart action and may be used daily long term. Give a low potency (IX, 4X) two or three times a day, or use the 30C when needed.

Convallaria majalis (lily of the valley) increases heart action energy and regulates heart rate. There is difficult breathing and dropsy, angina, palpitations from the least exertion and lung congestion. *Digitalis purpurea* (foxglove) is used after faintness or prostration following exertion. The pulse or heartbeat is abnormally slow, the animal may collapse, she may have a blue tongue and liver involvement. By giving a tablet (6X) after each attack, attacks become less frequent and less severe.

Apis mellifica (bee venom) is indicated when there is edema (water retention, dropsy); use a 6X potency three or four times a day for ten days. *Strophanthus hispidus* (kombe-seed) is for heart weakness due to valve problems; there is a weak, irregular pulse, difficult breathing, and the animal may be obese and with chronic itching and edema. *Adonis vernalis* (pheasant's eye) is a cardiac tonic and diuretic. It regulates the pulse and aids dropsy. Use a low 3X potency, three times a day for thirty days. *Carbo veg* (vegetable charcoal) aids breathing; use a 200C potency daily for seven days or as needed. *Spongia tosta* (toasted sponge) is for the dry cough of heart disease; use one dose daily for ten days in 30C potency, also for asthma. The animal's breath may sound gasping.

In case of an actual heart attack, *Aconite* (monkshood) is a first aid measure. *Cactus grandiflorus* (night-blooming cereus) has the symptom picture of constriction of the heart and arteries, and is also used in emergencies. Symptoms for *Cactus* include angina, palpitations, heart pain, edema, breathing difficulty, arteriosclerosis, valve insufficiency, and general heart dis-ease. Where the animal does not respond to other remedies, she may respond to *Cactus. Crataegus* and *Cactus* are probably the two primary remedies for animals or people with heart dis-ease and hypertension (high blood pressure).

Injuries, Cuts and Burns: Aconite napellus (monkshood) is the first aid remedy for trauma and shock; it is useful in all kinds of accidents and its primary symptom is fear. *Arnica montana* (leopard's bane) is the remedy for bruising, falls, blows, soreness, and septic conditions. It is used internally in potency after any accident, and used externally as an ointment or tincture (compress) when the skin is unbroken. The Mother Tincture of *Arnica* is not for internal use, and is not for external use

when the skin is cut or broken. The animal fears touch or being approached, is nervous, oversensitive, and wants to be left alone. For shock due to grief, use *Ignatia.*

Hypericum (St. John/Joan's wort) prevents tetanus in puncture wounds and is for any injuries that affect the nerves (a crushed tail-tip or toes). Its main symptom is great pain, which the remedy relieves. It is used after surgeries for recovery, after injuries from animal bites in fights, and for spasms and asthma attacks. *Hypericum* is used as pellets internally and in ointments or liquids topically. There may be shock or melancholy in the animal that requires it and always pain.

Urtica urens (stinging nettles) is used to relieve the pain of skin burns, scalds and rashes. Give as pellets internally and the liquid or ointment externally. *Calendula officinalis* (marigold) is for the rapid healing of open wounds, wounds that will not heal, wounds with pus, and ulcers. Though marigold is contraindicated as an herbal for cats, Anitra Frazier still uses calendula on her animals. It comes in ointments and tinctures and is a remarkable healer.

Injuries with strains respond to *Ruta graveolens* (rue) for the periosteum (bone covering) and cartilages, tendons, bruised bones, lameness after sprains, or body pain. The dog or cat is highly restless, or lethargic, weak and despairing. Long-term effects of injuries respond to *Hamamelis virginica* (witch hazel). *Ledum* (marsh-tea) is used for puncture wounds and animal or insect bites. If the wounded parts feel cold, this is the remedy, used as pellets internally. Ledum antidotes spider poisons.

Burns respond primarily to Calendula, Hypericum or Urtica urens, usually in external tinctures or lotions. For first degree burns (redness only) use Calendula tincture or lotion topically, and *Urtica urens* (stinging nettles) internally every few hours for pain. For second degree burns (with blistering), use Hypericum or Urtica urens tinctures topically, taking care not to break the blisters. Cut the hair away from the burn. After the blisters break of themselves, use Calendula topically, and internally use *Urtica urens* for stinging burning, *Causticum* for burning, rawness, soreness, or *Cantharis* for raw burning pain. Third degree burns (charred flesh) require veterinary care. No topical applications are used until the burn is almost healed. Use *Cantharis* (Spanish fly) internally for pain.[16] If the animal is in shock, use *Aconite* (monkshood) first, then *Arnica* (leopard's bane) internally.

Skin and Coat Ailments: Clearing skin and coat ailments in dogs or cats depends primarily on changing to a preservative free, optimal nutrition diet with supplements. Avoid steroids or cortisone at all costs, and these drugs will also interfere with homeopathic treatment. *Sulfur* is a primary remedy for chronic skin conditions and dry eczema, and often works when other remedies fail. Animals that prefer cool places respond to this remedy; they dislike getting wet, have very red body openings, and dry, hard hair and skin. Animals that prefer warmth, and have great thirst and dry skin with discharges and burning pain respond to *Arsenicum album* (arsenic). There may be dry, scaly eczema with itching, inflammation and swelling of the area.

When the skin eruptions start as fluid-filled blisters that the animal bites and scratches at, the remedy is *Rhus tox* (poison ivy). *Graphites* (black lead) is for skin conditions with sticky discharges, and *Cantharis* (Spanish fly) for scaly eruptions with burning and itching, often around the genitals. Use *Mercurius solubilis* (mercury) for wet eczema, with pustular eruptions and pimples, much discharge and yellowish brown crusts. The dog or cat is weakened by exertion and is worse at night. For eczema with intolerable itching, try *Mezereum* (spurge olive).

A dry, scaly skin with dandruff, responds to *Arsenicum album;* or use *Sulfur* for red skin with dandruff. Again, diet is the key here. *Petroleum* (crude oil) is the remedy for cracks in the skin, especially between the toes, that bleed easily. *Cortisone* may be used in homeopathic preparation (not the drug) for stubborn skin inflammations.

For cats with miliary eczema and alopecia (baldness), a dis-ease that appears after neutering, *Staphisagria* (stavesacre) is the first remedy to try, particularly for the animal that is angry about the surgery. If these do not heal the skin, try homeopathic hormone replacement—potentized *Ovarinum* and *Folliculinum* in females or *Testosterone* in males (30C).

Newton Laboratories has a skin combination for eczema, mange and fungus, that contains in 10X potency: *Mezereum* (spurge olive), *Graphites* (black lead), *Lachesis* (snake venom), *Antimonium crudum* (black sulphide of antimony), and *Croton tiglium* (croton oil).

Some cell salts for skin dis-eases include *Ferrum phorphoricum* (*Ferrum phos.,* iron phosphate) alternated with *Natrum phosphoricum* (*Nat. phos.,* sodium phosphate) for the acute phase of inflammation. *Kali phosphoricum* (*Kali phos.,* potassium phosphate) can be substituted for the *Nat. phos.* if the animal is irritable and upset. For long-term itchy and greasy or dry scaly skin check thyroid function, and try the following tissue salts. For a nervous animal with greasy hair, odor and itching, try *Kali phosphoricum* (*Kali phos.*). For the animal with greasy, oily skin that is irritated and itchy, use *Natrum muriaticum* (*Nat. mur.*)—the animal may have a thyroid imbalance. *Silicea* is for the cat or dog with pimples or pus-like eruptions. She is oversensitive and irritable, and the problems sometimes begin after vaccinating. If an animal has hair loss and a poor nutritional background, try *Calcarea phosphorica* (*Calc. phos.,* calcium phosphate)—and be sure to correct the diet. These are all in 6X potency and used twice a day; the information on cell salts is from Richard Pitcairn.

Spinal Problems: Remember vitamin C here, and chiropractic or acupuncture are strongly recommended. Says holistic veterinarian Gloria Dodd, "99.9% of all injuries to the spine require adjusting (chiropractic) for complete healing and correction of blockages to the chi flow."[17] Homeopathy can be a good support to this treatment and is known to have effected many miracles of its own. With an animal injured in this way, use all the methods and resources available.

Nux vomica (poison nut) in low potency is the place to start for pain, tightness and hindquarter symptoms, especially as soon after they begin as possible. Dr. Richard Pitcairn who suggests this remedy, also suggests tissue salts *Kali phosphoricum* (*Kali phos.,* potassium phosphate) or *Magnesia phosphorica* (*Mag. phos.,* magnesium phosphate) in 6X potency. These can be used in alternation or alone, three times a day for several weeks.

If there has been an injury or sudden "going out" of the back, use *Arnica* (leopard's bane) initially, every two hours. If the animal is sensitive to cold and the spine sensitive to touch, try *Hypericum* (St. John/Joan's wort) internally and as external compresses. If the symptoms worsen in damp weather or seem to improve after the dog or cat starts moving, the remedy is *Rhus tox* (poison ivy); if worse with movement, use *Bryonia* (wild hops)—the animal has a staggering gait, wants to be alone, and may bite or howl. *Conium macalatum* (hemlock) is for rear end paralysis. There is stiffness, difficult gait, trembling, loss of strength and weakness, often in older animals.

For motor paralysis affecting a front or hind limb, try *Lathrys* (chick-pea); there is a rigid, spastic gait, tottering, the knees may knock together when walking. A limb hanging down may be swollen or look emaciated. *Gelsemium* (yellow jasmine) may be the remedy in mild cases where the cat or dog is noticeably lethargic. *Plumbum metallicum* (lead) may help in motor paralysis, paralysis of the lower limbs. There are cramps and twitching, with the animal in evident pain; the paws are cold and symptoms are worse at night and with motion. Light pressure on the spine eases pain. *Silicea* (silica) in 200C potency (not cell salt 6X) may help a lean or undernourished pet with hardening of the nerve sheaths (spondylosis). If motor paralysis is persistent despite homeopathy, Dr. Dodd suggests considering pesticide poisoning (especially Malathion or methyl carbamate), and/or Rabies vaccination toxic energy as cause. Try nosodes.

When there is a slipped disc, *Ruta graveolens* (rue) is used for injuries effecting bone and cartilage, and for the vertebrae. It can be used along with *Hypericum,* as a pain reliever and for the nerves, particularly when the problem is in the lower part of the spine. When used with *Ruta,* alternate the remedies. If the slipped disc resulted from an injury, use *Arnica* (leopard's bane) first, then dose with *Symphytum* (comfrey) in 30C as needed; the two can also be alternated. *Augustura vera* (bark of galipea cusparia) is used for nerve damage and spinal cord injuries; it may limit nerve damage from the protruding disc. Symptoms include stiffness of muscles and joints, paralysis, great difficulty walking and pain worse with pressure. There may be twitching or jerking along the back; the animal bends backward and is highly oversensitive. Gloria Dodd uses *Ruta* and *Hypericum* together in 10M potency for disc injuries and protrusions, one to three times daily.

A combination remedy for backache, indicated for slipped disc and rheumatism from Newton Homeopathics contains in 10X potency: *Rhus tox* (poison ivy), *Ruta graveolens* (rue), *Guiacum* (resin of lignum vitae), *Strychninum* (strychnine), and *Colchicum* (meadow saffron).

Urinary Tract Infections, Kidney and Bladder Disease: For cats or dogs with urinary obstruction and inability to urinate due to stones, try *Thlaspi bursa pastoris* (shepherd's purse) as an emergency first aid. Dose every half hour until the animal urinates, but if there is no relief within two or three hours, a veterinarian must be seen immediately. This is an emergency situation that re-quires catheterization if the remedy fails. Give a dose of *Aconite* (monkshood) also, to reduce fear, as the animal will be highly distressed.

For cystitis, a bladder infection without blockage, there is frequency of need to urinate, little flow, and possibly blood in the urine. *Cantharis* (Spanish fly) is the primary remedy here; with the above symptoms, there may be high anxiety or crying. *Urtica urens* (stinging nettles) is for the cat or dog with urinary infection that wants warmth and is reluctant to move. She wants to be left alone. There may be blood in the urine. George Macleod recommends a 6C potency, Richard Pitcairn a 6X. *Apis mellifica* (honeybee venom) is for the animal that refuses heat, rather than seeks it. The urine is highly concentrated, odorous but without blood, and is passed in small amounts. *Rhus tox* (poison ivy) is for the cat particularly that develops bladder infections from sitting on cold cement and getting chilled. Once sick, she prefers warmth and wants to be touched. She is restless and moves frequently, and the urine is scanty but dark and may contain blood. Again, use *Aconite* if the animal is distressed, and *Pulsatilla* (wind flower) may be a good overall remedy for affectionate cats with feline urologic syndrome (FUS).

When cystitis (FUS) is chronic or after the acute and inflammatory stages above, try *Equisetum* (horsetail grass); the animal urinates frequently and worse at night, but is still uncomfortable. There is little straining. Use 30C potency daily for ten days. *Eupatorium perfolatum* (boneset or thoroughwort) is for urinary "gravel" and high albumen content in chronic form. Where the bladder has become thickened, and the urine has sediment and an ammonia smell, the remedy is *Pareira brava* (virgin vine). There is constant urging, much straining and thick, dark or bloody urine. *Causticum* (Hahnemann's tinctura acris sine Kali) can be used to follow *Cantharis* when bladder infections recur or become chronic. This especially benefits the older animal.

Veterinarian Gloria Dodd treats feline urologic syndrome as follows:

I use the combination homeopathics: *Cantharis* 6X (for painful burning sensation), *Belladonna* 6X (antispasmodic to the urethra and bladder sphincter), *Cuprum metallicum* 50M (very strong antispasmodic which you need to overcome the basic smooth muscle spasms of the urinary tract), *Berberis vulgaris* 6X (because most cases of cystitis are associated with liver and kidney dysfunctions), and *Hydrastis* 6X (lymph drainer of all epithelial lined organs). If there is blood I add *Ferrum phos.* 6X. For kidney or urinary bladder stone problems I add liver supportive treatments, for the liver pathology is the basic source of the stone formation in the urinary tract. Again the stone formation is due to a liver toxic with drugs, chemicals and vaccination effects.

While bladder infections are more frequent in cats, and are too often the cause of their deaths, dogs get them also though less frequently. Dogs more often develop urinary stones and kidney problems. In female dogs after spaying, stones can be the result of hormone imbalance. Kidney problems (chronic nephritis) in older dogs is a cause of many early dog deaths. Use *Mercurius solubilis* (mercury) for this and follow the animal's reactions. If there is blood in the urine, try *Cantharis*; the *Materia Medica* suggests potencies from 2C to 30C.

Newton Homeopathics' combination remedy for Kidney Help (cystitis, stones and incontinence) includes the following in 10X potency: *Solidago virgo* (goldenrod), *Berberis vulgaris* (barberry), *Cantharis* (Spanish fly), *Equisetum* (horsetail grass), and *Lycopodium* (club moss).

Viral Dis-eases: At first onset, when the animal appears restless and the dis-ease may not yet be defined, use *Aconite* (monkshood) 30C; this has been known to abort many illnesses when used early. Give a dose an hour for four hours, then discontinue. Symptoms will either worsen or disappear. The next step for influenza/distemper type dis-eases is *Gelsemium* (yellow jasmine); there is apathy, drowsiness and trembling, complete relaxation. There may be respiratory problems and sore throat. If neither of these stop the illness, go to *Distemperinum* (distemper nosode) or a nosode of the diagnosed dis-ease in 30C twice a day until the animal is well.

For cough, give *Bryonia* (wild hops); there is difficult, rapid respiration, a full hard pulse, and fever. If the animal is hot, feverish, with glaring eyes, restlessness and an excited mental state, try *Belladonna* (deadly nightshade). When there are flu symptoms, fever, loose cough or sneezing, great thirst and soreness; the remedy is *Eupatorium perfoliatum* (boneset or thoroughwort).

Homeopathic goldenseal, *Hydrastis canadensis,* can be used in advanced viral dis-ease, where there is yellow mucus discharge from nose or eyes, and depression. There may be skin eruptions. For a weak, depressed, cold animal with vomiting and diarrhea, worsened by drinking water,

use *Veratrum album* (white hellebore). Dr. Pitcairn suggests a 6X potency every hour or two, decreasing the frequency as the animal responds. When there is vomiting, diarrhea with bad odor and a blood tinge, restlessness, and the animal craves frequent small sips of water, the remedy is *Arsenicum album* (arsenic). For high fever and weak pulse with putrid, bad-smelling discharges *Pyrogen* (artificial sepsin) may be the remedy that works. The animal is highly restless and delirious—and seriously ill.

Remember the megadose vitamin C therapy and fasting, as well as Juliette de Bairacli Levy's herbal information. Herb tinctures can be made into homeopathic remedies by Dr. Pitcairn's formula. Do not force feed an animal with fever.

Homeopathy is an exact science and is more difficult to learn and use than some other methods of holistic healing. The rewards for the work make it well worth it, however, with results that can sometimes only be described as miraculous. It is my sincere wish that many more veterinarians and laywomen gain expertise in this system of healing. With careful use of a guidebook or *Materia Medica* and a basic homeopathic remedy selection, much healing for pets and people can be accomplished in the safest and easiest ways. Several places for ordering homeopathic remedies by mail are included in the Resources section. Most of these sources, and many health food stores, also carry books on using homeopathy for pets.

[1]Dana Ullman, *Homeopathy: Medicine for the 21st Century* (Berkeley, CA: North Atlantic Books, 1988), pp. 47–50.
[2]Francis Hunter, MRCVS, *Homeopathic First-Aid Treatment for Pets* (Great Britain: Thorsen's Publishers, Ltd., 1984), p. 12.
[3]William Boericke, M.D., *Pocket Manual of Homeopathic Materia Medica* (New Delhi, India: Jain Publishers Pvt., Ltd., 1987), p. 507.
[4]Dana Ullman, *Homeopathy: Medicine for the 21st Century,* p. 7.
[5]Francis Hunter, MRCVS, *Homeopathic First-Aid Treatment for Pets,* p. 15.
[6]Anitra Frazier with Norma Eckroate, *The New Natural Cat: A Complete Guide for Finicky Owners* (New York: Plume Books, 1990), p. 260.
[7]Francis Hunter, MRCVS, *Homeopathic First-Aid Treatment for Pets,* p. 16.
[8]Richard Pitcairn, DVM and Susan Hubble Pitcairn, *Dr. Pitcairn's Complete Guide to Natural Health for Dogs and Cats* (Emmaus, PA: Rodale Press, 1982), p. 193.
[9]Diane Stein, *All Women Are Healers* (Freedom, CA: The Crossing Press, 1990), pp. 214–215. And Dana Ullman, *Homeopathy: Medicine for the 21st Century,* pp. 25–28.
[10]Anita Frazier, *The New Natural Cat,* pp. 265–266.
[11]Richard Pitcairn, DVM, *Dr. Pitcairn's Complete Guide to Natural Health for Dogs and Cats,* pp. 250–252.
[12]George Macleod, MRCVS, DVSM, *Cats: Homeopathic Remedies* (Essex,

England: C.W. Daniel Co., Ltd., 1990), p. 145.

[13]Richard Pitcairn, DVM, *Dr. Pitcairn's Complete Guide to Natural Health for Dogs and Cats,* p. 155.

[14]William Boericke, M.D., *Pocket Manual of Homeopathic Materia Medica,* p. 629.

[15]George Macleod, *Cats: Homeopathic Remedies,* pp. 157–159. And Richard Pitcairn, DVM, *Dr. Pitcairn's Complete Guide to Natural Health for Dogs and Cats,* pp. 193–194.

[16]Cindy Brown, M.D., in Diane Stein, *The Natural Remedy Book for Women,* p. 135.

[17]Gloria Dodd, DVM, Personal Communication, June 22, 1992.

Animal Acupuncture & Acupressure

Acupuncture, the piercing of specific body-map points with fine needles, and acupressure, stimulating the points without needles using hand pressure, are two of the oldest methods of healing known. Acupuncture was used in paleolithic times—needles and tools have been discovered as old as 5000 BCE—and was developed for use on both large animals and people. Early Asians (and modern Chinese) paid little attention to healing dogs and cats but kept draft animals healthy for economic reasons. The method was highly regarded and thoroughly researched in ancient China and Asia for thousands of years, but fell into disuse and disfavor and was forbidden in 1822. The Communist regime in China revived acupuncture, which had gone underground, relegated to the low status of "folk medicine," in the same way that traditional healing has been degraded and ridiculed in the west.

Acupuncture for people was brought to the west relatively recently, first by Jesuit missionaries in the seventeenth and eighteenth centuries, and later as result of China's opening of relations with the west. The lessening of east-west tensions for about fifteen years before Tiananmen Square fostered an exchange of information that established acupuncture in the United States. Veterinary acupuncture was developed in Europe, taking Chinese information on human and large animal acupuncture and transferring it for use on small animals (dogs and cats). Both Asian and European (and ancient and modern information and treatment maps)[1] techniques are now being used, with some confusion among various systems. At this time there are acupuncture point charts used for dogs, cats, horses, camels, cows and pigs.[1] The information seems the most complete for horses (ancient information brought from China), and least complete for cats (modern European and American development), but the points and their uses are described as the same in all animals.

In modern use, acupuncture is becoming widely known and used for humans, and increasingly for animals in this country, with differences in various locales. When I lived in Pittsburgh, acupuncture was virtually unavailable and unknown, though several women did acupressure and reflexology. In Florida it is readily available with a number of practicing Chinese and Caucasian doctors, some of whom work on pets, and at least one trained veterinary acupuncturist in the area. In veterinary use, the method is described as giving successful cures in seventy to seventy-five percent of animals cases, many of them listed as incurable by standard veterinary medicine.[2]

The method is used to treat such dis-eases as hip dysplasia, spinal and disc problems, arthritis, lameness, nerve deafness, dermatitis and behavioral problems. In addition, it has been used with high success rates for pain, chronic digestive disturbances, nerve injuries, lick granulomas, epilepsy, chronic respiratory dis-eases, allergies, distemper and feline leukemia. Acupuncture is not recommended for healing animals with cancer, as it may stimulate the dis-ease. A total number of about a thousand individual acupuncture points are used. Needles are inserted from one-eighth to three-eighths of an inch into the animal's skin; there is surprisingly little fight or resistance from cats and dogs during the treatment; it seems to sedate them. In China, acupuncture is also used for anesthesia, during surgeries.

Points used for animal acupuncture in the west follow those used in Asia:

1. Points along the meridian lines.
2. Local points close to the ailment site.
3. Local and distant points along the same meridian combined.
4. Bilateral (both sides) paired points.
5. Paired points on the forelegs and hindlegs.
6. Matching points on dorsal and ventral (top and underside) parts of the body.
7. Matching yin and yang points.
8. Points indicated for specific diseases.
9. Points from human and other veterinary use, and/or as described by other acupuncturists.[3]

There is a variety of methods for stimulating the points once the needles are inserted, the best known being the use of moxibustion, heating the points with mugwort herb. The points may also be stimulated electrically or by soft laser, or by injecting sterile water, pain relievers, or vitamin B-12. Tiny metal beads or staples can also be surgically inserted into meridian points for permanent stimulation, for example in chronic pain relief or epilepsy—permanent action on a particular point. There are fourteen major meridians classically used in animals, energy pathways in pairs along which the acupuncture points are located. Dr. Reinhard Voll discovered sixteen new meridians in modern times, which he termed "vessels." The meridians relate specifically to ten major body organs. Organs can be stimulated by these meridian points with the needles and other stimulation methods. Diagnoses of dis-ease are also made by palpating specific points. If an organ is impaired (the chi to it is imbalanced), the points that relate to that organ will be sensitive. Treatments last from five to twenty minutes, and few animals require more than eleven treatments for serious chronic dis-ease. Most require less.

Veterinary acupuncture with needles requires a highly trained technician, and is not a method for the untrained to use at home. The International Veterinary Acupuncture Society lists 500 members who have completed the four-week intensive training for veterinarians (300 in the United States).[4] A list of practitioners is available from IVAS, Meredith L. Snader, DVM, 2140 Conestoga Rd., Chester Springs, PA 19425, (215) 827-7245. An additional number of practitioners may be found among traditionally trained Chinese doctors working in the west, some of whom will treat pets. (Laws on this vary from state to state.) Acupressure, however, is done without needles, using pressure from thumb, finger or hand. The same points may be stimulated in this way, though not as deeply as with needles, and the laywoman can safely use the method.

The points in animals are a bit harder to locate than they are in humans. The same slight depression under the skin is felt over a meridian point as is felt in people, but the animal's coat makes it harder to discover. A blocked point feels sensitive to the animal, as it does to a person. Reflexology, balancing the points through the palms of hands or soles of feet, is also possible in animals, but it is more difficult, especially in dogs because of the hard

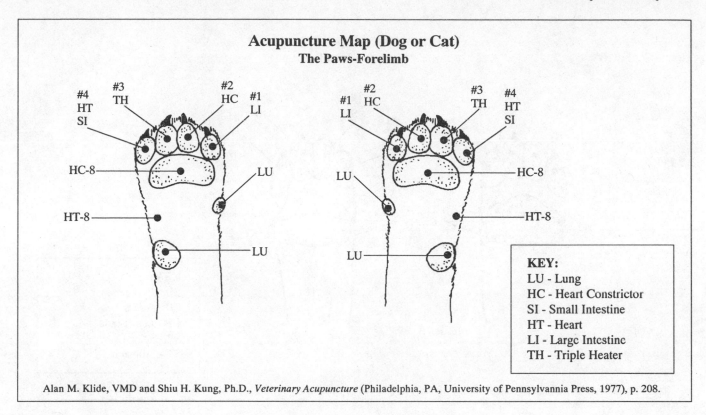

Acupuncture Map (Dog or Cat)
The Paws-Forelimb

#4 HT SI · #3 TH · #2 HC · #1 LI · HC-8 · LU · HT-8 · LU

#1 LI · #2 HC · #3 TH · #4 HT SI · LU · HC-8 · HT-8 · LU

KEY:
LU - Lung
HC - Heart Constrictor
SI - Small Intestine
HT - Heart
LI - Large Intestine
TH - Triple Heater

Alan M. Klide, VMD and Shiu H. Kung, Ph.D., *Veterinary Acupuncture* (Philadelphia, PA, University of Pennsylvannia Press, 1977), p. 208.

pads. Cats have soft feet but a very small area to work with, and most cats and dogs are highly foot shy. The body map and meridian endings, however, are there in animal physiology on the paws as they are in the human palms and soles. A full body map of meridian points is also located in dog and cat ears, as it is in human ears, and massaging the whole ear gently effects a whole body of healing that most animals welcome.

For the woman familiar with acupressure or reflexology in people, pet acupressure is a challenge and the results are as useful as they are in humans. Acupressure and reflexology were based on acupuncture (acupressure may have developed sooner), and the information and body maps shown for use with needles also work without puncturing the skin. The maps in this chapter are therefore maps for both acupuncture and the needleless acupressure. Also see the information and body map available for human use. See the material in Diane Stein's *All Women Are Healers* (The Crossing Press, 1990) on the methods, and *The Natural Remedy Book for Women* (The Crossing Press, 1992) for specific dis-ease points. For information on Chinese healing theory, see Ted

Kaptchuk, OMD, *The Web That Has No Weaver* (Congdon an Weed, Inc., 1983). The same information, meridian points and maps transfer over for use on dogs and cats.

When applying acupressure, find the points carefully, feeling under the animal's fur for the depression under the skin. The animal may twitch or flinch when a congested point is contacted—it's a strange sensation. There will be a pulsing in the point, usually a quite heavy feeling, until the point is released. When the point is located, apply gentle, steady pressure to it—never use force or cause pain. When the point is released, and energy balance and flow are regained, the point begins to pulse again, but in a different way and with a lighter feeling.

This takes some experience to understand and is easier to feel by touch than to describe in words. Once the point is located and released, move to the next one on the body map. Work from head to foot along the back of the body, and foot to head up the front, along one meridian line at a time. Points are never directly on the spinal cord, but are in the muscle above or beside it. A series of points for a variety of dis-eases are shown later in this chapter.

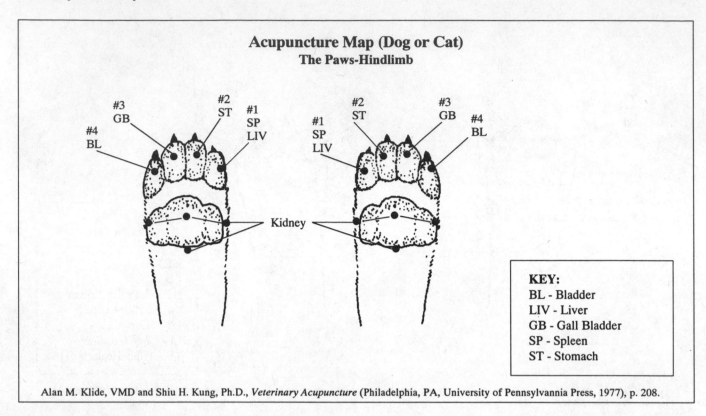

Acupuncture Map (Dog or Cat)
The Paws-Hindlimb

KEY:
BL - Bladder
LIV - Liver
GB - Gall Bladder
SP - Spleen
ST - Stomach

Alan M. Klide, VMD and Shiu H. Kung, Ph.D., *Veterinary Acupuncture* (Philadelphia, PA, University of Pennsylvannia Press, 1977), p. 208.

An acupressure point generally takes about thirty seconds of gentle direct pressure to release. It is easiest initially to use one finger (index finger) to find and work the points.

Why does it work? Particularly why does acupuncture work when veterinary/medical methods have failed? Acupuncture works with the electrical energy of the living body. Or to put it in metaphysical terms, it affects the nonphysical energy bodies and the chi (life force) that animates the physical level from the place of these nonphysical bodies. Chi is the life force energy, life itself (Goddess/nature). It moves into and through the body to animate it by the fourteen meridians or flow passageways. (Remember Marion Wehl-Former's energy flow charts in Chapter One.) As long as energy is moving freely, the body is in perfect health. When the energy is impeded, blocked so that too little flows through one area and too much in a corresponding area, dis-ease results. By inserting the acupuncture needles or finger acupressure on the point of blockage, the energy is rebalanced, and good health returns.

The meridian pathways are the animal or human body's tree of life. The two central channels, called by the Chinese the Great Central Vessels, are the Conception Vessel and the Governing Vessel. These run up the center front and down the center back of the body, along the spinal cord or central nervous system. (They are called the Ida and Pingala or the Shakti and Shiva in India.) Other meridian channels feed major organs, including the Small Intestine, Large Intestine, Liver, Lungs, Spleen, Gall Bladder, Stomach, Kidneys, and Heart. There are two additional meridians: The Heart Constrictor or Pericardium (Heart Protector) reaches the area surrounding the heart, and the Triple Heater is equivalent to the metaphysical solar plexus. In humans, the energy of the central channels runs directly through the chakras; in animals the chakras are along on this straight line, and other meridians/organ channels feed the chakra centers, as well.

The energy lines also spread out from the meridians into branches or smaller pathways; these nerve pathways of the body are called in Japanese the nadis. These in turn end in the (human) palms of hands, soles of feet, and in the ears. These endings are called the *seiketsu* (Japanese word). By freeing the chi in the meridian pathways, energy is released and freed to flow through the entire system of the living Be-ing—dog, cat or human. Free flow of chi through all the meridians, chakras, nadis and

Ear Acupuncture
(Dog, Cat or Horse)

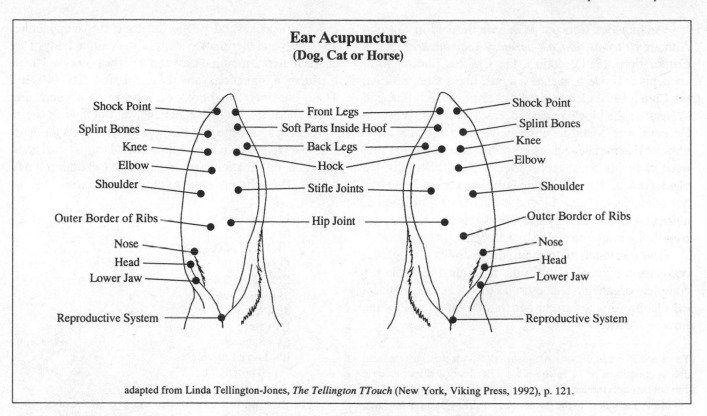

Shock Point — Front Legs — Shock Point
Splint Bones — Soft Parts Inside Hoof — Splint Bones
Knee — Back Legs — Knee
Elbow — Hock — Elbow
Shoulder — Stifle Joints — Shoulder
Outer Border of Ribs — Hip Joint — Outer Border of Ribs
Nose — Nose
Head — Head
Lower Jaw — Lower Jaw
Reproductive System — Reproductive System

adapted from Linda Tellington-Jones, *The Tellington TTouch* (New York, Viking Press, 1992), p. 121.

seiketu means good health. Once lost, good health can be regained through acupuncture or acupressure.

By balancing the meridian points with needle insertion or external pressure, the energy system of the body is brought into balance. All the chakras are balanced, the organs are balanced and freed for full energy life flow, and energy movement is cleared throughout the body. Meridian points that are stimulated are like removing the boulders that impede the flow of a rushing river. The snags and shallows are removed and there is no further roughness or undertow, only smooth free sailing. Disease states that have resulted from the blockage of chi are then removed when the normal free flow is regained. The animal returns to health. Like homeopathy, acupuncture is another method that bridges the healing of the physical and nonphysical body levels. It is a form of vibrational medicine, the medicine of the future (and of the matriarchal past). The changes have been measured by modern electrical means and photographed by Kirlian photography, but science has no better explanation for what happens than the ancients.

As advanced as acupuncture is in its theory and methods, remember that it is more ancient than any other healing or medical method now known on the planet, except possibly herbalism. Acupuncture tools of over 5000 years old have been found in Korea, and both China and Korea claim invention of the method. It was used in India and Sri Lanka, on elephants, more than 7000 years ago and may also have been discovered there. The *Nei Ching* (*Huang Ti Nei China, Yellow Emperor's Classic of Internal Medicine*) was written by Huang Ti who lived around 2700 BCE. According to this earliest medical book, acupuncture was developed in Southern China, moxibustion in Northern China, herbalism in Western China, and massage or acupressure in Central China. These healing systems were combined and codified during the Han Dynasty (206 BCE to 220 CE). The earliest verified written record of Chinese veterinary medicine was written in the Shang Dynasty (1766 BCE to 1066 CE), with animal healing information known in Babylonia, Egypt and India earlier. Acupuncture and Chinese medicine were used throughout Asia by the sixth century, brought to Europe in the seventeenth century and to the United States in the nineteenth century. [5] The methods and philosophies reflect a sophistication lost to modern culture and western medicine.

Archimedes Concon, MD, in an article in Sheldon Altman's *Introduction to Veterinary Acupuncture* (Chan's Corporation, 1981), defines the Chinese philosophical concepts in modern science's terms. In his interpretation, the Chinese five elements (Metal, Earth, Wood, Fire, and Water) are the biochemical processes of the life of a cell. He compares Metal to will, the psychic stimulus/nerve impulse that initiates action. Earth is minerals, the essential trace elements that support life. Wood is vitamins, the plant world and nutrition. Fire is the hormonal system (the hormone insulin burns fat and insures the assimilation of nutrients). Water is enzymes—cells require proper water balance/hydration to maintain well-being.

The meridians with their energy flows through the body are a movement from the individual cell into the complete organism. He describes the body as a "biological electric direct current generator" and describes the flow as follows:

There are 14 channels which transmit direct electric current from one acupuncture point to the next. The flow of direct electric current through the anterior of the patient is from a head to foot direction, secondary to the influence of the flow through the large arteries (magnetohydrodynamic principle). The flow of direct electric current through channels on the posterior of the patient is from a foot to head direction, secondary to the influence of the flow of blood through the large veins. The cells in channels have consistently ten times more sodium and potassium (which make good electrolytes), as compared to cells outside channels. Insoluble structural proteins behave as semiconductors. The combination of both properties make channels excellent conductors of direct electric current.[6]

This basically says what the ancients did in their theories of the movement of chi through the body. The information was known at least seven thousand years ago in what were probably matriarchal times. It has taken male science, which is quite young and arose from what was left of the matriarchies, centuries to discover it again. The Chinese concept of yin and yang, also a major factor in acupuncture, could be compared to the plus and minus poles of an electrical charge. We have perhaps come full circle, or are beginning to.

The next several pages illustrate the acupuncture body map and meridian system of the animal body. The charts illustrate a canine skeleton, but the points and their meridian designations are the same for cats as well. There are only two books on veterinary acupuncture available in the English language, and neither of these contains acupuncture charts for cats. The charts for dogs and cats were drawn from human and large animal acupuncture information and transferred to small animal bodies. The abbreviations for the channels are:

BL - Bladder
LIV - Liver
GB - Gall Bladder
LU - Lung
HC - Heart Constrictor (or P - Pericardium)
SI - Small Intestine
SP - Spleen
HT - Heart
ST - Stomach
LI - Large Intestine
TH - Triple Heater

The two additional meridians are the Conception Vessel (CV) and the Governing Vessel (GV), the central channels.

The following charts are highly technical. A numbered chart, called the Shin (or Chen) Dog Chart is also used, giving the points in number sequence with a Key. Each point number has a name, meridian designation, technical location, anatomical notes, needle technique notes, and major uses. There is a similar and simplified chart for cats (from Judy Fireman's *Cat Catalog*) suggested for acupressure. The Dog Chart and Key are contained in both of the English language books on veterinary acupuncture (Klide and Kung, *Veterinary Acupuncture*, and Sheldon Altman, *An Introduction to Veterinary Acupuncture*). These are easier to use for acupressure and are given here as well. Sixty-one meridian points are given in the Shin Dog Chart, twenty-six in the chart for cats.

Dog or Cat Acupuncture Body Map

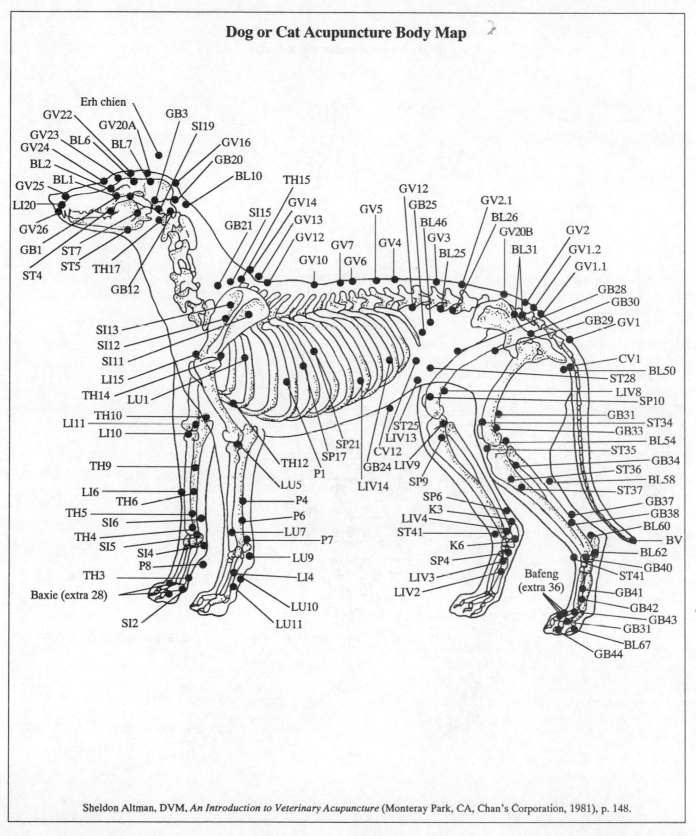

Sheldon Altman, DVM, *An Introduction to Veterinary Acupuncture* (Monteray Park, CA, Chan's Corporation, 1981), p. 148.

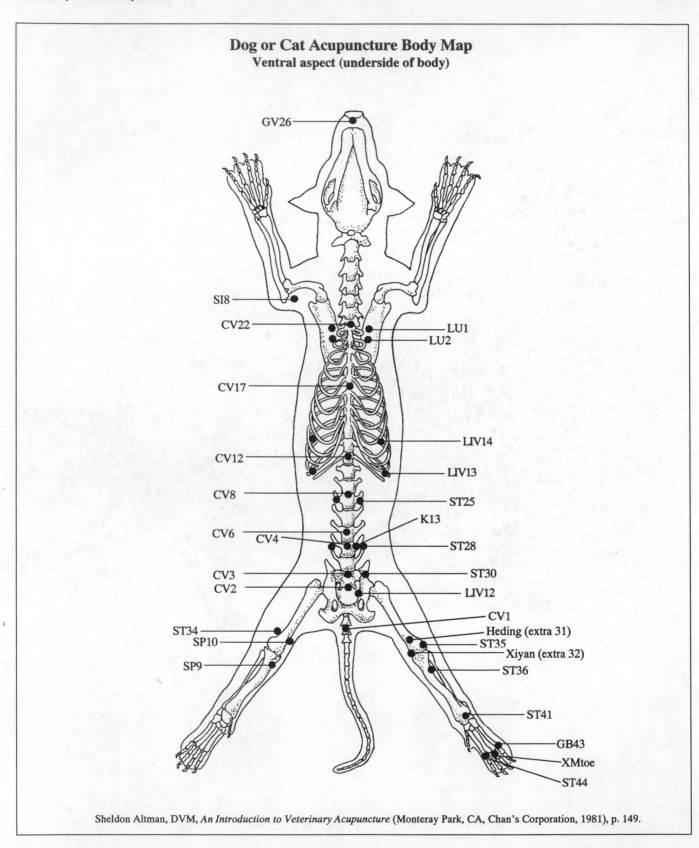

Dog or Cat Acupuncture Body Map
Ventral aspect (underside of body)

GV26

SI8

CV22

LU1

LU2

CV17

LIV14

CV12

LIV13

CV8

ST25

K13

CV6

CV4

ST28

CV3

ST30

CV2

LIV12

CV1

ST34

Heding (extra 31)

SP10

ST35

Xiyan (extra 32)

SP9

ST36

ST41

GB43

XMtoe

ST44

Sheldon Altman, DVM, *An Introduction to Veterinary Acupuncture* (Monteray Park, CA, Chan's Corporation, 1981), p. 149.

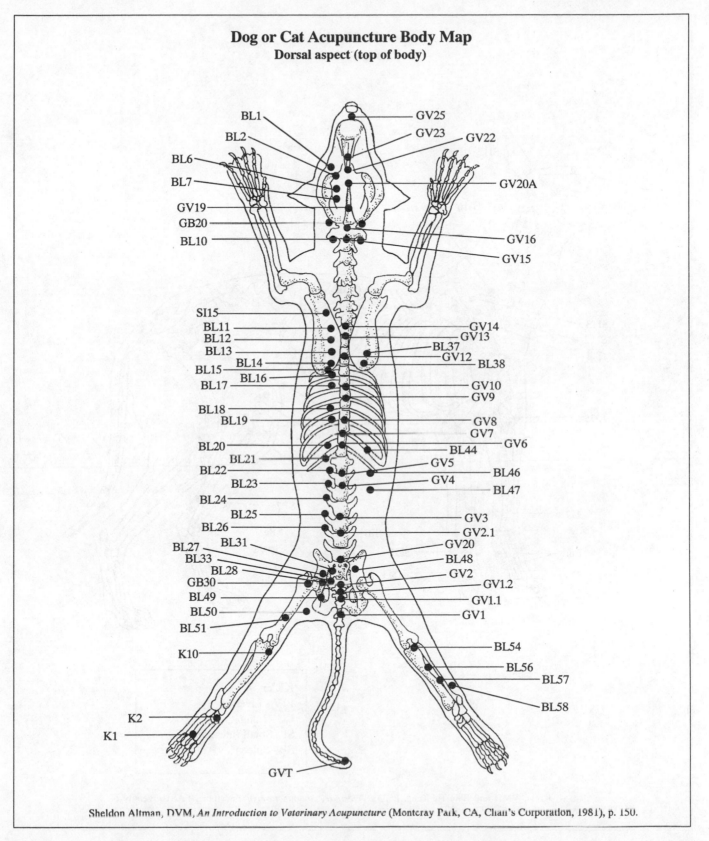

Dog or Cat Acupuncture Body Map
Dorsal aspect (top of body)

Sheldon Altman, DVM, *An Introduction to Veterinary Acupuncture* (Monterey Park, CA, Chan's Corporation, 1981), p. 150.

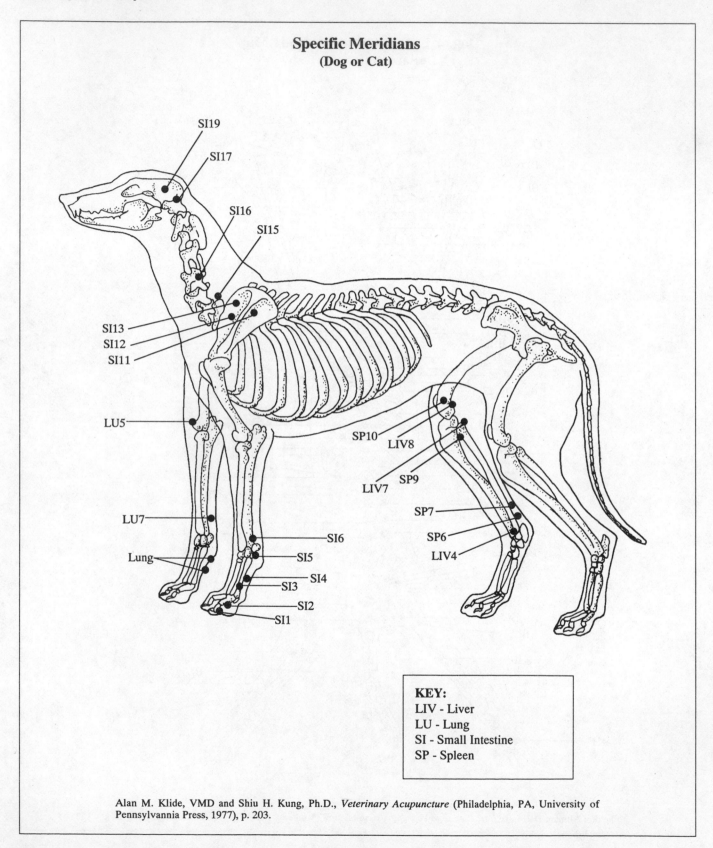

Specific Meridians
(Dog or Cat)

SI19
SI17
SI16
SI15
SI13
SI12
SI11
LU5
LU7
Lung
SI6
SI5
SI4
SI3
SI2
SI1
SP10
LIV8
LIV7
SP9
SP7
SP6
LIV4

KEY:
LIV - Liver
LU - Lung
SI - Small Intestine
SP - Spleen

Alan M. Klide, VMD and Shiu H. Kung, Ph.D., *Veterinary Acupuncture* (Philadelphia, PA, University of Pennsylvannia Press, 1977), p. 203.

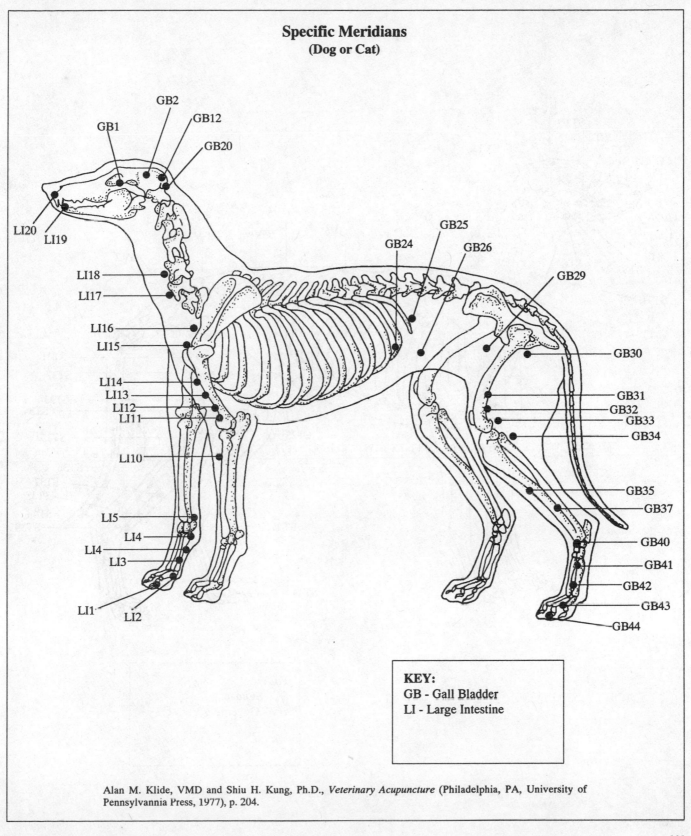

Specific Meridians
(Dog or Cat)

GB2
GB12
GB1
GB20
GB25
GB24
GB26
GB29
LI20
LI19
LI18
LI17
LI16
LI15
GB30
LI14
LI13
GB31
LI12
GB32
LI11
GB33
GB34
LI10
GB35
GB37
LI5
LI4
GB40
LI4
GB41
LI3
GB42
GB43
LI1
LI2
GB44

KEY:
GB - Gall Bladder
LI - Large Intestine

Alan M. Klide, VMD and Shiu H. Kung, Ph.D., *Veterinary Acupuncture* (Philadelphia, PA, University of Pennsylvannia Press, 1977), p. 204.

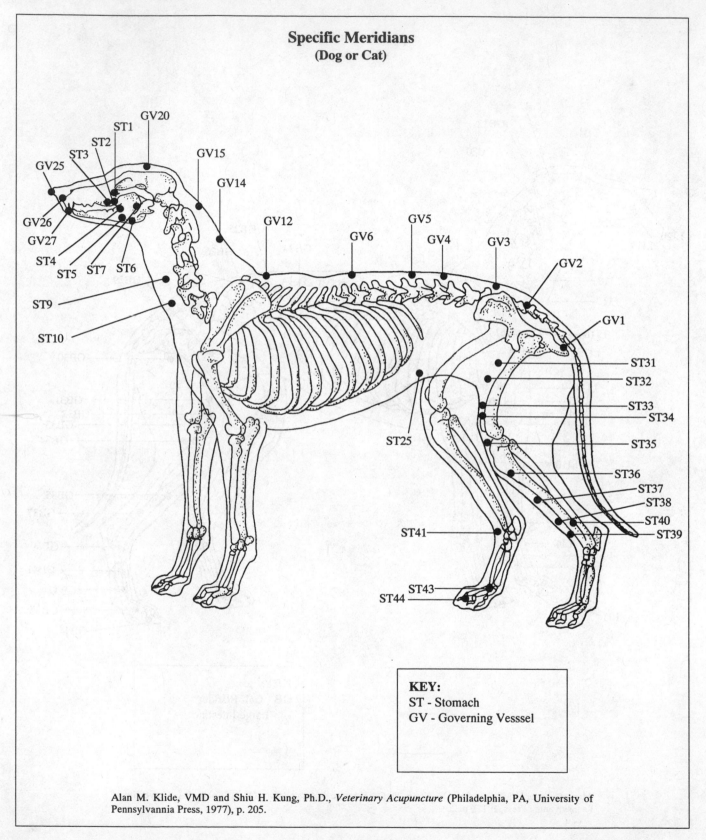

Specific Meridians
(Dog or Cat)

GV20
ST1
ST2
GV15
ST3
GV14
GV25
GV12
GV5
GV6
GV4
GV3
GV2
GV26
GV27
ST4
GV1
ST5 ST7 ST6
ST9
ST31
ST10
ST32
ST33
ST34
ST35
ST25
ST36
ST37
ST38
ST40
ST41
ST39
ST44 ST43

KEY:
ST - Stomach
GV - Governing Vesssel

Alan M. Klide, VMD and Shiu H. Kung, Ph.D., *Veterinary Acupuncture* (Philadelphia, PA, University of Pennsylvannia Press, 1977), p. 205.

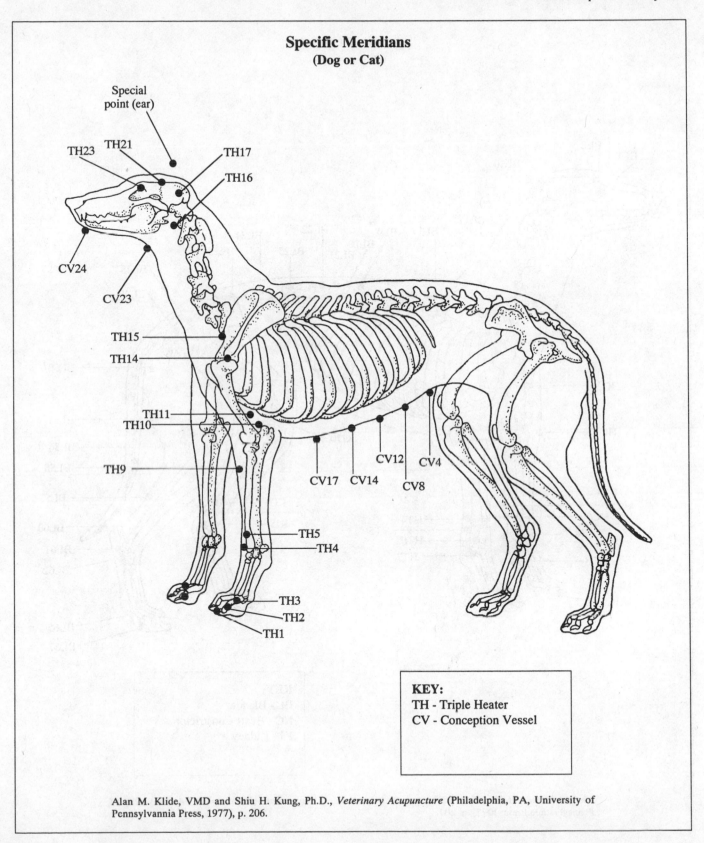

Specific Meridians
(Dog or Cat)

Special
point (ear)

TH23   TH21   TH17

TH16

CV24

CV23

TH15

TH14

TH11
TH10

TH9

CV17   CV14   CV8   CV4   CV12

TH5

TH4

TH3
TH2
TH1

KEY:
TH - Triple Heater
CV - Conception Vessel

Alan M. Klide, VMD and Shiu H. Kung, Ph.D., *Veterinary Acupuncture* (Philadelphia, PA, University of Pennsylvannia Press, 1977), p. 206.

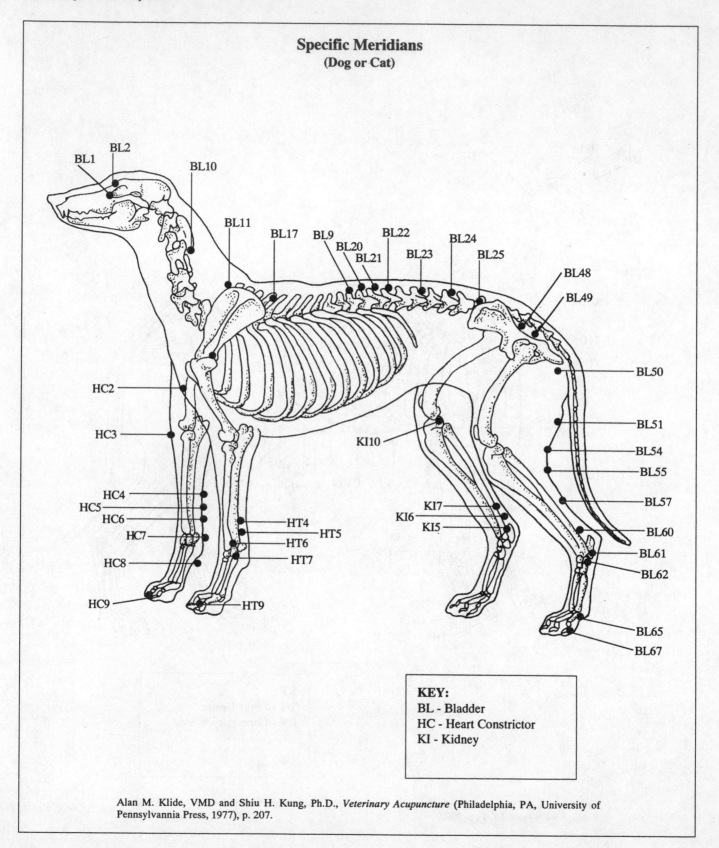

Specific Meridians
(Dog or Cat)

KEY:
BL - Bladder
HC - Heart Constrictor
KI - Kidney

Alan M. Klide, VMD and Shiu H. Kung, Ph.D., *Veterinary Acupuncture* (Philadelphia, PA, University of Pennsylvannia Press, 1977), p. 207.

Acupressure Points for Immune Stimulation—Bilaterally
(Dog or Cat)

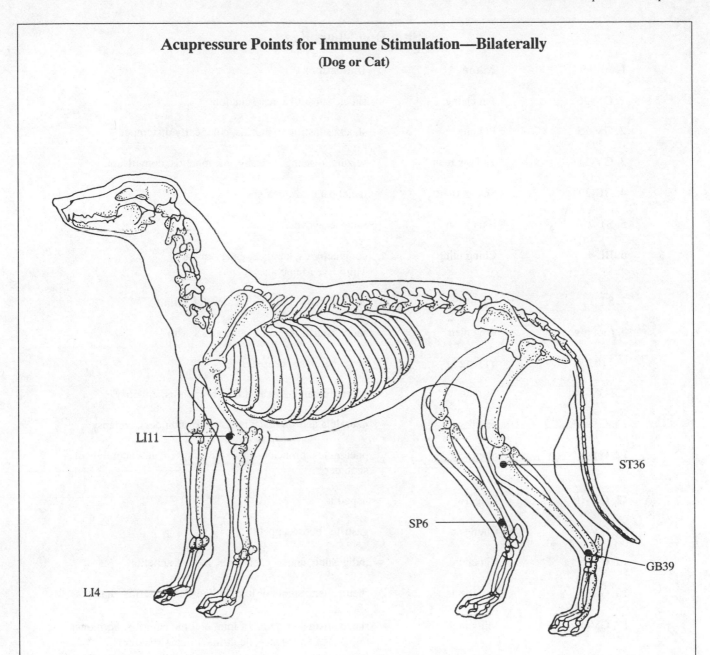

LI11

ST36

SP6

GB39

LI4

Press each point with thumb or forefinger for about 60 seconds 1-2 times daily as needed, both right and left sides of animal.

Gloria Dodd, DVM, © 1987.

Shin Dog Chart Key

Number	Name	Indications
1. GV-26	Jen chung	shock, sunstroke, resuscitation
2. GV-25	Pi liang	shock, sunstroke, sinusitis, cold, early distemper
3. GV-16	Ta feng men	seizure, distemper, tetany, encephalitis, convulsion
4. GB-3	Shang kuan	facial paralysis, deafness
5. ST-7	Hsia kuan	same as above
6. BL-1	Ching ming	conjunctivitis, keratitis, enlargement of Third Eye Membranes
7. ST-1	Cheng chi	conjunctivitis, optic nerve atrophy, retinitis
8. (not given)	Erh chien	shock, sunstroke, cold, colic and spasm
9. TH-17	Yi feng	facial paralysis, deafness
10. GV-14	Ta chui	fever, neuralgia, rheumatism, bronchitis, epilepsy
11. GV-13	Tao dao	neuralgia and sprain (forelimb and shoulder), epilepsy
12. GV-12	Shen chu	pneumonia, bronchitis, distemper, sprain and neuralgia of shoulder
13. GV-10	Ling Tai	hepatitis
14. GV-7	Chung su	gastritis, boosts appetite
15. GV-6	Chi chung	indigestion, diarrhea, enteritis, lack of appetite
16. GV-5	Hsuan shu	rheumatism, sprain of loin, indigestion, enteritis, diarrhea
17. GV-4	Ming men	rheumatism and sprain of loin, chronic enteritis, hormonal imbalance, impotence, nephritis, urinary disorders, lack of appetite
18. GV-3	Yang kuan	hypogonadism, endometritis, metritis, ovaritis, cystic ovary, atrophy of ovary or uterus, prolonged estrus, rheumatism and sprain of loin
19. GV-2.5	Kuan hou	endometritis, cystic ovary, cystitis, paralysis of large intestine, constipation
20. GV-20B	Pai hui	nervous disorders, sciatica, posterior paralysis, prolapse of rectum

Number	Name	Indications
21. BL-31	Erh yen	posterior paralysis, neuralgia
22. GV-2	Wei ken	posterior paralysis, paralysis of tail, anal prolapse, diarrhea, constipation
23. GV-1.2	Wei chieh	same as above
24. GV-1.1	Woei kan	same as above
25. GV-T	Woei chien	shock, sunstroke, gastro-enteritis
26. CV-1	Chiao cho	Diarrhea, prolapse of rectum, paralysis of sphincter muscles
27. LU-1	Fei yu	pneumonia, bronchitis, cough
28. P-1	Shin yu	mental stress, heart dis-ease
29. LIV-14	Kan yu	hepatitis, jaundice, eyes
30. GB-24	Wei yu	gastritis, stomach distension, indigestion, enteritis, lack of appetite
31. LIV-13	(not given)	enteritis, intestinal spasm, diarrhea
32. GB-25	Pl yu	indigestion, chronic diarrhea, lack of appetite
33. BL-23	Shen yu	urinary disorders, nephritis, sex hormone imbalances, sterility, impotence, sprain of lumbar region, rheumatism
34. BL-46	Yi yu	pancreatitis, indigestion, chronic diarrhea, diabetes
35. BL-25	Nuan cho	hormonal insufficiency disorders, cystic ovary
36. BL-26	Tzu kuan	cystic uterus, endometritis, metritis, hypotrophy of uterus, rheumatism of lumbar region
37. GB-26	Pung kung yu	cystitis, urine retention, bladder spasm, hematuria
38. ST-25	Tien shu	enteritis, diarrhea, abdominal pain, intestinal spasm
39. CV-12	Chung wan	acute gastritis, gastric disorders, vomiting, indigestion, anorexia
40. SI-11	Kung tzu	neuralgia, paralysis and sprain of shoulder; paralysis of scapula nerve, rheumatism of shoulder
41. TH-14	Chien ching	neuralgia, paralysis and strain of shoulder and foreleg

Number	Name	Indications
42. LI-15	Chien juan	same as above
43. TH-10	Chou yu	arthritis, neuralgia, paralysis and sprain of elbow and foreleg
44. LI-11	Chih shang	sprain, neuralgia and paralysis of foreleg, paralysis of brachial and radial nerve
45. LI-10	Chih chu	same as above
46. TH-12	Ch'ing feng	general anesthesia, nervous disorders of forelimb
47. TH-9	Chien san li	paralysis of radial and ulna nerves, neuralgia and rheumatism of foreleg
48. TH-5	Wai kuan	same as above
49. TH-4	Yang chi	sprain of digits, neuralgia and paralysis of forelimb
50. SI-6	Yang chu	neurologic disorders of thoracic limb, sprain of carpal tendons, paralysis of radial nerve
51. SI-5	Wan ku	same as above
52. (extra point)	Pa feng	sprain and paralysis of digits
53. P-8	Nei kuan	neurologic disorders of thoracic limb, stomach and intestinal spasm, colic
54. GB-30	Huan tiao	posterior paralysis, neuralgia and paralysis of pelvic limb, sciatica, paralysis of femoral nerve
55. ST-34	Chi shang	Neurologic disorders of pelvic limb
56. BL-54	Chi hou	same as above
57. ST-35	Chi shia	sprain, neuralgia, arthritis of knee
58. GB-34	Hou san li	posterior paralysis, neuralgia and paralysis of pelvic limb, gastroenteritis, intestinal spasm and colic
59. ST-41	Chih shi	sprain, neuralgia and paralysis of hindfoot
60. LIV-4	Chung fong	same as above
61. K-6	Hou Kon	same as above

Sheldon Altman, DVM, *Introduction to Veterinary Acupuncture*, p. 131-136, and Alan M. Klide, VMD and Shiu H. Kung, Ph.D., *Veterinary Acupuncture*, p. 113-118. Altman adds meridian designations. Material is abbreviated.

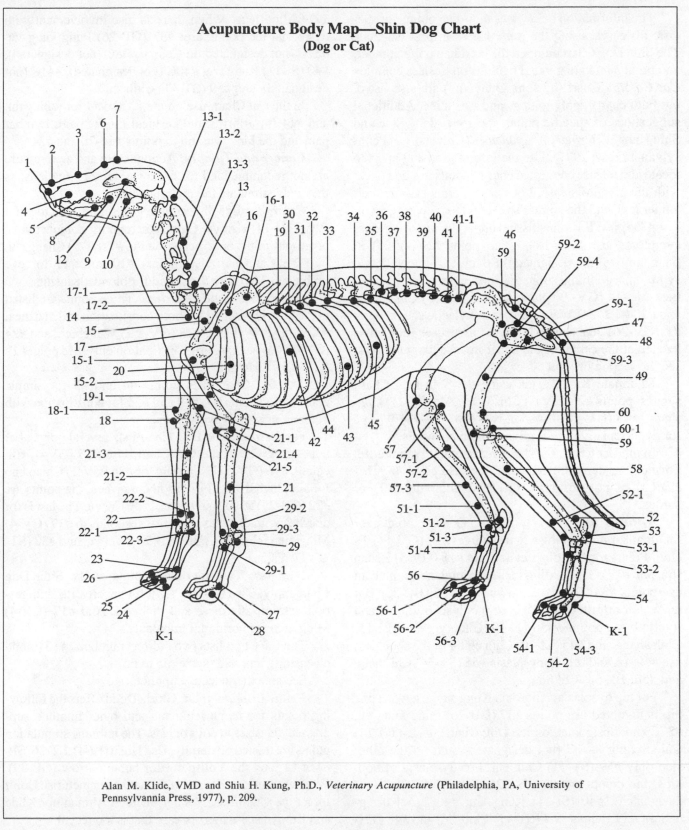

Acupuncture Body Map—Shin Dog Chart
(Dog or Cat)

Alan M. Klide, VMD and Shiu H. Kung, Ph.D., *Veterinary Acupuncture* (Philadelphia, PA, University of Pennsylvannia Press, 1977), p. 209.

The information below lists meridian points for specific dis-eases, using the same list as in past chapters. The Shin Dog Chart number, the meridian point number, and point name are given. Positions on the less complex *Cat Catalog* Chart (by John Ottaviano) are also listed, but both charts apply to dogs and cats alike. Additional suggestions of specific points are from Alan Klide and Shiu Kung, *Veterinary Acupuncture* (University of Pennsylvania Press, 1977). Use the information and maps to locate and release congested energy points in a dog or cat with the given dis-ease. Locate the points also by their tenderness, and the animal's reaction to palpating them.

Allergies: For sinusitis and upper respiratory allergy symptoms, use Shin Dog Chart point #2 (GV-25) Pi liang, and #8 (not designated) Erh chien. When allergic symptoms are indigestion, diarrhea and/or lack of appetite, use #14 (GV-7) Chung su, #15 (GV-6) Chi chung, and #30 (GB -24) Wei yu. For anaphylactic shock, point #1 (GV-26) Jen chung is used for resuscitation. It is located at the center of the upper lip, see diagram. Also see the section on skin dis-eases.

Klide and Kung, again using the Shin Dog Chart, suggest points #26 (CV-1) Chiao cho, #44 (LI-11) Chih shang, #13 (GV-10) Ling tai, and #30 (GB-24) Wei yu for hypersensitivity to foreign protein materials.[7]

In the Cat Chart, the shock/resuscitation point is #8. For itching, dermatitis or coughing, use point #5. This chart does not designate meridian point numbers or names.[8]

Arthritis and Hip Dysplasia: General points for rheumatism on the Dog Chart include: #10 (GV-14) Ta chui. Points for the loin area include #16 (GV-5) Hsuan shu, and #17 (GV-4) Ming men. For lumbar rheumatism use points #33 (BL-23) Shen yu, and #36 (BL-26) Tzu kuan. For arthritis, neuralgia or paralysis of elbow and forelimb see points #43 (TH-10) Chou yu, #44 (LI-11) Chih shang, and #45 (LI-10) Chih chu. For the shoulders use #40-42, and for hip dysplasia #55 (ST-34) Chi shang and #56 (BL-54) Chi hou.

For hip dysplasia, Klide and Kung suggest when one hip is involved use points #37 (GB-26) Pung kung yu, #37C (not designated on the Dog Chart), #41, (TH-14) Chien ching, #41C (not designated), and on the other side only #59 (ST-41) Chih shi. For dysplasia of both hips, the points are #38 (ST-25) Tien shu, #38C (not designated), #40 (SI-11) Kung tzu, #40C (not designated), #59.1 and #59.2 (ST-41) Chih shi, and #46 (TH-

12) Ch'ing feng. When there is disc involvement with dysplasia, the points are: #37 (GB-26) Pung kung yu, #37C (not designated on Chart), #38C (not designated), #40 (SI-11) Kung tzu, #40C (not designated), #41C (not designated), and #59 (ST-41) Chih shi.[9]

In the Cat Chart, use points #3 and #4 for joint pain, and #14 for arthritis and cervical (neck) pain. Lumbar pain and the hips respond to points #16-20 and #24.

Cancer and Tumors: Acupuncture and acupressure are not recommended for cancer or tumor situations, as they may stimulate the malignancies.

Cataracts: Eye dis-eases in general respond to point #29 (LIV-14) Kan yu. Cataracts, retinitis, conjunctivitis, or atrophy of the optic nerve refer to #7 (ST-1) Cheng chi.

The Cat Chart lists points #10 and #11 for eye problems. Also note #15, used for blood cleansing.

Constipation and Diarrhea: Three points are listed in the Shin Dog Chart for both constipation and diarrhea: #22 (GV-2) Wei ken, #23 (GV-1.2) Wei chieh, and #24 (GV-1.1) Woei kan. For constipation only, use point #19 (GV-2.5) Kuan hou.

The Cat Chart lists points #4 and #5 for simple constipation, and #17, #19 and #25 for constipation with hip pain or spinal involvement.

For diarrhea: The Dog Chart lists several poitns, but none are given in the Cat Chart. Use #15 (GV-6) Chi chung, #16 (GV-5) Hsuan shu, or #26 (CV-1) Chiao cho for simple diarrhea. For chronic diarrhea, the points are #32 (GB-25) Pi yu, and #34 (BL-46) Yi yu. The last is for diarrhea with diabetes. Enteritis responds to #17 (GV-4) Ming men (chronic), #30 (GB-24) Wei yu, and #38 (ST-25) Tien shu.

Diabetes: Two meridian points in the Shin Dog Chart apply: #34 (BL-46) Yi yu for pancreatitis, indigestion, chronic diarrhea, and diabetes. And #17 (GV-4) Ming men for hormonal imbalances.

The Cat Chart lists two indirect numbers: #15 (blood cleansing), and #22 (systemic tonic).

See an experienced acupuncturist.

Feline Leukemia: Dr. Gloria Dodd offers the following points for feline leukemia and other immune suppressed dis-eases in dogs or cats. The immune stimulation points are treated bilaterally. Use Hoku (LI-4), ST-36, SP-6, LI-11, and the Voll point for bone marrow (GB-39). Work with an experienced veterinary acupuncturist. Don't forget the vitamin C. Neither Sheldon Altman nor Klide and Kung discuss this dis-ease that is too recent.

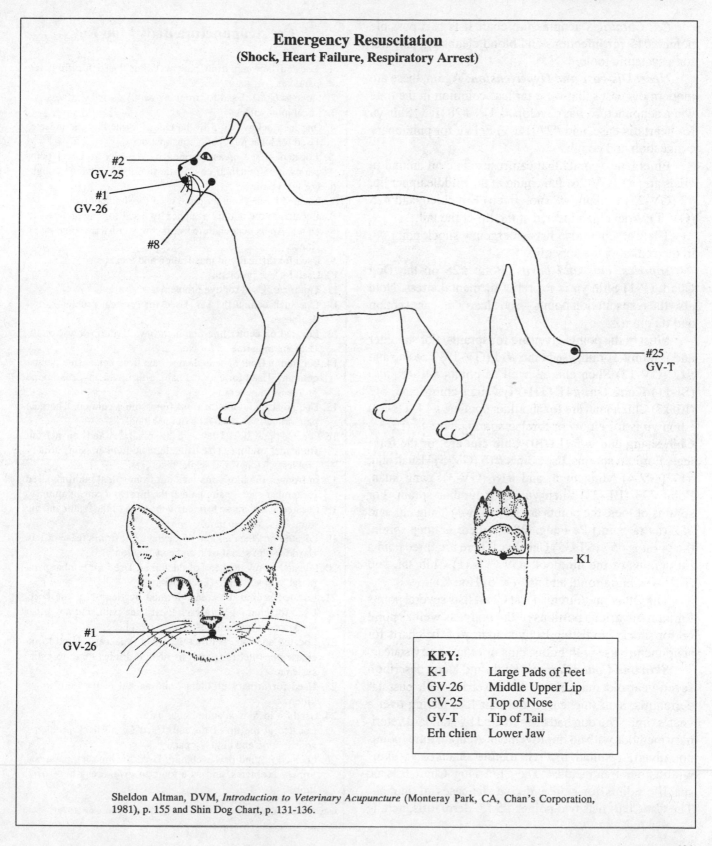

Emergency Resuscitation
(Shock, Heart Failure, Respiratory Arrest)

#2
GV-25

#1
GV-26

#8

#25
GV-T

K1

#1
GV-26

KEY:

K-1	Large Pads of Feet
GV-26	Middle Upper Lip
GV-25	Top of Nose
GV-T	Tip of Tail
Erh chien	Lower Jaw

Sheldon Altman, DVM, *Introduction to Veterinary Acupuncture* (Monteray Park, CA, Chan's Corporation, 1981), p. 155 and Shin Dog Chart, p. 131-136.

Cat Catalog's acupressure chart lists two possible points: #15 for infections and blood cleansing, and #22 for a systemic tonic.

Heart Dis-ease and Hypertension: Again, these are modern dis-eases that were far less common in the time when acupuncture was developed. Use #28 (P-1) Shin yu for heart dis-ease, and #27 (Lu-1) Fei yu for pulmonary congestion and cough.

Emergency points that can resuscitate an animal in crisis are: #1 (GV-26) Jen chung at the middle upper lip, #2 (GV-25) Pi liang, #8 (not given) Erh chien, and #25 (GV-T) Woei chien located at the tip of the tail.

The Cat Chart also lists emergency shock point #8, in the center of the upper lip.

Injuries, cuts and burns: Point #28 on the Dog Chart, (P-1) Shin yu is for relief of mental stress. Note also the resuscitation points—see Heart Dis-ease section and diagram.

Most of the points given are for sprains. For shoulder and forelimb sprain, use points #11 (GV-13) Tao dao and #12 (GV-12) Shen chu, as well as points #40-45. #40 (SI-11) Kung tzu, #41 (TH-14) Chien ching, and #42 (Li-15) Chien juan are for shoulder sprains; #43 (TH-10) Chou yu is for elbow or foreleg sprain, and #44 (LI-11) Chih shang and #45 (LI-10) Chih chu are for the forelegs. For loin sprains, use points #16 (GV-5) Hsuan shu, #17 (GV-4) Ming men, and #18 (GV-3) Yang kuan. Point #33 (BL-23) Shen yu is for lumbar sprain. For sprains of toes, the points are #49 (TH-4) Yang chi, and #52 (extra point) Pa Feng. Where there is knee sprain, the point is #57 (ST-35) Chi shia. There are three points for sprains of the hindfoot, #59 (ST-41) Chih shi, #60 (LIV-4) Chung fong, and #61 (K-6) Hou kon.

The Ottaviano/Fireman Cat Chart lists several points for pain in various portions of the body, as well as point #8 for shock. No listing is given in any of the charts for acupuncture use with burns, cuts or other injury states.

Skin and Coat Ailments: Klide and Kung describe a seven-year-old male Kerry Blue Terrier with pustular dermatitis, skin thickening and hair loss lasting over a year's time. The dog had been treated by standard veterinary methods with no improvement. Acupuncture (points not given) resulted in "remarkable changes in skin" within four treatments.[10] The Shin Dog Chart lists no specific points for skin and coat dis-eases in animals. The Cat Chart lists two points: #5 for dermatitis, itching

---

Cat Acupuncture Body Map Key

1. Located between front paw webbing. Used for front leg paralysis.
2. Same as No. 1. Used for front leg paralysis and deafness.
3. Local joint pain.
4. One inch below No. 5 in the crease formed by the muscle. Used for local joint pain, constipation.
5. Located in the crease formed by the elbow. Local pain, paralysis of front limb, constipation, dermatitis, itching, cough.
6. For local pain.
7. Located in the shoulder joint, used for shoulder pain.
8. Located in the middle of upper lip, used for emergency and shock. Apply acupuncture by pinching with thumb and index finger.
9. Used for difficulty in mastication and local pain.
10. Used for eye problems.
11. Tip of ear. Used for eye problems.
12. One inch behind the ear. Used for cervical problems, and deafness.
13. Located on center line one inch inward and below No. 12. Uses are the same as for No. 12.
14. Located in front of scapula one inch from center line (spinal column). Used for cervical pain, arthritis in any joint, bone problems in general.
15. Behind scapula one inch out from spinal column. Thoracic pain, infections, cleansing of the blood.
16. Located opposite the navel on the spinal area and one inch out from that midline. Used for thoracic-lumbar pain, urinary problems, kidney and sexual disorders.
17. In front of the ilium one inch out from spinal midline. Used for lumbar-sacral pain, pain at the hips, and constipation.
18. Located at the crease formed by the head of the femur and hip joint. Used for hip pain.
19. Located one inch up and 45 degrees out from crease of tail. Used for hip, sacral pain and constipation.
20. Located below the head of the femur. Used for lumbar pain, sacral pain and stifle (knee) pain.
21. Located behind the crease formed by flexing of the knee. Used for hind leg paralysis, local knee pain, and any other weakness of lower limbs.
22. Located one inch below the patella (kneecap). Used to increase appetite, for paralysis of hind limbs, tonic to entire systems.
23. Used for urinary problems, and an aid in the delivery of kittens.
24. Used for local pain and lumbar pain.
25. Located at the tip of the tail. Used for all back problems, constipation and hind leg paralysis.
26. Located in hind paw webbing. Used for hind leg paralysis, urinary problems, and as a tonic to give strength to lower limbs.

Judy Fireman, *Cat Catalog* (New York: Workman Publishing, 1976), p. 240.

Cat Acupuncture Body Map

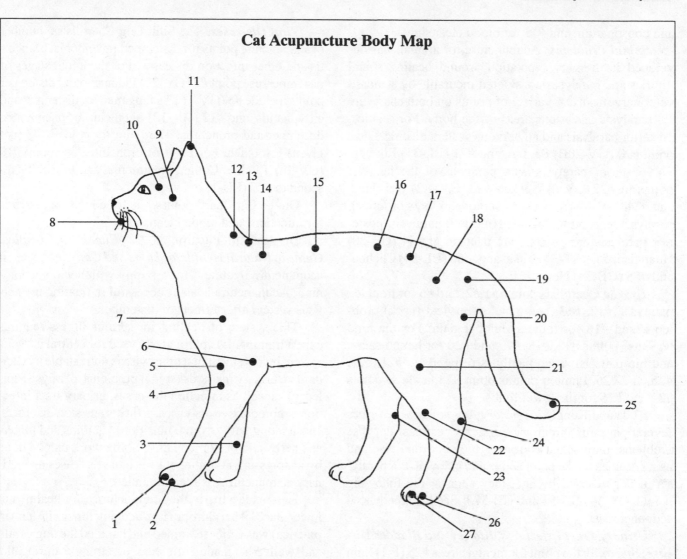

To use this chart, locate the general area which corresponds to your cat's problem. When a point is in need of pressure, the cat will respond by showing slight pain during palpation of the acupressure point. Massage gently for 1-10 minutes. This technique can be used as often as desired to provide relief to the cat. Use massage; only a trained acupuncturist can use needles. Home acupressure treatment cannot replace the advice of a veterinarian. (See key, previous page).

Judy Fireman, *Cat Catalog* (New York: Workman Publishing, 1976), p. 240.

and constipation, and #15 for blood cleansing.

Spinal Problems: Acupuncture for animals has developed its primary reputation around healing spinal injuries and paralyses considered incurable by standard veterinary means. A variety of points on both charts are for paralysis of various areas of the body. For sciatica, posterior paralysis and all nervous system disorders, use point #20 (GV-20B) Pai hui, and #21 (BL-31) Erh yen. For posterior paralysis with paralysis of the tail, the points are #22 (GV-2) Wei ken, #23 (GV-1.2) Wei chieh, and #24 (GV-1.1) Woei kan. Shoulder, elbow or foreleg paralysis respond to #40-47. Hindlimb paralysis, posterior paralysis and sciatica are needled at #54 (GB-30) Huan tiao, #55 (ST-34) Chi shang, #56 (BL-54) Chi hou, and #58 (GB-34) Hou san li.

The Cat Chart lists points #1,#2, and #5 for front leg paralysis, #12, #13, and #14 for cervical (neck) problems, and #16 for thoracic-lumbar pain. For the hind legs, use points #17, #18, #19 and #20 for lumbo-sacral and hip pain. Hind leg paralysis responds to #21, #22, #25, and #26. Lumbar pain is point #24, and use points #21 and #26 for the lower limbs.

Klide and Kung's *Veterinary Acupuncture* describes several pages of spinal and paralysis healings. For disc problems, they suggest locating the abnormal disc and using needles on the point above and below it. For paralysis in dogs caused by age, they suggest the following points: GV-19, GB-34 and GB-37.[11] See an experienced acupuncturist.

Urinary Tract Infections, Kidney and Bladder Disease: Start with the point for mental stress #28 (P-1) Shin yu. For urinary disorders and nephritis, use #17 (GV-4) Ming men, and #33 (BL-23) Shen yu. Use point #37 (GB-26) Pung kung yu for cystitis, urine retention, and blood in the urine.

The *Cat Catalog* Chart uses points #16 and #26 for urinary and kidney problems, and #23 for urinary infections and for easing delivery of kittens.

Klide and Kung's *Veterinary Acupuncture* describes treatment of a male cat with stones blocking the urinary outlet. He had been catheterized several times in quick succession with the blockage still recurring. A total of four acupuncture sessions a week apart were used, focusing on BL-38, BL-40 and BL-41. The cat responded immediately to the treatments, requiring no further medication or catherization from the first session.[12]

Viral Dis-eases: The Shin Dog Chart lists a number of acupuncture points for distemper, pneumonia, bronchitis and other infection dis-eases. For the initial stages of distemper, use point #2 (GV-25) Pi liang; other distemper points include #3 (GV-16) Ta feng men for distemper and encephalitis, and #12 (GV-12) Shen chu for pneumonia, distemper and bronchitis. The point for colds is #8 (not given) Erh chien. For fever or bronchitis, use point #10 (GV-14) Ta chiu. Cough, pneumonia, and bronchitis respond to #27 (LU-1) Fei yu.

On the Cat Chart, point #5 is for coughs, and #15 is for infections and blood cleansing.

Dr. Richard Pitcairn, in *Dr. Pitcairn's Complete Guide to Natural Health for Dogs and Cats,* describes an acupuncture treatment for a puppy with acute pneumonia.[13] Acupuncture is also successful in treating the nervous system after-effects of distemper.

This system of healing for serious illness requires expert training. It is particularly used for central nervous system involvement that otherwise is untreatable by standard veterinary methods (spinal problems, paralysis, epilepsy) as well as infection dis-eases, urinary tract infections, reproductive dis-eases, arthritis and skin disorders. Use it along with optimal nutrition, vitamins and minerals, herbs and/or homeopathy. Some work can be done by acupressure at home, but for most dis-eases a veterinary acupuncturist is recommended.

Kali made a trip to the acupuncturist, for healing her lower back. The chiropractor-acupuncturist (in human practice) was Chinese trained and handled the dog gently and well. She made little fuss or struggle during the treatment, it seemed to relax her. Several needles were inserted along her lower back, hip and right leg with electro-stimulation. The dog objected to only one of the needles that was placed in her right paw. She flinched for a moment when the electrical pulse was started, then relaxed and made no further fuss. The doctor said that animals usually sleep through the treatments.

It was determined that her rear end weakness is from an injury to the scapular joint on the right side, and that torn ligaments are the source of pain and restricted motion. The total session, including the examination, lasted about half an hour. After it, Kali wanted to sleep and was quite relaxed; she did not seem upset by the experience. A day later, she seems to have freer movement and to be more active on the injured leg; there is less awkwardness and distress at getting up and sitting or lying down. The acupuncturist suggests four to six sessions for complete healing, but with other methods also being used, my feeling is that fewer visits will be needed.

[1]Alan M. Klide, VMD and Shiu H. Kung, PhD, *Veterinary Acupuncture* (Philadelphia, PA, University of Pennsylvania Press, 1977), p. 67.

[2]Faith A. Uridel, "Alternative Therapies," in *Dog Fancy Magazine*, March, 1992, p. 44 and 46.

[3]Sheldon Altman, DVM, *An Introduction to Acupuncture for Animals* (Monteray Park, CA, Chan's Corporation, 1981), p. 243.

[4]Faith A. Uridel, "Alternative Therapies," p.46.

[5]Sheldon Altman, *An Introduction to Acupuncture for Animals*, p. 13-14.

[6]Archimedes A. Concon, MD, "Energetic Concepts of Classical Chinese Acupuncture," in Sheldon Altman, *Introduction to Veterinary Acupuncture*, p. 66-68.

[7]Alan M. Klide, VMD and Shiu H. Kung, PhD, *Veterinary Acupuncture*, p. 230.

[8]All John Ottaviano Cat Chart points are from: Judy Fireman, Ed., *Cat Catalog: The Ultimate Cat Book*, (New York, Workman Publishing Co., 1976), p. 240.

[9]Alan M. Klide, VMD and Shiu H. Kung, PhD, *Veterinary Acupuncture*, p. 231.

[10]*Ibid.*, p. 247.

[11]*Ibid.*, p. 230-231.

[12]*Ibid.*, p. 247.

[13]Richard Pitcairn, DVM, PhD, and Susan Hubble Pitcairn, *Dr. Pitcairn's Complete Guide to Natural Health for Dogs and Cats* (Emmaus, PA, Rodale Press, 1982), p. 150.

Massage & Touch

One of the things that bring women and their cats or dogs together is touch. Animals *feel* good, and people feel good stroking them. Animals like the stroking and come to humans to receive it. The bond that develops between women and their animals is primarily a tactile bond. In our sexually repressed western culture, people are not allowed to touch each other, so we touch our pets. The dogs and cats respond, and the relationship eases loneliness, lowers high blood pressure, and extends life spans. Pets take the place of some of what's missing in our over-stressed, over-extended, always rushing world. To come home from a long day and stroke soft, warm fur is one of the rewards of living on Goddess Earth. To lie on a bed or warm rug and have one's fur stroked, is one of the cat's and dog's greatest joys.

Touch is highly important, but of the senses, it seems to go less noticed:

Touch affects the whole organism, as well as its culture and the individuals it comes into contact with. "It's ten times stronger than verbal or emotional contact . . . and it affects damn near everything we do. No other sense can arouse you like touch; we always knew that, but we never realized it had a biological basis. If touch didn't feel good, there'd be no species, parenthood, or survival . . . Those animals who did more touching instinctively produced offspring that survived, and their genes were passed on and the tendency to touch became even stronger. We forget that touch is not only basic to our species, but the key to it.[1]

Touch is basic to the human-animal bond, as far as domestic pets go, and it's no surprise that touch can be a major healing technique. Dogs and cats get the same benefit from massage as people do. Animals heal women

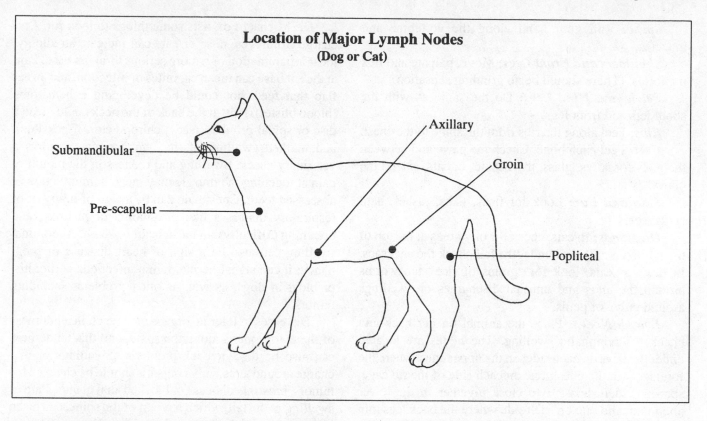

Location of Major Lymph Nodes
(Dog or Cat)

Submandibular

Pre-scapular

Axillary

Groin

Popliteal

by feeling good to touch and women can heal animals by returning the favor. It's done daily without thinking about it to communicate, comfort and praise. But massage and touch are also used in focused ways for focused healing. the deprivation of touch does harm to both pets and people, and adding touch for healing to daily petting and stroking benefits both participants.

Says Ouida West in *The Magic of Massage*:

Regularly massaging your pet strengthens the bond of friendship and love that already exists between the two of you. The more energy and time you invest in strengthening this bond, the greater your returns. You will be rewarded with a more happy, playful, alert, intelligent, responsive, protective and loving pet. To elicit these results, an occasional pat on the head is not enough. Regular massaging is required.[2]

The first thing to use healing massage touch for is to check the dog's or cat's well-being. This should be done at least weekly. By a simple going over with gentle hands, pending problems are discovered (and usually corrected) early. The animal experiences the process as a game, a more thorough than usual stroking and loving session. The touch is always gentle and comfortable for

both woman and pet. The animal not used to this can be eased into it gradually and soon learns to enjoy it. Any gentle, loving touch deepens the animal-human bond.

Diagnostic massage means simply feeling every part of your cat's or dog's body. By knowing your pet's body well, when something is unusual, you will be aware of it. Watch for lumps or sores, swollen nipples, fevers, eye or sinus discharge, and places that the pet may react to by snapping, flinching or crying out. An otherwise gentle animal may react to pain by what seems an aggressive action—biting, for example. Do not punish. If you are familiar with your dog's or cat's body and such reactions happen, you know that something is wrong. A sore can be given first aid, a tick removed, fleas discovered before they get out of hand, and injuries, cysts or tumors discovered and treated early by the weekly diagnostic touch.

The following checklist is from Judy Fireman's *Cat Catalog: The Ultimate Cat Book* (Workman Publishing Co., 1976).[3] It applies very well to dogs and cats both.

Head: Feel the skull, the jaw muscles in the cheeks and temples, and the bump behind the ears.

Neck: Feel the spine and neck muscles, and the sides of the neck and throat.

Spine: Run your hand along the vertebrae and muscles.

Shoulders and Front Legs: Move, palpate and flex the joints. (There should be no grinding sensation.)

Pelvis and Hind Legs: Do the same as with the shoulders and front legs.

Ribs: Feel along the ribs from the spine to the chest.

Feet: Feel each bone. Check the paws and between the pads for sores, glass, thorns, etc. In cats, extend the claws.

Skin and Fur: Look for fleas, ticks, rashes, bald spots, sores.

Oil glands: In cats, check for oily areas at the top of the tail (stud tail), and under the tail check the anal sacs. In dogs or cats, look for "grains of rice" tapeworms around the anus and unusual discharges or swellings around vulva or penis.

Lymph Nodes: Place the animal on her back and check for lymphatic swelling. The nodes are located under the jaws on each side; on the upper chest where the forelegs join the chest; one on each side of the rib cage, spaced widely apart; two close together in the lower abdomen; and one on each side where the back legs join the body. Check the nipples as well; they should not be swollen unless the female is pregnant or in heat.

Eyes, Teeth, Ears, Mouth: Look for discharges, discolored teeth, or very pale gums.

Pulse and Temperature: If you want to take your pet's pulse, find it at the femoral artery inside the hind legs. Normal pulse rate in a cat is 110-130 beats per minute, and in a dog is 70-130 beats per minute (at rest). If your pet has a fever, you will be aware of it by touch; I like to feel the inside of my dogs' ears for this. Normal temperatures for a cat is 101-102.5° F; a dog's normal temperature is 100-102.5°F (average 101.3°). Puppies' and kittens' normal temperature may be slightly lower.

A series of basic points on the dog or cat may cause a pain reaction in the animal if something is wrong. The points are actually acupuncture points, known as alarm points. A map of them follows. If an animal shows pain at one of these areas, though nothing is evidently wrong yet, further attention may be needed. Otherwise, look for signs of pain, heat, swelling or atrophy.[4] If unsure, compare the area with the same area on the other side of the body. Becoming familiar with the pet's body while she is well is important, because later when she is not well, anything unusual stands out.

Dr. Michael Fox lists some things to look for. Discharge from eyes, nose or ears can indicate an allergy, local inflammation or a more serious viral dis-ease. Pain at the ear base can mean ear mites or infection, and an ear flap that feels hot could be developing a hematoma (blood blister). Pain at the back of the neck could mean a disc or spinal problem (see a chiropractor, if possible), and marked swelling of the lymph nodes requires a veterinary check. Swelling and redness in the mouth or pain at touching the muzzle may mean gum infection or abscessed teeth. Chest pain can be a sign of injury or of respiratory dis-eases like pneumonia or pleurisy, and breathing difficulty can mean heart dis-ease. Abdominal swelling can also be a sign of heart dis-ease or pregnancy; it can signal hernia, feline infectious peritonitis, or bloat in dogs, as well as other problems including tumors.

Dis-eases of internal organs may result in tenderness of the alarm points along the spine, and this tenderness can also be disc or back problems. Swellings or discharge around anus, vulva or penis should be checked for tumors, prostrate dis-ease or blocked anal glands. Pain or swelling in the tail, which is a part of the spine, can be an injury or wound. In the legs, look for swellings, wounds, pain around the joints, or pain when the leg is flexed. Painless swelling can indicate edema from heart dis-ease, and hard swellings on the long bones can indicate bone cancer, especially in some large dog breeds. Look between the toes for cysts, thorns or injuries. Check the lymph glands; swelling can indicate infections in that body area, while several swollen glands can indicate feline leukemia or cancer.[5] For anything other than minor, evident skin sores or known difficulties, see a veterinarian for early diagnosis and treatment.

Hopefully, no problems will appear and the diagnostic massage becomes a weekly time of pleasure for both human and pet. Even without knowing anymore about massage than the diagnostic process, a beginning of luxurious pleasure is achieved. Full body massage is the next step. Massage should always be fun; it is not a wrestling match to hold the cat down long enough to put your hands where she thinks you have no business. Full body massage can help to treat joint dis-ease, speed recovery from illness or injury, serve as a tonic for elder animals, and help fast growing, large breed puppies avoid growing pains. As in acupuncture, massage stimulates the animals' brain to release endorphins—natural

Diagnostic Points in Dog or Cat

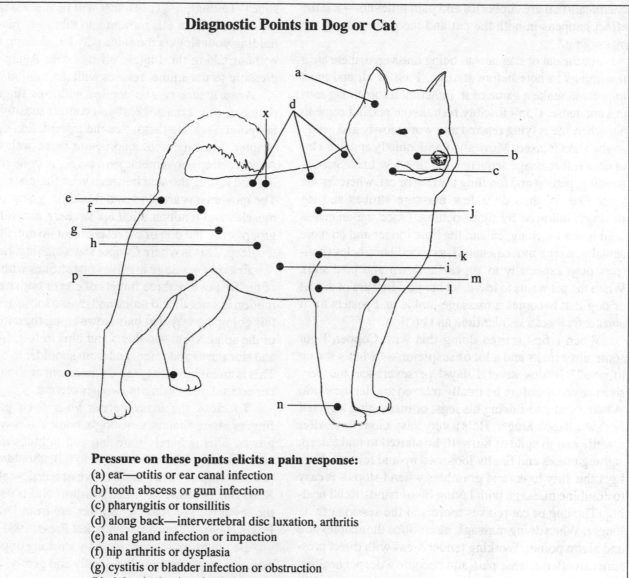

Pressure on these points elicits a pain response:

(a) ear—otitis or ear canal infection
(b) tooth abscess or gum infection
(c) pharyngitis or tonsillitis
(d) along back—intervertebral disc luxation, arthritis
(e) anal gland infection or impaction
(f) hip arthritis or dysplasia
(g) cystitis or bladder infection or obstruction
(h) abdominal pain—foreign body obstruction, infection, peritonitis
(i) low abdominal pain—hepatitis, pancreatitis
(j) chest region—pleurisy, pneumonia
(k) heart region—pericarditis, endocarditis
(l) elbow—arthritis, bursitis
(m) shoulder—arthritis
(n) forepaw—foreign body, cyst or referred pain from l, m, k, or d
(o) hindpaw—foreign body, cyst or referred pain from p, f, g, or d
(p) knee—patella dislocation or torn cruciate ligament
(x) kidney region—nephritis

Note: Dr. Gloria Dodd, DVM adds to (i): from low to *high* abdominal pain for liver, pancreas (right side), spleen (left), stomach, gall bladder and bile ducts.

Dr. Michael Fox, *The Healing Touch* (New York: Newmarket Press, 1981), p. 99.

chemicals that are euphorics and pain relievers—and the effect happens in both the pet and the person doing the massaging.[6]

For the cat or dog new to being massaged, there are a few things to note before starting. First of all and most important, make a game of it, rather than something serious and tense. Don't forcibly restrain the pet, but come to her when she is lying relaxed and work slowly and gently so she stays relaxed. Move and speak quietly and don't try to do a full massage sequence the first few tries. Start by stroking, petting and fondling the dog or cat, wherever she most likes it, then do a few massage strokes and leg flexings, followed by more petting. Once the animal is used to the touching, extend the time longer and do more actual massage movements. Basic obedience helps (it directs dogs especially to sit, or lie down and hold still). When the pet wants to leave, let her go.[7] Beware of the cat or dog that becomes a massage-junkie and pesters for it constantly—set a regular time and be firm.

When I first started doing this with Copper, I got some dirty looks and a lot of suspicion—"what's she up to now?" It took several days' perseverance and very short sessions before he finally relaxed and let me work. When it came to flexing his legs, or massaging legs, tail or paws, it took longer. He's a very suspicious boy. After a while and in spite of himself, he started to make deep, sighing noises and finally loosened up and relaxed. Now I get the dirty looks and grumbles when I stop. It is easy to combine massage with laying on of hands/Reiki healing. The dog or cat relaxes more and the session can be longer. When doing massage, also notice the acupressure and alarm points. Working tender areas with direct pressure can often release pain and become a deeper healing.

There are several basic massage strokes used with pets. In the first, called *effleurage*, use an open palm and fingers to stroke slowly and lightly along the animal's body. Gradually increase pressure and do about fifteen of these per minute, going with the lay of the fur. Start by stroking down the back, then from shoulder to hip to foot. In *fingertip massage*, hold two or three fingers together and move the skin in small circles over the muscles underneath. As the dog or cat relaxes, increase the pressure, but never so hard that it hurts. Use one hand for this, with the other holding the animal still by placing it flat on her side or head. When working on the legs, use the other hand to steady the leg you are massaging. This finger pressure movement is the basis of Linda Tellington-Jones' Tellington TTouch that will be discussed later in the chapter. Turn this motion into vibratory massage by holding your fingers the same way but shaking the wrist without taking the fingers off the skin. Again increase pressure as the animal relaxes with the motion.

Acupressure can be applied with one finger or the thumb during a massage. If you contact sensitive meridian points, release them. See the information of the last chapter. Massage and acupressure work well together. Another deep movement, *petrissage*, is done by kneading and rolling the skin between your fingers and thumb. The movements are slow and rhythmic, going across the muscles and tendons. Pick up, squeeze and roll muscle groups once the dog or cat relaxes, but do not pinch or go too deep. This is where Cooper starts sighing; he loves it.

Friction massage involves fast strokes with the balls of the first two or three fingers of one or both hands. The motion is smooth and quick and makes loose hair fly. Do this going the way that hair grows along the entire length of the spine, from shoulders and hips to feet, from chest and ribcage to abdomen, and from shoulder to rear flank. This is an invigorating, rapid movement at about a stroke per second, increasing to two per second.

To close the massage run your open palms and fingers along the cat's or dog's body the way the hair grows. This is barely touching and lightens to become aura stroking. Move from nose to tail, shoulder to front paw, and hip to back paw. Do five or ten slow strokes. In Reiki this is called the Reiki brushoff and is used to end the sessions. The massage strokes are from Dr. Michael Fox's *Healing Touch* (Newmarket Press, 1981).[8]

Begin the massage session by stroking or petting the dog or cat, approaching her quietly and gently. Start with the animal's favorite spot to be touched, and leave the tender parts (usually the feet and legs) for last, when she is as fully relaxed as possible. Start with light pressure that increases gradually but that is never so heavy as to be uncomfortable or scary. Watch the animal's reactions and honor them; if she seems uneasy or frightened talk gently to her and ease up. Work generally in the direction the fur grows, having some idea of the anatomy of the pet's body. When massaging the limbs, the movements are in the direction toward the heart. No massage oil is used with pet massage; the animals' fur allows your hands to move freely without it, and you don't want an oiled dog to jump on your furniture after the massage. For an animal new to this, know when to stop—and keep trying for short daily sessions.

Ouida West, in *The Magic of Massage* (Putnam Publishing, 1983), describes a pet massage sequence. She begins with the dog's or cat's feet and legs, then moves to abdomen, spine, side of body, neck, head and ears. You may wish to begin with the spine and work in different order: spine, head and neck, shoulder and front legs, chest and abdomen, hip and hind legs (Michael Fox's sequence). The steps are numbered but can be rearranged, providing a simple way to begin.[9]

1. Foot and paw massage: Gently massage the foot and then the pads between them. Animals are foot shy, so move slowly.

2. Leg massage: Next, starting just above the paw, massage up the leg toward the animal's body. Work the hind leg muscles and encourage the pet to relax and keep the leg limp.

3. Abdominal massage: From the legs move to the abdomen, most dogs will roll on their backs for this, or lift a hind leg to begin. Cats may take longer to accept their stomachs being touched. Make circular motions over the abdominal area, with your two palms for larger animals, or your thumb and fingers in a gentle squeezing motion with one hand for cats and smaller dogs.

4. Body massage: Massage one side at a time, using large circular motions from back legs to neck.

5. Spinal massage: Massage along either side of the spinal column, not on it, using middle and index finger or index and thumb. Watch for reactions here; these are acupuncture association points (Bladder Meridians, paired). Release sore spots and note where they are on the diagnostic map. Don't forget the tail.

6. Neck, Head and Ears: Massage these areas thoroughly and spend more time where the animal seems to most like it. Massage the neck on both sides of the spinal column, as for the spine. Work around the nose, mouth and eyes being careful not to poke. The ears contain a full acupressure body map, so spend time stroking them from base to tip, or pull them between fingers and thumb gently. Most animals like being touched there.

This is a simple sequence, and Copper approves, even starting at the feet he is so wary of. Of all the chapters in this book Copper likes this one best. It got me to practice massage on him. Michael Fox's massage sequence in *The Healing Touch* is more complete and I recommend it highly. His is the only book that I have found devoted entirely to pet massage. Some books on human massage

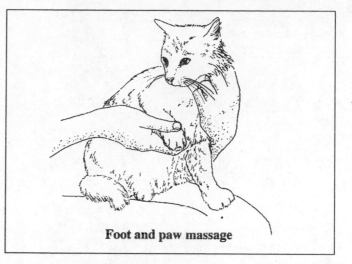

Foot and paw massage

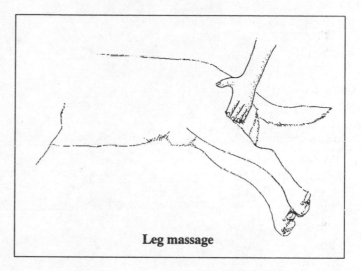

Leg massage

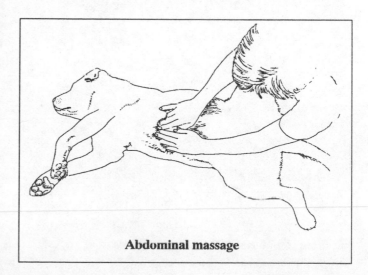

Abdominal massage

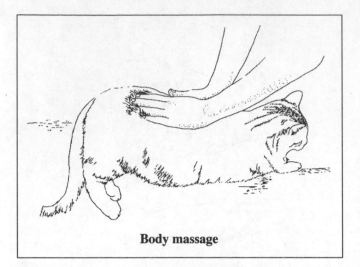

Body massage

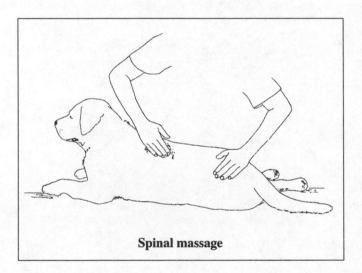

Spinal massage

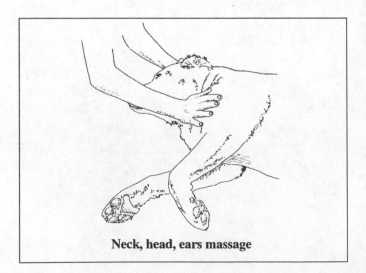

Neck, head, ears massage

mention pets or show a brief pet sequence, but they are few and far between. I found that using massage on Copper makes a positive difference in our rapport, and seems to lessen his tenseness and help with his willingness to be obedient. After about a week of sour grapes and suspicion, he started to visibly enjoy it and want more. Starting lightly, slowly and gently, gradually increase the movement and pressure as the animal relaxes.

Massage is contraindicated (not recommended) with sprains until the swelling is gone, broken bones or broken skin injuries. Do not use massage if an animal has an infectious dis-ease, feline leukemia, cancer, or is in shock. If the cat or dog is sick and wants to be left alone, honor her wishes. In these cases, use laying on of hands or Reiki/aura healing instead, placing your hands gently on the animal and in her aura above the body. After the acute stage, recovery can often be speeded by massage done gently. When in doubt, ask an experienced massage therapist for people or an informed veterinarian. Remember to do diagnostic massage frequently, and to follow up on discovered problems.

Arthritis and hip dysplasia, joint pain, muscle cramps or stiffness, skin problems, and spinal problems can respond well to gentle massage, being careful not to cause the animal further pain. Massage stimulates circulation and increases lymph flow and, as in acupressure, releases blocked chi. In puppies massage can help minerals to be absorbed from the blood into the bones where they are needed, and this is especially important in large and giant breed puppies. If a young puppy or kitten is orphaned, massage and touch can be highly important for the baby's survival and later socialization. After sprains and broken bones are healed, massage helps to increase movement and facilitates full recovery and function. After injuries, surgery or dis-ease, massage can help complete a full recovery more quickly.[10] Animals under physical or emotional stress are aided by massage, as well, and the technique reduces high blood pressure in pets as it does in people.

For pets with behavior or temperament problems, particularly for animals with a herstory of past abuse or trauma, massage can increase trust immensely. It aids socialization and cooperation. The ability to communicate with a cat or dog increases by doing massage regularly on her, enhancing both her receptivity and yours. When a dog or cat needs attention, massage works wonders. In every step of the process, be aware of the animal's needs, fears and tolerance level, especially in the beginning. Keep it fun and don't work longer than the animal seems to like it. Try the various types of movements, starting always lightly, and always being sure that the pet is comfortable and receptive. She will develop her preferences—honor them.

One specific massage technique, by animal behavior expert Linda Tellington-Jones, works wonderfully for modifying negative behaviors, taming wild or unsocialized animals gently, increasing trust and reducing aggressiveness, and for healing. The technique is named by its inventor the Tellington TTouch. It is derived from the human technique of Feldenkrais. This is a method that opens new neurological pathways to the brain by use of nonhabitual movements. The concept is based on the life-force intelligence of each cell of the body, each cell's connection with the whole organism animal or human, and between organisms—animal and human. "At the cellular level," says Linda Tellington-Jones, "we're all the same."[11] The TTouch stimulates cell intelligence, and "so turns on the corresponding brain cells like so many light bulbs."[12] Central to the TTouch technique is the idea of communication and co-creative partnership between human and pet.

When the TTouch is done properly (the circles closed), it generates all four brain-wave patterns in the animals receiving it—alpha, beta, theta and delta. Normal daily activity uses the beta pattern, alpha is equivalent to human concentration or meditation, theta is deep trance, and delta is the level below consciousness usually associated with sleep. Use of the TTouch to stimulate the body cells and corresponding brain cells activates the brain and changes old habits and patterns. It enables the horse, dog, cat or wild creature to think a situation through rather than automatically reacting by instinct. Instead of the habitual fight or flight response, the animal evaluates the situation—and calms down.[13]

A dog or cat (or other animal) that thinks is able to make choices and to learn to trust. Animals do think, of course, but traditional handling of most animals, including in dog and horse training, discourages them from it. Training by force without conscious communication can do more harm than good, resulting in a pet that develops negative behavior habits, irrational fears, stubbornness, resentment, over-submissiveness, aggressiveness, or unreliability. By asking and allowing the animal to think, and by an attitude of conscious respect and cooperation

with her, the cellular intelligence becomes two-way communication. The result is behavior and personality changes, along with increased speed of healing for wounds, injuries or stiffness.[14] By releasing body tension and opening the neural pathways, emotional tensions release as well. The dog's or cat's body relaxes, its ability to think is activated, and communication by touch does the rest.

All this happens with less than an hour's training for the human end of the partnership, and a few daily sessions of around fifteen minutes for the cat, dog or other animal. (TTouch is also successful for people). What accomplishes these miracles is a method that can tentatively be classified as massage (or acupressure perhaps), though it does a lot more and goes further than most massage methods attempt. There are a total of fifteen hand positions, but the method is based on a single hand motion:

The heart of the TTouch is a series of small, randomly placed circles "drawn" on the animal. Imagine a clock face, and beginning at six, push the skin gently clockwise all the way around past six and finish at eight. No one, including Tellington-Jones, knows exactly why it works. But . . . its success is overwhelming.[15]

When doing this, maintain an even constant pressure and make sure to close the circles. When you reach eight o'clock, pause for a moment, then lift your fingers from the animal's body gently, and begin again somewhere else. The circles are placed at random, anywhere—there is no pattern to doing this. Avoid circling in the same spot, as there is a tendency to do, but complete the circle, then lift your hand and move. Doing three circles in a row before moving seems to be a tendency for beginners—but it is not the TTouch and will not accomplish the miracles. Make only a circle and a quarter at each spot, then move and do it again elsewhere. Use your middle three fingers as one, allowing them to relax and move with the rotation. Rest your wrist, thumb and little finger against the animal's body to steady your hand. Make the circles round, and make them in a single flowing movement. Linda Tellington-Jones calls this basic movement The Clouded Leopard TTouch.

In the beginning of the session, make the circles quickly, about one per second. As the cat or dog begins to relax and "enters a state of bodily listening" slow the circles to half the speed, about two per second. When you reach eight o'clock on this slower circle, pause, push in a little, then lift your fingers gradually. The faster beginning circles awaken the dog's or cat's body, and the slower ones that follow allow deep relaxation, release muscle tension, deepen and enhance respiration, aid physical and emotional healing, and open animal-human communication. The practitioner need concentrate on nothing but making the circles. Keep your breath even and steady and pay attention to the animal's response.[16]

TTouch pressure ranges on a level from one to ten, using as little as one light finger or as much as the whole open hand. You will know when you have the pressure right by the pet's reaction and how it feels. Try attuning your breathing to the cat's or dog's and working in rhythm, and the pressure regulates itself. The practitioner is relaxed, breathing easily and moving rhythmically and fluidly. Says Tellington-Jones, "If you're getting tired it means you're doing something wrong."[17] Smaller animals or sensitive body areas require lighter touch, as does working over pain areas. Do not avoid these areas, but make sure not to cause the animal discomfort.

The Tellington TTouch was developed on horses, though it has been proven effective on every kind of animal, including dogs and cats. Kathy Witkowsky describes a TTouch session on a horse that also describes how to work with dogs and cats:

Starting with the horse's ears, Tellington-Jones slides her fingers from the base to the tip. This she says, relaxes an animal, and can normalize pulse and temperature and relieve colic . . .

As Tellington-Jones moves her hands to the horse's mouth and gums, ignoring his attempt to nip, she explains her technique: "Animals often hold their tension in their mouths. Until you get this horse to relax his mouth, he'll be distracted." (She) moves back along the horse's body drawing small imaginary circles on its skin, which is visibly loosening during the session.

Finally, she takes hold of the base of the horse's tail, rotating it in both directions, then stands directly behind it and gives one long, steady pull. Because a horse's tail is an extension of its spine, she explains, this stretches its back. The horse shifts its weight, rocks back and forth, and sighs with what could only be relief. All this in about fifteen minutes.[18]

The above description, plus the information of making tiny random circles on the skin that start at six o'clock and go around a circle and a quarter to eight o'clock, was all the information I had when I decided to try the TTouch. Copper was my subject, and it was his first experience with massage. After a circle or two I was amazed that he hadn't gotten up and left, and after less than five minutes the dog was blissed out in a way I had never seen before. He started to sigh and groan, and rolled over on his back for me to reach his belly. His tongue hung out to one side, and his body softened more than I had ever previously felt it. He especially liked the work with his ears. After the session, he followed me around for hours, and when I sat down put his head into my lap.

He has never been a major behavior problem, so there was no significant change to look for, but he was definitely more relaxed and less vigilant and hyper. After I got Kali, he showed some early distress and jealousy (though he loves her), and I used a TTouch session to help him through it. It clearly worked, especially when I used the TTouch around and in the dog's mouth, and I saw definite changes in Copper's jealousy. It was a combination of added attention, feeling wonderful, and the miracles of the TTouch itself.

Kali came to me traumatized and was a frequent biter for the first two months I had her. Along with the other healing, I did a TTouch session with her the night I brought her home and watched a definite change in her traumatic fear. A few sessions relaxed her and it was during them that she first began communicating with me. This is a puppy that loves any form of touch, and it seemed to reach through her recent on-the-street abuse. The biting has almost stopped. I tried it on a cat that had never seemed to like me and got a clear change of attitude from that point on, with only one session of less than ten minutes. The technique clearly and definitely reduces animal aggressiveness, tension and fear reactions, speeds the healing process, and increases two-way conscious communication.

Tellington TTouch is an exciting process, and like most profound breakthroughs, is extremely simple. It's a good method to teach children, and if you have read this far you already know how to use it. Just do it, and don't forget to close the circles. The healing can be done anywhere by anyone and requires little or no equipment. (Tellington-Jones uses some simple aids, particularly with horses and wild animals.) She considers four components as the basics of the method: a mental attitude of concentrating on the movements and approaching the animal with respect; the hand and finger movements; breath awareness; and finding the optimal pressure.[19] Much of the work is learned by doing it. What actually happens and why it works is still a mystery; just doing it is enough.

The method is an important healing tool, though Linda Tellington-Jones refuses to call herself a healer. Several women work with the TTouch in the Denver area humane shelters and see remarkable results in physical and emotional healing. Says Pam Beets, one of the workers:

By gently stimulating certain areas we are able to re-route messages from the body to the brain traveling along tiny neural pathways. These re-routed messages open us to new ways of thinking or feeling or reacting.

These newly opened neural pathways can help a frightened animal calm down, a sick animal feel better, and a misbehaving animal improve its behavior. Meanwhile, it strengthens the bond between the animal on the receiving end of all the gentle touches and pats and the human doing it.[20]

Beets demonstrated the TTouch on a sullen dog, a cat that had been injured by a fan belt, and a rooster that was attacking shelter workers. All three responded and changed dramatically and quickly. Sharon Jackson, of Colorado Horse Rescue, is quoted in the same article:

From minor ailments to severe starvation the (Tellington TTouch) methods and practices are a critical partner in the care we give. We can visibly see swelling go down, horses relax, appetite improve and fear subside.[20]

These are amazing responses for a technique so simple, which has remarkable results with no scientifically accepted explanation. Says Pam Beets again:

We know it works, but we don't really know why. The theory is that touch is the fastest way to access the brain. The brain pays attention to something that's not in its regular habit.[20]

The Tellington TTouch is used for dogs in a number of ways. It is useful in healing and is important for healing behavior and temperament problems. An overly aggressive dog learns to cooperate and listen by working with the TTouch, an overly passive/submissive animal gains confidence, and a nervous hyper one calms down. Instead of confrontation with a hostile, aggressive or terrified animal, the TTouch stimulates cooperation. Some of this is as simple as changes of body posture:

When dogs (and many other animals) feel aggressive, they tense up and hold their heads high. It seems like a miracle, but as soon as you get them to lower their heads, they give up their resistance, relax and begin to respond.[21]

To start this relaxation, Linda Tellington-Jones begins by working the dog's ears and then going to the neck and chest areas.

The dog's aggressive reactions are a learned automatic pattern of ingrained tension, fear and threat. The TTouch with its nonhabitual gentle motions gives the animal a chance to change the pattern and to relax. For overly timid animals the same thing holds true. For dogs who are fear-biters, timid or with phobias (as to thunder) try working with TTouch on the animal's hindquarters. Keep the dog standing up. For animals whose aggression or nervousness is the result of chronic pain, the TTouch used on the whole body will identify the problem areas, and done gently and repeatedly alleviate them:

If your dog is unusually belligerent or snappish, go over his (sic) whole body with the TTouch and look for painful areas. At the beginning, you might find it useful to note the areas where the dog is nervous about certain types of circles and where he is not. You'll discover that over a period of several days the areas that you can touch without nervous response will enlarge. For instance, a dog that will not let you touch him on the hindquarters will slowly begin to accept the TTouch, and will cease to sit down or growl at you each time you try.[22]

Work the areas of the head, neck, and particularly the muzzle and inside the mouth. The dog will relax enough to allow it, though maybe not on the first session. Work slowly and gently. There may not be a change in the first session, or a change during the session in the animal's behavior. Do short sessions (five to fifteen minutes) daily. The method works for dogs who are chronic chewers—work the mouth areas here, also.

For problem barkers, Linda Tellington-Jones rewards them when they *stop* barking by giving them the attention they crave with the TTouch. Again by changing the animals' body language, the habit is changed:

A dog who is nervous and barking will hold his (sic) head stiffly erect and tense his hindquarters, blocking the neural impulses that allow him to sense the rest of his body and thereby undermining his self-confidence. So, in a vicious cycle, he barks because he feels insecure and he feels insecure because he's barking.[23]

Work on the animal's hindquarters and neck. After the dog's head lowers, raise the muzzle with your hand and work the head and mouth areas. Tellington-Jones uses the TTouch for cooperation in grooming, veterinary trips, and to relieve Fourth of July firecracker and thunder (loud noise) fears.

She relates a story about a hyper-nervous Irish Setter. The woman who lived with the dog spent time petting her every day after work, but the dog wanted more and more, and it was never enough. She tried the TTouch one day for three minutes, after seeing it demonstrated on television. Afterwards, the dog was satisfied and lay quietly while she made dinner. Tellington-Jones explains why the dog was satisfied:

The circles activate the dog's awareness at a cellular level so that unlike stroking, which leaves no imprint, the experience remains with the dog even after you've stopped petting him.

Secondly, by making the circles you have changed the quality and type of attention you are giving your dog. Slowing yourself down and breathing into the circles means that you yourself are relaxing. Instead of patting the dog while your mind is on making dinner or whatever it is you want to do next, you become focused and grounded and so make a *real* connection to your dog. Animals are wonderfully honest—the only way you can truly connect to them is by being fully present.[24]

She also uses the TTouch on puppies that are orphaned, premature or refuse to (or are too weak to) nurse. Five minute session working on the ears and inside the mouth can start them nursing. She uses the TTouch on and around puppies' tails before and for a few days after tail docking. Circles around the young puppy's anal area with a warm wet sponge help an orphaned pup eliminate in a way similar to how a mother dog does it. In elder animals, use the TTouch in daily sessions to increase stamina and lengthen life. Abalone Circles (TTouch using the whole flat palm) on the chest aids labored breathing. Also focus on the ears and paws of older pets, as working these areas aids in heart problems.[25]

For cats, use the TTouch for the animal that refuses to be petted or handled. This is often a cat who has not been handled young enough or has been semi-wild:

When faced with a nervous cat—or any nervous creature for that matter—the best way to introduce the TTouch is by jumping all over the body with fast circles so that the animal doesn't know where your hand will land next. This focuses the animal's attention on you at the same time as it breaks the pattern of nervous reaction . . . . Because the animal can't anticipate, he or she very quickly gives up struggling.[26]

At first use some circles that aren't completely closed, starting at six o'clock and ending at four o'clock, for cats that are extremely nervous and upset. Tellington-Jones describes working with a cat in this way. After four days of capturing the tomcat she'd long been feeding but had never been able to handle, the cat became a lap cat and never left her again. Make a sling with a towel for a cat that really struggles, holding her restrained in it while starting the TTouch circles. She suggests the TTouch as aids to getting a cat into carrier case, for car travel, trips to the vet's, and for other handling. The technique does wonders for socializing.

As with dogs, for aggressive cats that claw or bite in hostility or too rough play, use the TTouch paying special attention to working on the mouth, lips and gums. There seems to be a neurologic connection between the mouth and the brain's emotional center (the limbic system). Working these areas very gently and totally without force can create major behavioral changes. They also work for erratic or uncontrollable behaviors.

In healings with cats, Linda Tellington-Jones describes using the TTouch on a snow leopard cub that seemed to be dying of respiratory dis-ease. She worked the area around the animal's face, sinuses and ears, then its neck, head, mouth, lips and gums. She worked the legs next, including the paws and between the pads, and the spine from head to tail tip. The massage took twenty-five minutes, and the animal began to recover immediately. She used visualization on the other two cubs in the litter that she hadn't been able to touch, visualizing that they received the massage as well. All three cubs, which were assumed to be dying, survived. During her work, all three of the cubs relaxed and calmed down.[27] This is healing work to consider for cats (or other animals) with infectious dis-eases or feline leukemia.

She also describes working the TTouch with cats who have been neurologically damaged in accidents, and

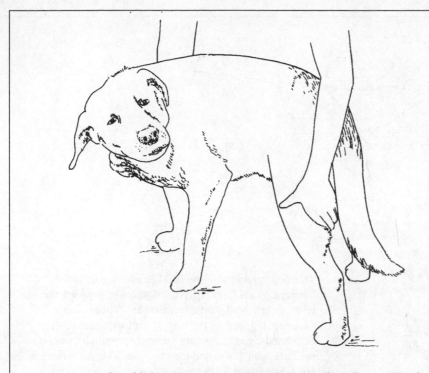

The TTouch on the hindquarters is particularly beneficial for dogs who are fear-biters, overly timid or afraid of thunder and lightning or gunshots. Some dogs will be concerned when you work this area and will try to sit down. Should this occur, lighten your TTouch and reassure your dog with your voice. Asking your dog to stand while working the hindquarters helps to release the fear more quickly than if you work while he is lying down.

text from Linda Tellington-Jones with Sybil Taylor, *The Tellington TTouch: A Breakthrough Technique to Train and Care for Your Favorite Animal*, (New York, Viking Press, 1992), p. 74-80.

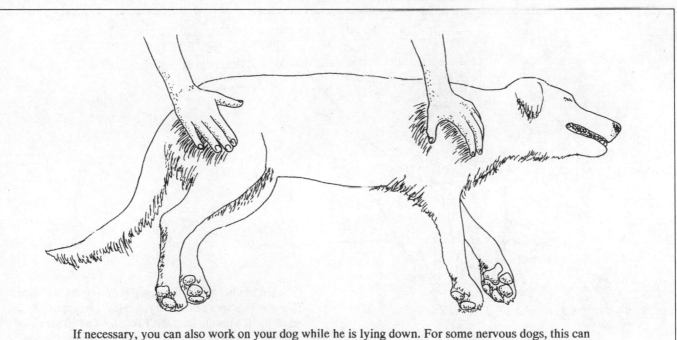

If necessary, you can also work on your dog while he is lying down. For some nervous dogs, this can be threatening at first, so gently but firmly keep your dog quiet with your right hand as you make the circles with your left. If a dog is overactive or very submissive, he may lick or try to get up, and it may take a few lessons for him to learn to focus and relax.

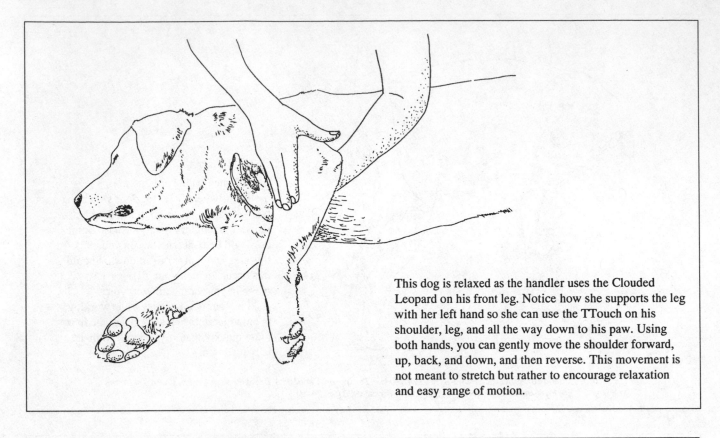

This dog is relaxed as the handler uses the Clouded Leopard on his front leg. Notice how she supports the leg with her left hand so she can use the TTouch on his shoulder, leg, and all the way down to his paw. Using both hands, you can gently move the shoulder forward, up, back, and down, and then reverse. This movement is not meant to stretch but rather to encourage relaxation and easy range of motion.

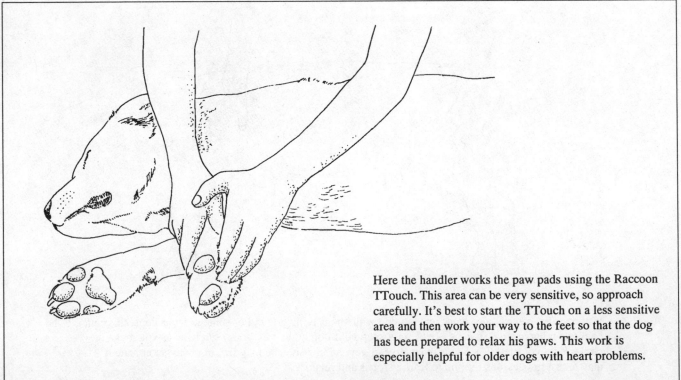

Here the handler works the paw pads using the Raccoon TTouch. This area can be very sensitive, so approach carefully. It's best to start the TTouch on a less sensitive area and then work your way to the feet so that the dog has been prepared to relax his paws. This work is especially helpful for older dogs with heart problems.

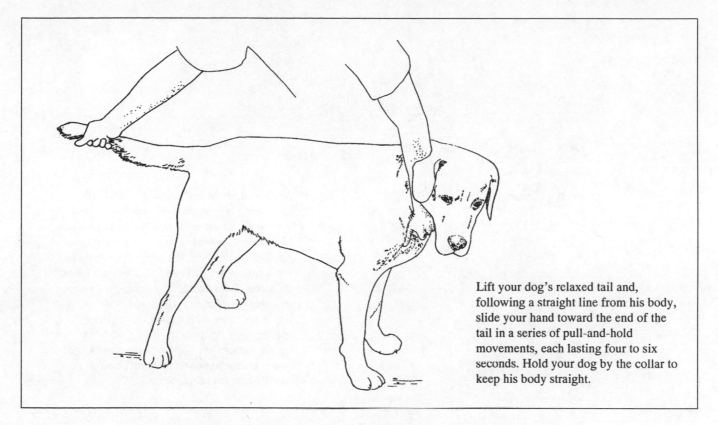

Lift your dog's relaxed tail and, following a straight line from his body, slide your hand toward the end of the tail in a series of pull-and-hold movements, each lasting four to six seconds. Hold your dog by the collar to keep his body straight.

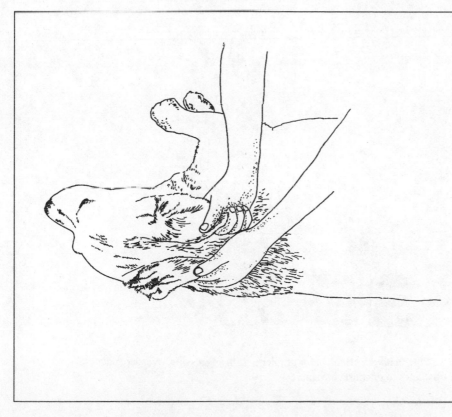

Starting a session with the ears is a good idea, since this work is eagerly accepted by most dogs. Gently but firmly slide down and out, holding your dog's ear between your thumb and bent forefinger, as shown. Repeat this movement several times from the base of the ears to the tips, covering a different portion of the ear with each slide.

Make tiny circles as you slide from one place to the other all over the ear. The thumb provides a base while the forefinger circles, or vice versa. Robyn used this TTouch on her old dog Stash, who was fourteen. He had fluid around the heart, and would often have trouble breathing and sleeping. After Robyn worked his ears for a few moments, he was able to get comfortable and drift off to sleep.

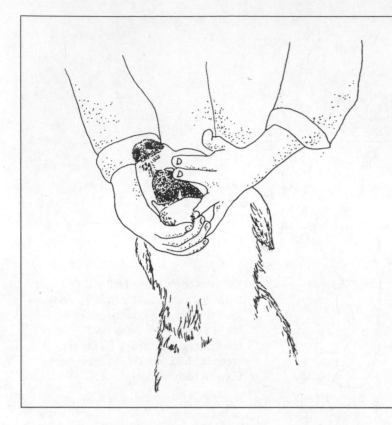

Sit so you are behind the dog's head and supporting his muzzle with one hand. Be careful not to squeeze, which could cause him to fight. use the index finger or your other hand to carefully lift the upper lip. Gently rub the inside of the lips and make tiny circles on the gums. If the inside of your dog's mouth is dry, wet your fingers with warm water. If your dog is unhappy with this work, begin by making very light circles on the outside of his dewlap before you slip onto the gums. Quiet perseverance over several short sessions usually brings acceptance.

Working dogs with the Homing Pigeon is very effective for problems with aggression, overdependency, or anxiety. Use a variety of obstacles to encourage focus

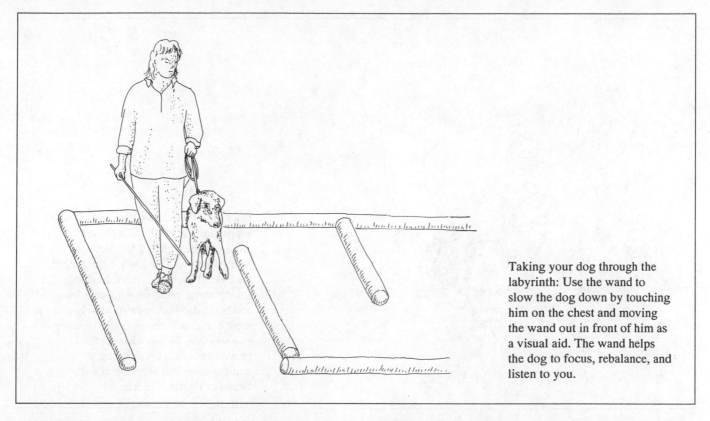

Taking your dog through the labyrinth: Use the wand to slow the dog down by touching him on the chest and moving the wand out in front of him as a visual aid. The wand helps the dog to focus, rebalance, and listen to you.

with elder cats. When working with elder animals, keep the pressure very light around the spine and put no pressure directly on the spinal column. This is more important with sensitive cats than with dogs, but a good precaution with both. When working cats' tiny ears, work very gently.

Here is the Tellington TTouch massage sequence for working with a cat. The information is from Linda Tellington-Jones' *The Tellington TTouch* (Viking Press, 1992):[28]

1. Hold the cat in a lying position on your lap supporting the head in your left hand. Use the basic Lying Leopard TTouch alternated with a touch that uses both fingers and the heel of the hand (Clouded Leopard TTouch). Make slow circles at random over the cat's body, experimenting with pressure levels.

2. Holding the cat's head, stroke her ears with both thumbs. Make tiny light circles first on the outside, then on the inside (gums, inner lip) of the cat's mouth.

3. Use tiny circles with the tip of the index finger on the inside and outside of the cat's ears. Slide your fingers from base to tips, as well.

4. Holding the leg in one hand and working with the other, make circles down the leg to the paw. Stroke the paw, and make tiny circles around the pads. (This is a behavior aid for cats who claw, and helps also with nail clipping).

Start slowly and work gently, especially at first before the cat is accustomed to the TTouch. Animals relax and enjoy this, and the TTouch does wonders for healing, for behavior modification that is gentle and without force, and for communication.

For more information on this technique, I highly recommend Linda Tellington-Jones' two books. The first focuses on horses and is called *An Introduction to the Tellington-Jones Equine Awareness Method* (Breakthrough Publications, 1988). The second, which focuses on a variety of animals including dogs and cats, is *The Tellington TTouch* (Viking Press, 1992). The information for this section on the TTouch comes primarily from the newer book. This is an exciting method of healing that can work wonders for cats and dogs on many levels.

When I began ordering material for reference before writing this book, my women's bookstore that patiently

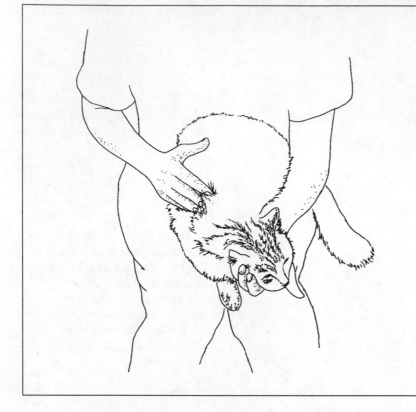

Hold the cat as shown with the left hand supporting the head under the chin. Alternate the Clouded Leopard and Lying Leopard TTouches, beginning at the base of the neck. Move randomly from place to place on your cat's body and make each circle fairly slowly—in most cases each circle should take one to two seconds. To see what depth of pressure your cat prefers, begin with number three and experiment with a firmer or lighter TTouch.

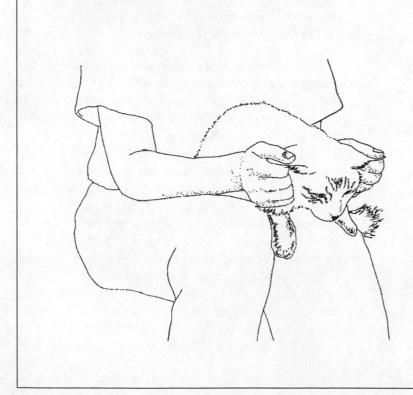

The ear has acupuncture points for all parts of the body, so working the ears at random can benefit the entire body. Treating your cat's ears gently, as though they were rose petals, make tiny circles with your forefinger on the inside of the cat's ear. You can also slide your fingers from the base to the tips of the ears, holding them between thumb and forefinger as shown. Not all cats like ear work, so be sure to start out gently.

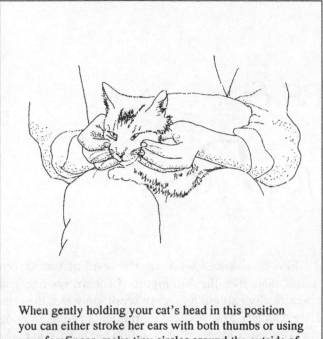

When gently holding your cat's head in this position you can either stroke her ears with both thumbs or using your forefinger, make tiny circles around the outside of the cat's mouth, gradually moving to the gums under the upper lip.

Support your cat's leg as you use your thumb to make TTouch circles down the leg to the paw. At the paw, gently stroke it, and then make tiny circles around the pads. This is a good procedure for cats who use their claws indiscriminately and as a preparation for nail clipping.

did the ordering teased me. They said I was reading "how to massage your horse books" and they were going to start a "how to massage your horse book section." And in fact, Patty Callahan of Brigit Books did just that. Joyce Weaver, of Treasures Bookstore in Tampa, did the same. It seemed funny at the time, but it's not a bad idea. If information like Michael Fox's *The Healing Touch* and Linda Tellington-Jones' *Tellington TTouch* were more known, there'd be many happier animals and their people. My own dogs' reactions to massage and TTouch bear this out, not to mention my own pleasure when I have a massage. There's something in it for everyone.

The next chapter uses flower essences for healing, and describes the technique of applied kinesiology muscle testing for dogs and cats.

[1] Diane Ackerman, from *A Natural History of the Senses*, in Jean Liedloff, "Babes in Arms: Why Infants Need to be Held," *Natural Health Magazine*, July-August, 1992, p. 48.

[2] Ouida West, *The Magic of Massage* (New York, Putnam Publishing Co., 1983), pp. 24-25.

[3] Judy Fireman, Ed., *Cat Catalog: The Ultimate Cat Book* (New York, Workman Publishing Co., 1976), p. 184

[4] Dr. Michael Fox, *The Healing Touch* (New York, Newmarket Press, 1981), p. 98.

[5] *Ibid.*, pp. 100-107.

[6] Karen Murchland, "New Frontiers in Pet Treatments," in *Massage Magazine*, June-July, 1989, pp. 26-27.

[7] Dr. Michael Fox, *The Healing Touch*, pp. 26-27.

[8] *Ibid.*, p. 64-69.

[9] Ouida West, *The Magic of Massage*, pp. 146-149.

[10] Karen Murchland, "New Frontiers in Pet Treatments," pp. 26-27.

[11] Kathy Witkowsky, "Tiny Circles on the Skin," in *American Way* (Vol. 24, no. 20), October 15, 1991, p. 60.

[12] Linda Tellington-Jones with Sybil Taylor, *The Tellington TTouch: A Breakthrough Technique to Train and Care for Your Favorite Animal* (New York, Viking Press, 1992), p. 18.

[13] Kathy Witkowsky, "Tiny Circles on the Skin," p. 58.

[14] Linda Tellington-Jones, *The Tellington TTouch*, pp. 23-25.

[15] Kathy Witkowsky, "Tiny Circles on the Skin," p. 58.

[16] Linda Tellington-Jones, *The Tellington TTouch*, pp. 23-25.

[17] *Ibid.*, p. 26.

[18] Kathy Witkowsky, "Tiny Circles on the Skin," pp. 56-58.

[19] Linda Tellington-Jones, *The Tellington TTouch*, pp. 70-71.

[20] Rebecca Jones, "Animal Tamer," in *The Rocky Mountain News*, April 9, 1992, p. 71. Also personal communication.

[21] Linda Tellington-Jones, *The Tellington TTouch*, pp. 70-71.

[22] *Ibid.*, pp. 84-85.

[23] *Ibid.*, p. 88.

[24] *Ibid.*, p. 94.

[25] *Ibid.*, pp. 94-97.

[26] *Ibid.*, p. 44.

[27] *Ibid.*, pp. 40-42.

[28] *Ibid.*, pp. 59-61.

Flower Essences & Muscle Testing for Pets

Flower essences work on the level of the unseen bodies, and like the Tellington TTouch, no one can scientifically explain how they work, only that they do. They operate on the level of vibrational healing, moving at a faster rate of speed and vibration but in a similar way to homeopathic remedies. Essences work in a subtle way, primarily on the emotional, mental and spiritual (soul level) bodies. Since energy moves through all the bodies to create an animal's or human's health, and since stress and emotional feelings are high factors in the creation of dis-ease or well–being, flower essences play a part in healing on all the levels.

An animal with a physical dis-ease will also have mental–emotional symptoms. Whether the dis-ease created the emotional state or the emotional state created the dis-ease can be a chicken and egg discussion. The point is to heal them both. Using flower essences to treat the mental-emotional level while using physical healing methods to treat the dis-ease, treats all the bodies and results in fuller healing. When dis-ease is healed physically but not emotionally-mentally, it may recur or become another dis-ease. Flower essences reach the vibrational unseen bodies that physical level healing methods cannot.

When an animal in physical good health becomes stressed, angry, depressed, jealous or traumatized, the emotions can move through the bodies to become physical illness. A cat nearly hit by a car, for example, can become so distressed and frightened that, though she was not physically injured, dis-ease results. She may harbor the pain emotionally to the point where she develops a dis-ease, perhaps a respiratory infection. Or she may turn the emotional fright into behavior problems, like wetting indoors on the rug, and the dis-ease becomes mental. By healing the initial trauma, the respiratory infection and the out-of-box wetting are prevented. If they have already manifested, healing the trauma helps the cat to heal the other dis-eases, which are physical and mental symptoms of the emotional fear.

Physical dis-ease caused by an emotion does not respond readily to antibiotics or chemical drugs, and resists other forms of physical level healing as well. This is because the ailment is a symptom and not the dis-ease itself. Healing that works on just the physical level in this case is only temporary. A dog that develops cancer because she is grieving the death of her human companion needs healing for the grief before she can heal the dis-ease. If the grief is not addressed, the tumor may be surgically removed but another appears, and eventually the animal dies. If the grief is released, the tumor shrinks with no intervention or the surgery to remove it is all that is needed, and the cancer does not recur.

Animals adopted from Humane Societies and other shelters are highly traumatized, and most of them arrive in new homes with some form of illness. The primary causes of the physical dis-eases in these dogs and cats are the abuse they may have suffered, the grief at losing original families, and the fright of being in a strange place with scary sounds and smells with nothing (no one) familiar nearby. Animals also absorb the emotions around them from other dogs and cats and take them into themselves. Exposure to dis-ease is less the cause of illness than emotional trauma in these pets. If the animals had not been terrified, stressed and lost, the same dis-ease germs would pass them by without harm.

The first six months or so in a new home for such a dog or cat is traumatic and scary as well. The abuse and fear of the past take time to release, and it also takes time for the pet to make new bonds and learn to trust new people and places. After a week in a noisy, threat-filled animal shelter, a dog or cat may be afraid of loud noises, wary of choke collars, and may tend to growl or snap when a hand approaches. The animal may suffer a series of dis-eases, not as much "brought from the pound," but as manifested from the its terror.

Even pets that do not come from a shelter suffer emotional trauma. Leaving their mother is the earliest traumatic situation most puppies and kittens face, and most are taken from the nest very early. A trip to the veterinarian or a stay at a boarding kennel can be a traumatic situation, especially the first time. ("What if she doesn't come back? Where is she? Doesn't she love me anymore? What am I doing here?") Being chased by a larger animal, teased by a child, a near-miss or hit with a car, coming in season, or facing outright abuse are all stresses and traumas in animal lives. Obedience training, done today with force and so little caring by some trainers, is another stressful time. Spaying or neutering, though necessary with the number of homeless and unwanted animals, is traumatic—it's major surgery and the animal may be angry about it. Any cat or dog that moves from one home to another, no matter how gently, is put under stress and is traumatized.

Pets also mirror human emotions. It may be part of their role as caretakers of people, but they suffer from it and need help. They become buffers to protect people and take on the pain:

Dogs and cats, for example, will absorb the raw emotional energy that is released during an argument and then act on it by coming to the people involved and insisting on attention—kind caring attention—something the people arguing need to do for themselves. Other times, a companion animal will respond to what it's absorbing by simply reflecting the emotion in its own behavior—withdrawing inside itself, showing hurt and distrust, getting manic, whining, jumping around. None of these reactions is in response to something that's happened to the animal directly, but rather to the emotionally imbalanced energy that's flying around the room [1]

These emotions, if frequent or long lasting, can result in mental, emotional or physical dis-ease in the dog or cat. Pets living with healers tend to take in the energy released from people during healings, and they may manifest dis-ease in themselves if they do it long enough. Though they do this voluntarily, it is best that they be protected, sent to another room or outdoors during arguments or other releases of human pain or emotion, and given comforting. An animal that lives in an unhappy house is not a happy or healthy pet.

Communicating with your cat or dog is an immense help in healing emotional traumas of whatever kind. A little petting and TLC can go a long way. Dogs or cats, however, have their own perspectives of the world, and can misunderstand or still be frightened after even a clear attempt at conscious communication after a trauma. They may not accept your explanation, or they may accept but not understand it, or still have pain despite it. They may feel you don't understand and also be unable to explain what's worrying them, what they are feeling and suffering. There may be trust issues involved, especially in a new home or if an animal has a herstory of abuse. Even the most loving of two-way conscious talk can fail to relieve the trauma, or fail to reach the source of it. Something more is needed.

That something is flower essences to heal the emotional, mental and spiritual body levels. Gem elixirs, which are made from the energies of minerals and precious or semiprecious stones, are similar. Flower essences are made from a distillation of the vibrational energies of plant blooms. Or, as Perelandra Flower Essence developer Machaelle Small Wright defines them:

Flower essences are liquid, pattern-infused solutions made from individual plant flowers, each containing a specific imprint that responds in a balancing, repairing, and rebuilding manner to imbalances in humans on their physical, emotional, mental and spiritual or universal levels.[2]

The definition works as well for dogs and cats (and other animals of all sorts) as it does for people, and the healing that takes place in using them on animals is as profound. Says Machaelle Small Wright again:

Flower essences operate in their body in exactly the same way as in our body—only with animals it's less complicated. When I work with animals, I feel as if the nervous system and the electrical system are both right on the surface just waiting for the flower essences.

We use the essences with our animals any time they are sick, injured, in need of surgery, when there's an unusual behavior change, and in preparation for death.[3]

Essences may be purchased or made at home. They are made basically by placing a plant bloom in pure water and sunlight, then storing the water in bottles with an alcohol preservative. Each type of flower has different healing properties and works for a different emotional or mental state. There are excellent books that define essences. If you wish to make essences at home, the recipe follows.[4] You will need some simple equipment: a clear bowl with no design that holds at least twelve ounces of water; pure, distilled or spring water (not tap water); brown glass storage bottles; a glass (not plastic) funnel; labels for the bottles; and brandy to use for a preservative. A pyramid is recommended.

First sterilize the glassware in hot water, in a glass, enamel or stainless steel pot for about ten minutes. Then take the bowl outside and place it near the growing flowers but not on concrete. Fill the bowl with pure water. Pick the healthiest blooms from several plants of the same type and put them on top of the water, touching them as little as possible (use sterilized tweezers). Cover the whole water surface with the flowers if you can; if not, a single bloom can make the essence. Leave the bowl and flowers in the sun for three hours, longer on a cloudy day or if starting after early morning. It is best to prepare essences as early in the day as possible, on days that are cloudless, and preferably in spring or summer.

After three hours, fill up to half of each storage bottle with good quality brandy. Remove the flowers and any debris from the water, without touching it by using tweezers or a crystal or leaf to scoop. Pour the water into the bottles using the funnel, filling them the rest of the way, and label the bottles. Make only one essence at a time or wash your hands between handling different bowls. Place the finished bottles under a copper pyramid for two more hours to finish the process, keeping different essences separate from each other. A crystal grid used with or without the pyramid can also be used.

This process results in what is called the Mother Essence, similar to the Mother Tincture in homeopathy. Once in the storage bottles, the Mother Essence may be homeopathically potentized by shaking, tapping or striking the bottle sharply against your hand fifteen to twenty times. A Stock Bottle is next made by taking two drops of the potentized Mother Essence and placing it in a one ounce dropper bottle filled twenty-five to fifty percent with brandy and the rest with pure water. Potentize it again. This is how flower essences are sold, and they can be used directly from this Stock Bottle, which I recommend.

The essences can be diluted once more into a Dosage Bottle, which may contain several different remedies together for use over a period of time. Place two drops from the Stock Bottle of each essence chosen in a one ounce bottle of pure water with a teaspoonful of brandy. The animal is dosed from this bottle, though I personally prefer to dose directly from the Stock Bottle with one less dilution. Unlike homeopathic remedies, flower essences do not grow more potent with each dilution, and the second dilution to me seems more effective. If using a Dosage Bottle, I also recommend using more than two drops of each Stock Bottle remedy—at least five to ten drops. Use only a few essences together at a time, generally three to five in a Dosage Bottle. Stock Bottle essences are individual.

Some notes on the process. The brandy is necessary as a preservative to keep bacteria from growing in and contaminating the essences. Brandy keeps the flower essence potent indefinitely, and as the essences are used by the drop there is very little alcohol actually ingested. Flower essences can be preserved with cider vinegar, but are less stable or permanent that way. Stock and Dosage Bottles are made from glass eyedropper bottles, with glass droppers, and the bottles are best tinted (usually amber, brown or blue). They can be bought at pharmacies or from flower essence sources. Make sure to label the bottles—they are not as evident as they look—and this includes Dosage Bottles which may contain several remedies for one pet (while a second bottle for another or yourself contains a different list of remedies).

When dosing, if the eyedropper touches the dog's or cat's mouth, rinse it off before returning it to the Stock or Dosage Bottle. Otherwise the essence may contaminate, and despite the brandy, grow a sour film that looks like algae. The remedy at that point needs replacing.

When making flower essences at home, make special psychic effort to connect with the Garden and Plant Devas that the flowers are coming from. Ask for insights on which blooms to put into the essence bowl, and ask the Nature Devas and spirits for help in making a potent healing remedy. Ask each plant from which a bloom is harvested for permission to take it, and refrain if you feel a negative response. After picking the flowers, thank the garden energies and the plants and blooms themselves. And when the process is completed, don't forget to return something to the energies and spirits of the garden. That something might be a watering session, or an organic gift. I once buried a grape at the foot of each plant I used a flower from; I felt it was accepted and appreciated. After the essences are potentized in the pyramid, charge them again with the energy from your hands. This is especially effective if you have Reiki training, and increases the ability of the essences.

Compared to homeopathic remedies, flower essences are very stable. They do not require waiting after meals or not drinking water for twenty minutes, as homeopathics do. They are not easily antidoted (I have never found mine

canceled by anything at all). I carry mine on airplane trips and am assured by inner guidance that the security machines do not damage them, nor have I observed a lessening of potency. Having the box of essences outdoors in the hot Florida sun has not damaged them either, though I don't recommend it. I can carry them everywhere, and do so. They may also be used along with any other healing method, including homeopathy.

To give flower essences to animals, my preferred way is to use them as I do for myself, placing one drop from the Stock Bottle directly on the animal's tongue. Once a day is enough unless the situation is acute. You can also lift the dog's or cat's lip and place the remedy either in the cheek pouch or on the gum. The Bach Flower Remedy pamphlet, "Animals and the Bach Flower Remedies," suggests using flower essences four times a day, except in crises or extreme stress. In this case they may be given as often as every half hour. Rescue Remedy in crises can be given as often as every five to eight minutes.[5] There is no risk of overdose.

Other ways to use essences include placing one to four drops from the Stock Bottle into the pet's waterbowl daily or twice a day, or putting four to seven drops on the dog's or cat's food or on a treat. For large animals, flower essence practitioner Mary Ann Simonds places ten drops of essence in an eight ounce sprayer bottle filled with water. The spray can be misted on to the animal's skin, in the air around her, or sprayed into the mouth. They can be used for aquatic animals (fish, frogs, etc.) by placing four to ten drops of flower essence directly into a twenty gallon aquarium of water.[6] Also place drops of essence directly on the animal's nose or ear; it will be absorbed from there. This is especially good for infant kittens and puppies.

Flower essences are available already prepared from a growing number of sources. The Bach Flower Remedies were the first of the essences and are best known. They can often be purchased in health food stores, and the list of thirty-eight remedies offers a guide for humans that works as well for animals. There are a number of books available on the Bach Remedies. They can be ordered from Ellon Bach USA, Inc., 644 Merrick Rd., Lynbrook, NY, 11563, (516) 593-2206 for eight to ten dollars each.

The Flower Essence Society (FES) is the second newer source, with a selection of seventy-two major essences plus twenty-four that are defined but still in the research stage (of about two hundred essences now under research at the center). They sell individual essences and essence kits, books about flower essence use (none so far on animals), and an extensive repertory book. Individual essences cost three to eight dollars, and kits run from thirty dollars and up. Ask for their catalog, and ask about the extensive repertory.

The address for the Flower Essence Society is P.O. Box 1769, Nevada City, CA 95959, 1-800-548-0075. They also carry essential oils for aromatherapy.

A further source for flower essences is Gurudas' Pegasus Products (POB 228, Boulder, CO 80306, 1-800-527-6104), which also makes gemstone elixirs. Gurudas' book *Flower Essences and Vibrational Healing* (Cassandra Press, 1983) is a pioneer in the field and contains much information for animal healing.

A newer source of flower essences, which I have worked with extensively for both animals and people, is Machaelle Small Wright's Perelandra Essences. I recommend her books and essences highly and have had amazing successes using them for myself and my dogs. Write for their fascinating catalog at Perelandra Center for Nature Research, POB 3603, Warrenton, VA 22186, or call (703)937-2153 (twenty-four hour machine). The remedies and kits come with a guidebook.

When I first got my Perelandra Basic Kit, I started testing (see below for the process) them daily on myself (more on this in a moment), and had the idea one day of testing Copper. The dog is in good health, and I was not surprised that nothing seemed to test for him, but he did test "yes" for one remedy, Comfrey. Comfrey in the Perelandra kit is defined as "Repairs higher vibrational soul damage that occurred in present or past lifetimes."[7] This made sense, since though I've had the dog for four years, he came to me abused and sick. I gave him the remedy, and he reacted with a deep afternoon sleep. He never tested as needing it again, and I can only assume that the remedy removed some last residue of his past.

Then I got Kali. For her first few days with me she tested for White Lightnin', a Rose Essence described for "Synchronized movement. Stabilizes the inner timing of all . . . levels moving in concert and enhances the body/soul fusion."[8] I have observed that this essence appears useful in times of extreme trauma and distress, and this also fit the situation. I additionally added the Bach Rescue Remedy and Bach Walnut to the dog's water at first. The Rescue Remedy tested "yes" for the first week, and Walnut for two

weeks longer. Kali tested for Comfrey as well, and tested daily for it for a month. During the period of using the essences, the dog has stabilized, calmed down, and become emotionally, mentally and physically stronger. I also use flower essences along with Machaelle Small Wright's Nature healing coning system (see the section on Communication and Psychic Healing), both for the animals and myself.

How are flower essences chosen for a cat or dog? First, by scanning the lists and seeing what looks as if it fits the animal's needs or personality. This is working mentally and is less effective than working directly with the pet's subconscious. Next test the remedies on the cat or dog directly, bypassing the conscious level (yours and the pet's) and connecting into the animals higher self. To do this, use a process called surrogate muscle testing. This may be done by pendulum, which is how I do it, or by applied kinesiology muscle testing. There are two ways to use muscle testing, the first requiring two people, plus the dog's or cat's presence, the second only one person. When using muscle testing or pendulum, you may be surprised at what the animal tests for; it may or may not fit your mental assessment but the testing always proves out.

In the basic muscle testing method, a woman emotionally close to the dog or cat touches the pet with one hand, holding her other arm out straight. A second woman puts a flower essence bottle into the extended hand, then presses down gently on the extended arm just above the wrist. As she does this, she asks to be connected to the animal's higher self as well as to her own higher self, and then asks, "Is this remedy good for Kali?" or "Does Kali need this remedy?" and asks the other woman to "hold." The woman tries to keep her arm steady against the pressure behind her wrist. If the essence is not needed by the animal, the arm goes down, as a "no" answer. If the essence is needed, the woman's arm remains firm, as a "yes." There are only yes and no answers in muscle testing.

For best results, the woman who is the surrogate (touching the pet) goes through the essence testing process for herself first, taking a drop of each flower essence she tests "yes" for before testing the dog or cat. Otherwise, her own essence requirements may interfere with what is testing yes or no for the animal. Next she asks to be connected to the animal's higher self, and verifies by testing whether or not that connections has been

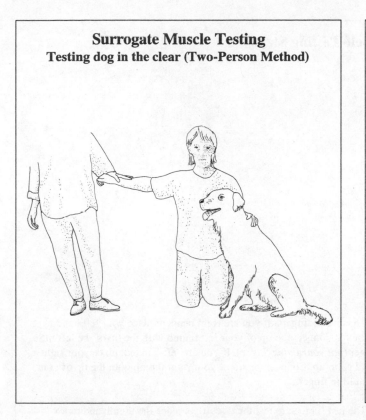

Surrogate Muscle Testing
Testing dog in the clear (Two-Person Method)

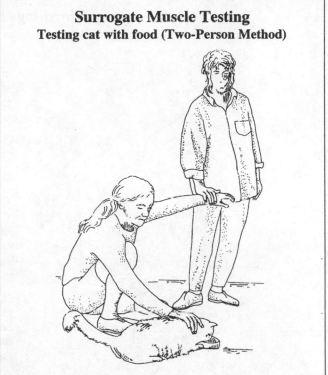

Surrogate Muscle Testing
Testing cat with food (Two-Person Method)

made. This process can be used for any number of things, asking if a pet (or person) needs a particular vitamin or herb, asking if a particular item in the food is an allergen (hold a piece of the food in your hand or in the animal's mouth while testing), asking if a particular kind of pet food is positive or negative for the cat or dog. Questions must be phrased clearly and very simply, with no possible ambiguity, and must require a yes or no answer.

The major disadvantage of this is that it requires two people. The second way, using muscle testing to bypass the conscious mind and access deeper levels, requires only one person who has the use of both hands. The method is from Machaelle Small Wright. To use it, again have the animal beside you and focus upon her while doing the test.

Practice this method until you are comfortable and confident, then use it to test for flower essences for yourself or your cat or dog. When testing for an animal, always test for yourself first and take whatever remedies you test "yes" for at that time. Then ask to be connected with the animals higher self, and verify by testing. Since animals so often mirror their people, do not be too surprised if you test for some of the same essences as

your pet does. When testing for the dog or cat, keep your mind focused on the animal and allow no distractions. Test initially to see if you are in link with the pet and do not proceed until the answer is "yes."

Next place the flower essence bottles one at a time in your lap and test yes or no for each. I like to test daily and administer the essences required each day. If the animal tests "yes" to an essence, administer one drop of it onto her tongue, then go on to test further. Remain focused on the process the entire time; if you are distracted, you may get a wrong answer. An unnessary essence will do no harm, but you may also miss a needed one. Pay attention. I like to keep a daily record of results and watch the changes over time.

I also use my pendulum for this and for a lot of other things. It works accurately. For information on using pendulums and the two-person method of surrogate testing and kinesiology, see Diane Stein, *All Women Are Healers.* For more information on the one-person finger method, see Machaelle Small Wright's *Flower Essences* (Perelandra Ltd., 1988). I especially like the Perelandra essences for use with animals and myself because they are a fully unified set with a relatively low number of

Kinesiology Self-Testing Steps

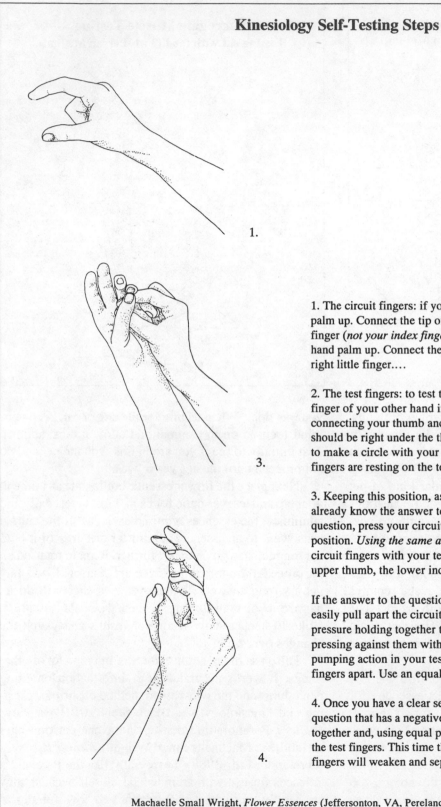

1.

2.

3.

4.

1. The circuit fingers: if you are right handed: place your left hand palm up. Connect the tip of your left thumb with the tip of the left little finger (*not your index finger*). If you are left-handed: place your right hand palm up. Connect the tip of your right thumb with the tip of your right little finger....

2. The test fingers: to test the circuit . . . place the thumb and index finger of your other hand inside the circle you have created by connecting your thumb and little finger. The thumb/index finger should be right under the thumb/little finger, touching them. Don't try to make a circle with your test fingers . . . .It will look as if the circuit fingers are resting on the test fingers.

3. Keeping this position, ask yourself a yes/no question in which you already know the answer to be yes . . . .Once youve asked the question, press your circuit fingers together, keeping the tip-to-tip position. *Using the same amount of pressure*, try to pull apart the circuit fingers with your test fingers. Press the lower thumb against the upper thumb, the lower index finger against the upper little finger....

If the answer to the question is positive . . ., you will not be able to easily pull apart the circuit fingers....Important: Be sure the amount of pressure holding together the circuit fingers is equal to the amount pressing against them with your testing fingers. Also, don't use a pumping action in your testing fingers when trying to pry your circuit fingers apart. Use an equal, steady and continuous pressure....

4. Once you have a clear sense of the positive response, ask yourself a question that has a negative answer. Again press your circuit fingers together and, using equal pressure, press against the circuit fingers with the test fingers. This time the electrical circuit will break and the circuit fingers will weaken and separate....

Machaelle Small Wright, *Flower Essences* (Jeffersonton, VA, Perelandra Ltd, 1988), p. 58-61.

bottles to test for. They can also be used with other essence systems, if you wish. Whatever essences you choose, test each bottle individually to see what your animal needs.

Though muscle testing or pendulum are the clearest way to pick which flower essences your dog or cat needs, there are dozens of essences available. If you are not using a unified set like Perelandra or Bach, it helps to have some direction. *The Flower Essence Repertory* (Flower Essence Society, 1992) is a good place to begin, as is the Ellon Bach repertory pamphlet "Animals and the Bach Remedies" (Ellon Bach, 1990). The Bach pamphlet lists Bach Flower Remedies for a number of dog and cat needs. As these are the most familiar flower essences, a part of this repertory is given below, from the Bach pamphlet:[9]

For Dogs: Aspen is for the submissive, nervous dog that is fearful especially in unfamiliar circumstances. The animal has sometimes been trained too harshly. Sometimes she is a nervous wetter. Use *Chestnut Bud* to correct harsh early training and for effective behavior modification. *Chicory* is for the extremely affectionate dog that always wants attention. She is constantly underfoot, in your lap, easily jealous, and upset when left alone. *Clematis* helps new puppies start breathing and helps in waking up after anesthesia. This is for the dog that does nothing but sleep and seems to be barely here.

Use *Holly* for jealousy, or aggressiveness due to past abuse; this is for the dog that threatens and may attack. This flower essence is best used along with Star of Bethlehem. *Honeysuckle* is for the grieving dog whose person is permanently gone and for the animal that is homesick in a boarding kennel. Star of Bethlehem should be used with Honeysuckle if the animal's person has died. *Mimulus* is for the dog that fears known things, like thunderstorms or trips to the vet. If there is terror, use Rock Rose or Rescue Remedy. Use Olive (with Star of Bethlehem) for an exhausted, ill or traumatized pet.

Scleranthus helps with car sickness, use it with Rescue Remedy. *Star of Bethlehem* is for abused animals, and dogs who are traumatized physically or emotionally. Always use it for dogs who have come from animal shelters. *Vervain* is for high strung, nervous, over exuberant dogs to help them slow down. *Water Violet* helps the dog who is an aloof loner. This is an animal socialized late, or one that is wild or partly wild (part-wolf, part-coyote, etc.).

For cats: here is a sample list of frequently used Bach Flowers,

again from "Animals and the Bach Remedies." *Aspen* is for the shy, scared cat that startles easily; if the animal has a herstory of abuse, use it with Star of Bethlehem. *Beech* is an essence for the cat who will not tolerate a second cat or some particular person; use it with Walnut when two cats in a household fight. *Chicory* is for the affectionate cat that can be too possessive and tends to jealousy. *Clematis* is for beyond-typical sleep, for help in the animal's regaining consciousness, and to help newborn kittens start breathing.

Honeysuckle is for the cat that is grieving for a lost person or an animal friend. Use it with Star of Bethlehem for these things or with Walnut when moving to a new house. *Hornbeam* is for fatigue, to strengthen a sick animal. *Larch* builds a cat's self-esteem. *Mimulus* is for fear of particular circumstances or things; when fear becomes terror, use Rock Rose or Rescue Remedy. *Star of Bethlehem* is for all trauma, especially good for cats that have come from shelters. *Vine* is to mellow the cat that bosses the household. Use *Walnut* for changes and transitions—moving, a new pet, new baby, etc. *Water Violet* is a cat constitutional remedy, for keeping cat interactions with people in good balance.

Rescue Remedy is the best known of Bach flower essences; it is used for any situation of stress, injury or trauma, for dogs, cats or people. When your pets needs Rescue Remedy, you probably do, too. It comes in both a first aid cream and the alcohol-preserved liquid, and contains a combination of five flowers.

The *Flower Essence Repertory* gives an additional list of essences for animals and pet care. The following suggestions are for both dogs and cats and the remedies are available from the Flower Essence Society:[10]

Arnica as an essence is used for shock, trauma, illness or surgery much in the same way that the Bach Rescue Remedy is. *Borage* helps a depressed animal that may be ill or elderly, and *Chamomile* for barking dogs, or for emotional upsets that cause digestive symptoms in dogs or cats. To aid two-way conscious communication try *Cosmos*. This flower essence is also for establishing a psychic bond with a pet, for training, and where a number of strange animals are gathered together (dog shows, boarding kennels, etc.). Both humans and pets can take this essence.

Mariposa Lily is for young animals entering a new home. It also aids the mother-infant bond and helps when a kitten or puppy must accept a surrogate mother. *Penstemon* is for illness or trauma, giving strength in adverse circumstances, and *Pink Yarrow* helps pets that mirror people's emotions or take on human pain. *Red Clover* is an important cat remedy; it calms anxiety and helps in frightening circumstances. *Self-Heal* awakens vitality and the will to live, and aids healing on any level. It can be added to any flower essence combination. *Snapdragon* is for animals that bite, chew up furniture, lick sores on their own bodies, bark chronically, or for any other negative mouth-centered symptoms. Use *Tiger Lily* for aggression or hostility in cats or dogs, while *Wild Rose* helps listless, apathetic animals.

Gurudas, in his comprehensive book *Flower Essences and Vibrational Healing* (Cassandra Press, 1983) lists animal healing uses for flower essences in his directory of a hundred and twelve flowers. The material on pets is more complete than any other published source, but often the remedies duplicate or have uses that are too specific to be considered universal. For example, a remedy for shock and injury such as *Arnica* or *Rescue Remedy* has universality—it is helpful to many animals and people at any given time. But a remedy like *Blue Flag,* for use by pets whose creative people take the same essence for frustration, becomes too esoteric to be truly important to many. Unlike most of the flower essence systems, however, a number of entries are for specific physical ailments in dogs and cats.

The book's flower entries are divided into two sections, the first, Flower Essences Effecting Primarily the Physical Body, and the second, Flower Essences Affecting Primarily Ethereal and Psychological States. Here is a selection of essences for pet use from Gurudas' *Flower Essences and Vibrational Healing;* they can be ordered from Pegasus Products or the Flower Essence Society.[11]

Essences For Physical States: *Almond* is for the mother-infant animal relationship, from birth to six months and through adolescence. Use *Aloe Vera* for behavior problems due to stress. *Avocado* helps animal growth spurts, and assimilation of diet and supplements. Use *Banana* to help release food addictions and combat the toxins and chemicals in commercial pet foods. *Bells of Ireland* aids in rejuvenating elder animals, and *Blackberry* flower essence releases environmental factors that cause depression and enhances learning new skills. *Bottlebrush* aids cooperation between animals, and helps group animals that have been separated. *Camphor* is a detoxifier, and *Cedar* detoxifies environmental contaminants and aids hair loss—use them together with Camphor first and Cedar following.

Energy problems, old age, arthritis or bursitis respond to *Centaury Agave. Coffee* flower enhances quickness of thought and decision making in animals, and *Cotton* is for mange and fur problems, especially in dogs that swim a lot. *Dandelion* deepens a cat's or dog's earth attunement and is for difficult sleep states. When pets absorb human worries, they are helped by *Date Palm,* and *Fig* enhances breeding, conception and fertility in female animals. *Forget-Me-Not* is a first aid remedy for accidents and for learning that "there are no accidents," and *Four Leaf Clover* enhances learning and mental acuity in pets.

Khat essence strengthens the nervous system and thought processes, aids learning new things, and helps when reuniting a parent animal with grown offspring. *Lilac* is for strengthening the many dogs and cats who are healers. Use *Loquat* to help change a pet to a better diet, and *Luffa* for skin allergies. Nervous tics and twitches in animals respond to *Mugwort,* and *Pansy* helps feline AIDS and feline leukemia. For older dogs, cats with feline urologic syndrome, or dogs or cats with arthritis, blood problems, or kidney/bladder dis-ease, the flower essence is *Redwood. Saguaro* builds stamina and strength in all animals.

Spruce helps animals that want to be alone; it increases and strengthens the pets' ability to self-heal. *Squash* aids the female uterine system, balances animals' sexual behavior toward humans, and helps puppies and kittens up to three months of age. *Star Tulip* is for hypersensitivity in dogs or cats, and allergies with hair loss. *Sugar Beet* aids in breaking food addictions, especially to sugar, and helps animal diabetes. *Watermelon* is for pregnancy; use it until a week after giving birth for cats or dogs. Emotional problems caused by grief or moving, where the pet shows digestive disturbances, respond to *Wisteria.*

Essences for Ethereal and Psychological States: For an animal that shows extreme behavior changes, or extreme difficulty in adapting to a new environment or new people, try *Angelica* flower essence. For previously abused pets, *Bleeding Heart* enhances the ability to accept love and kindness and aids emotional recovery; *Bloodroot* is for heart healing. *Chaparral* aids cats or dogs experiencing difficult sleep states. These are pets that lead humans on astral journeys during sleep. When an animal presents behavior problems and resistance to learning, the remedy is *Daffodil,* and *Daisy* is for mother-baby early learning. Use *Dill* for arthritis, bone spurs, kidney stones or stiffness.

Garlic as a flower essence helps to repel fleas and ticks; it takes about three weeks of daily use to begin working. *Harvest Brodiaea* aids cats or dogs in adjusting to a new environment or to new behavior in their people. *Helleborus* is for animals with degenerative dis-eases, cancer, old age, arthritis, or bladder and kidney dis-eases. Use *Henna* for general strengthening, and *Hyssop* for understanding new patterns and self-forgiveness for mistakes. *Lavender* enhances the spiritual bond between human and animal, both take the essence, and *Lemon* increases a pet's ability to understand mental pictures. *Lotus* deepens the dog's or cat's connection to the earth and their person, and it creates bliss in the relationship.

McCartney Rose is for AIDS and Epstein-Barr syndrome in pets. Animals that are distressed by being neutered or spayed respond to *Mallow,* and the essence eases fears in old age. Use *Mango* for energy and meridian balancing after animal injuries, or *Maple* or *Morning Glory* to enhance energy balancing and psychic healing methods (like Reiki, acupuncture/acupressure, homeopathy, etc.). *Nectarine* helps when rebalancing aggressive behavior with dietary changes. When bringing a new pet into a home with an older one, *Papaya* helps both animals to adjust. It is especially effective when the first pet is highly bonded to the person. *Passion Flower* releases an animal's sense of guilt and allows acceptance and love.

Peach helps pets when human emotional problems transfer to them; it aids longevity and creates a sense of playfulness in the cat or dog. *Pennyroyal* essence is a cleanser and strengthener that repairs holes or tears in the aura. It's important for animals that are exposed to human negative thought forms. Use *Petunia* in animal training to break bad habits and establish beneficial behavior patterns, and *Pimpernel* is for nervous disorders, nervous tics, and behavior aberrations. For pregnancy and nurturing of the mother dog or cat use *Pomegranate. Prickly Pear* is for cats or dogs that have to be left alone too much; it also aids stress between animal mates, and enhances greater patience between pets that share a household.

Queen Anne's Lace and *Rose Webbiana* are for animals that are disturbed by human psychic development, channeling or psychic phenomena. *Rosemary* balances the animal's emotional body, eases difficult behavior, and increases the pet's receptiveness to human thought forms. Use *Sage* for circulatory cleansing, heart dis-ease and high blood pressure, *St. John's Wort* after injuries to release fear and pain, and *Scullcap* for nervous system dis-eases. *Stinging Nettles* is for cleansing and arthritis, as well as recovery from blood loss. *Sunflower* aids an animal with sunburn or heat stroke, and also attunes the pet to the healing qualities of the sun.

Sweet Flag prepares a cat or dog for stress, as before moving or travel, and *Wood Betony* is used before spaying or neutering , as a preparation and for faster recovery. *Tuberose* enhances acupuncture, massage or any form of hands-on healing when used with dogs or cats. Many of these plants used as flower essences are familiar from herbal healing or homeopathy. Each of the methods uses the energy qualities of plants to heal animals and people on physical, emotional, mental and spiritual levels. Of them, only flower essences reach all of the levels and bodies.

The Perelandra Essences have a slightly different emphasis, aiming for and achieving universality, where Gurudas' essences are specific. The Rose Essences I are similar to Gurudas' Ethereal and Psychological category, and the Garden Essences, many made from the flowers of garden vegetables, are equivalent to his Physical Body category. The categories are not clearly divided, however, and while the Rose Essences work primarily but not exclusively on the unseen bodies, the Garden Essences affect physical, emotional, mental and spiritual levels. For pets, the remedies definitely apply, though it may take muscle or pendulum testing to choose them—they will not so easily stand out on scanning the definitions.

Flower essences are also extremely helpful as supports to healing physical level dis-eases. Refer to Perelandra Rose Essences charts on pages 158-160. They can be as powerful for cures as any antibiotic, and in dis-eases where emotional-mental factors are prime causes, they can be the catalysts for true healing. I have attempted below to use the Bach, Perelandra and Gurudas/FES flower essences for the list of physical dis-eases discussed throughout this book. The essences are representative rather than definitive, as individual animal's responses to a particular dis-ease may differ. One cat with

Bach Flower Remedies
(Adapt for Pet Use)

Agrimony For those not wishing to burden others with their troubles and who cover up their suffering behind a cheerful facade. They are distressed by argument or quarrel, and may seek escape from pain and worry through the use of drugs and alcohol.

Aspen For those who experience vague fears and anxieties of unknown origin, they are often apprehensive.

Beech For those who while desiring perfection easily find fault with people and things. Critical and at times intolerant, they may overreact to small annoyances or idiosyncracies of others.

Centaury For those who are over-anxious to please, often weak willed and easily exploited or dominated by others. As a result they may neglect their own particular interest.

Cerato For those who lack confidence in their own judgment and decisions. They constantly seek the advice of others and may often be misguided.

Cherry Plum For fear of losing mental and physical control, of doing something desperate. May have impulses to do things thought or known to be wrong.

Chestnut Bud For those who fail to learn from experience, repeating the same patterns of mistakes again and again.

Chicory For those who are overfull of care for others and need to direct and control those close to them. Always finding something to correct or put right.

Clematis For those who tend to live in the future, lack concentration, are daydreamers, drowsy or spacey and have a half-hearted interest in their present circumstances.

Crab Apple For those who may feel something is not quite clean about themselves, or have a fear of being contaminated. For feelings of shame or poor self image. For example, thinking oneself not attractive for one reason or another. When necessary, may be taken to assist in detoxification, for example, during a cold or while fasting.

Elm For those who at times may experience momentary feelings of inadequacy, being overwhelmed by their responsibilities.

Gentian For those who become easily discouraged by small delays or hindrances. This may cause self-doubt.

Gorse For feelings of hopelessness and futility. When there is little hope of relief.

Heather For those who seek the companionship of anyone who will listen to their troubles. They are generally not good listeners and have difficulty being alone for any length of time.

Holly To be used when troubled by negative feelings such as envy, jealousy, suspicion, revenge. Vexations of the heart, states indicating a need for more love.

Honeysuckle For those dwelling in the past, nostalgia, homesickness, always talking about the good old days, when things were better.

Hornbeam For the Monday morning feeling of not being able to face the day. For those feeling some part of the body or mind needs strengthening. Constant fatigue, tiredness.

Impatiens For those quick in thought and action, who require all things to be done without delay. They are impatient with people who are slow and often prefer to work alone.

Larch For those who, despite being capable, lack self confidence or feel inferior. Anticipating failure, they often refuse to make a real effort to succeed.

Bach Flower Remedies

Mimulus For fear of known things, such as heights, water, the dark, other people, of being alone, etc.

Mustard For deep gloom which comes on for no known reason, sudden melancholia or heavy sadness. Will lift just as suddenly.

Oak For those who struggle on despite despondency from hardships, even when ill and overworked, they never give up.

Olive For mental and physical exhaustion, sapped vitality with no reserve. This may come on after an illness or personal ordeal.

Pine For those who feel they should do or should have done better, who are self-reproachful or blame themselves for the mistakes of others. Hardworking people who suffer much from the faults they attach to themselves, they are never satisfied with their success.

Red Chestnut For those who find it difficult not to be overly concerned or anxious for others, always fearing something wrong may happen to those they care for.

Rock Rose For those who experience states of terror, panic and hysteria; also when troubled by nightmares.

Rock Water For those who are very strict with themselves in their daily living. They are hard masters to themselves struggling toward some ideal or to set an example for others. This would include strict adherence to a living style or to religious, personal or social disciplines.

Scleranthus For those unable to decide between two things, first one seeming right then the other. Often presenting extreme variations in energy or mood swings.

Star of Bethlehem For grief, trauma, loss. For the mental and emotional effect during and after a trauma.

Sweet Chestnut For those who feel they have reached the limits of their endurance. For those moments of deep despair when the anguish seems to be unbearable.

Vervain For those who have strong opinions and who usually need to have the last word, always teaching or philosophizing. When taken to an extreme they can be argumentative and overbearing.

Vine For those who are strong willed. Leaders in their own right who are unquestionably in charge. However, when taken to an extreme they may become dictatorial.

Walnut Assists in stabilizing emotional upsets during transition periods, such as puberty, adolescence, menopause. Also helps to break past links and emotionally adjust to new beginnings such as moving, changing or taking a new job, beginning or ending a relationship.

Water Violet For those who are gentle, independent, aloof and self-reliant, who do not interfere in the affairs of others, and when ill or in trouble prefer to bear their difficulties alone.

White Chestnut For constant and persistent unwanted thoughts, such as mental arguments, worries or repetitious thoughts that prevent peace of mind, and disrupt concentration.

Wild Oat For the dissatisfaction with not having succeeded in one's career or life goal. When there is unfulfilled ambition, career uncertainty or boredom with one's present position or station in life.

Wild Rose For those, who for no apparent reason, have resigned themselves to their circumstances. Having become indifferent, little effort is made to improve things or find joy.

Willow For those who have suffered some circumstance or misfortune, which they feel was unfair or unjust. As a result they become resentful and bitter toward life or toward those who they feel were at fault.

Bach Centre USA, "The Bach Flower Remedies" (Woodmere, NY, Centre USA, 1983), p. 8-9.

Flower Essence Descriptions

Allspice—Promotes Memory	*Crab Apple*—Mental Cleansing
Almond—Maturation/Rejuvenation	*Cyclamen*—Channeling
Aloe Vera—Personal Survival	*Dog Rose*—Enthusiasm
Amaranthus—Immune System	*Elm*—Strength/Confidence
Amaryllis—Crown Chakra	*Eucalyptus*—Breath/Grief
Angelica—Urban Stress	*Eyebright*—Psychic Perception
Angel's Trumpet—Stimulates Visions	*Fig*—Mental Clarity
Apricot—Gaiety & Lightness	*Fireweed*—Transmuting Karma
Banana—Male Sexuality	*Fuchsia*—Childhood Issues
Beech—Greater Acceptance	*Garlic*—Eases Anxiety
Birch—Female–Interpersonal Relationships	*Ginseng*—Mental Clarity
Birch—Male–Interpersonal Relationships	*Goldenrod*—Spiritual Inspiration
Black-Eyed Susan—Improves Self-Esteem	*Goldenseal*—Emotional Scars
Bleeding Heart—Peace & Harmony	*Green Rose*—Psychic Balance
California Bay Laurel—Flexibility/Wisdom	*Heather*—Self-Confidence
California Poppy—Psychic/Spiritual Balance	*Hibiscus*—Female Sexuality
Carob—Empathy/Group Interaction	*Jimson Weed*—Stimulates Dreams
Cedar—Cleansing/Stress	*Jojoba*—Massage Therapy
Celandine—Communication	*Kidney Bean*—Hidden Fears
Cerato—Self-Reliance	*Koenign Van Daenmark*—Left/Right Brain
Chervil—Spiritual Identity	*Lemon*—Mental Activity
Cinnamon—Emotional Expression	*Lima Bean*—Grounding
Clematis—Enthusiasm/Stability	*Live Forever*—Higher Guidance
Coffee—Decisiveness	*Lotus*—Emotional/Spiritual Harmony
Comfrey—Telepathy	*Luffa*—Cleansing
Corn-Sweet—Urban Dwellers	*Macadamia*—Friendship/Bonding

feline distemper may be severely depressed, for example, while another may be panicky instead. As with homeopathy, tailor the flower essences specifically to the individual animal's needs. Use muscle testing or pendulum kinesiology to find precisely which essence(s) to use. The Bach Flower suggestions below come from Anitra Frazier's *The New Natural Cat*, under her information for each dis-ease. Gurudas and Machaelle Small Wright are the other sources.[13]

Allergies: Try Bach *Rescue Remedy* during an allergic reaction, then *Crabapple* as a detoxifier. Gurudas suggests *Banana* for releasing food addictions and to counteract the chemicals and toxins in pet foods, and *Camphor* for gentle cleansing. *Star Tulip* is for hypersensitivity in animals and for hair loss, and *Pear* is for hypersensitivity, also *Luffa* is for skin allergies. Of the Perelandra Essences, *Sweet Bell Pepper* stabilizes during times of stress, and *Tomato* helps in cleansing and

throwing off toxins.

Arthritis and Hip Dysplasia: Anitra Frazier suggests the following three Bach remedies for arthritis; *Crabapple* to detoxify, *Hornbeam* and *Larch* to increase strength and self-worth. Gurudas' essences include: *Centaury Agave, Helleborus* and/or *Redwood* for arthritis and old age, *Dill* (also Perelandra) for arthritis and stiffness, and *Stinging Nettles* for cleansing the blood and for aching limbs. Perelandra essences include *Comfrey* (suggested by Gurudas as an inner healer), *Cucumber* to lift depression and aid attachment to life, and *Tomato* for cleansing, shattering and throwing off toxins.

Cancer and Tumors: Bach's *Mimulus* is to reduce fears, *Olive* strengthens energy, and *Gorse* for depression and despair. *Crabapple* for cleansing is also suggested. Gurudas lists *Apricot* as a general strengthener, and also for animals whose people have

Flower Essence Descriptions

Mango—Energizer
Maple—Yin/Yang
Milkmaids—Self-Esteem
Nectarine—Psycho-Spiritual Balance
Nutmeg—Past Life Therapy
Oak—Perseverance
Onion—Emotional Cleansing
Orange—Psychological Counseling
Orchid—Dream Clarification
Papaya—Higher Self-Assimilation
Passion Flower—Christ Consciousness
Pennyroyal—Psychic Protection
Peony—Honest Communication
Periwinkle—Higher Spiritual Concepts
Pineapple—Chakra Amplification
Plum Tree—Inspiration/New Ideas
Pomegranate—Nurturing
Potato—Dimensional Exploration
Purple Nightshade—Soothing Calm
Quinoa—Kundalini Opening & Grounding
Raspberry—Self-Expression
Rosa Banksla—Divine Intellect
Rosa Beggeriana—Increases Intuition
Rosa Chinensis Mutabilis—Creative Forces

Rosa Gallica Officinalis—Spiritual Rejuvenation
Rosa Macrophylla—Greater Love
Rosa Sinowlisonii—Clairaudience
Rosa Webbiana—Earth & Angelic Attunement
Rosemary—Inner Peace
Sandalwood—Aroma Therapy
Self Heal—Fasting Assistance
Sensitive Plant—Shyness
Shooting Star—Astrological Awareness
Silversword—Spiritual Awakening
Skullcap—Massage/Psychic Healing
Solomon's Seal—Psychic Grace
Squash-Zucchini—Youthfulness
Strawberry—Stimulates Visions
Tree of Life—Upliftment
Tree Tobacco—Smoke-Free
Vanilla—Balanced Weight Loss
Watermelon—Emotions of Pregnancy
Wintergreen—Past Life Therapy
Witch Hazel—Spiritual Healing
Yarrow-White—Psychic Healing
Ylang Ylang—Earth Attunement
Yucca—Transforms Anger
Zinnia—Laughter

Pegasus Products Inc., P.O.B. 226, Boulder, Co., 80306, 1-800-527-6104.

cancer; the essence releases negative miasms. *Koenig Van Daenmark* is also for animals contracting dis-eases usually associated with humans, and helping animals whose people may have such dis-eases. Pets can emotionally absorb and mirror human pain and manifest it in themselves physically. *Helleborus* is for cancer, old age and degenerative dis-eases in humans or pets. In the Perelandra Essences, *Celery* restores immune balance, *Cucumber* lifts depression and restores the will to live, and *Tomato* is for cleansing and throwing off dis-ease. Test also for the Rose Essences here, especially *Peace, Eclipse* and *Orange Ruffles*.

Cataracts: Use Bach's *Crabapple* for cleansing. Gurudas' *Banana* counteracts chemicals and toxins in pet food that may be a cause of this dis-ease. *Camphor* and *Hawthorn* are also for cleansing, and try *Sugar Beet* when cataracts come with diabetes. Perelandra Essences include *Okra* for seeing the positive in life, and *Tomato* for cleansing and shattering.

Constipation and Diarrhea: Anitra Frazier suggests Bach *Crabapple* for cleansing, *Vine* to relax, and *Aspen* to calm fears. Of Gurudas' essences, *Camphor* is for gentle cleansing, and *Cedar* detoxifies environmental contaminants and poisons. Use *Chamomile* for emotionally caused digestive upsets. *Loquat* or *Pawpaw* help during dietary changes, and *Clover* aids anxiety. Perelandra Essences suggest *Celery* to restore the immune system if the cause is bacterial or viral, *Tomato* for cleansing, and *Sweet Bell Pepper* for calm during stress.

Diabetes: Bach Flowers to reduce stress include *Mimulus* for fear and *Hornbeam* for strengthening and self-confidence. Gurudas uses *Sugar Beet* for sugar dis-eases and addictions, and *Sage* for circulatory system and blood cleansing. Perelandra suggestions include *Cucumber* for depressions, *Salvia* to restore emotional stability during stress, and *Tomato* for throwing off dis-ease and cleansing. Test for all the essences, including the

Perelandra Garden Essences

Broccoli: For the power balance which must be maintained when one perceives himself to be under siege from outside. Stabilizes the body/soul unit so the person won't close down, detach, and scatter.

Cauliflower: Stabilizes and balances the child during the birth process. Stabilizes body/soul balance in adult.

Celery: Restores balance of the immune system during times when it is being overworked or stressed, and during long-term viral or bacterial infections.

Chives: Re-establishes the power one has when the internal male/female dynamics are balanced and the person is functioning within a state of awareness within this balance.

Comfrey: Repairs higher vibrational soul damage that occurred in present or past lifetime.

Corn: Stabilization during universal/spiritual expansion. Assists translation of experience into useful, pertinent understanding and action.

Cucumber: Rebalancing during depression. Vital reattachment to life.

Dill: Assists individual in reclaiming power balance one has released to others. Victimization.

Nasturtium: Restores vital physical life energy during times of intense mental-level focus.

Okra: Returns ability to see the positive in one's life and environment.

Salvia: Restores emotional stability during times of extreme stress.

Snap Pea: Rebalances child or adult after a nightmare. Assists in ability to translate daily experience into positive, understandable process.

Summer Squash: Restores courage to the person who experiences fear and resistance when faced with daily routine. Shyness. Phobia.

Sweet Bell Pepper: Inner peace, clarity and calm, when faced with today's stressful times. Stabilizes body/soul balance during times of stress.

Tomato: Cleansing. Assists the body in shattering/throwing off that which is causing infection or disease.

Yellow Yarrow: Emotional protection during vulnerable times. Softens resistance and assists the integration process.

Zinnia: Reconnects one to the child within. Restores playfulness, laughter, joy, and a sense of healthy priorities.

Zucchini: Helps restore physical strength during convalescence.

Perlandra Center for Nature Research, P.O.B. 3603, Warrenton, VA, 22186, 1-703-937-2153.

Rose Essences. Has the pet experienced a shock or grief? If so, focus on releasing that emotion.

Feline Leukemia: Anitra Frazier uses Bach *Mimulus* for fears of illness, *Aspen* for fear of the unknown, *Crabapple* for cleansing, and *Hornbeam* as a strengthener. Gurudas' *Pansy* and *McCartney Rose* are for feline leukemia and feline AIDS specifically. Try Perelandra *Celery* for immune system balance, *Cucumber* for depression, and *Tomato* for throwing off dis-ease. Test for Rose Essences I and II.

Heart Dis-Ease and Hypertension: Use Bach's *Oak* for patience during illness, *Impatiens* for the "type A" nervous cat or dog, and *Hornbeam* for strengthening and fatigue. Gurudas suggests *Hawthorn* for vitality, blood cleansing and chronic conditions, *Bloodroot* for heart healing, and *Sage* for the heart, blood and circulatory cleansing. *Bleeding Heart* is for emotional heart healing and the ability to accept love. Of Perelandra Essences, test for *Cucumber* (depression, vitality), *Salvia* (stability under stress), and *Sweet Bell Pepper* for inner peace. Also test for the Rose Essences.

Injuries, Cuts and Burns: Rescue Remedy is the Bach classic, with *Rose Rose* for extreme fear and/or *Star of Bethlehem* for trauma or injury. Gurudas essences include: *Arnica* for trauma and bruising, *Forget-Me-Not* for accidents and first aid, *Comfrey* (also Perelandra) for first aid and nerve regeneration, *Grapefruit* for spinal injuries from falls, *Mango* for energy balancing after injuries, and *St. John's Wort* to release pain and fear. Perelandra's *Salvia* restores emotional stability during times of stress, also *White Lightnin'* of the Rose Essences.

Skin And Coat Ailments: Bach's *Crabapple* is for cleansing and *Larch* aids self-confidence. Gurudas suggests *Camphor* and *Cedar* together for cleansing and hair loss, *Cotton* for mange and fur problems, or *Luffa* for skin allergies and karmic skin problems. *Star Tulip* helps hypersensitivity and hair loss. Perelandra suggestions include *Tomato* for cleansing, shattering and throwing off dis-ease; test for other essences.

Spinal Problems: Use the Bach *Rescue Remedy*, *Rock Rose* for extreme fear and *Star of Bethlehem* for serious injury. Gurudas' *Grapefruit* is for injuries to head, neck, spine or pelvis caused by falls; *Comfrey* is a nerve regenerator and first aid essence, and *St. John's Wort* is for releasing fear and pain. *Scullcap* helps nervous system dis-orders.

Perelandra Rose Essences

Gruss an Aachen: Stability. Balances and stabilizes the body/soul unit on all PEMS levels (physical, emotional, mental, spiritual) as it moves forward in its evolutionary process.

Peace: Courage. Opens the individual to the inner dynamic of courage that is aligned to universal courage.

Eclipse: Acceptance and insight. Enhances the individual's appreciation of his own inner knowing. Supports the mechanism which allows the body to receive the soul's input and insight.

Orange Ruffles: Receptivity. Stabilizes the individual during the expansion of his sensory system.

Ambassador: Pattern. Aids in seeing the relationship of the part to the whole, in perceiving pattern and purpose.

Nymphenburg: Strength. Supports and holds the strength created by the balance of the body/soul fusion, and facilitates the individual's ability to regain that balance.

White Lightnin': Synchronized movement. Stabilizes the inner timing of all PEMS levels moving in concert, and enhances the body/soul fusion.

Royal Highness: Final stabilization. The mop-up essence which helps to insulate, protect and stabilize the individual and to stabilize the shift during its final stages while vulnerable.

Note: PEMS= Physical, Emotional, Mental and Spiritual

Perlandra Center for Nature Research, P.O.B. 3603, Warrenton, VA, 22186, 1-703-937-2153.

Urinary Tract Infections, Kidney and Bladder Dis-ease: Bach Flower Remedy suggestions include: *Mimulus* for fears, *Star of Bethlehem* for shock, *Hornbeam* for fatigue and courage, *Gorse* to aid hopelessness, and *Rescue Remedy* for trauma. Gurudas essences include *Redwood* and *Helleborus,* specifically for kidney, bladder and urinary dis-eases. In the Perelandra Essences, test for *Celery* for immune boosting, *Cucumber* for depression, *Salvia* for stability under stress, and *Tomato* for throwing off/shattering the dis-ease. Also test for the Rose Essences, especially *Peace* for courage and *Gruss an Aachen* to stabilize the bodies.

Viral Dis-eases: Anitra Frazier suggests *Mustard* to dispel gloom, *Hornbeam* for strength and *Crabapple* for cleansing; use *Rescue Remedy* during crises. Gurudas' essences include *Apricot, Saguaro* or *Self-Heal* as a general strengthener, *Camphor* for cleansing, *Nasturtium* (also Perelandra) to strengthen the nervous system and *Sage* for blood cleansing. Of Perelandra Essences, test for *Celery* for immune system balance, *Tomato* for throwing off dis-ease, *Salvia* for stability during stress, *Cucumber* for depression and *Zucchini* for convalescence. Test for the Rose Essences, and Rose Essences II.

It is difficult or impossible to choose flower essences accurately without testing them for the specific animal and dis-ease, so use the above as a beginning guideline only. Test whatever essence selection is available to you, scanning them for emotional states, mental states and the physical dis-ease itself. Using the right flower essence(s) for the animal's needs can make a significant difference in her healing. They are as potent for dogs and cats as they are for people, and they are very potent for people. If using a system of essences like Perelandra, test for all of the remedies, not only what seems evident. Your animal may need something you wouldn't have expected, and that unusual essence can be the key to her healing. Often humans and pets will test for the same flower essences; you take them, too.

The next chapter discusses the difficult topic of death and reincarnation and its role in healing animals and people.

Perelandra Rose Essences II

1. *Blaze Improved*: Softens and relaxes first the central nervous system and then the body as a whole, thus allowing the input from an expansion experience to be appropriately sorted, shifted and integrated within the body.

2. *Maybelle Stearns*: Stabilizes and supports the sacrum during an expansion experience.

3. *Mr. Lincoln*: Balances and stabilizes the CSF pulse while it alters its rhythm and patterning to accommodate the expansion.

4. *Sonia*: Stabilizes and supports the CSF pulse after it has completed its shift to accommodate the expansion.

5. *Chicago Peace:* Stabilizes movement of and interaction among the cranial, CSF and sacrum during an expansion experience.

6. *Betty Prior*: Stabilizes and balances the delicate rhythm of expansion and contraction of the cranial bones during the expansion.

7. *Tiffany*: Stabilizes the cranials as they shift their alignment appropriately to accommodate the input and impulses of the expansion.

8. *Oregold*: Stabilizes and balances the cranials, central nervous system, CSF and sacrum after an expansion process is complete.

Note: CSF= Cerebral Spinal Fluid

Perelandra Center for Nature Research, P.O.B. 3603, Warrenton, VA, 22186, 1-703-937-2153.

Flower Essences & Muscle Testing

[1]Machaelle Small Wright, *Behaving As If the God in All Life Mattered* (Jeffersonton, VA: Perelandra Ltd., 1987), pp. 164–165.

[2]Machaelle Small Wright, *Flower Essences* (Jeffersonton, VA, Perelandra Ltd., 1988), p. 3.

[3]*Ibid.*, p. 215.

[4]Gurudas, *Flower Essences and Vibrational Healing* (San Rafael, CA: Cassandra Press, 1989), pp. 17–20, and Diane Stein, *The Natural Remedy Book for Women* (Freedom, CA: The Crossing Press, 1992), pp. 79–80.

[5]Ellon Bach USA, Inc., "Animals and the Bach Remedies" (Lynbrook, NY: Ellon Bach USA, 1990), p. 7. Pamphlet.

[6]Mary Ann Simonds, "Essences for Animal Care" (Nevada City, CA: Flower Essence Society, 1989), p. 2. Pamphlet.

[7]Machaelle Small Wright, *Flower Essences*, p. 45.

[8]*Ibid.,* P. 47.

[9]Ellon Bach USA, Inc., "Animals and the Bach Remedies," pp. 3-6.

[10]Patricia Kaminski and Richard Katz, *Flower Essence Repertory: A Comprehensive Guide for the Natural Health Practitioner* (Nevada City, CA: Flower Essence Society, 1992), pp. 23–24.

[11]Gurudas, *Flower Essences and Vibrational Healing,* pp. 77–220.

[12]Machaelle Small Wright, *Flower Essences,* pp. 45–46.

[13]Anitra Frazier with Norma Eckroate, *The New Natural Cat: A Complete Guide for Finicky Owners* (New York Plume Books, 1990), pp. 273–412, Gurudas, *Flower Essences and Vibrational Healing,* pp. 77–220, and Machaelle Small Wright, *Flower Essences,* pp. 29–47.

Death & Reincarnation

Tiger was with me from five weeks old until the age of twelve. We had a deep rapport and the dog was a healer far beyond my own understanding at the time. One day I came home from a trip, the Michigan Women's Music Festival, and the sitter informed me that though acting normally, the dog had not eaten the entire time. "She's been giving the food to Dusty," she said. I watched Tiger closely for the next week; she didn't eat at all and I took her to the vet. My vet of the time was a gay man who had an ability to see auras, something he seldom talked about, and he verified what I saw as well. "She's dying, you know," he said. "There's nothing we can do." He suspected lymphatic cancer, and said just to leave her alone. "Should I put her down?" I asked. He said, "She's in no pain. Keep her comfortable and you'll know when."

The next two and a half months were among the hardest times of my life. Tiger refused totally to eat and totally withdrew. We had talked all through her life and now she refused to speak to me. When her daughter Dusty approached, she chased her away, as well. "Go away, I'm not here now," she said. I pleaded with her, begged her, raged at her—"Why are you doing this? Don't you love me? Won't you at least eat? You can't do this." But she continued to starve herself, no matter what I tempted her with, no matter how I begged. Chocolate ice cream was the last thing she ate and very little of that. She passed everything else on to Dusty. She refused to speak to me, but told a priestess friend, "I'm old and tired, I'm ready to die, just leave me alone."

The dog grew thinner and weaker by the day. By the time she was too weak to take her walks outside she was light enough for me to carry easily, and I hauled her up and down the apartment steps three times day. She never puddled in the house. She had never been large for a Siberian Husky. She was my first black and white one (all my others have been redheads). She had the largest turquoise eyes, freckles on her face, and long tiger stripes running across her chest. Now she was as small and lightweight as as stuffed toy, and it felt as if there was very little dog left inside all the fur. At night, I would carry her upstairs and put her in my bed, and sleep touching her all night, as we had done all through her life.

One bedtime I was meditating as usual before sleep, when the dog crawled off the bed and came to me. She put her head in my lap and said, "I love you, but I have to go now." The next morning she was unconscious and I took her to be put down. I was not permitted to remain with her during the injection, but Tiger was already gone.

Two weeks later I did a Hallows ritual (October 31) with two adult women and a five year old girl. As soon as I cast the circle, I felt Tiger enter the room through the door, run counterclockwise around the circumference of the circle, then plop herself down beside me. She put her head in my lap, and I could feel the motion of her breathing and the softness of her fur. She stayed until I opened the circle, then left through the closed door of the room. After the ritual, the little girl said, "I saw a dog come to be with us. She said she loves you." Tiger appeared at Hallows every year for the next several years, and after that I often saw her with one of my spirit guides. I was promised that she would reincarnate and be with me again, but though she seemed to enter another puppy I had briefly she left again and has not reappeared. After six years, I'm still looking for her. I always had the feeling through the years with Tiger that she was never a dog, but an evolved spirit who had come to me as a guide.

Her daughter Dusty grieved when Tiger died; they had been inseparable. She obeyed Tiger's wishes to stay away while she was dying, but I often saw her lying quietly beside her and Tiger allowed that. After Tiger's death she searched for her behind every door and in every closet, even looking under the bed and furniture. She searched daily for months, and if she heard Tiger's name she went and looked again. Dusty lived to thirteen years. I lost her two years ago. She suddenly began having desperate panic attacks for no obvious reason, sometimes keeping me awake all night. Her breathing became labored but it was also a very hot summer. The vet said she had a large mass in her lungs, cancer again,

and that the panic was either from lack of oxygen, or from senility, or because the cancer had spread to her brain. We tried broncho-dilators and tranquillizers but they didn't help. The dog was in pain.

I couldn't bear to see a long drawn-out agony as I had alone with Tiger. A little more aware now, I linked with Dusty asking, "Do you want to die?" She said, "Yes." I asked her, "Do you want the vet to put you down?" She agreed, and I promised I would take her the next day. She walked into the office like a young, strong dog ready to take on the world; she actually dragged me in there on her leash, crying. That night meditating I saw her—young, strong, tail wagging and prancing in a green field. I heard a voice say, "You did the right thing, she'll be back." Copper grieved for months and seemed to blame me for taking her away. I tried to explain to him, but he wouldn't listen, and his reproach made my own grief harder. I have grieved her for two years.

Kali came to me five months ago. I did not see her before she arrived. A friend found her for me in a California shelter and said, "That's Diane's dog." She adopted her, called me, and we arranged for air shipping. When Kali came out of her flight box my first impression of her was, "She looks just like Dusty." For the puppy's first two days with me I couldn't name her because I kept wanting to call her Dusty. The second or third night I made psychic contact with her and asked her, "Were you Dusty?" The puppy said, "Yes." I asked her, "Do you remember living with me when you were Dusty?" and she said "yes" again. "But it wasn't here." I had moved to Florida since Dusty's death in 1990. This puppy was angry and traumatized, and I asked her, "Will you live with me again?" And she said, "Yes, I was supposed to find you." She seemed to have the impression that since this was a different life and different place for her, it must be a different life for me also. I decided to name her Kali, since she is a gift to me from the Goddess of the Underworld. When her photo and Dusty's are placed side by side, you can't tell which dog is which.

It seems a great tragedy of human life that our dogs and cats live such short lifes pans and can't stay with us while we live. They are as much family as our sisters and children, and their deaths—which seem to come so often—hurt us as much as the death of any other friend or family member. It is also a tragedy that we live in a time and culture that in general gives little value to animals and regards human grief for a lost pet as something embarrassing or inappropriate. When a pet dies, the response is, "Too bad, you'll get another one." Or, "Well, it was just a cat, don't worry about it." Or, "She was getting old anyway and was too much trouble." But that's not the way it is.

Those of us who adopt an animal and make her a part of our family for life go through the same mourning process at the dog's or cat's death as we would for a person. In a culture that has too little caring for people and not enough contact with Goddess/Nature, this fact can be ignored, suppressed, or just misunderstood. The stages of grief and the process of recovery and acceptance after an animal's death are the same as the process of grieving a human loss. The stages, as defined by Elisabeth Kubler-Ross in her classic book *On Death And Dying* (MacMillan, 1969), are denial and isolation, bargaining, anger, depression, and acceptance. They may be experienced in different order or with some of the stages at once, and acceptance may come and go before the final resolution. Barbara Meyers, certified grief therapist with the Holistic Animal Consulting Center in New York, adds a sixth stage, reinvestment. Other emotions can include guilt, and just not being able to cope or go on.

The shock of a pet's death, especially if sudden but even if it's expected, puts the person in a place of denial and isolation at the beginning. You are stunned and refuse to accept the reality of what's happening; the mind shuts down as a buffer for the pain. Yet this is the time when too many decisions have had to be made; to euthanize or not, to allow more treatment or surgeries, or how to dispose of the cat's or dog's body after death. You may or may not have had time to say goodbye, especially if the situation is sudden or the animal is under veterinary care and away from you. You may or may not be present at the death. You come home and the dog's or cat's energy is still in the house and all around you. You go to call her for dinner, or pick up a toy, and she seems to be everywhere. Or, you need to "go home and feed the cat"—but the cat is no longer there.

For women in metaphysics or the Goddess craft, some of this time is made easier. First of all, there is a knowledge that death is a transition and not an ending, and an awareness that the body is not the whole Be-ing. The pet's energy is still in the house, she *is* still there. Many women receive manifestings of their dog or cat shortly after her death, and this is accepted as natural and

a comfort. She has left this plane, but is still there. One pamphlet on pet loss, from the respected American Animal Hospital Association, describes these visitations as "hallucinations,"[1] which they are not. It's a cruel term for something that a lot of people experience, and denying its reality only adds to the grief process particularly in this early stage when it usually happens. Know that you are not going crazy; this is real but you may feel very much alone.

The second stage is *bargaining*, and may come before or after the cat's or dog's actual death. It goes something like, "If my dog lives, I'll never do _____ again." Or, "If my cat comes home, I'll give you _____." The bargaining is with the Goddess, with yourself, with the veterinarian, or with the pet, and is actually a part of the denial stage. At this point, the animal's death may not be final but still pending. The person is willing to make any sacrifice to turn the clock back, but it just cannot be so.

Next is an*ger*, which may feel out of control and overwhelming. It may be directed at oneself, the animal, the veterinarian, or anyone else who happens to be there. There may be general outbursts of hostility at others who are involved or not. "Why do you care if she died, you never even knew her?" Or anger directed at anyone who was there: "You're the veterinarian, you could have saved her."

Some of the worst anger may be directed to oneself: "If only I had _____," or "If only I hadn't done _____ the cat would have lived." Blaming the veterinarian is probably typical but within their own medical value systems most animal doctors are caring people and genuinely do their best. They also grieve for animals they may have treated for many years and watched grow old, or for the sudden deaths. The veterinary medical model, particularly to someone involved with holistic healing, feels terribly cold and uncaring. It can use technology beyond all common sense. It is up to the woman whose pet is dying to know when to call a halt and not to feel guilty for doing so.

Guilt is a frequent part of the death and grieving process. After Dusty died, my guilt was a fear that I had put her down too soon, that she could have lived longer, and I had taken something away from both of us. Copper's reproaches didn't help. This feeling lasted until Kali came, and lasted even though I had every assurance—

from Dusty, from the veterinarian, from channeled messages later, and from my own common sense—that it was done at the right time. After Tiger's death and during her long dying, I beat myself mentally and emotionally for not having been able to do more. Strangely, as hard as Tiger's death process was, I didn't blame myself for letting her go through it in her own way. It was her express wish, no matter how hard it was for me. Yet, I doubt I'd let another animal do it that way again.

It is all too easy to blame oneself for an animal's loss. If she has gotten out and been killed by a car, it's even easier. Even if there is nothing to take blame for, too often people create it. The patriarchal culture that so terribly denies death and dying, that ignores the meaning of a loved pet's death, that is embarrassed by grief and tries to suppress it, is all too good at encouraging women to feel guilty. The other side of this is that animals have their lifespans and karma just as humans do, and when it is time to die, death comes. If the cat hadn't gotten loose and died that way, something else would have happened if it was the animal's time to die. Pets have also been known to use themselves as sacrifices to protect their people from death or injury. This does not encourage negligence, but attempts to ease the guilt and pain. Life and death are decisions given to conscientious people in only very limited ways.

Says animal grief expert Mickie Gustafson in *Losing Your Dog:*

Guilt feelings are understable and extremely common in the course of the grief process. These feelings are almost always unfounded, however—a fact which the bereaved eventually comes to realize.[2]

Depression and grieving are the fourth stage of the process. This is the time of emptiness—the dog or cat is gone, the anger and denial are gone, only emptiness remains. Home feels lifeless, and no warm furry friend sleeps at the foot of the bed. No one is there to beg for pizza, hide your shoes, to take for a walk or buy catnip mice for. The woman left alone may experience a variety of physical-emotional reactions at this time, like wandering aimlessly around the house wondering what to do next. She may experience sleep disturbances—nightmares, insomnia, oversleeping, dreaming of the lost animal—and/or eating disturbances—overeating, food binging, lack of appetite.

Wendy Nelson describes this after the death of a cat:

The mourning cat owner may go through ". . . waves of sadness," accompanied by crying and feelings of hopelessness. The owner may feel listless and unmotivated, perhaps even questioning his or her ability to continue living without the cat. Most people work through these stages on their own, probably because they don't know they have a choice.[3]

Numbness, fatigue, loneliness, depression and sadness, confusion, restlessness, anxiety, irritability and crying are all expressions of depression and grief in this stage. Other animals in the family may be grieving, too.

Only time can bring acceptance, and the amount of time varies from person to person. Eventually, the good times shared with the dog or cat while alive take the place of the horror of final crises. After a few months, the animal may start to psychically manifest again in meditation or quiet times. Some animals never reappear, however. (Tiger did frequently, but Dusty only once, the night following her death.) Eating pizza or walking on the pet's favorite walk route no longer are painful, only gentle memories of her. You can look at her pictures again and bear to have them around your home. Though you will always remember and love the cat or dog that is gone, her memory is no longer so painful. Grief can last as long as months or years, and the best way to move through it is to allow the process and allow yourself to feel and grieve.

Reinvestment is learning to love again, accepting another animal into the home. The new pet can never replace the one that died, but is lovable in her own way and needs to be cared for and loved. Some people want another pet immediately, often to stave off the grieving process for the dead one. This may not be fair to the newcomer and can serve to stuff emotions that only make the process harder. But women who have love to give need someone to give it to, and if they are animal lovers they eventually choose another pet. It may take varying amounts of time. Presenting a new kitten to a woman who has recently lost her cat should not be done without talking to the woman about it first. She may or may not be ready, and should not be rushed.

Women involved with metaphysics, the Goddess Craft, or psychic work have an easier time moving through the grief process than is typical in our starved and uncaring culture. The faith is there that there is no death, only transition into something else that will eventually be another birth. Death is an intrinsic part of living. With the concept of reincarnation, women know that their animals will come back to them, in this life or another. Friends are not separated forever. With the concept of a life beyond the physical plane, there is knowledge that though the dog or cat is not "here" she is still present, still in existence on other planes and dimensions. Cats and dogs have souls just as people do, and souls are immortal however transient bodies may be.

Says psychic Laurel Steinhice:

Animals do reincarnate in tandem with their human companions, and with each other. The closer the interspecies bonding, the more likely and more frequent the reincarnation is to occur.

Canine and feline bodies are freely interchangable (dogs can reincarnate as cats, and vice versa), and there is much flexibility with regard to most other species as well.

When your beloved companion lets you know she is considering leaving the body behind, it is a loving kindness to let her know you understand . . . and that you will welcome her into a new body, a new incarnation in which her spirit can continue to share a close bonding with you.

When your beloved companion gives up the body in death, know that love always finds its own again: she is near to you in spirit presence. And when you choose a new pup or kitten she will guide you in the selection of a new embodiment for her Lifeforce essence.

And when you yourself move into a new reality, a new dimension, we invite you to know . . .that your nonhuman companions on life's journey will as surely be there to greet you as your human companions. They will choose to be with you again, as you will also choose to be with them.[4]

With this information, there are other ways to view death than is typical in western culture, and these alternative viewpoints make the whole process much gentler for both animals and humans. Death with dignity can be achieved, even if the pet must be euthanized. The veterinary medical system has less denial of death than does the human medical system. The issue becomes quality of life, and the woman living with the dog or cat needs to ask what is truly best for the animal. Lessened suffering and death with dignity are more easily achieved with a knowledge of reincarnation and communication.

Marion Webb-Former tells of Earl's death and their agreement:

As he grew beyond the life expectancy of a German Shepherd we began to have "conversations" about when he would leave me. He would "call" me to the window and I'd see him sitting or lying in the sun, peeping out from his favorite willow tree, or standing on "his hill." He'd "tell" me that these were the places where he wanted to be scattered because we had agreed that on his death he would be cremated and his ashes would be scattered by me in the back yard . . .

Above all, I reinforced the fact that if this was his time to go, I wouldn't try to hold onto him . . . It was also at this time that we made an agreement that whenever he was ready to leave, he would tell me and I would honor his decision. We would say our "goodbyes" with love and joy at having shared such a close friendship.

In the summer of 1986 (he died on August 1st) he began to tell me that his time was coming. And so we spent our quiet times together, sharing loving farewells and the promise that we would again at some point be reunited.[5]

There is a different feel to death when it is treated in this way, a much more loving, dignified and gentle way. In this perspective, whether or when to euthanize a beloved pet becomes a calmer, clearer, less guilt-ridden situation. In the way of conscious communication, ask the animal what she needs and wants. Dusty told me that she wanted to go. With Tiger, I fought her leaving so hard that I couldn't ask, and yet I knew when it was time. (Machaelle Small Wright, in *Flower Essences*, talks about animals starving themselves the way Tiger did. She doesn't let it happen, asserting to the animal that it find another way.[6] With Tiger, I did not know I had that option.)

Says Machaelle Small Wright on the subject of animals and dying:

I find that the primary thing keeping people from thinking clearly about how to assist an animal through death is their reluctance to accept the sorrow of separation and the inevitable grief. It clouds our ability to make clear decisions based on what is best for the animal. One thing to remember about animals is that they are not at all sentimental about death . . . I feel that they see death as a natural part of life and, if we allow them, they will move through it with extraordinary grace.[7]

In this context, if an animal is clearly entering the death process, Wright asks her whether she wants veterinary help. The animal usually does not. She then keeps the animal physically comfortable in a quiet place, and watches for the withdrawal and privacy-seeking that generally signals the coming death. She makes the decision of euthanasia on three considerations: (1) veterinary advice and information, (2) the animal's quality of life if it continues living, and (3) the animal's own wishes. If the pet is ready to die, or the decision is made that it is time based on the above things, she uses kinesiology and flower essences to support her through the death process, whether the animal dies at home or is put down.

Since Machaelle Small Wright is the developer of the Perelandra Flower Essences, her method of helping the animal's transition is by using the essences. Here is the process. In a natural death where the pet is able to die peacefully at home, an entrance into the death phase is usually evident. The animal seeks privacy, stops eating and may sleep all the time; there is a change in its daily behavior that communication verifies. To support the animal, first test yourself for flower essences and take the essences indicated, then focus on the dog or cat, test and give the pet what she tests for. Next ask what essence(s) are needed to help the animal prepare for death. It is simpler to test daily, but you can also use the testing process to find out how many days to use an essence and how many times a day. When the first test period ends, test again.

When the animal has died, as soon as possible, test yourself again for essences and take what is called for, then link with the pet. Verify the link by pendulum or muscle testing, and test the animal for essences, placing a drop of each essence on the animal's body over the chest area. Next wrap the body in a towel and allow it to lie in a quiet place for three hours (or one hour for a wild animal). This is the time needed for the animal's spirit to separate from the physical body, and by the end of this period the body usually feels empty, the life consciousness has gone. Just before burial, test yourself again for flower essences and take what are needed, then test the animal again, placing the essences on the towel wrapping the body. The animal may not need more essences at this time. Complete the burial.[8] Use the essences for yourself during the grief process.

For sudden death caused by injury, first test yourself and take the flower essences indicated, then link with the animal and test her for essences. If the cat or dog is still alive, place them on her lips or in her mouth. Use the question, "What essences are needed to stabilize this animal for death?" and test again, administering those essences. Repeat every two hours, linking with the pet and asking, "Are the stabilizing essences needed again?" Check every two hours, giving the essences tested for. After death, do the same as for a natural death. If you find the dog or cat already dead, and the death has occurred less than three hours before, do the testing and give the essences. After three hours, the pet's spirit has separated from the body and you won't be able to link with it to do the process.[9]

If the decision to use euthanasia has been made, test yourself for flower essences first and take what are needed, then link with the pet. Ask, "Do you wish to die now?" Machaelle Small Wright reports that she has never gotten a "no" to this question. If the pet wishes to remain living, consider all the information, but the decision is yours. Clearly tell the animal what is coming, what it will be like, what will happen to the body, etc., and ask if she agrees. (Verify by testing with pendulum or kinesiology.) If the pet disagrees, ask her if she wishes to die naturally. Again, you can choose not to go along with it—ask her to cooperate and likely she will. Test again to verify.

Next, by testing, ask how many days the animal needs to prepare for death. She will probably choose to go immediately; make the veterinary appointment and inform the cat or dog. Then start testing the question, "What essences are needed to stabilize this animal for death?" and test periodically, including right before the trip. If at that time the animal indicates she is not ready for death, test for essences again and give her what she tests for. She will then indicate she is ready. Don't forget to test yourself first, you need it as much as the pet does. Do the after-death process the same as in a natural death.[10] Handling the process in this way offers the animal and her person a death with dignity, peaceful and loving for both. No one claims it to be easy, but the grieving is clearer and guilt free, with far less trauma than the usual situation.

Sometimes the circumstance isn't what it seems. I was asked with a friend to do healing for a ten year old greyhound dog. He had been accidently poisoned with lawn chemicals and was severely bloated, lying on his side and evidently in pain. I had been aware for some time that Matt was old and seemed to be getting tired. When my friend and I did healing for him, I did Reiki while she boosted me psychically without touching. I asked the dog, "Matt, are you going to die?" He said, "No, not for another year or so." I asked him, "Can you get well from this?" He said, "Yes." I asked him what he needed, and his reply was, "An enema."

The conversation was silent, but just at that moment, my friend doing the healing with me commented, "If he were my child at this point, I'd give him an enema." She verified my estimate also that the dog was not dying and, despite appearances, could survive this dis-ease. I told the dog's person what we had learned and offered to help her obtain a child's Fleet Enema and administer it. I suspected one would not be enough but that one would tell us if we were on the right track. The owner refused politely and the next day had the dog put down.

At what turned out to be the time of death, Matt came to me psychically, thanking me for trying and stating again that he didn't have to die and didn't want to. He came to me every day for the next three days, until finally on the third day I surrounded him with flowers and called his guides in to help him finish the transition. I asked him if he had gone to see his person, and he said he had tried but "she wouldn't see me." It took three days to calm the dog's anger and help him understand that his person had done her best. When I last saw him, he told me, "I'll see you again."

How do you know medically when it's time for a pet to die, whether more medical care would save her or only increase suffering? Beyond the animal's assessment, how do you know when is the time? Veterinary information and cooperation are important here, when the decision is a medical one, but the person living with the pet is likely to be the first to know:

Tiger Paws, a deaf sixteen-year-old cat, began hanging around inside the house, demanding to be held one Monday. By Tuesday, he looked as if he'd lost five pounds and his coat was dull. He drank water and a little milk, but he wasn't his normal, piggy, independent self. By afternoon, he was clearly going rapidly downhill.[11]

The veterinarian concurred that death was within a few days, and the cat's person opted for euthanasia.

Loss of awareness or interest in life is a primary signal that the death process is beginning, and the signs may be highly subjective. The animal may sleep more and be hard to rouse. She may lose her lifelong house training to eliminate in the house, or in or near her sleeping place. With loss of appetite and later a refusal of water, death occurs within a day or two. An animal that goes through this process naturally may die in her sleep. When there is illness, cancer or injury there is more suffering to consider. There may be pain, vomiting, diarrhea, difficulty breathing and signs of distress like crying or restlessness. Ending the suffering should be considered.[12]

This is so hard to do. My first Siberian Husky was Cinde, who was a retired show dog that came to me when she was four years old. She was also my first dog, in my first apartment, and I had her for five years. At the age of nine, she developed a large, soggy looking swelling in her abdomen over the line of nipples. The dog had had one litter but never been spayed. I took her to the vet who said it was an abscess, gave her antibiotics and told me to bring her back in a week. In a week's time, the area was topped by a large running sore, which when lanced drained over two cups of fluid. The fluid came back and over a couple of weeks required lancing two or three more times. Each time I held Cinde for it, and she was obviously in great pain. Each time the amount of fluid that left her body seemed amazing.

Finally, the vet suggested surgery. I asked him if he thought she had cancer and told him that when he opened her up if she had cancer or couldn't heal, would he please end her suffering. The dog went through the surgery, losing five nipples and was stitched together so tightly she almost couldn't move her legs to walk. I was sure at that time it was cancer, and regretted that the dog had been revived. Within two weeks after the surgery, the animal's body developed dozens of grape-sized external tumors along the line of the incision. The incision never closed or healed.

Cinde refused food, accepting only water, and just lay on her rug, withdrawn. I brought her back to the veterinarian, and asked that she be put down. A week after her death, the biopsy returned with the verdict of cancer; it had been taken at the time of the surgery. My guilt in the grief process for Cinde was that I had let her go through so much suffering.

But there are no easy answers. Tiger, I let die at home without veterinary intervention and that wasn't easy, either. With Dusty I did my best; when I knew she was suffering and that it was irreversible I had her euthanized, then grieved that I had maybe done it too soon. There are no easy answers to losing a pet, and the grieving is painful whatever the circumstances. We can only do our best and do it with love.

Anitra Frazier in *The New Natural Cat* gives a list of signs that the time for euthanasia has come. Any one or more of these in a cat is indication, and for dogs the information is the same or similar:

1. *Confusion.* Inability to locate the litter box or to get back to bed.
2. *Extreme weakness.* Staggering, leaning against things, collapsing to rest.
3. *Sitting or lying in the litter box.*
4. *Sitting with head over the water dish.*
5. *Subcutaneous hydration therapy no longer being absorbed.*
6. *Body temperature drops below normal.*
7. *Refusing warmth*, though the animal feels cold or the environment is cold.
8. *Constant uninterrupted purring for no reason.*
9. *Lying or crouching and staring off into space.* Eyes unfocused, not caring what you do or don't do to care for her.
10. *Rapid breathing through partly open mouth.*
11. *Abdomen heaves with each breath.*[13]

Euthanasia is supposedly painless and without fear or trauma for the animal. In the case of irreversible suffering it is the humane way. Many people suffering drawn-out, agonizing deaths from cancer or losing their mental ability through Alzheimer's Dis-ease wish the option were available to them. In a less technological time it might have been, and in a more caring future. I have past life memories of working in a temple, helping people to leave their bodies when the time was right, but no idea of when or where that may have been. Death is treated with denial in modern times; ignoring it won't make it go away, and it seems only responsible to help prevent unnecessary suffering. If the dying pet wants to go, putting her down is not cruel.

A veterinary assistant describes the process:

The euthanasia solution we use is called T-61. We give the solution intravenously 95 percent of the time, with 5 percent of the animals, we administer it directly into the heart. T-61 is a fast-acting fluid made of several chemicals. To put to sleep a pet takes less than 30 seconds, and the pet never suffers any pain. All it feels is a little pinch from the needle, and it becomes unconscious very quickly.[14]

Machaelle Small Wright describes the experience:

Within seconds, I can feel the animal's body begin to relax. I'll use my hands to gently guide them down to the towel we placed under them before we began. Although I am usually speaking to the animal in a low voice, encouraging him to relax, and assuring that everything is fine, this has been a very quiet and gentle moment. We wait for a couple of minutes, then the vet will check for heart activity, verifying death. We spend perhaps another twenty minute or so in the room, all of us quietly talking, usually reminiscing about our friend, while getting our hearts back out of our mouths. Sometimes the animal will twitch or move during this time, but this is just the body and its nervous system naturally letting go. It can be a bit weird to see if you're not prepared for the possibility. Then we wrap the animal in the towel and take him back to Perelandra for burial. Our experience with this, although tough emotionally, has always been special. I think it is good for our friend to die in loving and caring hands, and I think it is good for us to experience the peace and tranquility of the moment.[15]

Once the animal's spirit has separated from her body, the death process ends. Psychics have described visually watching the spirit separate from the body, and past life regression work reports that dying is far easier than being born and happens with more joy. Suffering happens in the body, not out of it. Many pets hang on long after their time out of responsibility for taking care of their people. I might have done that to Tiger, but she was wise enough not to let me.

Linda Tellington-Jones, in her beautiful book *The Tellington TTouch*, suggests using ritual to help in the letting go, both before and after a beloved dog's or cat's death:

Death makes no distinction between humans and animals, and neither does love. Why shouldn't we celebrate, mourn, and remember our animal friends as we do our human ones, with a ceremony that takes joy in the life that was, and that allows us to grieve and also to heal our grief? . . .

When we think of ourselves as midwives helping in the process of dying, it makes the going that much easier. Communicate your feelings to your pet. When you do—crying if you want to, but bringing the good times you had together joyously to mind, too— your animal will feel the strength of your friendship and will know that you will never forget him or her. Mourn and celebrate at the same time, and don't try to cut the emotional bonds.[16]

The animal that has lost an animal companion, or one that has lost her people (to death or other losses) also grieves. These dogs or cats are in mourning and need comforting and reassurance as much as the person who has lost a pet. Communicating, caring, flower essences, massage and TTouch, homeopathy and other methods are important in helping the animal overcome loss and choose to survive. The grief process in people can also come without a death, but by a change in life circumstances, such as the woman who must move to government housing because of age or disability and loses her cat or dog. Or the woman who must enter a nursing home or give up her own home and independence in other ways. A woman who is ill may need to find homes for her dogs and cats. The mourning and grief process also happens when a pet is stolen, lost or missing with the outcome unknown. The animal may be gone permanently or temporarily, and the not-knowing can be worse than certainty.

Ignatia is a homeopathic remedy that helps grieving in either human or animal. It is used for behavior or physical symptoms that occur after a death or deep loss. A number of flower essences are helpful in the grief process: Bach Flower Remedy's *Honeysuckle* is used with *Star of Bethlehem* for the animal whose person is permanently gone (or the person whose pet is). Gurudas/FES *Pear* flower essence helps a dog or cat that has lost its family and must adjust to a new one. Use *Amaranthus* for the pet that has lost her animal friend, and *Eucalyptus* for one that blames a human for her grief.

Apricot or *Koenig Van Daenmark* are for animals whose person has cancer. *Angel's Trumpet*, *Angelica* or Perelandra's *Royal Highness* help an animal (or human) to prepare for death and go through the process gently. *Bleeding Heart* helps the person or animal to let go, and *Borage* to overcome grief. Bach *Rescue Remedy* or *Star of Bethlehem*, or Perelandra's *White Lightnin'* help with shock and the trauma of the early process.

Physical level healing is less effective or important for a human or pet in this circumstance, but scullcap herb is a relaxant and nervous system calmative, and valerian is for emotional or physical pain. While these are not addictive, it is important for the grieving human not to become psychologically dependent upon them or to use them to stop feeling. The only cure for grieving is time and going through the process. Acupuncture can help a person or animal with depression, as can flower essences (like *Cucumber*) or homeopathy, and some herbs (scullcap, passion flower) or vitamins (B-complex). The

Tellington TTouch is highly recommended for pet or person, either dying or in grief.

Death is the beginning of the process of rebirth, and an end to suffering and pain. When the dog's or cat's body is worn out, give her release and permission to let go, and do not deny the grieving in yourself. The separation is not a final ending, there are no final endings. People recovering from near-death experiences often describe their already dead cats or dogs waiting for them, ready to escort them to the other world when the time to leave truly arrives. There are countless stories of dead animals manifesting, as Tiger did for me in yearly Hallows rituals, and a number of recorded stories of ghost dogs or cats returning to a house they lived in before their deaths.

Bill Shul has made a collection of these stories, in *Animal Immortality: Pets and Their Afterlife* (Carroll and Graf Publishers, 1990). In one story[17], Norma adopted a large collie she named Corky, having found the dog near death from a bullet wound in the throat that permanently affected his bark. She had the dog for many years. Two years after the dog finally died, Norma moved to a New York apartment and was awakened one night by Corky's distinctive, damaged voice. The dog's insistent barking saved three people from a fire.

Here is Barbara's near-death experience, from the same book:

During a clinical death experience she found herself walking along a path in a meadow and there, trotting alongside, was her cat Lilly who had died two years before. Suddenly, feeling called back to the site of her body, she hurried back along the path, with Lilly running beside her. Then the cat stopped as though knowing it could not go farther, and sat down in the path as though to wait.[18]

One of the stars of my book on psychic development, *Stroking the Python: Women's Psychic Lives* (Llewellyn Publications, 1988) is Lady, the German Shepherd that was Mimi's friend in life and after. Mimi sent me this story:

I woke this morning to a scratching and weight on my blanket. Looking over the side of the bed I saw Lady. She walked over to the window, whiffed at the air as if the window were open, telling me she wanted to go out. I started to get out of bed and stepped into my slippers when it occurred to me that Lady is not alive. She looked at me as if to say, "Well?" This amused me and I told her, "Hey Lady, you came in through the wall, now go out the same way." She looked at the window again and disappeared through the wall. It was four o'clock in the morning, it was dark and cold outside. I went back to sleep.[19]

Nan's cat had lived in their apartment before they rented it, and a former tenant had put it to death after its person moved. The cat was young and not ready to die, and remained.

We moved into our apartment in July. From practically the minute we stepped in the door, we just had this sense that there was a cat in the house. We didn't say anything to each other, but we were both feeling it just the same. We would find ourselves automatically blocking the way with a leg when we opened an outside door, so that "the cat wouldn't get out." We haven't had a cat of our own for over three years. We could see the cat in the doorway to the bedroom or walking around the corner of the refrigerator in the kitchen, sitting in an outside window. As Samhain (Hallows) approached, we both began to see it more clearly.

One day, I came in from outside, kneeled by our gerbil cage, and right in clear sight was a cat walking straight up to me. It vanished about a foot away. I told my partner about it: that's when we first compared notes . . . Around Samhain the sightings were much clearer, and we each felt the cat touch us on a few occasions. Nearer Yule we decided to have a ritual and tell the cat it had died and that it had the choice to go on to the other side. We both cried. Since then we've seen it less often and less clearly, but it's not gone altogether. As I was writing this, I must have summoned the cat in my thoughts, because three of the gerbils started doing their "danger thump" without any noise or sudden movement on my part to instigate it.[20]

I experienced this cat for myself, in Nan's house. Sleeping in Nan's apartment on a visit, I felt the cat come in to bed with me. It stepped on to the mattress and the bed moved, walked across my leg, stared at me, then curled up against my knees. It was a large orange cat.

Eileen Garrett, noted psychic and author of a number of books in the 1940s, describes the separation of soul from body in dead ducklings she saw as a child:

The ducks were quiet but there was a movement going on all around them. I saw, curling up from each little body a grey smoke-like substance, rising in spiral form. This fluid stuff began to move and curl as it arose and gradually I saw it take on a new shape as it moved away from the bodies of these little dead ducks. Fear had now given way to amazement in the face of this spectacle. I was joyful because I knew that in a moment the ducks were "coming alive" again. I had forgotten about their dead bodies lying limp below and waited, with tense expectancy, to see them take on a new shape and run away.[21]

One of a friend's three dogs died. Intermittently after, she watched her other animals seemingly playing with nothing, and playing as they had done when the three dogs were together. The remaining dogs thought nothing of it; their friend had come back to visit. A similar cat story is described by Bill Shul. The cat's name was Fingal:

Shortly after Fingal died, the tapping at the French window commenced again. It would be so insistent that the family would open the window. It would then cease. On several occasions they were convinced they heard purrs from Fingal's favorite yellow cushion.

One afternoon a friend of the family brought her Siamese cat along for a visit. When the cat approached the chair containing Fingal's yellow cushion, he arched his back in fright. His eyes seemed to follow something as it moved toward the window. When the window was opened, the visiting feline—apparently aware that the original occupant of the chair had left—settled down on the vacant cushion.[22]

Many psychically aware women who have had and lost a dog or cat will have similar stories. There are no explanations, but so many stories that they can only be considered real. The only conclusion from them that can be made is the immortality of the soul, both human and animal. Says Marion Webb-Former:

Animals are far less preoccupied with the physical than the humans with whom they share Earth. Even though there is a much smaller fragment of soul consciousness within them, they are far closer to the true reality than humans. Their matrix is the consciousness of *All That Is* which I will term Source consciousness.[23]

My own term for "Source consciousness" or the "All That Is" is Goddess. Marion describes the oneness between human and animal that begins with conscious communication, but that only begins there:

Indeed, for some there is the beginning of soul rejoining which continues on and does not cease at the point of physical separation, for many owners and their pets are of the same essence, the same oversoul. They are being reunited with a fragment of their total Be-ing.[24]

Death is not death but a reuniting and a new beginning. There may be no more to say. Or as Laurel Steinhice puts it, "We are all One."

For the woman who has lost her cat or dog, pet loss support groups are springing up in cities nationwide. For information on locating one, ask your veterinarian, or write or call the Delta Society, POB 1080, Renton WA 98057-1080, (206) 226-7357. The number of books in print on pet loss and on grief and recovery can also help, as will metaphysical books on reincarnation. A number of therapists are also now specializing in grief recovery work including recovery from the loss of a pet. Find these through the veterinary medical schools, or contact the Grief Recovery Hotline at 1-800-445-4808. A woman who has lost her dog or cat is experiencing deep grief, but light appears at the end of the tunnel eventually.

[1]American Animal Hospital Association, "*Pet Loss and Bereavement: The Loss of Your Pet*" (Denver, CO: AAHA, 1989), p.2.

[2]Mickie Gustafson, *Losing Your Dog: Coping With Grief When A Pet Dies* (New York: Bergh Publishing, Inc., 1992) p. 20.

[3]Wendy L. Nelson, "When Your Best Friend Dies," in *CatFancy*, March, 1992, p. 37.

[4]Laurel Steinhice, "Energy Centers (Chakras) in Dogs and Cats," Personal Communication, 1992.

[5]Marion Webb-Former, Personal Communication, December 1991.

[6]Machaelle Small Wright, *Flower Essences* (Jeffersonton, VA: Perelandra Ltd., 1988), pp.225–226.

[7]*Ibid.*, pp. 224.

[8]*Ibid.*, pp. 231–232.

[9]*Ibid.*, pp. 232–233.

[10]*Ibid.*, pp.233–236.

[11]Robert Anderson, DVM and Barbara Wrede, *Caring for Older Cats and Dogs* (Charlotte, VT: Williamson Publishing Co., 1990), p. 135.

[12]*Ibid.*, p. 136.

[13]Anitra Frazier with Norma Eckroate, *The New Natural Cat: A Complete Guide for Finicky Owners* (New York: Plume Books, 1990), pp. 193–194.

[14]Deborah Papio, in Wendy L. Nelson, "When Your Best Friend Dies," p. 38.

[15]Machaelle Small Wright, *Flower Essences,* pp. 229–230.

[16]Linda Tellington-Jones with Sybil Taylor, *The Tellington TTouch: A Breakthrough Technique to Train and Care for Your Favorite Animal* (New York, Viking Press, 1992), p. 206-207.

[17]Bill D. Shul, *Animal Immortality: Pets and Their Afterlife* (New York: Carroll and Graf Publishers, Inc., 1990), pp. 112–113.

[18]*Ibid.*, p. 199.

[19]Diane Stein, *Stroking the Python: Women's Psychic Lives* (St. Paul, MN: Llewellyn Publications, 1988), p. 136.

[20]*Ibid.*, p. 135.

[21]*Ibid.*, pp. 323–324.

[22]Bill D. Shul, *Animal Immortality,* p. 116.

[23]Marion Webb-Former, Personal Communication, December 10, 1991.

[24]Marion Webb-Former, Personal Communication, May 16, 1992.

Appendices

These following are by Dr. Gloria Dodd, DVM and are used with her permission.

I. Scientific Methods of Detecting the Nonphysical Anatomy

There *are* scientific methods of detecting the nonphysical anatomy (the etheric organs) and the EMF of the body.

(1) *Electrically and quantitatively* in millivolts, one can measure the health of any organ by the millivolt reading from that organ's specific acupuncture point. It is read by a sophisticated solid state machine which was discovered by a doctor who was educated in Germany and received a double degree in electrical engineering and in medicine. Dr. Reinhold Voll, whom I had the pleasure of studying with in Germany and there learned his EAV (Electroacudiagnosis according to Voll) method in human medicine. I then devoted 2 years of my life to applying it to animals (dogs and cats), found the methods and treatments were identical for animals, published my results and taught other veterinarians in this country. It was *the* essential linch pin of my practice. Voll called the original machine the Dermatron. There have been numerous copies. Some are hooked up to computers: the Vega System, The Interro, etc., but all use Voll's basic tenets of mechanisms and conclusions.

I cannot say enough about this method. It is true preventative medicine, for it can detect the health of an organ's energy field before it happens in the physical organ (hence before any known laboratory or orthodox testing methods); and through its use of testing homeopathic remedies made from the offending substance, bacterial, viral, fungal, parasitic, drug or chemical, the ensuing health hazard can be aborted. Also orthodox resistant dis-eases can be completely cured by this method.

I could give you hundreds of animal cases that I miraculously turned around with this method, that I could not have begun to help in any other way.

I used the acupressure points on the toes of the animals themselves; later I found this energy value can be transferred to a surrogate human and the toes and finger of that human (touching the animal or having the animal sit in her lap) and I would be reading the value of the animal not the person—this was verified by reading the person's points first. This is much like doing applied kinesiology using a person to read the animal's muscle by touching or making contact with the animal but using the person's arm for testing.

(2) *Visually by Kirlian Photography*—the non-physical can be photographed by a special camera utilizing a current to expose the film in a light-free environment. What is captured on film of fingers and toes, is the EMF of these or the "aura" as some term it. This was done originally in man, but some Europeans have very large plates and have photographed sheep and cattle. I have a Kirlian Camera and used it as a diagnostic of the health of the associated acupuncture meridians with their specific organs flowing on each side of the finger (forepaw and toes) and the toes of the hindfoot and paw. These meridian auras coincided with my findings on the Dermatron with the EAV analysis. I also used it in my original research showing the beneficial affects of quartz crystal therapy, and the effect of the "Energyzing Halter" I developed on the body's organ EMFs. Please see Kirlian photos taken of healthy cat, a cat with Feline Leukemia, a puppy with Canine Distemper, and a dog with Chronic Dermatitis; each before and after wearing the halter.

Working in the nonphysical is where true healing occurs. This is a statement and basic principle vehemently contested by the medical community in this country. I have photographed it and measured it quantitatively down to the millivolt level of emission from the body's cells. I have seen these changes in energy fields turn from degenerative readings to normal readings with holistic treatment, then seen these manifest clinically in a recovered animal.

It is interesting to see Kirlian photography of a hands-on healing between healer and patient (both people). In a series of photos it shows the large strong aura of the healer being transferred to the patient's weak one (finger photos). Then the last photo shows the patient's weak one (finger photos). Then the last photo shows the patient's aura strong, and the healer's weak. This is why so many holistic healers are sick themselves—they give away their own aura constantly to the sick (that goes for holistic veterinarians who heal from their heart chakra and don't protect themselves). We participate with the animals. We're literally draining our own etheric fields continually.

One way to protect one's self is to discharge any noxious energies picked up from your patient, by grabbing a water faucet in your left hand and running the water—monitoring your energy with a pendulum or muscle testing. Also practicing what we teach too—good diet, exercise, rest, using our own healing therapies to help us strengthen our etheric field.

Healing with Crystals: Magnificent Concentrators of Energy[1]

My first case of crystal healing involved my own dog Duffy, a 14-year-old female poodle who had a grade three left-sided heart murmur. Despite homeopathy and acupuncture, she had reached a plateau and her heart condition was not improving. Blood tests showed an elevation of certain heart muscle enzymes, which indicated current heart muscle damage. Although eating well, she had a cough. The murmur persisted.

I placed a quartz crystal pendant around her neck at the location of the thymus gland, and applied smooth-tumbled quartz crystals to her nylon harness, with one crystal over each heart valve, right and left, and one at the top and bottom center of her chest. These lined up as a double pyramid encircling the heart chakra.

Within six days her coughing stopped, her murmur disappeared and her blood test results showed normal heart enzyme levels. I have monitored Duffy for two years now, and she continues to show no signs of congestive heart condition. She plays vigorously with my daughter's male Boston terrier.

To me, this is incredible. In my 24 years of veterinary practice—both conventional and holistic—I had never seen such a reversal.

Laying the Foundation: But what are crystals? How do they heal? What's a chakra?

In 1974 I began my studies into alternative methods of treatment and preventive health care in animals. I began with acupuncture and homeopathy, but in 1983 I discovered the healing power of quartz crystals.

I should say I rediscovered the healing power of crystals, because the history of using quartz for relieving pain and stimulating recovery goes back into antiquity. Randall and Vicki Baer, in their book *Windows of Light,* write that the oldest and most famous civilization, Atlantis, used crystals as central technological building blocks. Quartz was used as the primary source of generating all energy forms as well as for healing.

Physically, crystals are simply fossilized water. They come into existence when water combines with an element in the presence of pressure, temperature and energy. When conditions are right, water will cause, or allow, the element to grow as a crystal. Silicon (sand) and water produce quartz crystal.

Quartz has a uniqueness all its own: it amplifies, transforms, stores, focuses and transfers energy.

If you are wearing a quartz watch, you should know that it's the ability of quartz to vibrate at precise rates that makes it so valuable in the creation of extremely accurate timepieces.

Quartz stores energy. The huge amounts of "memory" in a computer are stored on a tiny slice of quartz in a microcircuit.

When quartz is squeezed, it generates electricity. It's at the heart of the waves known as radio and television signals. Quartz also focuses energy. In lasers, crystals allow us to measure the distance to the moon in seconds, burn through steel walls, or perform delicate eye surgery.

Crystal healing is energy medicine. Energy medicine is based on the premise that energy flows harmoniously through a healthy body; in an unhealthy body it is unbalanced at the disease site and prevented from flowing properly. To reestablish health we must bring that energy into equilibrium and harmony. "Healing, in general, is the harmonizing of imbalanced energy fields toward their inherently perfect state of functioning," say the Baers in *Windows of Light.*

When something affects the flow of energy to the cells, the organs begin to die. The body becomes sick. When balanced energy is brought back to the area, new cells will form, rebuilding the organs, and the body gets well. In its simplest form, that's all there is to know about healing.

All the techniques of modern medicine are for the purpose of getting energy to the cells so that they can repair themselves. No doctor or healer can really heal anyone except himself. All anyone can do for someone else is get energy to the cells so they will repair and heal themselves.

We use the amplifying ability of the quartz to give us this extra energy and we direct that energy to the area calling for it. This way we can speed up the healing process and reduce pain naturally rather than rely on pain killers, which can interfere with the healing process.

Pain killers coat the nerve endings so the signal from the cells never gets to the brain. The brain feels no pain, but since it does not know the cells are in trouble, it does not send the energy needed and the condition of the cells worsens. This is one reason why painful diseases are often debilitating. They get progressively worse. Arthritis is a good example.

With the crystal we feed energy to the cells instead of blocking the pain signal. The cells can now repair themselves and then turn off the pain because that signal is no longer needed. This is the natural healing way.

Aura Scan: Crystals are magnificent healing instruments. One healing practice you can do at home is called the aura scan.

Here is how it works: Have your pet lie down on his right side. Hold your crystal lightly between the thumb and the first three fingers. Start at the top of head, holding the crystal about an inch away from the body.

When you feel heat or a tingling sensation, begin to move the crystal slowly over the body.

Be aware of any change—a resistance to your movement, a sense of heat, a tingling sensation, coolness, or simply a feeling that something is there even if you have no physical sensation. When you come to such a change, stop and begin making a circular counter-clockwise motion around the center of the disturbance. Keep making

this motion until you feel the crystal get heavier, pulling your hand down toward the body. Stop the circular motion and touch the tip of the crystal to the body in the center of the circle.

Continue to move the crystal down over the front and sides of the body, making corrections with the counter-clockwise motion whenever you find a difference in the feel of the crystal.

Once you reach the feet and have finished, go back to the top of the head and move the crystal from the head to the foot in a sweeping motion. Imagine your patient has feathers sticking out all over his body and you are smoothing down these feathers. This will align the auric energy pattern into a smooth, even movement.

Turn your pet over and do the left side. When you are completely finished, imagine a zipper at the tail. Reach down and grasp this zipper and pull it all the way to the top of the head. This will close the chakras.

Your pet's whole body will now be in balance. In a short time he should feel rested and stronger; aches and pains and tension will lessen and there will be a sense of well being.

In terms of energy, the reason you could detect the change in the areas needing correction is because this is where there was an imbalance of energy. The pet's body was sending out a pain signal, and you could detect this abnormality in your pet's energy field by using the crystal. The counter-clockwise motion reduces the signal, eventually equalizing the energy flow again, restoring the body by eliminating the disturbance in the distribution of energy. With little or no resistance, the energy can flow more efficiently, making the overall body stronger.

Since aura scanning balances and relaxes the whole body, I use it for preparing a patient for surgery, for chiropractic or massage work, where muscle tension and resistance hinder the healing process, and as part of the therapy in any illness or disease.

Chakras: are energy centers in both people and animals. There are seven major and five minor chakras.[2] They correspond to various areas on the body, beginning with the root chakra in the genital area and progressing upward to the seventh chakra on the top of the head. The heart (fourth) chakra is in the center of the chest and works with the thymus gland which is the seat of the immune system.

Pink rose quartz and citrine quartz work on the emotional body. Natural citrine, in light orange to brown, balances the lower three chakras—the groin, splenic, and solar plexus. This is especially important with pets who suffer liver, kidney and digestive organ illnesses. Green quartz interacts with the endocrine glands to keep the physical body balanced.

Tumbled flat crystals can be used to energize your pet's bed and water bowls. They can be applied in bandages to painful areas of the body.

Crystals are healing and transforming gifts from Nature. They are abundant and easy to acquire. They are energy medicine.

[After Dodd researched the effects of crystals on the body's aura—and recorded them using Kirlian photography (a special medium of photography developed in Russia by a husband and wife team, the Kirlians)—she developed a pet halter based on crystal energy.]

[1]Holistic Animal News, Vol. 3, No. 1, Winter, 1987. Reprinted by permission.
[2]There are differing diagrams of dog and cat chakras, see the first chapter of this book.

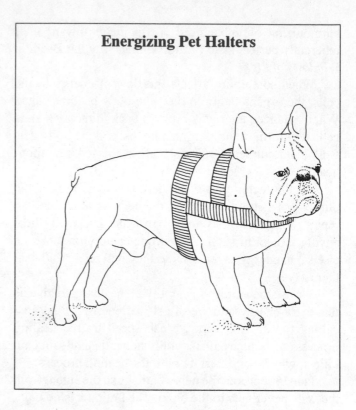

Energizing Pet Halters

Energizing Pet Halters

To balance the body's Electromagnetic Field which stimulates the natural healing mechanisms.

Three energy principles are incorporated into this halter:

(1) Color Therapy: Green is the color vibration that stabilizes the organs of the physical body and acupuncture energy flow.

(2) Quartz Crystal Mandalas: Quartz Crystals have been used for centuries for healing the body due to the unique piezo-electric field force exerted by the crystal. I have found the mandala (crystal symbol) produces the same electrical charging affect on the body's electromagnetic field (EMF) as the stone, according to Kirlian photography and electrical measuring machines (Dermatron) of the acupuncture point energy emissions I have been researching.

(3) Pyramid Configuration Energy: The specific 51°51' angle of a triangle (such as the Great Pyramid at Giza Egypt exerts a powerful electromagnetic field, known for centuries to kill bacteria, increase growth of plant seedlings, sharpen razor blades, etc.)

I've placed the 4 crystal mandalas on the green halter in a double pyramid configuration, worn at the body's heart chakra, with one of the mandala's located at the site of the body's Thymus Gland (one of the immune system glands).

All acupuncture meridians of all the body's organ and tissue systems intersect within the Heart Chakra (one of the 7 major energy centers of the body). Therefore, charging the Heart Chakra and Thymus gland would lead to energizing all the body's organs and immune system, to better physiological health.

Balancing the acupuncture meridians and amplifying the EMF around the toes of the animals by this halter has been verified through Kirlian Photography.

Kirlian photographs

Kirlian photographs of energy fields of acupuncture meridians on the toes (footprints) of dogs and cats follow. Normal or healthy animals compare to the various sick animals before and after wearing the energy halters. Please note the breaks in the aura and the low amplitude of energy of the sick animals' footprints before wearing the halter, and how the halter increased the amplitude and

Canine Distemper Dog-control

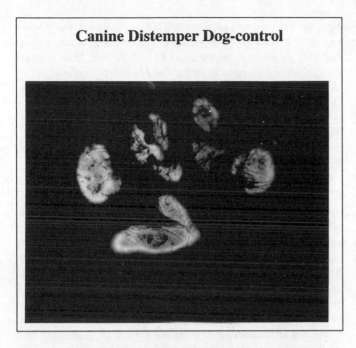

Canine Distemper Dog Wearing Energy Halter Fifteen Minutes

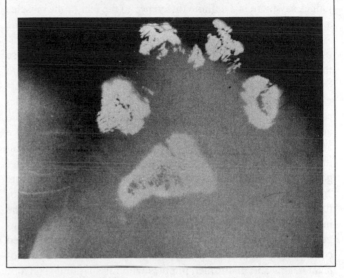

filled in the breaks of the auric fields in the Kirlian photos. This proves the energizing affect of the halter on the body's electromagnetic field, normalizing the energy flow which has been found to stimulate the body's healing mechanisms.

II. Ethoxyquin in Pet Foods: A Letter to the FDA

[The following is a letter summarizing current research submitted by Gloria Dodd, DVM, to the Federal Food and Drug Administration, Division of Animal Feeds, on the subject of the pet food preservative Ethoxyquin.]

August 17, 1992

Dr. David A. Dzanis
Veterinary Nutritionist
Div. of Animal Feeds; FDA
HFV-222
7500 Standish Place
Rockville, MD 20855

Dear Dr. Dzanis;
I am writing to you about the dangers of *Ethoxyquin* used as a preservative in many pet foods and human foods. Since you are responsible for pet food issues within the FDA and will be meeting with two concerned dog breeders next month concerning

the safety of this chemical, I wish to present my own experiences and knowledge of *Ethoxyquin's* toxic affects, first hand.

First of all, let me introduce myself; I am a veterinarian, a graduate from the University of California Veterinary Medical School, Davis, California, class of 1960. I had a small animal practice in San Ramon, California (a rapidly growing area east of San Francisco) for 31 years and am now retired. During those many years I saw a change emerging in the disease and illness of animals presented to me. In the early 1960s, our concerns were primarily those of infectious agents causing Canine Distemper, Feline Distemper, Hepatitis, Leptospirosis, staph and strep infections, etc.

However during the 1970s and to the present time we are seeing an epidemic of chronic degenerative diseases. True, the widely accepted program of preventative vaccination programs virtually wiped out the viral caused diseases and antibiotics helped stem the bacterial infections, but something else is operative here. We are now seeing both in the animal and human populations, a sharing of chronic degenerative diseases such as generalized allergies, arthritis, dermatitis, congestive heart failure, kidney failure, liver pathologies, diabetes, AIDS, tumors and cancer. Also, lifespans of animals have shortened during this period.

I remember, as a kid growing up in Nevada seeing Basque sheepherders with working dogs living to be 20–25 years of age. These dogs were still herding sheep at that age, and the bitches were delivering litters of healthy puppies at 20 years of age! Today, we are lucky to find dogs living to be 10 years old, and many of these suffering from various forms of chronic degenerative disease. Of course in the 1940s our air, water and food was clean and virtually free of chemicals. My shepherd friend's dogs worked in clean air, ate fresh lamb stew and vegetables and home-baked bread along with his master. As a dog show veterinarian I have heard many judges say there is a definite difference to the feel of the muscles and skeleton of dogs in Australia than those of America. The Australian dogs' muscles are firm, bones firm and strong compared to the "mushy" feel of the American dogs. Why? Because these animals' diets are vastly different. The Australian dogs were being fed (until recently—now there is an emergence of commercial pet food) trimmings from the freshly killed beef and sheep carcasses, vegetables and fresh grains, ours on commercial kibble and canned dog food with every chemical residue and preservative and coloring in the book! And forget all the highly touted advertising and P.R. by the pet food industry—I say put garbage in—get garbage out! In the good old days, the family pet ate from the same "pot" so to speak, as the owner/family did, and were healthier for it. Not only are chronic degenerative diseases of pets on the increase, but breeders complain of increasing frequency and numbers of reproductive problems: irregular estrus cycles, missed conceptions, stillborns, "fading puppy" syndrome, increased neonatal deaths and malformed puppies with missing limbs, organs, hydrocephalus, cleft palates, etc.

Historically, I was first alerted to *Ethoxyquin's* (heretofore being referred to as "E") possible health hazard to dogs, when Midge Harmer, a breeder of German Shepherd show and obedience dogs in Newark, Delaware contacted me on February 12, 1988. She related her heartbreaking experience of losing four of her young champions to liver cancer. Since she had changed nothing in her program of rearing these dogs except switching their diet to feeding ANF (Advanced Nutritional Formula), she looked into the ingredients and found "E" as a preservative. She asked me if I had any experience with this preservative and its affect on animal health. Thus started a four-year quest into finding out all we could on this chemical. I hadn't any known knowledge about "E" or its related toxic affects to animal health until I started looking into it. I next met a breeder at the Golden Gate Dog Show in San Francisco that same year. She told me of suddenly developing 82% mortality in her puppies (Min. Pinchers, and Boston Terriers). Out of 27 puppies born she was lucky to save 5. Many others were stillborn and malformed with cleft palates, and hydrocephalus. These problems were atypical. She had not changed any variables (including breeding stock) except for changing the diet to ANF because of the highly favorable advertising put out by the manufacturers.

I contacted the Dept. of Agriculture for toxicology information on "E." They sent me a copy from their Farm Chemical Handbook listing "E" as a pesticide, used in fruit scald control. It is also used as a rubber preservative. I have since learned "E" is FDA approved for use as an antioxidant for carotenes vitamin A and E and the prevention of the development of organic peroxides. It is approved at 150 ppm in paprika and chili powder, and

because it is used as a preservative in livestock feed, the following residue allowances in human consumed animal products as follows: 5 ppm in or on the uncooked fat of meat from animals except poultry; 3 ppm in or on the uncooked liver and fat of poultry, 0.5 ppm in or on the uncooked muscle meat of animals, 0.5 ppm in poultry eggs, and zero in milk.

We have learned "E" is used as a preservative in such widely marketed dog foods as ANF, Eagle Dog Food, NutriMax, Hills Prescription Diet W/D (sold in vet hospitals!), Nutro, Purina, IAMS, Royal Canine USA; and in livestock feeds by Willowbrook Mills in Petaluma to preserve Lay Crumbles for laying chickens, and dehydrated forage crops of alfalfa, barley, clovers, corn, oats, wheat, fescue and various grasses. The above information brings up the question why the FDA allows such a small amount of "E" residue (5 to .5 ppm) in human consumed foods yet allows such high amounts (150 ppm) to be used in petfood and livestock feeds? In the case of the dog, pound for pound, a dog weighs 1/5 to 1/10th the weight of a human (except for giant breeds of dogs) yet is consuming 300 times more "E" than allowed for people. Also many dog food manufacturers are not listing "E" as an ingredient on the packaging. Only under much investigation will they admit it. Isn't there an FDA regulation about labeling ingredients? Truth in labeling is another issue—ANF, which incidentally is one of the *most* expensive dog foods, is touted by the manufacturer as an *"all natural formula"* with no preservatives, yet lists "E" as an antioxidant which they claim to be quite safe.

Correspondence with various people revealed other dog owners/breeders having sad experiences with pets eating "E" preserved dog food:

1. A breeder of Rottweilers lost a dog with liver cancer after switching to feeding ANF for 6 months.

2. A German Shepherd breeder lost a stud dog to cancer of the mouth, feeding dog food containing "E."

3. A woman had skin allergies develop in her German Shepherd fed on NutroMax ("E" preserved) and then switched to Solid Gold (no "E") with the dermatitis allergy disappearing.

4. Dr. Pia Peters, Ph.D. claims that when she was studying in Ireland for her degree in agriculture (1983–84) she became interested in a news story relating that farmers in Italy suddenly had calves born with eyes on the backs of their heads, no ears, two or three legs only, or legs developing turned backwards, etc. Dr. Peters claims the culprit was "E" in the animal feed fed to the breeding stock.

5. A breeder first of Poodles, then Collies, had been free of whelping problems; her bitches came into estrus every 6 months "like clockwork," and all whelped normal healthy litters, then a

few years ago she began noticing changes in the dogs' overall appearance. She was now seeing dry, lustreless coats, flaky skin, and nose pigmentation fading. A friend of hers who raises Labradors, Newfoundlands, Collies, and Old English Sheep dogs, had similar problems. Then Elaine's Blue Merle stud dog (sire of all her dogs) began drooling and bleeding from the mouth. From a biopsy, her veterinarian diagnosed an immune breakdown triggered by a virus or chemical. Her bitches who had not previously come into estrus were now delivering litters of malformed puppies; two were born without legs, tails or any sex organs. the problems in these two kennels were traced to a change in diet fed the dogs, from one free of "E" preservative to a dog food with "E" preservative.

6. Another German Shepherd breeder in Pennsylvania lost a puppy fed Pro Plan ("E" preserved) to a fast growing cancer in both hips.

Some of the damning information on "E" comes from Monsanto's own cautionary warnings in using and handling this product. They warn that it may cause allergic skin reactions, irritation to the eyes and skin. They advise that workers must wear eye and respiratory protection. The container of "E" has a very prominent skull and crossbones with POISON written in capital letters. "E" is listed and identified as a hazardous chemical under the criteria of the Osha Hazard Communication Standard (29 CFR 1910, 1220). Monsanto further states the disclaimer regarding the use of "E," that "Although the information and recommendations set forth herein are presented in good faith . . . Monsanto Company makes no representations as to the *completeness* or *accuracy* thereof. Information supplied upon the condition that the persons receiving same will *make their own determination* as to its suitability for their purposes prior to use. Monsanto will not be responsible for damages of any nature whatsoever resulting from the use of or reliance upon information." If the company who makes it won't stand behind it, how can the general public accept its safety as a preservative for their pets' food and directly for themselves (and indirectly as residues in human consumptive food products from "E's" use in livestock feed?)

I further learned from the Chemical Toxicology of Commercial Products (Ref. Gosselin et al., 1984) that "E" has a toxic rating of 3 (on a scale of 1–6, with 6 being super toxic requiring less than 7 drops to produce death), slowly developing depression, convulsions, coma and death; skin irritation and liver damage.

I wrote a letter to my Board of Examiners in Veterinary Medicine, expressing my concern about the safety of feeding dogs foods with "E" as a preservative. I urged them to look into the matter and suggested that with such information wouldn't it be prudent to recommend to the FDA to ban "E" as a preservative until more definite safety studies be made? The Board responded that I was "overreacting" without scientific proven evidence that the food is the cause of problems cited and that I "refrain from voicing my opinions until there is proven scientific and official evidence that those opinions are true." The Board was complacent with the FDA approval of "E" based on a five-year safety study done on dogs by Monsanto some 30 plus years ago. That study, I found was grossly incompetent.

Let me tell you about what I learned about this so-called "scientific" study by Monsanto. The study is fraught with incompetent, slip-shod methods, and erroneous conclusions that by today's standards of testing would be laughed out of the room. For example, there were never any truly controlled studies on these dogs with the only variable being the feeding or not feeding of "E" and then evaluating the health results. Instead, bitches were kept with males, some dogs were kept indoors, others outdoors, there was no preventative care of vaccination and parasite control so all dogs could start equally—many dogs in the study succumbed to Canine Distemper, Hepatitis and one from Heartworm. Many showed heavy parasite infestations, and fight wounds, etc. "E" was fed on a one time a day, 5 days a week basis instead of twice daily 7 days a week which is routinely done in the "real world" by dog owners. Of the 67 puppies who were unfortunate enough to be born during this 5 year study, 32 puppies died. That's a 50% mortality rate! The "scientists" claimed the deaths were due to "under developed and weak puppies"! Isn't that exactly what we are seeing in litters from breeding stock fed dog food preserved with "E"? To my knowledge nothing was reported in the study of the appearance of coat, pigmentation of the nose, skin health, etc. Changes like these would be an early indicator of liver and immune system pathology. Another discrepancy is the lowered frequency of feedings and relatively short time of the study (5 years vs. 6 or more years of feeding "E" preserved food and seeing cancer developing.) Nothing, to my knowledge, was reported in the study of the nature of the reproductive cycles in the bitches; numbers of missed or irregular estrus, sterility) as we are seeing clinically. Was any blood work done? Liver and thyroid panels? I believe not. I believe it is highly *unethical* for self serving employees to be the scientists in charge of evaluating a product's safety manufactured by the company who pays their salaries! I would like the FDA to foster safety studies on products by independent testers other than the manufacturer of the product. Perhaps such a plan could be funded by a safety study "fee" levied on the manufacturer who is applying for FDA approval of their product. These monies could then be paid directly by the FDA to the independent testers, thus minimizing possible bias in the report findings.

While we're on the subject of product safety studies using live animals I *must* voice a deeply felt objection to the use of live animals in any research study. It has been proven many times that there are viable alternatives to live animal models, i.e., computer model software, tissue culture and embryo studies. Why not use the tissue cultures of the target organs affected by chemicals? These as you know are the brain, nervous system, endocrine glands (pituitary, adrenal, testes and ovaries, thyroid, thymus, pancreas, etc.) as well as those of the immune system (spleen, liver, lymph nodes, bone marrow, etc.), and are the most acutely sensitive to any toxic substance or radiation. This is where pathology starts *immediately*. It's months or years later before the whole organism shows signs of illness. I firmly believe all animals were created equal with man by our Creator, and that the Animal Kingdom has given its silent permission to man to provide him with sustenance, creature comfort, transportation, as beasts of burden and in the case of our pet animals, their unconditional *love*. Is this how we repay them? Dr. Dzanis, both you and I have a covenant with the Animal Kingdom from the day we graduated from Vet School and took the Hippocratic Oath. We solemnly swore to safeguard the health and well being of all animals and to n*ever* do anything to harm them. I have kept my promise, as I am sure you are keeping yours, but it would do well for all mankind to take and uphold that oath—in today's growing moral bankruptcy, people are too willing to turn a blind eye and squeeze every cent out of a transaction at any costs. Perhaps we should rename it the "Hypocritical Oath"?

III. Aluminum Toxicity

Plants not only take up minerals but heavy metals in the soil as well. If these levels are at toxic levels, the health of the animals and people are at jeopardy. I had a serendipity event happen with my 19-year-old black cat Sambo that led me to 6 years of intensive testing of every pet food, bottled water variety, and some food for humans that was being routinely fed to animals in the home and in vet hospitals. I began to notice Sambo's glossy black coat was turning to a dry grey. I had been feeding home prepared meals but had switched to the heavily touted holistic Cornucopia brand of cat kibble and canned food.

It was at this time that I was beginning to use hair analysis of ill animals to give me information on the ratios of electrolyte and mineral balances in the body. I took some of Sambo's hair and sent it to Analytical Research Labs in Phoenix, Arizona. They analyze samples by the very most critical methods of atomic absorption. Flame photometry is not as exacting, although more commonly used in other hair/food/water analytical labs. From Sambo's deranged mineral levels Dr. Eck decided to run a heavy metal screening on his hair. The heavy metal panel consists of lead, mercury, cadmium and the mineral aluminum which at high levels is toxic just like the heavy metals are. Dr. Eck found toxic levels of lead and mercury

but *extremely* high levels of aluminum (45 ppm whereas .05 ppm is allowable or at tolerable levels in man).

Dr. Eck called me personally on the phone from Phoenix to ask if this cat was still alive, for he had never seen such high amounts of aluminum before—either in man or animal. I said he was still alive and was puzzled as to the source of this aluminum. He suggested I test the food and water. The Cornucopia Stars (dry food) was in the several hundreds ppm (ppm = parts per million) and was several 1000 times more than the allowable in food for people. And this was a little 9 pound cat. I treated Sambo with the homeopathic nosodes *Mercury, Cadmium* and *Aluminum* metallicum and he recovered.

Aluminum is omnipresent—not only from man's conscious addition of it in our food and water chain (in baking powder, as a dehydrant as aluminum oxide to prevent caking in packaging, in aluminum cans, cookware, and the public health's common use of it to precipitate solids in our drinking water as part of their purification system), but the most serious contamination comes from the acid rain falling on earth's soil. Aluminum is a mineral that makes up 30% of the earth's crust as serpentine rock. It is held in a molecularly bound state but is released to a free ion with acid rain. The aluminum ion is then freely taken up by roots of plants grown in that soil, or filters down into the subterranean waters and then contaminates wells, streams etc. Aluminum has a predilection for the nervous system: the brain, and systemic nerve ganglia that innervate every organ in the body; chronic degenerative changes in all organ systems ensue as well as neurological behavioral changes.

Every sick animal I tested on the Dermatron and included a hair analysis had aluminum at toxic levels. I documented 28 cases of sick dogs and cats, the studies of which were very well done, even with supportive orthodox tests (blood, urine, etc. lab tests) hair analysis results, food testing and clinical records. I sent these to the FDA and the head veterinarian of Animal Health and Public Health at the National Institutes of Health in Bethesda, Maryland. I never heard until I persisted with phone calls and letters. Finally they said they "were looking into it." They gave me this response every year for 4 years until I just gave up in disgust.

Aluminum is a very serious cause of chronic degenerative disease and has been implicated as one of the factors in mental illness (paranoia, schizophrenia) and learning disabilities. They have even found aluminum nodules in the brains of Alzheimer patients, at necropsy.

Aluminum lowers blood estrogen levels. It also competes with calcium in the body. I've since found it prevents hydrochloric acid production by the stomach's cells in carnivores (and man) thus producing improper digestion or metabolism of the proteins in the early stages of digestion. I found it in Gerber's baby food (veal, chicken and beef), Starkist Tuna, every dog and cat food on the market in 1985—the kibbled form was the worst because of the mechanics of drying the food— the aluminum content increases over that of wet or canned food. Many of the spring or drinking water sources in California all had Aluminum at varying levels and it differed with the time of year too—during the summer it increased (water underground is more concentrated during the dry times of the year). The symptomatology of chronic aluminum toxicity in the animals I saw were those similar for chronic chemical toxicity (especially the pesticide/herbicide/fungicide group).

Central nervous system symptoms: aberrant behavior, chewing wall boards and door knobs and trying to catch imaginary objects in the air, and aggressive, violent behavior. Many animals were switched into vagatonia (overriding of the parasympathetic nervous system to the sympathetic system).

Suppressed immune systems: chronic dermatitis, coryza and nasal discharges (and loss of black pigment on the nose pad).

Endocrine gland dysfunctions: hypothyroidism, hyperactivity of the parathyroid due to the lowered calcium levels of the body, adrenal hyperfunction at first then progressed to adrenal hypofunction as continued chemical stress influenced the medulla of the adrenals, hypoglycemia, diabetes, lack of pancreatic digestion enzymes, lowered stomach HCl (needed for protein digestion) resulted in signs of poor nutrition (dry, lustreless hair coat, skin dry and flaky) increased intestinal fermentation, constipation and dehydration, low grade fevers, liver, kidney and heart pathologies. Blood tests showed increased BUN and creatinine (kidney damage), decreased platelets in the circulating blood (for blood clotting) and elevated cholesterol levels (liver, pancreas damage). To even begin to treat these animals, I had to change the diet to home made and *detoxified,* for I found the grains, meat, oils, kelp and bone meal supplements were all contaminated with chemicals and heavy metals. I advise Dr. Parcell's method of detoxification of fresh foodstuffs by soaking in dilute clorox (1/2 tsp. per gallon of water) solution for 20 to 45 minutes as needed (dowse with pendulum or do muscle testing) until cleared, then rinsing in bottled water. I also used the corresponding homeopathic nosode of *Aluminum, Lead, Mercury,* etc. as well as other holistic supportive treatment and orthomolecular medicine, of vitamin mineral balancing (hair analysis results were invaluable here). Once the animals had the aluminum (and other chemicals) chelated out of their systems with the nosodes and the electrolyte/mineral balanced, they began to recover and did very well as long as a strict detox. diet was followed.

Resources

Ellon Bach USA, Inc.
644 Merrick Rd.
Lynbrook, NY 11563
1-800-433-7523
Bach Flower Remedies

Holistic Animal Consulting Center
29 Lyman Avenue
Staten Island, NY 10305
Barbara Meyers (718) 720-5548
Bach Flower Remedies/Grief Counseling

Newton Laboratories
P.O. Box 936
Lithonia, GA 30058
(404) 922-2644, 1-800-448-7256
Homeopathic Combination Line for Dogs, Cats, Horses

American Holistic Veterinary Medical Association
2214 Old Emmorton Rd.
Bel Air, MD 21014
(301) 838-7778
Referrals and Information

International Veterinary Acupuncture Society
Merdith Snader, VMD
2140 Conestoga Rd.
Chester Springs, PA 19425
(215) 827-7245
Referrals and Information

Analytical Research Labs
8650 N. 22nd Avenue
Phoenix, AZ 85021
1-800-528-4067.
Heavy metal analysis, mineral analysis

Dr. Goodpet Laboratories
P.O. Box 4489
Inglewood, CA 90309
(213) 672-3269, 1-800-222-9932
Homeopathics and vitamins

Noah's Park
13600 Wright Circle
Tampa, FL 33626
1-800-842-6624
Natural pet foods and products
Mail Order

Natural Life Pet Products
12975 16th Ave. N. Suite 100
Minneapolis, MN 55441-4531
1-800-367-2391
Natural Pet Foods

Nutro Products, Inc.
445 Wilson Way
City of Industry, CA 91744
(818) 968-0532
Natural Pet Foods (but uses ethoxyquin)

Solid Gold
1483 N. Coyamaca
El Cajon, CA 92020
(619) 465-9507
Natural Pet Foods and Products

National Center for Homeopathy
801 N. Fairfax St., Suite 306
Alexandria, VA 22314
(703) 548-7790
Homeopathy Referrals, Books

Institute for Traditional Medicine
2017 E. Hawthorne
Portland, OR 97214
1-800-544-7504
Chinese Herbs, Books

Beckett's Apothecary
1004 Chester Pike
Sharon Hill, PA 19079
1-800-727-8188
Homeopathic Remedies
Mail Order

Coyote Moon Herbs
Teresa Finkbeiner, MH
P.O. Box 312
Gainesville, FL 32602
(904) 377-0765
Herbs, Mail Order

Frontier Cooperative Herbs
P.O. Box 69
Norway, CA 52318

PetGuard, Inc.
P.O. Box 728
Orange Park, FL 32073
(904) 264-8500, 1-800-874-3221
Natural pet foods and Products
Call for free catalog

Wow-Bow Distributors
309 Burr Rd.
Northport, NY 11731
(516) 499-8572
Natural pet foods, supplements and products
Free catalog

Eco Safe Products
P.O. Box 1177
St. Augustine, FL 32085
1-800-274-7387
Herbal Products and Flea Products

All the Best
8047 Lake City Way
Seattle, WA 98115
1-800-962-8266
Natural pet foods, supplements, homeopathics, supplies

Cornucopia Products
Veterinary Nutritional Associates
229 Wall St.
Huntington, NY 11743
(516) 427-7479
Nonallergic Petfoods

Critter Oil
The SuDi Company
P.O. Box 12767
St. Petersburg, FL 33733
(813) 327-2356
Natural Flea-Rid Products, Pet Foods, Supplements, Supplies

Amrita Herbal Products
Rt. 1, Box 737
Floyd, VA 24091
(703) 745-3474
Herb Tinctures and Salves

Flower Essence Society
P.O. Box 459
Nevada City, CA 95959
1-800-548-0075
Flower Essences, Aromatherapy, Books

Standard Homeopathic Co.
P.O. Box 61067
Los Angeles, CA 90061
(310) 321-4284, 1-800-624-9659
Homeopathic Remedies and Books

Felix Co.
3623 Fremont Ave. N.
Seattle, WA 98103
(206) 547-0042
Cat-Care Products

California Holistic Veterinary Medical Association
c/o Beth Wildermann, DVM
17333 Bear Creek Rd.
Boulder Creek, CA 95006

Dr. Joanne Stefanatos, DVM
1325 Vegas Valley Dr.
Las Vegas, NV 89109
(702) 735-7184
Holistic Pet Care Video

Delta Society
P.O. Box 1080
Renton, WA 95057
(206) 226-7357
National Directory of Grief Counselors, Books on Grief, etc.

The Grief Recovery Hot Line
Grief Recovery Institute
1-800-445-4808
Monday–Friday 12 to 8 PM EDT

Perelandra Flower Essences
P.O. Box 3603
Warrenton, VA 22186
(703) 937-2153 Machine
Flower Essences, Books by Machaelle Small Wright

Natural Sales Company
P.O. Box 25
Pittsburgh, PA 15230
(412) 288-4600
Eucalyptus Honey for Cataracts

Morill's New Directions
P.O. Box 30
Orient, ME 04471
1-800-368-5057
Natural Pet Care Products

Boericke and Tafel
1011 Arch St.
Philadelphia, PA 19107
1-800-272-2820
Homeopathic Pharmacy, Mail Order Homeopathics

Pegasus Products Inc.
P.O. Box 228
Boulder, CO 80306
1-800-527-6104
Flower and Gemstone Essences

Gurudas
P.O. Box 868
San Rafael, CA 94915
Flower Essences, Gem Elixirs, Books

Laurel Steinhice
6712 Currywood Dr.
Nashville, TN 37205
(615) 356-4280
Channeling, Psychic Work

Marion Webb-Former
340 The Circle
Queen Elizabeth St.
London SE1 2ND
England
Channeling, Psychic Work

Dr. Gary Glum
Silent Walker Publishing
P.O. Box 92856
Los Angeles, CA 90009
(310) 271-9931
Essiac Herb Formula

Davida Johns
St. Petersburg, FL
(813) 521-3829
Feminist Photographer

Gloria Dodd, DVM
Everglo Ranch
P.O. Box 1242
Gualala, CA 95445
Audio-Tape Cassettes—$8.95 + $1.00 postage
For Pet Owner and Veterinarian
Note: Dr. Dodd is no longer in practice and cannot offer
consultations or advice.

Practitioners

Barbara Meyers
Holistic Animal Consulting Center
29 Lyman Ave.
Staten Island, NY 10305
(718) 720-5548
Grief Counseling, Bach Flower Remedies

Mary Ryan
Certified Bach Counselor
Lantana, FL 33462
(407) 588-5382

Mary Ann Simonds
Wisdom Stone Farms
17101 N.E. 40th Ave.
Vancouver, WA 98686
(206) 573-1958
Natural Healing, Consulting

Joanne Stefanatos, DVM
1325 Vegas Valley Dr.
Las Vegas, NV 89109
(702) 735-7184
Holistic Veterinarian, Video on Holistics and Pets

Ann Lampru, DVM
3816 W. Humphrey
Tampa, FL 33614
(813) 933-6609
Veterinary Acupuncture

John Fudens, DVM
29296 US Hwy 19 N.
Clearwater, FL 34621
(813) 787-6010, (813) 787-2960
Holistic Veterinarian

Sheldon Altman, DVM
2723 W. Olive Ave.
Burbank, CA 91505
(818) 845-7246
Veterinary Acupuncture

Linda Tellington-Jones
P.O. Box 3793
Santa Fe, NM 87501-0793
1-800-854-TEAM

Bibliography

Altman, Sheldon, DVM. *An Introduction to Acupuncture for Animals*. Monterey Park, CA: Chan's Corporation, 1981.

American Animal Hospital Association. "Pet Loss and Bereavement: The Loss of Your Pet." Denver, CO: AAHA, 1989. Pamphlet.

Anderson, Robert, DVM and Barbara Wrede. *Caring for Older Cats and Dogs*. Charlotte, VT: Williamson Publishing Co., 1990.

Arnold, Larry and Sandy Nevius. *The Reiki Handbook: A Manual for Students and Therapists of the Usui Shiko Ryoho System of Healing*. Harrisburg, PA: PSI Press, 1982.

Austen, Hallie Iglehart. *The Heart of the Goddess: Art, Myth and Meditations of the World's Sacred Feminine*. Berkeley, CA: The Wingbow Press, 1990.

Bach Centre USA. "The Bach Flower Remedies." Woodmere, NY: Bach Center USA, 1983. Pamphlet.

Balch, James F., MD and Phyllis A. Balch, CNC. *Prescription for Nutritional Healing*. Garden City Park, NY: Avery Publishing Group, 1990.

Belfield, Wendell O., DVM and Martin Zucker. *The Very Healthy Cat Book: A Vitamin & Mineral Program for Optional Feline Health*. New York: McGraw Hill Book Co., 1983.

Belfield, Wendell O., DVM and Martin Zucker. *How to Have a Healthier Dog: The Benefits of Vitamins and Minerals for Your Dog's Life Cycles*. New York: New American Library, 1981.

Bethel, May. *The Healing Power of Herbs*. N. Hollywood, CA: Wilshire Book Co., 1968.

Boericke, William, M.D. *Pocket Manual of Homeopathic Materia Medica*. New Delhi, India: Jain Publishers Pvt., Ltd., 1987.

Carlson, Delbert G., DVM and James M. Giffin, MD. *Dog Owner's Home Veterinary Handbook*. New York: Howell Book House, 1986.

Chaltin, Luc, N.D. *The Homeopathic Treatment of Common Ailments*. Lithonia, GA: SANUS, undated.

Chicago, Judy. *The Dinner Party: A Symbol of Our Heritage*. New York: Doubleday Books, 1979.

Church, Julie Adams. *Joy In a Wooly Coat: Living With, Loving, and Letting Go of Treasured Animal Friends*. Tiburon, CA: H.J. Kramer, Inc., 1988.

Cummings, Stephen, FNP and Dana Ullman, MPH. *Everybody's Guide to Homeopathic Medicine*. Los Angeles, CA: J.P. Tarcher, Inc., 1984.

Dodds, W. Jean, DVM. "Nutritional Approach Can Help Enhance Immune Competence." In *DVM: The Newsmagazine of Veterinary Medicine* (Vol. 22, no. 4), April, 1991. Reprint.

Dunbar, Ian, Ph.D., Bs.C., B. Vet. Med., MRCVS. *Dog Behavior: Why Dogs Do What They Do*. Neptune, NJ: TFH Publications, Inc., 1979.

Ellon Bach USA, Inc. "Animals and the Bach Remedies." Lynbrook, NY: Ellon Bach USA, Inc., 1990. Pamphlet.

Fireman, Judy, Ed. *Cat Catalog: The Ultimate Cat Book*. New York: Workman Publishing Co., 1976.

Fox, Dr. Michael W. *The Healing Touch*. New York: Newmarket Press, 1990.

Fox, Dr. Michael W. *Understanding Your Cat*. New York: St. Martin's Press, 1974.

Fox, Dr. Michael W. *Understanding Your Dog*. New York: St. Martin's Press, 1972.

Frazier, Anitra with Norma Eckroate. *The New Natural Cat: A Complete Guide for Finicky Owners*. New York: Plume Books, 1990.

Garfield, Leah Maggie and Jack Grant. *Companions In Spirit*. Berkeley, CA: Celestial Arts Press, 1984.

George, Jean Craighead. *How to Talk to Your Cat*. New York: Warner Books, 1985.

George, Jean Craighead. *How to Talk to Your Dog*. New York: Warner Books, 1985.

Getty, Robert, DVM, Ph.D. *The Anatomy of the Domestic Animals*. Philadelphia, PA: W.B. Saunders Co., 1975.

Griffin, Susan. *Woman and Nature: The Roaring Inside Her*. San Francisco, CA: Harper and Row Publishers, 1978.

Griffin, Susan R. *Winning the Flea War Naturally . . . Without Toxins*. St. Petersburg, FL: The SuDi Co., 1990.

Gurudas. *Flower Essences and Vibrational Healing*. San Rafael, CA: Cassandra Press, 1983.

Gustafson, Mickie. *Losing Your Dog: Coping with Grief When a Pet Dies*. New York: Bergh Publishing, Inc., 1992.

Harper, Joan. *The Healthy Cat and Dog Cookbook*. Richland Center, WI: Pet Press, 1988.

Hay, Louise. *You Can Heal Your Life*. Santa Monica, CA: Hay House, 1984.

Hunter, Francis, MRCVS. *Homeopathic First-Aid Treatment for Pets*. Great Britain: Thorsen's Publishers, Ltd., 1984.

Johnson, Buffie. *Lady of the Beasts: Ancient Images of the Goddess and Her Sacred Animals*. San Francisco, CA: Harper and Row Publishers, 1988.

Jones, Rebecca. "Animal Tamer." In *The Rocky Mountain News*, April 9, 1992, p. 71.

Kaminski, Patricia and Richard Katz. *Flower Essence Repertory: A Comprehensive Selection Guide for the Natural Health Practitioner*. Nevada City, CA: Flower Essence Society, 1992.

Kapel, Priscilla. *The Body Says Yes: Muscle Testing Tunes in to Your Body's Needs*. San Diego, CA: ACS Publications, 1981.

Kaptchuk, Ted J., OMD. *The Web That Has No Weaver.* New York: Congdon and Weed, Inc., 1983.

Kilbourne, Cheryl A. *For the Love of Princess: Surviving the Loss of Your Pet.* Beaverton, OR: Princess Publishing, 1987.

Klide, Alan M., VMD and Shiu H. Kung, Ph.D. *Veterinary Acupuncture.* Philadelphia, PA: University of Pennsylvania Press, 1977.

Kubler-Ross, Elisabeth. *On Death and Dying.* New York: MacMillan Book Co., 1969.

Lazarus, Pat. *Keep Your Pet Healthy the Natural Way.* New Canaan, CT: Keats Publishing, Inc., 1983.

Liedloff, Jean. "Babes in Arms: Why Infants Need to Be Held." In *Natural Health Magazine,* July–August 1992, pp. 46–49.

Juliette de Bairacli Levy. *The Complete Herbal Handbook for the Dog and Cat.* London and Boston: Faber and Faber Ltd., 1991. (First Published, 1955).

Macleod, George, MRCVS, DVSM. *Cats: Homeopathic Remedies.* Essex, England: C.W. Daniel Co., Ltd., 1990.

Macleod, George, MRCVS, DVSM. *Dogs: Homeopathic Remedies.* Essex, England: C.W. Daniel Co., Ltd., 1983.

Macleod, George, MRCVS, DVSM. *A Veterinary Materia Medica and Clinical Repertory with a Materia Medica of the Nosodes.* Essex, England: C.W. Daniel Co., Ltd., 1983.

Macleod, George, MRCVS, DVSM. *Homeopathy for Pets.* London, England: Wigmore Publications Ltd., 1981.

Murchland, Karen. "New Frontiers in Pet Treatments." In *Massage Magazine,* June–July, 1989, pp. 26–28.

Nelson, Wendy L. "When Your Best Friend Dies." In *CatFancy Magazine,* March, 1992, pp. 36–39.

Pitcairn, Richard H., DVM, Ph.D. and Susan Hubble Pitcairn. *Dr. Pitcairn's Complete Guide to Natural Health for Dogs and Cats.* Emmaus, PA: Rodale Press, 1982.

Plechner, Alfred J., DVM and Martin Zucker. *Pet Allergies: Remedies for an Epidemic.* Inglewood, CA: Very Healthy Enterprises, 1986.

Raphaell, Katrina. *The Crystalline Transmission: A Synthesis of Light.* Santa Fe, NM: Aurora Press, 1990.

Rosenberg, Marc, FMD. "Death of the Family Pet: Losing a Family Friend." Lehigh Valley, PA: ALPO Petfoods, Inc., 1992. Pamphlet.

Sams, Jamie and David Carson. *Medicine Cards: The Discovery of Power Through the Ways of Animals.* Santa Fe, NM: Bear and Co., 1988.

Sheppard, K. *The Treatment of Dogs by Homeopathy.* Essex, England: C.W. Daniel Co., Ltd., 1972.

Shul, Bill D. *Animal Immortality: Pets and Their Afterlife.* New York: Carroll and Graf Publishers, Inc., 1990.

Simonds, Mary Ann. "Essences for Animal Care." Nevada City, CA: Flower Essence Society, 1989. Pamphlet.

Smith, Penelope. *Animal Talk: Interspecies Telepathic Communication.* Point Reyes Station, CA: Pegasus Publications, 1989.

Stein, Diane. *The Natural Remedy Book for Women.* Freedom, CA: The Crossing Press, 1992.

Stein, Diane. *Dreaming the Past, Dreaming the Future: A Herstory of the Earth.* Freedom, CA: The Crossing Press, 1991.

Stein, Diane. *All Women Are Healers.* Freedom, CA: The Crossing Press, 1990.

Stein, Diane. *Casting the Circle: A Women's Book of Ritual.* Freedom, CA: The Crossing Press, 1990.

Stein, Diane. *Stroking the Python: Women's Psychic Lives.* Freedom, CA: The Crossing Press, 1988.

Stein, Diane. *The Women's Book of Healing.* Freedom, CA: The Crossing Press, 1987.

Tellington-Jones, Linda with Sybil Taylor. *The Tellington TTouch: A Breakthrough Technique to Train and Care for Your Favorite Animal.* New York: Viking Press, 1992.

Tellington-Jones with Ursula Bruns. *An Introduction to the Tellington-Jones Equine Awareness Method.* New York: Breakthrough Publications, 1988.

Tiekert, Carvel, DVM. "An Overview of Holistic Medicine." Handout of the American Holistic Veterinary Association, undated pamphlet.

Ullman, Dana. *Homeopathy: Medicine for the 21st Century.* Berkeley, CA: N. Atlantic Books, 1988.

Uridel, Faith A. "Alternative Therapies." In *DogFancy,* March, 1992, pp. 40–46.

U.S. Department of Commerce, Bureau of the Census. *Statistical Abstracts of the United States, 1991.* Washington, DC: U.S. Government Printing Office, 1991.

West, Ouida, M.Th. *The Magic of Massage.* New York: Putnam Publishing Co., 1983.

Witkowsky. "Tiny Circles on the Skin," In *American Way Magazine* (Vol. 24, no. 20), October 15, 1991, pp. 56–62.

Wright, Machaelle Small. *M.A.P.: The Co-Creative White Brotherhood Medical Assistance Program.* Jeffersonton, VA: Perelandra Ltd., 1990.

Wright, Machaelle Small. *Flower Essences: Reordering Our Understanding and Approach to Illness and Health.* Jeffersonton, VA: Perelandra Ltd., 1988.

Wright, Machaelle Small. *Behaving As If the God in All Life Mattered.* Jeffersonton, VA: Perelandra Ltd., 1987.

Wright, Michael and Sally Walters, Eds. *The Book of the Cat.* New York: Summit Books, 1980.

Index

A

acupressure/acupuncture, 11, 21, 66, 70, 82, 101-125, 128, 153, 170, 173, 174
    meridians, 21, 104, 105, 106, 173
    see also massage
AIDS, 12, 60, 61, 62, 68, 152, 153, 160, 177
allergies, 10, 51, 52, 55, 62, 64, 66, 76, 78, 88, 92, 102, 120, 128, 152, 153, 156, 177
Altman, Sheldon, 106, 107-109, 121
    Introduction to Veterinary Acupuncture, 106, 107-109, 121
aluminum toxicity, 1, 62, 67, 93, 180-181
Alzheimer's Dis-ease, 1, 169, 181
anatomy, 13-32
anemia, 52, 64, 65
Anubis, 8
arthritis, 10, 40, 52, 60, 62, 64, 65, 66-67, 71, 73, 78, 89, 92, 102, 120, 124, 132, 152, 153, 156, 159, 175, 177
artificial flavorings, 52
aura, 12, 21, 23, 24, 25, 42, 173, 174
    scan, 175
Austen, Hallie Iglehart, 2

B

Baba Yaga, 8
Bach, Ellon, 147, 151
    Bach Flower Remedies, 147, 148, 154-156, 157, 159, 160, 170
Baer, Randall and Vicki, 174, 175
    Windows of Light, 174, 175
Balch, James, M.D., 63
    Prescription for Nutritional Healing, 63, 65
Balch, Phyllis, C.N.C., 63
    Prescription for Nutritional Healing, 63, 65
Bast, 7
Bau, 8
B-complex
    see vitamins
bear, 7
behavior problems, 51, 52, 63, 102, 132, 133, 136, 152, 153, 157
Belfield, Dr. Wendell, 56, 57, 58, 63, 64, 67, 69
    How to Have a Healthier Dog, 63, 66
    see also supplements
    The Very Healthy Cat Book, 63, 66
beta-carotene
    see vitamin A

Bethel, May, 79
    The Healing Power of Herbs, 79
BHA, 51, 54
BHT, 51
big cats, 7, 8
biotin
    see vitamins
birds, 7, 10, 11, 85
bladder dis-eases/infections, 69, 82, 98-99, 124, 152, 153, 160
Boericke, William, 85, 94
    Materia Medica, 85, 87, 88, 94, 99
Boston Terriers, 90, 178
burns, 68, 81, 96, 122, 160

C

calcium
    see minerals
cancer, 10, 12, 49, 50, 51, 52, 60, 62, 63, 64, 65, 67, 71, 79, 80, 88, 92, 102, 120, 128, 132, 145, 153, 156, 159, 162, 168, 169, 170, 177, 178
Carson, David, 8
cat, 5, 6, 7, 8, 9, 11, 12, 13, 14, 17, 21
    anatomy, 13, 14
        internal organs, 18
        lymph nodes, 19
        muscular system, 17
        skeletal system, 16
    circulatory system, 14
    gestation, 14
    hearing, 14
    sensory system, 14
    size, 14
    smell, 14
    taste, 14
    teeth, 13
    urinary system, 14
    vision, 14
Cat Anna, 9
Cat Oil Mix, 55, 56, 61, 66, 81
    see also supplements
Cat Powder Mix, 55, 56, 61, 66, 67, 68
    see also supplements
cataracts, 52, 63, 64, 67, 79, 93, 94, 120, 157, 159
cell salts, 91, 92, 93, 94, 95, 97, 98
Cerberus, 8

V

W

Y